RICHARD M

THE R

E   ROPE

1945 – 1973

ANCHOR BOOKS

Anchor Press/Doubleday
Garden City, New York
1973

19990

The Recovery of Europe was originally published by Harper & Row, Publishers, Inc. in 1970.

Anchor Books Edition: 1973

ISBN: 0-385-07251-1
Library of Congress Catalog Card Number 73–81119

CONTENTS

PREFACE

This book is only incidentally a history of Western Europe since World War II. Its real aim is to investigate and make vivid the deep, powerful, and complex motives that Europeans have for seeking unity.

To anyone under the age of thirty, the Europe that emerged from war is virtually inconceivable. To anyone who remembers it, that Europe is a compelling nightmare. How the nightmare was banished, how a devastated Europe was rebuilt, how psychological wounds were healed and enemies reconciled—all this is a vital part of Europe's recent past, and essential to any understanding of the present and the future. No less vital, for anyone concerned with Europe's and America's place in world affairs, is to feel the force that drives Europeans in the direction of unity—against habit, tradition, narrow self-interest, stubbornness, lack of vision, and national pride. Today, the emerging European Community may look technical and humdrum. But its inspiration, and the grip it still has on men's imaginations, can only be seen by looking backwards, to its origins, its founders, and the world from which it sprang.

The bulk of this book, therefore, is concerned with a past that the young never knew and the middle-aged may have forgotten—a no man's land too recent to be history yet too distant to be current affairs. But because that recent past is so relevant to today's and tomorrow's news, I have tried in this book to trace the thread of it not only into the present but also into a conjectural future. As in Giotto's Florentine bell tower, I have deliberately distorted the perspective that most people expect, foreshortening what is near to us and lengthening what is now farther off. The result, I hope, is an accurate and balanced picture of a crucial, turbulent age.

THE RECOVERY OF EUROPE

A GENERATION OF CHANGE

Ask nothing of history except the past itself.

Ernest Renan[1]

Man is incredibly forgetful of his ancestors' living conditions and incredibly ungrateful for technological progress.   *Jean Fourastié*[2]

To most men, experience is like the stern lights of a ship, which illumine only the track it has passed.

S. T. Coleridge[3]

If it works, it's obsolete.   *Anon., c. 1950*[4]

In the world of today, we are all apprentices. Once, when change was less rapid, the only true novices were the young; for their elders, "experience" was the consolation-prize for sheer survival into middle age. Now, old and young start level, because a single generation has transformed our universe. The fact is so familiar that we tend to overlook it. Like drivers on an express highway, we forget how fast we are moving: our reflexes were trained at lower speeds. Time and again, statesmen whose formative years were the 1930s have found that "experience" can be a fallible guide. Yet just because the men who built the postwar world were survivors from its predecessor, any contemporary historian has a preliminary duty to look backward—not to seek analogies or lessons in the past, but to make clear how profoundly it differs from the present.

The task seems simple; yet its very simplicity is baffling. Those old enough to remember even the end of the 1930s may find it hard to realize vividly how remote that decade has become. Old fashion plates and family photographs reveal archaic strangers who were once our parents—or ourselves. Newsreels reanimate a restless Neville Chamberlain, with umbrella, wing collar, and mustache. Newspaper files preserve the moment's fears and crises, mummified in the language of thirty years ago. "I used a lot of my favorite words," wrote a well-known "thirties" novelist some time later, recalling a conversation from 1934: *"Gauleiter,* solidarity, *démarche,* dialectic, *Gleichschaltung,* infiltration, *Anschluss,* realism, *tranche, cadre."*[5] In a later generation, he might have written *"apparatchik,* confrontation, *détente,* credibility, charisma, massive, polycentrism, software, option, crunch." Reading today's newspapers, a Rip van Winkle awaking from thirty years' sleep would be bewildered by a whole new alphabet of technological, economic, and political change:

apartheid	JFK	Sputnik
Benelux	Kinshasa	Terylene
Comecon	laser	UNESCO
Dounreay	Mach 2	Vietcong
Eurocrat	NATO	WEU
FAO	overkill	Xerox
GATT	Pakistan	Yalta
Hiroshima	Quisling	Zimbabwe
Iron Curtain	Rapacki Plan	

With a new vocabulary, he would also face new surroundings. To restore even everyday life to what it was thirty years ago, a number of familiar objects would have to be subtracted from the present: nylon stockings, after-shave lotion, selective weed-killers, automatic gearshifts, motels, credit cards, supermarkets, frozen foods, tape-recorders, long-playing records. Some are relative newcomers. The mixed blessing of the transistor may be said to date from 1948, when Brattain and Bardeen produced the pioneer study that baptized it. Jet aircraft, atomic energy, rockets and missiles, artificial satellites, masers and lasers, DDT, various antibiotics—all are partly the product of wartime or postwar research. But just as the transistor has an earlier origin in the work on semi-conductors published by A. H. Wilson in 1931, so the best known of today's seeming novelties already existed in embryo at least a generation ago. What is really new is their sudden efflorescence.

Washing machines, for instance, were first patented as long ago as 1780, and first began to be built in the mid-nineteenth century. It was a hundred years before they came into household use in Europe; but within two decades there were some 25 million in Britain, France, Germany, Italy, Belgium, the Netherlands, and Luxembourg.[6] The beginnings of television go back to the 1920s: in London, the Baird company first put out experimental programs as early as 1929 from a studio in Long Acre and a transmitter in Oxford Street; and the BBC began a regular service from 1936 to 1939. Within twenty years of World War II, there were 13 million television sets in Britain, over 40 million in Western Europe, nearly 70 million in the United States, and 160 million in the world.[7] Plastics, likewise, had a lengthy history before their recent dizzy growth. The term first came to be used in the 1920s to describe such veteran man-made substances as celluloid and bakelite. Accustomed to these, some people were surprised or skeptical when experts in the early 1940s predicted a "Plastic Age," complete with plastic tiles, toys and table-tops, mugs, spoons and toilet articles, glues, flooring, pipes, clothes, shoes, book covers, and even plastic sailboats. Fifteen years later, the experts were vindicated. "It is astonishing," wrote two of them, "to find how far our prophecies have been fulfilled."[8]

Similar astonishment has been caused in more spectacular fields. In 1938, even Ernest Lawrence, the inventor of the cyclotron, remained very skeptical about the practical possibilities of "subatomic energy." "We are aware," he said, "of no greater prospect of destroying nuclear matter for power, than of cooling the ocean . . . and extracting the heat." Yet in the following winter, nuclear fission was achieved and proved; 1945 saw the first atomic explosions; and by 1951 experimental quantities of electricity were being produced by nuclear means. Within a further fifteen years, despite delays and disappointments, the world's output was already 16½ million kilowatt-hours, more than half of it in Western Europe.[9]

Space research, however, is the subject whose prophets have been most notably overtaken by events. In 1955 Sir George Thomson, the winner of the Nobel Prize for Physics, wrote that "there are many difficulties to inter-planetary travel besides the obvious one of getting off the earth, but there seems to be nothing that is really fundamental and one cannot help feeling confident that in the next fifty to a hundred years the ingenuity of engineers will have overcome them." Only two years later, the Soviet Union put into orbit the first man-made satellite, Sputnik. This had been predicted, accurately, by another expert writing in 1955; but the latter's further forecasts were too cautious by several years. The year 1957, not 1960, saw the first animal sent into space; in 1961, not 1965, the first human cosmonaut circled the earth; in 1962, three years ahead of expectation, the first television relay satellite came into service. By October 4, 1967, the tenth anniversary of Sputnik, nearly 600 satellites had been launched by the United States, the Soviet Union, France, Britain, and Canada. One rocket had reached Venus; a dozen had landed on the moon, and samples of its soil were soon to be collected by human visitors for examination on earth. The lunar landscape had been photographed as if it were the Sahara, and the planet earth as if it were the moon. Over a thousand man-made objects and fragments were in orbit, including nearly 300 artificial satellites, a third of them still transmitting signals. By the 1970s the total was to reach 7000. In all, about 150 tons of miscellaneous hardware were rotating in the skies.[10]

But even the headlong rapidity of the space race is only the most dramatic instance of what has happened in almost all fields of technology. For centuries, by comparison with our own day, many of life's material foundations scarcely seemed to alter. Empires rose and fell, dynasties succeeded each other, administrative groupings and methods changed, and frontiers were moved back and forth, often at great human cost. Within this shifting framework progress was discernible. Architecture, dress, weapons, tools, foodstuffs, language and thought all evolved. Agriculture improved, towns were built, commerce spread, prosperity grew, knowledge increased: yet the pace of change was relatively slow. Men invented few new substances and discovered few new sources of energy. The fastest means of travel remained a galloping horse. Then, with steel and the steam engine, came the first industrial revolution. The curve of technological change revealed itself as exponential: its imperceptible gradient began to rise quite sharply. Today, with plastics and electronics, we are learning to live on its vertiginous upward leap. Two centuries elapsed between the age of Copernicus and that of James Watt; one century between Watt and Michael Faraday; half a century between Faraday and the Wright brothers; a quarter of a century between the Wright brothers and Einstein. Since then, the intervals between major landmarks have grown ever shorter. New inventions snowball, themselves providing high-speed instruments that hasten further research. Even the milli-second is now no symbol of rapidity. Thirty years ago, the fastest computer took one hundredth of a second to process a single elementary datum. Its present-day counterpart takes one thousand-millionth of a second.[11] "A new sense of time," it is said, "was one of the outstanding psychological features of the industrial revolution."[12] One product of today's technological revolution is a new sense of speed.

In the lives of statesmen and citizens, speed makes its greatest impact through travel by air. In a single generation, this has become so commonplace that an effort is needed to recall its comparative novelty. The first British statesman to use an aircraft was Andrew Bonar Law, who flew on his rare visits to the Versailles Peace Conference after World War I.[13] Neville Chamberlain first traveled by air when he went to Munich to meet Adolf Hitler on September 15, 1938.[14] Cordell Hull, U. S. Secretary of State during World War II, made his first short journey by air in 1943.[15] The first transatlantic passenger service—by flying-boat—was inaugurated in 1939; but six years later, when President Harry S. Truman wanted to fly home from Europe after the Potsdam Conference, his advisers vociferously forbade it: "They all yell their heads off," he complained.[16] In America, the traditional whistle-stop rail tour, rather than a series of flying visits, was still a feature of the presidential election campaign in 1952. When Dwight D. Eisenhower became President, his personal aircraft was the piston-driven *Columbine*. Not until 1959 did he travel by jet—"an exhilarating experience," he characteristically recorded.[17]

Exhilarating or not, the experience is now widely shared. The world's commercial airlines at present operate more than a thousand jet aircraft. In these and others, they annually carry some 240 million people, a total of 275,000 million "passenger-kilometers," about a fifth of them in Western Europe. Since 1958, more travelers have crossed the Atlantic each year by air than by sea. In Britain alone, the number of air passengers has grown by over four thousand per cent in the past thirty years.[18]

Over the same period, moreover, the maximum speed of piloted engines has increased at almost the same rate. In orbit, a manned space capsule travels at about 18,000 miles an hour—some forty times as fast as any prewar aircraft. Even the ordinary passenger flights between London and Paris can break the 1939 world speed record: in a rocket-powered Bell X-15 it has been multiplied by ten. The 1939 land record is not far short of being doubled; and when Donald Campbell was killed on Coniston Water in January 1967, his Bluebird speedboat was traveling more than twice as fast as his father's had when it set the record for 1939. Meanwhile, as if accelerated by the pace of his own mechanical creations, man himself has attained running speeds once thought quite impossible. On May 6, 1954, Roger Bannister ran the first four-minute mile. Since then, his record has been broken more than fifty times.[19]

But not in every respect has man proved able to respond even so modestly to the pace of change. With dizzy speed, science and technology have provided new tools, new toys and new weapons. Economic life has changed more slowly; and the world's political organization lags further behind still. Most of men's present ills and dangers derive from the fact that their achievements in different fields are out of phase. Only latterly and painfully, that is, has man begun to find ways of using in economics and business the type of intelligence he displays in the laboratory; still less has he yet learned how to apply it to the political relations between states.

One result of scientific progress in the last thirty years has been a further marked improvement in health and sanitation.

Even in countries already industrialized, this has made possible a much greater expectation of life. Between 1930 and 1958, the average life-span in England and Wales rose from 58.7 to 67.5 years for men, and from 62.9 to 74 years for women. In Western Europe as a whole the death rate per thousand fell from 13.7 in 1938 to 10.2 in 1958.[20] In Britain, as in other European countries, far fewer people now die of tuberculosis, diphtheria, whooping cough, poliomyelitis, and measles, and far more from cancer and the typical afflictions of age—circulatory and respiratory diseases, and vascular lesions of the central nervous system, or "strokes." The proportion of older people in our society is therefore on the increase; but while this has led to loneliness and hardship in the midst of a sometimes uncaring society, the economic and political framework has not been disrupted by the benefits of modern medicine, except in so far as the medical services themselves—and their financing—have been put under strain.[21]

Quite different is the situation in the so-called "developing countries" of Africa, Asia, and Latin America. Here, too, better medical care—and even simple hygiene—have helped to reduce the death rate, but far more drastically. As late as 1946, the average expectation of life in India was only 32 years; today it is more like 50. In neighboring countries, infant mortality has been cut by 50 per cent in fifteen years. The consequence, as in nineteenth-century Britain, has been a startling increase in the total population. In 1939 there were just over two billion people in the world. Thirty years later there were nearly three-and-a-half billion. In a single generation, the rapidity of the change has outstripped the boldest forecasts: it has even overtaken some that have been made since World War II. Over the ages, the time taken for the world's population to double has shrunk from about a thousand years around the time of Christ to about a hundred years in the past century. Current estimates suggest that in the next three decades the population will double again. Even now, two-thirds of humanity are underfed—and it is they, broadly speaking, whose numbers are growing the fastest.[22]

To produce and distribute enough food for the world's

present population ought to be technically feasible: few purely scientific obstacles stand in the way. During the past generation, in Europe and the United States, agricultural machinery and chemical fertilizers have greatly increased farm productivity per man and per acre respectively, in many cases by well over 100 per cent. But in the poorer countries, for obvious reasons, both have grown far more slowly: in places, they have actually diminished. Even in Europe, the rise in food production has done little more than parallel the growth of population; and what is true of Europe is true of the world. At this rate, the proportion of those who go hungry may remain constant: but their numbers will undoubtedly grow. If the problem were scientific or technical, it might be solved relatively quickly—but it is not. It requires a vast and concerted program of material and financial aid, industrialization, instruction and birth control; and this in turn requires changes in habits and attitudes on the part of the rich countries as well as the poor. In short, because the organization of the world's economy has failed to keep pace with its technological progress, the plight of the world's poor is almost certain to get worse before it grows better. The term "developing countries" is in many cases not merely a euphemism, but a lie. And because politics, finally, lags even further behind economics, the resultant conflicts could endanger the whole globe.[23]

In the face of existing misery and prospective famine, there is much that seems repellent in the richer countries' pursuit of their own wealth. With some exceptions, we tend to behave as if two-thirds of our fellow human beings were scarcely real to us, although none is more than a few hours' flying time away. Shall we ourselves appear to future historians as callous and shortsighted as the nobles of the *ancien régime*? Good intentions, and private or public charity, are surely suspect unless they lead to adequate large-scale action —but so, on the other hand, would be misdirected guilt. In fact, no "developing country" would be better off if the industrialized nations gave up their apparently selfish struggle for faster economic growth. Their increasing wealth may widen the gap between them and the poor: but the attack on world poverty can only be really effective if the impetus of the rich countries' growth is maintained. To believe otherwise is to bring the mental habits of the past to an age of potential abundance. Thirty years ago, it was still just possible to feel that mankind's essential problem was the sharing out of resources that were ultimately limited: if the richer nations were not already robbing the poor, they were robbing posterity by stripping the earth of fuel and metal. Today, by contrast, the technological revolution offers a prospect of virtually limitless energy and countless new materials—as well as the future products of processes yet unknown. In this unprecedented situation, what is really remarkable is the double paradox of how little our most recent technology has so far affected the economy, and how great are the problems of adjusting to even this degree of change.

In thirty years, while man's technical knowledge has increased perhaps a thousandfold, the world's wealth has doubled. Today, men produce and use more than twice as much energy and three times as much steel as in 1939. Industrial production has nearly tripled, and the value of world trade has been multiplied by seven. Revenue per head has increased in all the industrialized countries: in some, real wages are twice as high as before World War II. In all of Europe, the total output of goods and services is more than 50 per cent greater, and production per head of population has risen by one-third. Unemployment has receded—in one case to less than a thirtieth of the prewar level. The amount per person spent on social security is four times as much as in 1930. Twice as many people as in 1939 now enter higher education. In general, Western Europeans work shorter hours with the aid of more machinery in larger productive units, more of which they now own either as stockholders or through nationalization. They invest 50 per cent more than in the 1930s; they employ more civil servants; they reserve fewer jobs exclusively for men. They eat more fruit, sugar, meat, and eggs, but fewer potatoes and grain products. They live in larger cities; they communicate more; they take more and longer holidays; they travel farther and faster. Together they now own—or are paying for by installments—seven times as many motorcars and motorcycles as were already crowding the roads a generation ago. In 1939 there were six million cars in Western Europe; twenty years later, there were sixteen million; today, after a further decade, there are forty-two million. If the process continued at this rate, the total would reach a hundred million within the next five years.[24]

The industrialized countries, in other words, are near the threshold of an age of plenty—the so-called "society of leisure." Their movement towards it is slower than technology theoretically warrants; but already it seems too fast for adjustment to be painless. Some have even claimed that we retard our own progress through unconscious fear of growing idle: we see to it, under "Parkinson's Law," that "work expands so as to fill the time available for its completion"; and while industrial working hours shorten, administrators multiply the unfinished paperwork they feel obliged to take home.[25] At all events, in Europe as elsewhere, men are discovering with some surprise the side-effects of affluence. Air-pollution, diesel fumes, smog, road congestion and accidents, automobile cemeteries, oil contamination of the beaches, chemical poisoning of rivers, rusting metal refuse and undecaying plastic litter—all are material proof of our inveterate improvidence. Sonic booms, the scream of jets, the roar of traffic, and the snarl of speedboats are some of the audible penalties of living in a machine age; standardized entertainment and preserved foods are equivocal examples of its benefits. Into cities appropriate for nineteenth-century numbers we crowd a vastly expanded population: the suburbs creep outwards to meet each other on the ruins of fields and woods. Telephones, teleprinters, tape-recorders, digital computers, and closed-circuit television might already make it possible to disperse and decentralize offices, if not to dispense with them; but competitive rivalry keeps them in the city centers, and a huge unhappy tide of commuters wells back and forth daily, in conditions reminiscent of the salt mines. Even the day itself is curiously organized. Work claims the better part of it: private life is squeezed into its margins. Most shops are closed when wage-earners are free to use them, and armies of housewives collect their families' requirements in small quantities several times a week. At night, as at the weekends, the business sections of any large city become expensive deserts of brick and concrete, and the roads into the dwindling countryside are choked with lines of cars.

In such an environment, man's nature seems almost to be transformed. Violence explodes out of boredom and alienation: the roadhog and the tearaway enact similar mute rebellions at the cost of human lives. Small wonder that students rebel, alert to tensions, contradictions, and futilities that their elders accept out of habit rather than choice. Stress diseases multiply, and some fail to be diagnosed; research discovers that smoking may cause lung cancer, but the complex causes of smoking remain obscure. Other drugs acquire new and younger addicts, seeking the spice of danger they feel that modern life denies. More sensible if no less sensitive, others find an outlet in deliberate, unnecessary physical effort: sport, camping, do-it-yourself, and gardening—apart from their practical value—are occupational therapy for a sickness the middle-aged share with the young. To palliate it, more and more people join the self-defeating quest for "unspoiled" holiday resorts, usually in the less-developed regions. Evoking the biblical simplicity of age-old fishing villages complete with water-skiing, the travel brochures echo and debase an understandable nostalgia—for societies in which, we tell ourselves, man still felt at home. And yet, bronzed and slightly disappointed, we often return with some relief from these excursions, glad to be back with the challenge and stimulus of our own strenuous civilization. Its blemishes, after all, are merely a reminder that "the price of pace is peace."

If this is a painful truth for private individuals, statesmen and politicians confront it in sharper form. A generation ago, it was a commonplace that motorcars, telephones, radio, and aircraft were reducing distances and bringing nations into closer contact, while men still organized their political affairs as if nothing had changed. Today, this assertion has as much a period air as 1930s roadsters, pedestal telephones, crystal wireless sets, and fixed-undercarriage biplanes; yet how much, even now, have we heeded its warning? Jet travel, artificial satellites, universal television and nuclear explosives have made the traditional forms of international relations still more obsolete and dangerous: but recent political history shows how halting are men's efforts to behave as if they realized the fact.

In a generation, that is, the scale of the world has altered. Already, at an early stage of the technological revolution, size became important: it was often a decisive advantage in the competition between private firms. Now it is even more so. The possibilities and needs of mass production, and the cost of research and development in the so-called "science-based industries," have led to mergers and takeovers, culminating in huge international corporations whose horizons are broader than even the largest nation state. At the same time, and increasingly during the past thirty years, the state itself has become more and more concerned in the economy—either as owner or part-owner of specific industries, or by accepting responsibility for welfare and for the stimulus and guidance of economic growth. Even in the least socialist of societies, government contracts and some degree of indicative planning have forced the administration into economic territory that once was alien; elsewhere, the conventional frontiers between the private and the public sector have become still more blurred. Large-scale business and industry have acquired some of the tone and features of national or international civil services; public authorities have assumed some of the functions of old-style private enterprise. Within the nation, this double process has raised political problems. Unnerved by monolithic institutions whose similar size may give them convergent interests, smaller concerns, workpeople, and individual citizens feel the need for some impartial "Ombudsman" to defend private rights.[26]

No less striking, however, are the international repercussions of modern welfare capitalism. By taking responsibility for national economies which are now so closely interlocking, governments once "sovereign" have become more involved with each other, notably in trade, investments, and monetary affairs. World trade, in particular, has expanded so much faster than gold production that its financing now depends on a complex network of credit, mutual confidence, and collective fear. This has severely limited national freedom of action—a fact most explicitly acknowledged in 1944, when the Bretton Woods Conference sought to codify international economic behavior, laying the foundations of what were to be the International Monetary Fund and the World Bank. But despite these preliminary efforts, governments have proved reluctant to allow the world's supply of money to be regulated by equitable international decision-making: rather than control their destinies jointly by pooling their sovereignty, they prefer to cling to its appearance while its reality leaks away. The international monetary system, such as it is, continues to be based on the so-called "key currencies" of the United States and Britain. Since neither now has adequate reserves, the one-time "gold-exchange standard," whereby holders of dollars or sterling could convert them freely into gold metal, has had to be virtually abolished, largely by gentlemen's agreements which have been well described as "threateningly precarious and short-term."[27] The outcome is general uneasiness, occasional danger, and —beginning in Britain but not confined to any one country —intermittent stagnation. Through attempts to evade the implications of interdependence, economic freedom has actually been reduced.

In politics, likewise, interdependence has proved to be inescapable. Statesmen now travel between continents in the time it once took to cross a single country. Heads of government converse directly on the scrambler telephone or, more slowly, via the teleprinters of the "hot line." One incidental result has been to devalue diplomatists and their dispatches —an unusual instance of the truism that our culture is now more oral and less literary than a generation ago. Radio and television, largely responsible for this last shift of emphasis, are themselves further elements in the growth of interdependence. Every night, the citizens of the richer countries have the chance to see from their own armchairs a little of other nations' lives. Very gradually, foreign affairs are being domesticated: countries and peoples once distant—"aliens"— are becoming real. Soon, with the aid of relay satellites, multiple polyglot versions of a single television broadcast may be addressed to the whole world, ignoring distances, the earth's curvature and national or political barriers: jamming, in this case, would be extremely difficult. The effects of such universal television can only be guessed at: much will depend on the honesty and skill with which it is used. But whatever the motives of those who exploit it, its political significance is incalculable. In this respect at least, for good or evil, the world is now potentially one.

Here once more, however, the organization of human affairs lags far behind human technology. Telecommunications may have shrunk our planet; yet the numbers of its separate nations have greatly swelled. The past generation has fostered more than fifty new sovereign states, with a total population of 800 million. Essentially, this is the outcome of postwar decolonization. The Italian colonies in North and East Africa, like the Japanese empire in the Far East, were dismantled at the close of hostilities. Armed rebellion spurred the ending of Dutch rule in Indonesia, and of French rule in North Africa and Indochina. Denmark granted independence to Iceland, France to Syria and the Lebanon, the United States to the Philippines, and Britain to a score of countries including India, Pakistan, Ceylon, Burma, Malaysia, the West Indies, Guyana, Cyprus, and Malta, while the Belgians, the French and the British have relinquished the greater part of Africa. Here, in particular, frontiers are more often the relics of colonial map-making than the expression of ecological boundaries. In some of the new nations this has led to regional tension and bitter conflict; elsewhere, economic logic calls for the integration or federation of adjacent territories, but natural pride, fear and sometimes jealousy stand in the way. With the large exceptions of India, Pakistan, Indonesia, and Nigeria, none of the newly independent states has a population of more than thirty-five million people; the majority of them have less than ten million, and a number of these have less than one million each. As a first step toward justice and equality, decolonization was long overdue; but allied with nationalism it has proved to be a splintering process—a grim paradox in a world of increasing interdependence, where technology puts a premium on size.

The growth of new giants, indeed, is a further decisive feature of the past thirty years. Its beginnings were discernible well over a century ago when Alexis de Tocqueville observed that "there are, at the present time, two great nations in the world which seem to tend towards the same end, although they started from different points: I allude to the Russians and the Americans." "Each of them," he added, "seems to be marked out by the will of Heaven to sway the destinies of half the globe."[28] In 1835, such prescience was visionary; but so familiar has the vision grown that we forget how little it was credited even a generation ago. In the '30s, America was still isolationist; only reluctantly and briefly had she entered the world scene. To many ordinary Europeans, "the typical American" was either a stereotype from the cinema or a stage "Yankee" with horn-rimmed spectacles, a name like "Hiram J. Rickenbacker," and a poorly imitated drawl. Viewed from Europe, the United States still seemed a distant land of hustle and skyscrapers, if not of cowboys and Indians. Yet by 1939 it was producing a third of the world's most widely used metals, a third of its coal and electrical energy, two-thirds of its oil, and three-quarters of its automobiles.[29] Today, although the percentages have dropped, the absolute figures are greater. America's standard of living, by any economic indicator, is twice as high as that of her closest competitors; and her total output of goods and services amounts to $756 billion—nearly seven times as much as any other country for which there are comparable figures.[30]

The missing exception, of course, is the Soviet Union. This too seemed very distant in the '30s, even if to some it appeared a precarious experiment in socialism or, as André Gide put it, "the land where the future is being born."[31] What astonished Western observers at that time was less the scale of Russia's industrial production than the speed of her growth. In 1929, the United States accounted for 42.2 per cent of the world's industrial output. By 1938 this had fallen to 32.2 per cent—not because American production was declining, but because the Soviet percentage had leaped from 4.3 to 18.3 in less than ten years. Since World War II, especially, Russia has begun to enjoy the fruits of her progress. She now produces two-thirds as much steel and energy as the United States; and although America remains predominant in many fields, the Soviet Union's achievements in space are symbol enough of her new status as the world's second giant.[32]

Beyond America and Russia, moreover, other giant powers are beginning to flex their muscles. Physically the biggest is Communist China. Before World War II, the Republic of China was ruled from Nanking by Chiang Kai-shek's Kuomintang. Today, the People's Republic has its capital in Peking; it has exchanged the Kuomintang for the Community Party, and the dictatorship of Chiang for that of Mao Tse-tung and Chou En-lai. But the essential difference is more fundamental. In 1939, with the disputed territories of Manchuria, Mongolia, Sinkiang, and Tibet, China comprised over four million square miles and 458 million people. Huge, undeveloped, largely uncolonized, and attractive to outside capital and commerce, it seemed fated to be a pawn in other countries' games of power. Thirty years later, with much the same area, China has a population not far short of 700 million, and increasing at the rate of 20 million a year. Cleared of invaders if not of civil strife, it has embarked on a ruthless program of modernization and mass education. The "Great Leap Forward" in agricultural production made in 1958 may well have been exaggerated, but it evidently took place; and similar if steadier progress has been made in industry. China's crude steel production has now reached twelve million metric tons—more than Italy's; its installed electrical energy capacity is in the region of fifteen million kilowatts—more than Sweden's; and its annual output of science and engineering graduates is well over sixty thousand—more than that of any other country except America and Russia. The most spectacular result of these endeavors has been China's development of nuclear weapons and ballistic missile systems—and, more recently, her first venture into space.[33] By comparison with the '30s, this is already an extraordinary change. Equally significant, although perhaps not surprising, is the fact that after some years of seeming to follow in the wake of the Soviet Union, Communist China is now beginning to steer a course of her own. This redoubles the contrast with the backward and passive Republic of a generation ago.

But while China's progress is the more obvious, no less remarkable is the growth of that smaller giant, Japan. This is no new phenomenon. It began toward the end of the nineteenth century, with a largely unassisted "great leap forward" from medieval feudalism to western technology in the space of some forty years. By 1938, Japan was supplying 3.5 per cent of the world's manufacturing output—more than Belgium, Canada, Italy, or Sweden.[34] Since World War II, the country's economic expansion has broken all comparable records. Even in 1964, when the brakes were applied to the economy, total production rose by nearly 14 per cent, and exports by 22 per cent. On average, Japan has maintained an annual growth rate of some 10 per cent for more than a decade—enough to quadruple her output within fifteen years. With 100 million people in an area more densely populated than Britain, she now produces more energy than France and more steel than Germany; her output of trucks is second only to that of the United States. She is the world's biggest shipbuilder, and by 1965 she was producing nearly half the gross tonnage launched. One day, by their sheer numbers, China and even India may eclipse her; but China is still very far from achieving her full potential, and India incalculably further. Meanwhile, Japan is already what *The Economist* has called "the greatest practical research laboratory of economic growth in our time."[35]

The past thirty years, then, have witnessed crucial changes. Technology has transformed men's everyday environment, given new meaning to notions of speed and distance, unlocked the power of the atom, and opened the way into space. Economic progress, although remarkable, has been less rapid: the world's growing millions remain undernourished, while the industrialized countries develop more quickly than is comfortable, but more slowly than they could. Men's political behavior, at the same time, adapts itself more sluggishly still. Most nation states have yet to accept the implications of their increasing involvement with the economy and with each other; and while the world grows smaller and its economic units larger, minute new nations proliferate alongside existing and emerging giants.

Amid this unprecedented turmoil and upheaval, Europe is responsible for the biggest change of all. It is not merely that today's technology, economics, and political organization are largely of European origin. What most sharply divides the present from past generations is still the grim landmark of the Second—European—World War.

In the six years from 1939 to 1945, war itself changed its nature. In previous conflicts, the state's defenses had been its frontiers or its front line: its armies acted as a carapace which might be dented or even fatally pierced, but which short of disaster sheltered the civilians—and many of the generals—in its rear. With air raids and conscription, this concept had to be modified. The civil population, as the phrase went, "was now in the front line." In the days of trench warfare, the metaphor still seemed valid; but it was certainly inappropriate by the time of World War II. Even before Hitler's armies invaded Belgium to turn the flank of the Maginot Line, blitzkrieg tactics had made static linear defense anachronistic. Mobility was the keynote of this new kind of warfare: parachute troops, commando raids, guerrilla skirmishing and sabotage by resistance circuits behind the lines were as typical of it as the lightning thrusts of the Panzer divisions. Mass air attack, flying bombs and rockets made the carapace concept even more obsolete by virtually abolishing the distinction between military targets and civilian victims—a process carried to the ultimate in the extermination camps and, on a smaller scale, in the aerial massacres of Dresden, Hiroshima and elsewhere. When the last of the ashes had settled on Nagasaki, the carapace and its contents were one.

Immense, impersonal, and indiscriminate, today's destructive weapons have dwarfed even those of World War II. The biggest bomb dropped on Germany in 1945 contained ten tons of TNT; the biggest since tested by the Soviet Union is the equivalent of ninety-seven million tons. The total explosive power now in existence is ten million times as great as in 1943. Intercontinental missiles, thermonuclear weapons and radioactive fall-out have robbed front lines and frontiers of most of their military meaning: such notions as "fortress America" are now doubly out of date. True, the carapace concept lingers. Perhaps its last vestige is the hope that antiballistic missiles might one day make nations invulnerable—a costly and precarious form of carapace in the sky. At present, no industrialized and densely populated country could hope to "win" a nuclear war, and all have an interest in preventing it. In 1969 the existing nuclear powers spent nearly $420 billion on "defense"; but unless they are willing to find still greater sums for an anti-ballistic missile race, their military strategy is in fact not defensive, but deterrent. They eye each other like poker players or stock-market speculators, acting on hypotheses about each other's future behavior rather than on their own plans. The survival of civilization must remain uncertain so long as it depends on such gambler's dexterity— especially if the number of nuclear powers continues to grow. Contrary to some expectations, however, even the "balance of terror" has not put an end to armed conflict. As Jean Cocteau once remarked: "If men offer to get rid of nuclear weapons, it is not to make war impossible, but to make it possible"; and under the virtual ban on nuclear and germ warfare imposed by men's fear of the consequences, "conventional" struggles continue, sometimes threatening the whole world. War has dramatized the interdependence of nations. Already brought closer in so many other ways, since 1945 they have been handcuffed together by military technology.[36]

Their response to this situation makes a further contrast with the world of a generation ago. The shock of war released political as well as technical inventiveness, quickened by the knowledge of what a third world war would mean. By 1939, the diplomatic nationalism of the past had revealed its antiquated bankruptcy: six years of war demolished its last pretensions: now was the chance for statesmen to start afresh. For once, they were impatient to do so. Within five years, in an extraordinary burst of creative energy, they endowed the world with almost all its present network of global institutions. The year 1945 saw the establishment of the United Nations Organization (UNO), the Food and Agriculture Organization (FAO), the International Monetary Fund (IMF) and the International Bank for Reconstruction and Development (IBRD or World Bank). In 1946 came the United Nations Educational, Scientific and Cultural Organization (UNESCO), the United Nations International Children's

Emergency Fund (UNICEF) and the International Court of Justice; in 1947, the General Agreement on Tariffs and Trade (GATT); in 1948, the International Refugee Organization (IRO) and the World Health Organization (WHO); in 1949, the United Nations Relief and Works Agency (UNRWA) and the International Confederation of Free Trade Unions (ICFTU).

The supreme aim of such co-operation was to build a world-wide system of what had once been known as "collective security," although its old embodiment, the League of Nations, had already proved disappointing when Maxim Litvinoff popularized the phrase in 1935. The practical outcome now was UNO, which despite its weaknesses has been stronger and more comprehensive than the League. But almost equally significant was a psychological change that accompanied postwar reconstruction; and this had its origins in World War II. Unlike most of its predecessors, the war had been ideological, concerned as much with principles as with power. Fascism and Nazism at one extreme, Soviet Communism at the other, each claimed a universal mission; and a similar universalism marked more moderate thinking about the future peace. It was hard, after what had happened, to go on regarding the nation state as more than a stage in the slow evolution of human society: still less did it now seem sacrosanct, a proud eternal solitary with no permanent friends or allies, but only permanent interests. If the 1914–18 struggle had been "the war to end war," the victors of World War II spoke more insistently of the need to "build a better world." The generation that now came to maturity found it natural to see that world as a unit, as if from an aircraft or a satellite, rather than from the arrow-slits or gun-turrets of separate national positions. Equally natural was the conclusion that international anarchy must soon be replaced by the rule of law.

Sometimes, this feeling was superficial and unpractical; sometimes it was Messianic; sometimes it reflected one or another great power's conviction that it alone knew best. In retrospect, the hope of world-wide law and order may seem premature or even Utopian—especially to those for whom nations are the sole political "realities" in a fundamentally unchanging world. But "realist," egotist or nationalist prognoses are often self-fulfilling prophecies, spells which summon the devils that they claim are already here. And however imperfect or tainted the ideals of the postwar generation, there was so much to be done when the war ended that to think in world terms was a practical necessity. It was also a significant break with previous mental habits; and it left its mark. So ingrained, now, is the notion of "building a better world" that many are unduly puzzled by the policies of statesmen who ignore it. A measure of its strength is that even out-and-out nationalists, in this sense deeply pessimistic, sugar their doctrines with hopeful universalist words.

But if the beginnings of peace aroused high expectations, these were quickly dashed by a partial legacy from the war. Instead of uniting, the world became polarized, split by the growing tension between America and Russia. The origins of this "cold war" have been variously interpreted: there was perhaps as much misunderstanding on both sides as there was malevolence on either. Nor is there a consensus about whether the "cold war" has ended. Fear, greater wealth, restiveness in Eastern Europe, and growing rivalry from Communist China have certainly been nudging the Soviet Union into a new relationship with the United States. In the 1962 Cuban missile crisis, Moscow overruled Havana in order to preserve peace; in 1963 came the nuclear test ban treaty, followed later by a draft agreement against the spread of nuclear weapons; in 1967, both Moscow and Washington stood aside from the Israeli-Arab war, and the meeting of President Johnson with Mr. Kosygin in Glassboro, New Jersey, seemed to confirm the bilateral link already established by the "hot line." Yet if the change is dramatic, it remains none the less gradual, as was dramatically shown when Russian tanks invaded Prague in 1968. The "cold war" may indeed be moving into the Far East, leaving a wary, uneasy complicity to grow between America and Russia: but in the meantime one of the essential differences between our world and that of the 1930s is still the twenty-year confrontation of these two giants across the former battlefields of Europe.[37]

Down the middle of Europe, in fact, runs this particular

division of the world. In a typical atlas of the '30s, the European map spanned two pages: it stretched from Reykjavik, 21° 20′ West, almost to Obdorsk, 66° 50′ East. This was still the traditional "Europe from the Atlantic to the Urals." Thirty years later, the map on the right-hand page has changed completely. With the growing industrialization of parts of Siberia, the Urals have lost their old significance as a boundary; to the West of them, the cartographer's expression "Russia in Europe" has acquired new, ironic overtones. Estonia, Latvia and Lithuania have become Republics of the Soviet Union, whose borders now also include what were formerly parts of Finland, East Prussia, Poland, Czechoslovakia, and Rumania. "People's democracies" of varying shades have been established in the eastern zone of Germany, in Poland, Czechoslovakia, Hungary, Rumania, Bulgaria, Albania and —*mutatis mutandis*—in Yugoslavia. The so-called "Iron Curtain" may no longer be impenetrable, but it still marks the borderline between rival forms of society. In political terms, the fold in the prewar atlas has become real.

On the left-hand page, the map shows fewer changes. The biggest and most serious is the division of Germany, crucial to the division of Europe and of the world. Nearly half its prewar area is now sealed off in the east. Of this, rather less than half, with a population of some sixteen million, is ruled by the so-called "German Democratic Republic"; the rest has been split between Poland and the Soviet Union. Berlin, the former capital, is divided by an ugly makeshift wall of breeze blocks, and its western sector forms an extensive but claustrophobic enclave within Eastern territory. In the 95,737 square miles that now make up the western half of Germany—the Federal Republic—there are sixty million people, the ninth largest nation in the world, and almost as many as lived in the whole German Reich before World War II. Their provisional capital is the small, unpretentious university city of Bonn, remote and a little sleepy in the muggy climate of the Rhineland. Despite the big new office blocks on the Adenauerallee leading south to Bad Godesberg, Bonn has scarcely even modernized its railways: four level crossings still hold up the traffic in the middle of the town. Like so much else in today's divided Germany, Bonn maintains a mute insistence that its present situation cannot last.

Compared with the division of Germany, the other changes in the map of Western Europe are small. Italy's northern frontiers have been adjusted; the Saar has passed back and forth between France and Germany; the Dutch have reclaimed more of the North Sea. But no major differences meet the eye of the map-reader, and few can be seen by a traveler looking down at Europe from the air. In places, the scars of World War II still show. Berlin, in particular, has made monuments of its ruins, like the broken spire of the Kaiser-Wilhelm-Gedächtniskirche, deliberately left unrepaired. Yet even such wounds as these seem less deep than the angular imprint of the World War I trenches, still just visible from the air like a palimpsest in Flanders fields replowed and planted for the past fifty years. Even the military graves of World War II, row upon row of standardized crosses, are far outnumbered—in Western Europe—by those of 1914–18.

A little more obvious to the airborne traveler are the signs of peace. The clustered lights of the cities are brighter and more widespread; more cars move faster along broader ribboning highways. Airfields are crowded; new towns have sprung up, anonymously modern; the steel-framed windows of ferro-concrete buildings flash in the sun. Europe's outward appearance has altered dramatically: but the biggest change of all can only be seen by looking at statistics.

In less than a generation, interrupted by six years of war, Western Europe has nearly tripled its wealth. Its total output, measured at constant prices, is almost three times as great as in 1939: so is its purely industrial production. Imports have tripled, exports quadrupled. Energy consumption has doubled. Hydroelectric power production has tripled; the output of crude oil has been multiplied by thirteen, and that of natural gas by 300. True, the population has increased also: but just as striking as the rise in output has been that of output per head. Since World War II, the average increase in productivity has been in the region of 3.5 per cent a year, compared with less than half that figure before 1939. The postwar economic expansion, moreover, although still uneven, has so far been spared the severe crises and depressions that recurred so regularly in the past; and although there have also been variations from country to country, even the laggards have shared, less spectacularly, in Western Europe's general, unprecedented and unusually self-conscious pursuit of growth.[38]

Paradoxically, however, these figures partly mask a relative decline. While Western Europe's industrial production has risen by more than 130 per cent, that of the United States has increased by 234 per cent. While Europe's trade has expanded, its share of world trade has diminished: its imports from 47 per cent to 42 per cent of the total, its exports from 57 per cent to 43 per cent. Its gold and currency reserves, which a generation ago covered 77 per cent of its annual imports, now cover only 48 per cent; and whereas Europe once met more than 90 per cent of its own energy needs, it now supplies only 70 per cent, depending on imports for the rest. Greater dependence is thus the obverse of Europe's new prosperity; and in some respects its growth has lagged behind that of the rest of the world.[39]

Europe's relative decline has been greatest, moreover, in some of the most crucial fields. At present, Western European countries pay some 200 million dollars a year more than they earn for technological knowledge, patents and licenses, while the United States has a comparable surplus on such earnings of more than 500 million dollars a year. Not for nothing has it become fashionable in Europe to speak of "the technological gap." In pure science the gap is just as evident. During the thirty-nine years from 1901 to 1939, Europe produced 109 Nobel Prize-winners in physics, chemistry, physiology, and medicine, compared with thirteen from the United States. In the twenty-three years 1943–65, Europe's score of fifty-six was almost equaled by the United States with fifty-four, while other countries—which before World War II had had only two laureates—now had thirteen, seven of them from the USSR.[40]

If Western Europe as a whole has thus lost ground over the past thirty years, its individual countries have done so even more. Even the largest of them is now dwarfed by the Soviet Union and the United States. A country that was in the same proportion to America as America is to, say, France would be gigantic—a nation of 800 million people in a territory of 60 million square miles. Each of its inhabitants would produce one-and-a-half times as much as the average American, and its standard of living would be twice as high. The sales of its biggest firm would be seventeen times those of General Motors. Its scientists might be experimenting with intergalactic travel, with the total prevention of aging, with custom-made newspapers electronically printed in every home. Nor would the disparity be confined to economics and technology. To pursue the comparison further, this hypothetical giant power would have 12 million men in its armed forces and an annual defense budget of more than 500 million dollars.

The psychological and political effects of such disproportion are very evident. Thirty years ago, Western Europe was still the bright and tragic stage on which the world's dramas were enacted. Its nations, in those days, could still see themselves as protagonists and arbiters. Today, this is no longer possible. Pageantry has replaced power in the chancelleries of Europe: the drama is now dominated by non-European giants.

In the past thirty years, then, Europe has gradually been forced to face a challenge of scale. But even more fundamental is the challenge to political maturity. Just because Europe thirty years ago was the world's cockpit, it was Europeans who paid most dearly for man's failure to match political wisdom to technological skill. The Fascist and Nazi regimes used the resources of civilization for ends that were plainly barbarous; the democracies, in self-defense, committed themselves to "total war," to the demand for unconditional surrender, to the bombing of Dresden, Hiroshima, and Nagasaki. The agony of the old Europe cost the lives of fifteen million of its citizens, half of them in extermination camps. Many had fought and died for a world and a Europe where such things could no longer happen. The task of the survivors was to make that hope a reality, and to honor their debt to the dead.

THE WASTE LAND

Though we had Peace, yet 'twill be a great while e'er
things be settled. Though the Wind lie, yet after a Storm
the Sea will work a great while.   *John Selden*[1]

War is no longer declared,
but continued.   *Ingeborg Bachmann*[2]

I preferred the war to that 'sickness' which, after the
Liberation, had soiled, corrupted, and humiliated us all.
          Curzio Malaparte[3]

The nightmare ended prosaically, in the small hours of a
Monday morning, inside a red-brick building not far from the
railway station of Rheims. This was the Boys' Technical High
School, taken over by General Eisenhower for Supreme
Headquarters, Allied Expeditionary Force. In the war room,
formerly used for recreation, a small crowd was gathered—
staff officers, journalists, newsreel cameramen. "The damned
war room," said Eisenhower, "looked like a Hollywood setting." Chairs were arranged at a long whitewood table; at
each place was a clean ashtray and a freshly sharpened pen-
cil. Around the table stood senior Allied officers: a Russian
general and two companions; a French commandant; an admiral, a general, and an air chief marshal from Britain; and
the Commander of the U. S. Strategic Air Forces in Europe.
Of Eisenhower himself there was no sign.

The door opened; in came the Supreme Commander's
Chief of Staff, General Walter Bedell Smith. He was followed
a moment later by two German officers, looking strained and
uneasy, holding themselves stiffly erect. One was Generalad-
miral Hans-Georg von Friedeburg: the other, set-faced, with
precise lips and cold, heavy eyes, was Generaloberst Alfred
Jodl. The principals took their places. Documents were set

before them; aides came forward with pens. In the bright glare of the newsreel floodlights, they signed. It was 2:41 A.M. on May 7, 1945. Those present had just witnessed the unconditional surrender of Nazi Germany.

It is often hard to live up to great occasions. Perhaps the participants feel, in the words of a perceptive novelist, "somewhat insincere, as any intelligent person is likely to feel who performs a symbolic action."[4] Perhaps, too, blunders are inevitable at the only performance of an unrehearsed drama. At all events, in the agony and exultance of those swift spring days, not much could be well stage-managed; and the early-morning ceremony in Rheims was followed by considerable confusion. As one of Eisenhower's aides commented: "I've learned the hard way that it is much easier to start a war than to stop one."[5]

There was uncertainty, first, about the time when hostilities were due to cease. Grossadmiral Karl Dönitz, Hitler's official heir as Reichspräsident, now established with his short-lived government in the quasi-exile of Mürwik-bei-Flensburg on the Danish frontier, had done his best to delay the capitulation, hoping that as many as possible of his troops would give themselves up to the Western Allies and avoid captivity in the East. The Rheims documents called for a cease-fire at one minute after midnight on May 8–9 DBST; the message received by Dönitz, however, gave the time as Central European Time—i.e. one hour later. According to German records, this was due to a mistake in transmission, and was quickly rectified. Whether it might have led to needless slaughter is problematical: isolated battles in fact continued for several days.[6]

Greater confusion marred the public announcement of the surrender. For some time, the Soviet Union had feared that the Nazis might make a separate peace with the West. This they had indeed attempted: but Eisenhower had been firm. Although he had allowed their armies in northeastern Germany, Holland, and Denmark to surrender to Field-Marshal Montgomery at Lüneburg Heath on the previous Friday, May 4, he insisted that this was a tactical, purely military proceeding, like the surrender of the German forces in Italy at Caserta two days before. The capitulation at Rheims, however, marked the end of the war in Europe; and the Allies had agreed to announce this simultaneously on Tuesday, May 8, at 9:00 A.M. Washington time, or 3:00 P.M. in Western Europe and 4:00 P.M. in Moscow. To respect the deadline, the press had been asked to hold the story for a day and a half. It was a long embargo for such momentous news; and in the event it was broken. At 12:45 P.M. on Monday, May 7, "to anticipate the enemy announcement and thereby maintain order," Dönitz's Foreign Minister read a proclamation over Flensburg radio: his speech was monitored by the BBC and rebroadcast in English that same afternoon. By 3:35 P.M. the story was on the news-agency wires. In London, excited crowds began to gather. Everyone now knew that the war in the West was over; but because of their prior agreement, the Allies were not due to admit the fact for nearly twenty-four hours.[7]

This seemed to Winston Churchill "an idiotic position." Within half an hour he was on the secret telephone to the Pentagon, arguing with Admiral Leahy, President Truman's Chief of Staff. Earlier that day he had already badgered Eisenhower with repeated attempts to have the embargo lifted; now, as Truman put it, "he was mad as a wet hen." "What is the use," he exclaimed, "of me and of the President looking to be the only two people in the world who don't know what is going on? The whole of this thing is leaking out in England and America . . . I feel it absolutely necessary to go off at 6:00 P.M., and I will telegraph to Stalin the very message that I am sending you . . . in view of the fact that the Germans have blasted it all over the world."[8]

Left to himself, Truman might have accepted this argument. Stalin, however, was still not convinced that the Germans on the eastern front would in fact surrender; and he was anxious to avoid an announcement that might be premature. Leahy sent an urgent teleprinter message to General Deane at the U. S. Military Mission in Moscow; but although he waited at the Pentagon in the hope of a quick reaction from Stalin, none came. Within the hour, Churchill was once more on the telephone: he too had had no reply from the Russians. In view of public feeling, he could delay no longer. "The Moscow people," he complained, "have no public opinion—

but you cannot control your press, nor can I control mine—that's the difficulty of living in a free country!" Reluctantly, he postponed his own broadcast to the nation until the official deadline; but "the thing must go forward." That evening, the British Ministry of Information made the announcement: the next forty-eight hours would be a public holiday, and V-E Day (for "Victory in Europe") would be tomorrow, Tuesday, May 8. That day had already dawned in Europe, and was already a few minutes old in Washington, when at last an answer came from Moscow. The Russians would not yet celebrate victory. Stalin wanted more time to examine the surrender terms.[9]

These, indeed, were the third source of that week's manifold confusion. In Rheims, at General Eisenhower's headquarters, they had already caused commotion during the previous night. Shortly after the surrender ceremony, the American career diplomat Robert Murphy, who was acting as the Supreme Commander's political adviser on German affairs, cast a routine glance at the document that had just been signed. To his astonishment, he found that it contained the wrong text. Two months earlier, he had sent to Eisenhower's Chief of Staff, General Bedell Smith, the surrender terms laboriously approved by the three Allied governments. Where were they now? Bedell Smith had by this time gone to bed. Roused by a telephone call from Murphy, he hastily dressed again and hurried back to the office. There, locked in his top-secret filing cabinet, was the big blue folder which Murphy had sent him. Had he simply forgotten it, as Murphy afterward claimed?

In fact, the explanation was more complex. Supreme Headquarters in Rheims had received several printed copies of the agreed surrender terms, and its representatives had discussed in some detail with the State Department the arrangements for their translation and signature. Apart from the fact that this text officially committed all the Allied governments, including the Russians, to the rudiments of an agreed policy, it was also the only legal basis for the exercise of Allied authority in Germany after the war. But military headquarters believed that to present so elaborate a document to the Germans would risk protracted argument with them; and while argument continued, so would fighting and loss of life. Two years earlier, in 1943, the military had unwillingly ceded to their civilian colleagues' insistence on elaborate surrender terms for Italy. This time, as one participant put it, they were determined to have their revenge. The document signed that morning, therefore, had been an improvisation, concocted on the basis of reference material as soon as capitulation had begun to seem likely; the Russian liaison officer who had certified and counter-signed it had clearly not realized that it was unofficial. Not until the evening of the previous Saturday, May 5, had news of the Rheims document reached the U. S. Ambassador in London, John G. Winant, who had helped draft the official terms. Only by strenuous efforts, including a talk with Churchill and an urgent telephone call to Bedell Smith, had Winant managed to secure the insertion in the Rheims document of an enabling clause providing for the Allies' later assumption of political authority in Germany. Even so, the military surrender terms just signed had still not been cleared at governmental level, except in London. While Murphy and Bedell Smith were comparing the two texts and wondering how to proceed, a priority cable arrived from Washington: Moscow had noticed the discrepancy too. Early that same Monday morning, Supreme Headquarters made a rueful announcement. The Rheims document had merely "formalized the surrender": "the official surrender" would take place in Berlin, as the Russians had requested, on Wednesday, May 9.[10]

At last, it might have seemed, the chapter of accidents was finished; but the Berlin ceremony itself was no model of order. First, the Western Allies had to wait five hours for Marshal Georgi Zhukov: when he arrived, they still had to wait for Andrei Vyshinsky, the Deputy Foreign Minister. As at Rheims, Eisenhower preferred not to participate: his place was taken by Air Chief Marshal Sir Arthur Tedder. As Deputy Supreme Commander, Tedder was to sign for all the Western Allies; but General de Gaulle insisted that General Jean de Lattre de Tassigny sign for France. It was therefore agreed with Zhukov that Tedder should act on behalf of Britain only, while General Carl Spaatz represented the United States. When Vyshinsky arrived, however, he would have none of it. Since Tedder was Eisenhower's deputy, he argued, there was no need for Spaatz. If so, Spaatz answered, there was no need for de Lattre. For two hours the problem looked insoluble; then Vyshinsky at last conceded that both could sign as witnesses lower down the page. Meanwhile, de Lattre had discovered that Red Army headquarters possessed no tricolor to hang with the other Allied flags behind the conference table; and when he had one made up by Russian seamstresses, they at first sewed the stripes horizontally, producing a Dutch flag. Even when they put right this mistake, the makeshift banner was still rather small. Finally, at the solemn moment of signature, a fist-fight broke out among the reporters and cameramen. The ceremony began at 11:30 P.M., and ended at sixteen minutes past midnight. By the time it was over, the first arrivals had been waiting about for more than fourteen hours.[11]

Nor, even now, was the confusion at an end. The double surrender had been negotiated with the representatives of Grossadmiral Dönitz—at Rheims with Friedeburg and Jodl, in Berlin with Friedeburg, Generalfeldmarschall Wilhelm Keitel, and Generaloberst Hans Jürgen Stumpff. But Dönitz's status was, to say the least, ambiguous. Appointed by order of Adolf Hitler, he had set up the apparatus of government at his headquarters in the Flensburg Naval College, complete with guards of honor and civilian personnel. He had not received the full list of ministers nominated in Hitler's "political testament"; but he had rejected those whose names Josef Goebbels had sent him in the telegram announcing Hitler's death. On Saturday, May 5, he had appointed what he called "a purely caretaker cabinet," with the avowed aim of "winding up as well as possible the practical problems arising at the end of the war, and thereby laying the basis on which to build anew." For some days the cabinet debated whether or not to stay in office. Although it went through the motions of governing, even bureaucratic routine could not quite sustain the illusion. "We do not even know," complained the ministers, "how far the German people outside the limited area of Flensburg even knows about or recognizes the Dönitz government."[12]

For understandable reasons, the attitude of the Allies was

equally uncertain. Dönitz had been a faithful follower of Hitler. When first appointed Reichspräsident, and still unaware that the Führer was dead, he had cabled back: "My loyalty to you will be unconditional." Earlier, he had been willing to serve under Heinrich Himmler; and although he soon dismissed the Reichsführer SS and other notorious party members, he and his ministers continued to exercise what was indisputably a Nazi mandate. Among those he dismissed was Josef Goebbels, whose suicide in Berlin was still unknown in Flensburg; but the policy he now appeared to advocate might have been dictated by Goebbels himself. The coming danger, Dönitz argued, was the Bolshevization of Europe: against it, Germany and the Western Allies must stand firm together. This, it was true, had been urged by some members of the German Resistance against Hitler; but by now it was the watchword of Himmler and Hermann Göring, most memorably voiced in the last doomed broadcasts made from Hamburg by the English-speaking Nazi propagandist, William Joyce. To Eisenhower, the stratagem seemed obvious. Dönitz, he concluded, "was trying to make trouble between SHAEF and the Russians," and he sent Robert Murphy and a senior staff officer to Flensburg to investigate. When they arrived, Dönitz repeated his anti-Bolshevik arguments. "He seemed totally unaware," wrote Murphy later, "that the entire continent hated and feared Germany more than Russia." Dönitz, in turn, was astonished by "the complete lack of understanding of this problem on the part of the Anglo-Americans": their "shortsighted, colonialist treatment of the German people further serves to throw us into the arms of the Russians." He was more astonished still on Wednesday, May 23, when he and his cabinet were taken into custody by military police. Both sides could plead some justification. Perhaps the aptest comment was the German war diarist's grim bureaucratic footnote on the Rheims surrender: "Over-all impression after thorough reflection and discussion: 'Es ging nicht anders.'" There was indeed no other way.[13]

The multiple confusion of these anxious weeks contained much future history in embryo. The chaos itself was revealing; and so was each of its components. The Germans' anxiety to avoid capture by the Russians was a measure both of Nazi atrocities in Eastern Europe, and of the savagery with which they were being avenged. Churchill's vain attempt to persuade Truman to override Stalin foreshadowed the ever clearer contrast between Britain's declining greatness and America's growing strength. Stalin's suspicion that the West might make a separate peace with the Nazis typified the insecurity of a nation with no natural western frontier, prone to what has been well called "defensive expansion," and hence a ready participant in the "cold war." General de Gaulle's characteristic concern for protocol was a similar presage of friction. Finally, the makeshift arrangements for the surrender reflected the sketchiness of the Allies' preparations for peace. For several years, the essential task of winning the war had had first claim on their attention. When Nazi resistance collapsed, they were like men bearing a battering-ram, carried headlong into the castle by the very impetus that had smashed down its doors. Few had realized the long-term implications of their call for "unconditional surrender." Natural and inevitable as it was in response to the nihilism of Hitler's "total war," it was bound to prolong the conflict; but this was not all. Interpreted as the surrender not just of a regime, but of a nation, it helped to create a divisive political void in the waste land that was now the heart of Europe.[14]

The continent that now lay open to its liberators had once been the richest in the world. This implied no special virtue in Europeans; nor was it necessarily due to a uniquely favorable providence. Just as the windings of a river across flat country may be the cumulative effects of once minute irregularities, so Europe's wealth may well have derived from a series of fortunate accidents, each favoring the next. Fertile, densely populated, with a temperate climate and many waterways, the continent was bounded to the north, south, and west by an unusually long coastline, dotted with islands and fretted with creeks and harbors; only to the east were there few natural barriers, merely the plains and steppes so often crossed by hordes from the vast Eurasian land-mass. From Europe's rocky backbone of the Pyrenees, the Massif Central, and the Alps, flowed the tributaries of its great rivers—the Garonne, the Ebro, the Rhone, the Rhine, the Po, the Danube, the Elbe. Some divided the nations; others linked them together. The Alps and the Rhine, in particular, separated three broad regions, each of which in turn had been the main focus of Europe's wealth. To the south were the lands of the Mediterranean, source of ancient civilizations, home of hardy, long-rooted plants and trees—lemons, olives, vines, figs, almonds—which conserve their secret moisture through the hot dry summers when the "trade winds" blow offshore. To the north of the Alps, in cooler regions, the westerly "anti-trade winds" brought rain to nourish the forests of oak, elm, beech and birch that once covered the continent, interspersed with dark conifers on the heaths and uplands. Gradually, men had cut back the forest to make way for fields and pastures: west of the Rhine, the land had grown especially green and lush. "France is just a plate of salad," cried the eight-year-old son of the King of Afghanistan when he saw it for the first time from the air.[15] In the east and northeast, some of the soil was poorer; but the earth below was rich. Here lay the mineral deposits—the coal and iron ore—that helped to forge the first industrial revolution. Here, spread diagonally across Europe, was the powerhouse of its prosperity from the nineteenth century onward, a huge populous workshop straddling the frontier between Romance and Germanic languages that stretched from the North Sea to the Alps.

Now, as so often in recent history, Europe's workshop had become its battleground; nor had other areas been spared. One after another, with the exception of the neutrals, most countries in continental Europe had been invaded or occupied: Austria, Czechoslovakia, Albania, Poland, Finland, Denmark, Norway, Belgium, Holland, Luxembourg, France, Latvia, Lithuania, Estonia, Rumania, Bulgaria, Hungary, Greece, Yugoslavia, Russia; then, when the tide turned, Italy and Germany. Many had been fought over twice in the same war.

No one who saw the results is likely to forget them. By 1945, beyond the joy and frenzy of liberation, beyond the panic of defeat and conquest, much of the continent shared a grim uniformity. Europe, and above all central and Eastern

Europe, was a land laid waste. In the cities, the skyline was jagged with destruction: amid the ruins and craters, rubble and wreckage blocked the streets. The spires of churches stood truncated, broken; machinery rusted in the bombed-out factories; doors hung askew on torn hinges; window-glass crunched and crackled underfoot. Roads were pitted with shell-holes; the abutments and piers of demolished bridges were left like the stumps of giant teeth. Railway tracks jutted over empty space, or reared in stiff contortions; skeletons of wagons, stripped for firewood, lay with their wheels in the air. Tunnels were flooded; in canals and rivers there were swollen corpses, drifting half-waterlogged, occasionally catching on submerged tugs and barges, whose wheelhouses broke the surface like huts in a swamp. Harbors were full of listing sunken ships.

Much of the countryside was charred and blackened. Mutilated trees, burned bushes, and fields plowed by tank tracks marked the site of battles; here and there, nothing was left of a village but crumbled walls, ashes and wisps of straw. Nature, once tamed, now retaliated. Grass grew between the paving-stones; rats multiplied; in some areas, unchecked by peasant bows and arrows, herds of wild pigs roamed the land for forage.

Yet amid the desolation there were people. Smoke curled from tin chimneys poking through boarded roofs and windows. Sheds on weekend vegetable plots became houses; cellars and caves were turned into homes. Now and then, there was a sudden crash of masonry and a choking explosion of dust. Peace had silenced the thud of bombs and mortars, the whistle of shells, the rattle of small-arms fire. Instead of the roar and shrill clatter of tanks, there came the more humdrum sound of army lorries, jeeps, and motorcycles; as well as the steady tramp of marching men, there was now the endless shuffle of the defeated, the captive, the homeless. To many of the troops who first encountered them, the people in parts of Europe seemed a population of cripples, of women and children and the very old. Some were starving; some were sick with typhus or dysentery; in the concentration camps, millions had already died. The survivors, gray-faced ghosts in parodies of clothing, trundled their salvaged belongings in home-made handcarts—rugs, threadbare overcoats, a kettle, an alarm clock, a battered toy. They waited at standpipes for a dribble of brown water; they queued for bread and potatoes; they rummaged for sticks and scraps. For them, this waste land of rubble, rags, and hunger was a prison without privacy or dignity; and like all prisons, it smelled. It smelled of dust, oil, gunpowder, and greasy metal; of drains and vermin; of sweat and vomit, dirty socks and excrement; of decay and burning and the unburied dead.

In all of Europe, not including the Soviet Union, at least five million houses had been destroyed, and very many more were badly damaged. In the Soviet Union, twenty-five million people had lost their homes. Out of ten million houses in France, the number destroyed was over half a million; those severely damaged were a million and a half. In Holland, the respective totals were 92,000 and 400,000; in overcrowded Italy, where losses were counted by rooms rather than houses, they were two million and four-and-a-half million. In Britain, the combined total was four million. In Germany it was ten million.[16]

Of Europe's capitals outside the neutral countries, only Brussels, Paris, Prague, and Rome had escaped large-scale destruction. Many cities, like London, Coventry, St. Nazaire, Toulon, Vienna, Trieste, or Lübeck, had whole sections gouged out of them. Others—Warsaw, Budapest, Rotterdam, Le Havre, Cologne, Frankfurt, Essen, Rostock—were largely in ruins. Some had been consumed by fire-storms: among the victims of these mass cremations were Hamburg, Wuppertal, Kassel, Stuttgart, Darmstadt, and Dresden. A few—Jülich, Düren, Nuremberg, Hanover, Düsseldorf—had been almost totally destroyed. The condition of Berlin, in particular, horrified those who came to it from the West. "I never saw such destruction," declared Truman; for General Lucius Clay, "it was like a city of the dead." Some 95 per cent of its urban area lay in ruins. There were three thousand broken water mains, and only twenty fire stations out of more than eighty were in operation; 149 of the city's schools had been demolished, and not one of its 187 Evangelical churches was untouched. In the streets were over 400 million cubic meters of rubble: one estimate reckoned that if ten trains a day with fifty wagons each were used to remove it, the process would take sixteen years.[17]

Between the devastated cities, communications had become difficult and slow. Many roads were closed to traffic. In the western regions of Germany, 740 out of 958 major river bridges were impassable. Many of the Seine and Loire bridges, and all those across the Rhine, had been demolished. When the war ended in Sicily, no permanent bridges had been left on the road from Catania to Palermo, and even a short journey of ten miles on the map could entail a drive of more than twice that distance across country. Vast numbers of vehicles had been destroyed or requisitioned. Nine-tenths of the trucks in France were out of action, and of the ten thousand needed to bring food to Paris, only two-and-a-half thousand were in use. Petrol, oil and spare parts were at a premium: early in 1945, most of the trucks produced by the French Renault company remained useless for want of tires.[18]

The railways were in a worse state than the roads. Long stretches of track were out of commission—4,000 kilometers in France, 12,000 kilometers in northwest Germany, two-thirds of the entire system in Yugoslavia and Greece. Many viaducts were down—more than two-thirds of those in Poland, and 2,395 in Germany. In Berlin, rowboats had to be used in the flooded subway. One-quarter of the railway tunnels in Czechoslovakia were blocked. Few locomotives were in working order—50 per cent in Germany, 40 per cent in Belgium and Poland, 25 per cent in Holland, 3,000 out of 17,000 in France. Rolling stock was scarce, and scattered all over Europe. In northwest Germany, only 5,000 out of 12,000 wagons were usable, and in France only 115,000 of 475,000.[19]

Europe's waterways, once so vital to its prosperity, were now equally paralyzed. Out of the 8,460 kilometers of French canals and rivers normally bearing traffic, only 509 kilometers were navigable at the time of the Liberation. About 90 per cent of the Oder barge fleet, and 35 per cent of the Rhine fleet, were destroyed. Many locks were badly damaged. Traffic on the Rhine was at a standstill. In its upper stretches, 754 barges had been sunk; to the north, the debris of 540 bridges was waiting to be removed from the canals. Antwerp and Bordeaux were the only large continental ports still functioning almost normally. In Hamburg harbor, fifty merchantmen, nineteen floating docks, and various other craft had foundered; the port of Toulon was encumbered with the scuttled gray wrecks of the French fleet. Most European countries, finally, had lost a large proportion of their merchant marine—Holland 40 per cent, Britain and Norway 50 per cent, Belgium 60 per cent, France 70 per cent, and Italy 90 per cent.[20]

The paralysis of transport in Europe was partly matched by that of industry. Everywhere, there were shortages—of machinery, of raw materials, and especially of fuel and power. European coal production outside the Soviet Union was down to two-fifths of its prewar level. The Ruhr, which had once produced 400,000 tons a day, was now producing 25,000. In Italy, the total output of electricity stood at less than 65 per cent of the 1941 figure, and less still in the center and south. Some items were particularly scarce: in France, coal production was held back by the shortage of pit-props, while the output of textiles had been greatly reduced by damage to the mills in the northeast. In southern Germany, with 90 per cent of the factories and 85 per cent of their plant out of action, industrial output was down to only 5 per cent of normal capacity. Production in Italy had fallen to less than one-quarter of what it had been in peacetime; in Belgium, France, Greece, Holland, Yugoslavia, and Poland, it had fallen to one-fifth.[21]

In money terms, World War II had cost more than the combined total of all European wars since the Middle Ages. In France, the expenditure was estimated at 36 billion dollars, or nearly three times the country's prewar annual income. Italy's national resources were reckoned to have been reduced by one-third. Even in Great Britain, which had been spared invasion, 10 per cent of the national wealth had been destroyed by bombing and by the running down of capital assets. Britain's biggest loss, however, was invisible. Government expenditure had risen during the war to five times its previous level, while the exports with which to pay for it had been reduced by 60 per cent. To try to fill the gap,

Britain had been obliged to liquidate £1,118,000,000 worth of overseas investments and other resources: but this still left an external debt of more than £3 billion. Within six years the world's biggest creditor nation had become the biggest debtor. Much of continental Europe likewise, had also been living on credit and aid. By October 1945, the United States had granted 46,040,000,000 dollars' worth of supplies on the "Lend-Lease" basis of permanently deferred payment. Of this, some 30 billion went to the British Empire, and 11 billion to the Soviet Union. The other main beneficiaries included France, the Netherlands, Greece, Belgium, Norway, Turkey, and Yugoslavia. When the war and Lend-Lease ended, Britain, France, the Netherlands, and Belgium found it necessary to raise American loans. In Germany, the public debt had increased from 40 billion marks to 357 billion; in Italy, the budget deficit for 1945–46 was 300 billion lire. Inflation plagued most European countries, although in varying degrees. Relatively mild in Britain, Denmark, Sweden, and Switzerland, it was worse in Belgium, Bulgaria, Czechoslovakia, Finland, France, the Netherlands, Norway, Spain, and Turkey; in Italy, prices rose to thirty-five times their prewar level. In Greece and Hungary, the currency collapsed completely. In November 1944, the Greek government devalued the drachma at the rate of 50 billion to one; and by the time that Hungary introduced a new monetary unit, the final quotation for the old one had reached the rate of 11,000,000,000,000,000,000,000,000,000,000 pengoes to the United States dollar.[22]

"Butter, chocolate, meat!" ran a front-page headline in the *Amsterdamsch Dagblad* on May 8, 1945.[23] Inflation might be an ominous symptom of Europe's longer-term problems; it might swallow up private savings and further demoralize an already shaken society: but even more immediate for most Europeans that summer was the search for food.

Throughout the continent, immense tracts of arable land had been laid waste. Nearly 40 per cent of Europe's livestock was gone, and countless farm buildings had been destroyed or damaged. The Ukraine had twice suffered from "scorched earth" devastation. In Italy, nearly two million acres of farmland south of the Apennines had been flooded, mined, or used for airfields; in the Netherlands, 540,000 acres had been flooded, 190,000 of them with salt water. In the whole of Europe, the area under wheat and rye had been reduced by 23 per cent; and when the war ended, it was too late for further sowing.[24]

The land still cultivated was in poor condition. Farming, like other industries, was subject to serious shortages—of seeds, pesticides, machinery, draft animals, manure. There was even a shortage of twine. Fertilizer output had fallen to one-fifth of its prewar level: this, coupled with severe drought, reduced yields per acre in 1945 by about 25 per cent. The wheat crop was 40 per cent below normal, and the total harvest of bread grains in continental Europe outside the Soviet Union was only thirty-one million tons, compared with an average of fifty-nine million before the war. The total, moreover, concealed wide variations. If Denmark's 1945–46 crops were 93 per cent of the prewar average, those in France, Belgium, Germany, and Italy were only a little above 50 per cent, and those in the Netherlands and Austria even lower.[25]

Hunger became commonplace in Europe. Even where agriculture had traditionally flourished, many remained underfed; and because the lack of transport made distribution difficult, there were notorious contrasts between the countryside and the towns. In France at the Liberation, while food in the provinces was adequate though meager, the average Parisian had lost nearly 42 pounds in weight. The official daily ration of bread, when available, was 275 grams or 500 grams for workpeople; the daily fats ration was ten grams; the meat ration, bones included, was 400 grams—less than a pound— to last for a month. On the Paris black market, bread was six times, butter ten times, and meat nearly three times the official price. For many Europeans, indeed, the black market had become a grudgingly accepted necessity; but for those unable to pay its prices, it was a bitterly resented privilege of the rich. At one black-market restaurant in Rome in 1945, old women and children crowded round the open-air enclosure to snatch food from the table; elsewhere in Italy at that time, bread was being sold by the slice.[26]

A man leading a sedentary life normally consumes between 2,400 and 2,800 calories a day, while a physically active man needs 3,200 to 5,500, depending on the nature of
his work. Long after the war was over, United Nations experts reported that 140 million Europeans were still receiving
fewer than 2,000 daily, and 100 million of them fewer than
1,500—less than the average inhabitant of India, and less
than the normal ration for a seven-year-old child. In the
last year of the war, many people in Holland had been
subsisting on only 900 calories a day.[27]

But war had not only pauperized Europe; it had also
taken unprecedented toll of human life. To the previous generation, World War I had seemed the ultimate Armageddon:
it had left twenty-one million wounded and eight and a half
million dead. World War II had killed thirty-two million,
twenty-three million of them on the battlefield: of the total
dead, more than fifteen million were Europeans. World War
I had been the first to claim more victims among conscripts
than among regular servicemen; World War II was the first
in which so many civilians had lost their lives. Of all the
belligerents, the Soviet Union had lost the most servicemen
—seven and a half million; the next largest loss was that of
Germany, with three and a half million men missing or killed.
When the war ended, 24 per cent of the Germans born in
1924 were either dead or missing, and 31 per cent were more
or less severely mutilated. In the western regions of Germany there were two million cripples. In the whole country,
out of a population of nearly seventy million, there were now
7,279,000 more women than men.[28]

Yet however grim the fate of so many civilian and service
victims of the actual war machine, the worst treatment of all
was reserved for those who died—and those, perhaps less
fortunate, who nearly died—in the concentration and extermination camps. Their story has been told so many times
that anyone who was not an inmate may well question his
own credentials, and perhaps the quality of his own motives, for returning to it. Needless repetition would be doubly
obscene. Nevertheless, the stripe-clad scarecrows condemned
to the "bone-mills" of Auschwitz, Bełżec, Sobibór. Chełmno,
Treblinka and the rest have their place in any account of

postwar Europe—no less than Stalin's forced laborers, the bombed victims of Coventry or Dresden, the women and children massacred in the church of Oradour-sur-Glane, the German plotters against Hitler, hanged on meat-hooks—and, indeed, the degraded, brutalized, sometimes frightened men who devised and ran the apparatus of extermination, and whose minds must surely be numbered among its victims. Altogether, at least six million people died in the camps before the war was over. When the Allied forces entered them, behind the look-out towers and the double barbed-wire fencing they found a total of some 670,000 survivors—befouled apathetic skeletons of men and women, huddled five to a shelf on multi-tier bunks, or lying, sitting and dragging themselves about amid the reeking, fly-covered litter of corpses outside their huts. To their liberators, many seemed half-human, reduced by cruelty to the very condition of *Untermenschen* that their captors' ideology prescribed for them— the most appalling circular argument in the history of mankind.[29]

The death camps set an absolute for human suffering: besides the long shadow they cast on history, few comparisons are valid. But among the ruins of Europe in 1945, suffering was not rare; and alongside the dead and the half-alive there were many more for whom sheer existence had come close to misery.

Between 1939 and the end of 1945, at least sixty million Europeans—not counting servicemen and prisoners of war— had been uprooted from their homes. Twenty-seven million of them had left their own countries, or been driven out by force. Four and a half million had been deported by the Nazis for forced labor; many thousands more had been sent to Siberia by the Russians. When the war ended, two and a half million Poles and Czechs were transferred to the Soviet Union, and more than twelve million Germans fled or were expelled from Eastern Europe. At one period in 1945, 40,000 refugees a week were streaming into northwest Germany. All told, the shifts of population involved fifty-five ethnic groups from twenty-seven countries. Some had been displaced more than once: one group—420,000 Karelians from between the Gulf of Finland and the White Sea—was shuttled to and fro no less than three times. By the summer of 1945, more-over, in addition to such refugees and "displaced persons," there were seven million prisoners of war in Allied hands in Western Europe, and more than eight million Allied troops.[30]

Statistics may indicate, but can hardly convey, the realities of such mass removals: the trains and cattle trucks crammed with human beings; the straggling processions with their baby carriages and cardboard suitcases; the women and children staggering under knapsacks; the roadside deaths; the weary fugitives limping across border zones in the darkness, their boots clogged with heavy mud. Several million died in the process; the impossibility of knowing how many is a rough measure of their ordeal. Of those who survived it, many were destitute. Germans expelled from Hungary were allowed to take 100 kilograms of personal belongings; from Czechoslovakia, 70 kilograms; from Poland, what they could carry: none was permitted more than a small quota of already inflated Reichsmarks. Europeans deported as forced laborers had naturally had even less; so had many of those who had fled from the advancing armies or escaped with only their lives from the air raids that had destroyed their cities. All were desperate for food and shelter—and for news of their families. At the center set up in Germany to trace missing persons, a staff of 240, using twenty-four languages, dealt with a thousand enquiries a day. With millions to be collected and cared for, lodged in converted factories, equipped with soap and blankets, fed on bread, thick soup, and coffee substitute, humanitarian efforts were bound to seem dehumanized. Alongside the refugees' own languages, alongside "Lagerdeutsch" and the polyglot scapegrace slang of postwar Europe—"comme ci comme ça," "Alles kaputt," "finito," "nix OK"—there grew up a new bureaucratic jargon: "DP" (for "displaced person"), "post-hostility refugees," "internal displacement," "infiltrees," "non-repatriables," "uncovered children," "unaccompanied children." It was a verbal device for facing the intolerable; but to some compassionate and sensitive observers it inevitably seemed cold. Others, at first, found equally disconcerting the unattractiveness of the unfortunate, at once aggressive and feckless, clinging to a few symbolic possessions; conspiring and often fighting to gain small material advantages; sometimes apathetic, often touchy and ungrateful, resenting the overworked helpers who were saving their lives.[31]

Such symptoms were part of the plight of the homeless and uprooted; and they were very widespread in the Europe of 1945. The destructive force of war had been more than physical. When peace came, many Europeans were deeply weary and demoralized. Inflation, rationing, the black market, the wealth and power of the occupying forces—all added to the disruption of normal ethics: looting, armed robbery, pimping, corruption and subterfuge were the result. And beneath the obvious signs of social disturbance there remained a legacy from dictatorship and defeat—a profound sense of impotence before alien authorities that was often taken for inherent submissiveness or cynicism. "*Der kleine Mann, was kann er doch machen?*" was a question continually asked me by prisoners of war. Nor was the feeling confined to Germany. Depicting the moral anarchy of postwar Naples, the novelist Curzio Malaparte added, "All of us in Europe . . . are more or less Neapolitan"; and a young French writer from the Paris suburbs, René Fallet, described with something of Malaparte's florid bitterness the world in which he and his contemporaries grew up:

We are the children of the occupation. In 1940 we were twelve, thirteen or fourteen. We began our life in an atmosphere of defeat, pillage and theft. We begged cigarettes from the Germans, on the roads of a country in ruins. We stuffed ourselves with swedes when what we wanted was bars of chocolate. We got in on the rackets. . . . For us, 'before the war' was a faded memory. Our years of discretion were years of utter absurdity, utter misery. . . . The older generation dropped us flat, although it was they who produced us! All they can do is keep on at us: 'In my day, we didn't answer our mothers back like that. . . . Young people today don't like work any more. . . . I don't know what's become of morality and honesty. . . .' So what? To hell with all the virtues that that lot couldn't preserve![32]

The tone was authentic and familiar: more radically than the celebrated "disillusion" of the 1920s, it expressed a general postwar mood. The writings of Jean-Paul Sartre, Max

Frisch, Cesare Pavese, Graham Greene, George Orwell; the films of Henri-Georges Clouzot, Marcel Carné, Wolfgang Staudte, Vittorio de Sica; the plays of Jean Anouilh; the verses of Jacques Prévert; the paintings of Francis Bacon—all on their different levels, whatever their affirmations, seemed to imply that happiness and hope were incompatible with intelligence or sensibility. Looking at the world in which they were welcomed, it was hard to disagree.

During the past six years, even in the democracies, a number of the civilized virtues had indeed had to be suspended "for the duration," like non-essential adjuncts to civilian life. For all the belligerents, violence, hatred and killing had become legitimate, patriotic, heroic; for resistance workers in the occupied countries, law-breaking, sabotage, and occasional necessary murders had become the norm. The skill of professional criminals had been recruited to combat crimes against humanity. Peaceable, kindly men and women had been taught cruel trades. To survive in such a moral climate, the sensitive had had to steel themselves; others had had to exploit, yet hold within limits, a natural aggressiveness that served their cause. Not everyone succeeded. When the great convulsion ended, when the Fascist and Nazi empires crumbled and the dictators went to their squalid deaths, some of the weapons that had defended freedom, peace and civilization proved to be double-edged. Nothing was more natural, more to be expected even by its victims, than the orgy of vengeance that broke out in Europe. Nothing was more inevitable: but it was an ugly sight.

At the elemental level, it took the form of what one writer bleakly called "the good old standbys of murder, torture, robbery, and rape." "There is a sad monotony," he commented, "about what one can do to a human being." For a time, there was lawlessness in most of the conquered and liberated countries. In Berlin and elsewhere the Red Army, its depleted ranks replenished from distant, primitive regions, earned a grim reputation for drunken violence, plunder, and indiscriminate sexual assault. In many parts of Germany, forced laborers and prisoners, suddenly freed, ran riot; and ordinary thieves and other criminals seized their chance, amid the general anarchy, to enrich themselves or pay off old scores. In the liberated countries, Nazi collaborators were rounded up and punished, sometimes summarily. The one-time conquerors' girl friends—what the Dutch called the *"moffenmeiden"*—were subjected to treatment in which long-pent anger, prurience, and puritanism seem to have had equal shares; but even they, paraded with shaven heads and some-times shaven bodies, were better off than some male col-laborators, reviled and bloodily beaten amid the smiles of peaceful-looking crowds. Many were executed on the spot. In France at the Liberation, at least 5,000 men and women were killed by their compatriots, and many more were im-prisoned without proper trial. By no means all of the victims had been collaborators; by no means all of those responsible were members of the Resistance. In some areas, the Com-munist underground Francs-Tireurs et Partisans used force to try to eliminate their rivals; but many cases of murder and torture—some rivaling those of the Nazi Gestapo—were simply the work of rapacious armed thugs. True, the picture was not entirely black. Many deserved their fate, and a num-ber of others showed restraint and courage. Just as, at the Ebensee concentration camp, two German Luftwaffe pilots turned guns on the guards and saved the inmates from last-minute massacre, so in the pillage of Berlin some Russian soldiers defended German women from their own drunken comrades. Even in that darkness there were points of light; and when some of the survivors in the death camps rounded on their SS captors, it could hardly be said that darkness was greatly deepened.[33]

"Revenge," wrote Francis Bacon the essayist, "is a kind of wild justice." At the end of World War II, certainly, much rough justice was done. But retribution, however deserved, is a questionable aim in international policy; and if it as-sumes judicial status, it may cause justice to be mistaken for a kind of pedantic revenge.

This, at least, is what happened when the victors of World War II set out to judge some of the vanquished, most no-tably in the first Nuremberg trial. In the dock were twenty-one defendants. A few of the Nazi ringleaders were absent: Hitler, Himmler, and the labor organizer Robert Ley had already committed suicide; Goebbels had had himself shot by an SS orderly; and Martin Bormann was missing, perhaps dead. The star defendant was the once plump Hermann Göring, also later to kill himself before he could be hanged. With him were some of the pillars of the Third Reich—Rudolf Hess, dazed and vacant, staring and fidgeting; Joachim von Ribbentrop, no longer the icy diplomat, but cowed and pallid; Karl Dönitz, looking to one observer "for all the world like a shoe clerk";[34] Wilhelm Keitel and Alfred Jodl, sitting sternly upright; Julius Streicher, angry and insolent; Ernst Kaltenbrunner, nervously chewing. They and their colleagues now seemed dim and unimpressive in their rankless uniforms and crumpled suits. For 216 days they sat in the big wooden enclosure, flanked by U. S. Military Police. From November 1945 to October 1946 the trial continued, with five million words of testimony and ten million words of printed record. The documents processed weighed several tons, and the published proceedings filled forty-two volumes. At the end of it all, three of the accused were acquitted; Hess, Dönitz, and five others were sentenced to varying terms of imprisonment; and the remaining twelve—including Göring, Ribbentrop, Keitel, Jodl, Streicher, Kaltenbrunner, and the absent Bormann—were condemned to death.

The verdicts, like the volume of evidence, were proof of the tribunal's anxiety to be fair. It attempted to blend British, American, and continental European procedure. Its president was Lord Justice Lawrence; each of the four main victorious powers supplied one distinguished judge and one alternate. The prosecution was conducted by eminent Allied counsel, and the accused were defended by lawyers of their own nationality, all but one of whom wore legal robes, as did all but one of the judges. Simultaneous interpretation, with adjustable headphones, ensured that all the testimony was instantly understandable. In the dock, the defendants were allowed to talk together; and Göring, at least, spoke so long when giving evidence that the chief American prosecuting attorney appealed to the president of the court to silence him—in vain. The records of the trial were of unique documentary importance: in the words of one scholar, they "threw valuable light upon the history of the war from the former enemy side."[35] More than this, they provided conclusive proof of Nazi barbarity: some of the atrocities they revealed would have earned the maximum penalty in any civilized court of law.

In this respect, the trial succeeded. It was no longer possible to deny with any honesty the nature of Adolf Hitler's "new order"—or the mediocrity of those who served it: Julius Streicher, for instance, who had so long preached "Jewish inferiority," proved to have the modest intelligence quotient of 106.[36] Nevertheless, if justice must not only be done, but also be seen to be done, the Nuremberg trial was a partial failure. It was perhaps too soon to be judicial about those who had caused unimaginable suffering: it was certainly too soon to appear so.

Despite the tribunal's fairness, in fact, it could hardly avoid the appearance of being both prosecutor and judge. The principle that men are innocent until proved guilty was understandably difficult to apply to the Nazi leaders. Before the trial, the Soviet judge had argued that they already stood convicted by proclamation of the Allies; and according to Sir David Maxwell Fyfe, British representative at the meetings preparing the trial, "Our work is to see these top-notch Nazis tried, condemned, and many of them executed." To enable all the prisoners to be kept in solitary confinement—forbidden to officers by the Geneva Convention—the defendants from the services were stripped of military rank. For reasons of security, none of the accused was allowed to speak alone with counsel, and all at first shared a small consulting-room a dozen at a time. In court, the prosecuting lawyers, unlike the defense, wore plain clothes or military uniform: also in uniform was the Russian judge. Finally, the gladiatorial nature of British and American court procedure, which predominated, was unfamiliar to the defendants' lawyers, for whom normal judicial proceedings were at least theoretically biased toward collective truth-seeking rather than attack and riposte. In the subsequent trial of the munitions manufacturer Alfried Krupp, arraigned in lieu of his senile father Gustav, there were serious clashes between the judges and defending counsel, who once walked out in protest and were briefly imprisoned for contempt of court.[37]

One argument before the Krupp tribunal, in particular, raised more clearly than most a question that was implicit in all the trials. "Much can be understood," the defense pleaded:

. . . only by him who experienced it himself: the extraordinary mixture of genuine love of one's country and unhealthy nationalism, of justified consciousness of one's self and [a sense of] racial superiority; the harmony between voluntary readiness for sacrifice and terroristic force, the intermingling of faith, self-deception, and betrayal.[38]

Such words could not bring back the dead, nor mitigate the enormities they helped explain; but they applied to many. There was and remains, in fact, a deep enigma in apportioning guilt and responsibility. When death and torture are inflicted on so many millions, it becomes more difficult than ever to draw a reasonable line between the obvious culprits and those whose co-operation, acquiescence, forced obedience, indifference, or voluntary ignorance helped make such things possible. Those who blame only the ringleaders may dishonor the active resistance—for whose members the concentration camps were partly intended—by tacitly grouping it with the inactive mass. Those, chiefly foreigners, who tend to depict Hitler as in some ways a normal statesman, thereby implicitly blaming a whole nation, seem not only to discount the Führer's long-avowed intentions, but also to have no logical grounds for totally absolving themselves: their countries too could have acted from outside to check the Nazis sooner—even if then it was still impossible to forestall them by establishing law and order on an international scale.[39]

In one respect, therefore, the Allied tribunals had an insuperable task. Inevitably, there were inequities if not injustices: some slipped through the net in which others, with similar records, were caught. To many, for instance, it seemed unfair that military men should be hanged for obeying orders, however iniquitous: a soldier's obedience, they claimed, should be unconditional. This dubious doctrine was convincingly answered by those who pointed out that every man, soldier or not, has an ultimate duty to his conscience, and that blind obedience was one of the evils against which the war had been fought. Their case would have seemed stronger, however, if Allied propaganda had analyzed less superficially the causes of World War II. As it was, "Prussian militarism" had been denounced alongside "Nazi tyranny"—despite the fact that a number of the plotters against Hitler had been "Prussian militarists" themselves.

Confusion of this sort was compounded by the double nature of the Nuremberg indictment. On the one hand it accused the defendants of war crimes and crimes against humanity, of which most of them were manifestly guilty, and were proved so; but on the other it made the much more general charge of "waging aggressive warfare."

"Aggression" was a word from the political vocabulary of the '30s; perhaps because it was so familiar, it was never adequately defined. The impulse behind its use was a groping toward some system that would make war illegal, as Henry L. Stimson—later, ironically, to be U. S. Secretary of War—had declared it to be as early as 1932. In 1939, Russia had been expelled from the League of Nations for violating the Kellogg-Briand Pact by attacking Finland; "aggression" of this kind was now "a crime." At Nuremberg, at least, this became a prosecution thesis. Robert H. Jackson, the American prosecutor, claimed that "no political, military or other considerations justify going to war . . . The law . . . requires that the status quo be not attacked by violent means." Sir Hartley Shawcross, for the British, was only a little less categorical: "It is a fundamental part of these proceedings," he declared, "to establish for all time that international law has the power . . . to declare that a war is criminal . . ." But however well-meaning, arguments such as these were juridically and morally precarious. In the opinion of the French delegate at the preparation of the tribunal, "If we declare war a criminal act of individuals, we are going further than the actual law." On this count, moreover, the Allies themselves—including the Russians—were by no means immune from reproach.[40]

At the safe and comfortable vantage point of more than twenty years' distance, therefore, the Nuremberg trials reveal many imperfections. To condemn these now would simply be to echo them; it has to be recalled how very different, to most people, the whole question looked at the time. In their context, the trials were a marvel of impartiality; then, perhaps only the saintly—or the insensitive—could be truly detached. Yet, in historical perspective, the mood of those concerned seems fatally tainted by the moral climate of war. Hatred and cruelty had called forth hatred, even on the part of the innocent; in some cases, elsewhere, they had called forth further cruelty as well. Writing in the shadow of Europe's collective tragedy, the American critic Edmund Wilson drew the stark conclusion: "Our whole world is poisoned now, and we must recognize that outlawing the enemy makes it easy to dislike one's allies."[41]

THE NEW FRONTIER

This war is not as in the past; whoever occupies a territory also imposes on it his own social system. Everyone imposes his own system as far as his army has power to do so. It cannot be otherwise.   *Joseph Stalin*[1]

Stalin was always asking for as much as he could get.
    Harry S. Truman[2]

The King was evidently very uncomfortable at having to sit down between the two giant creatures: but there was no other place for him.   *Lewis Carroll*[3]

The East-West confrontation had begun on Wednesday, April 25, 1945, when Russian and American troops had met on the Elbe. At least three separate advance parties from the American side pushed forward across the last strip of enemy territory between them and their Allies; recollections and dramatic reconstructions differ about who met whom first and where. Was it at Torgau or at Strehla? Was it a rowboat or a sailboat that the Americans paddled across the river with their rifle butts? Did the meeting take place at 12:05, 1:30, 4:40 or 4:45? In fact, a man in a fur hat riding on a pony seems to have been the first Russian sighted, in the village of Leckwitz, a mile from the Elbe; he was hailed from a jeep by Lieutenant Albert Kotzebue of the 69th Division of the V Corps. The time was about 11:30 A.M. Shortly afterward came the first encounter on the river itself. There, photographs were taken; a public relations officer appeared as if from nowhere, to have them posed and retaken with officers of higher rank. There was laughter, friendly babel, handshaking and gesturing with the flags that hung limp in the still air. Toasts were drunk; little speeches were made for posterity. Then the war continued. In Europe, it was almost over: but for anyone who sought them, that day's thin sunshine was already casting new shadows. At Torgau, an American patrol had come under Russian fire before it could establish its identity; later, to the Americans' surprise, the Russians dug themselves into further defensive positions—facing west.[4]

Both these incidents arose from routine battle drill; but they symbolized the fact that the world's two giants now confronted each other, warily, across a prostrate continent. The sequel, although neither may have consciously intended it, was the partition of Europe.

To impute "inevitability" to historical processes can be a tempting substitute for investigation and thought. But now and then comes a moment in history when circumstances conspire against men's efforts to change them; and one such moment was the last winter of the war. By that time, all the belligerents were weary. All three of the statesmen then supremely responsible in the struggle against Hitler had reached what in many less demanding professions would have been the retiring age. Joseph Stalin was sixty-five, and long tainted by what his opponents later called "the cult of personality." Winston Churchill, at seventy, was "very tired"[5] by the crushing burdens he had borne for more than four years, and he had recently been shaken by two attacks of pneumonia, one of them extremely severe. Franklin Roosevelt, although only sixty-two, was a haggard semi-invalid already close to death. Weighed down by the day-to-day tasks of war, obliged to deal pell-mell with problems as they presented themselves, they were even less able than statesmen ever are to transform the basic situation from which the problems arose. In many respects, therefore, their efforts for the future peace were bound to fit into a predetermined pattern. It was unfortunate, and ironical, that the pattern should largely have been set by Adolf Hitler.

All three of the leading Allied powers had originally been "insular." Britain was an island in the literal sense; her traditional aspiration had been non-involvement in continental Europe, whose peace she had sought to ensure by using a casting-vote to maintain successive balances of power. The

United States, more decisively protected by a broader ocean patrolled by the British navy, had tended to regard non-involvement as not merely prudent, but virtuous: Europe was an Old World from which many Americans' fathers and grandfathers had been glad to escape. Russia's historical situation had been different. Lacking the natural protection of a western coastline, it had fought to establish on its European borders a defensive ring of cowed or conquered territory; internally, it had developed a siege mentality, becoming autocratic in order to survive. But while in these respects it had been the opposite of America, at a deeper level its experience had been similar. It too had lived alone. Communism, with its revolutionary mission, had modified Russia's traditional solitude; but defensiveness ran deep. It was even intensified by the Communists' belief—or their claim—that they alone were building the good society. In their various ways, in fact, all three Allies had been "right little, tight little islands," with the typical islander's sense of superiority—shared, for slightly different reasons, by the fourth Ally, France.

Hitler, by destroying the old Europe, had destroyed the Allies' isolation and had brought them face to face. The crippling of France and the impoverishment of Great Britain ensured that the confrontation was now essentially between America and the Soviet Union. America, which had distrusted the balance of power in Europe, was forced into similar balance on the world scale. For a while, she seemed to grope for the role of arbiter that had once been played by Britain: Roosevelt, in particular, sometimes saw himself as a mediator between Russian Communism and Churchillian "imperialism." But the British Commonwealth could be no real counterweight to the Soviet Union; and in the end America entered and almost filled one side of the global balance. The other, as in the past, was occupied by the strongest power on the continent of Europe. Until very recently, that power had been Germany; but now, Hitler's "total war" and its corollary of "unconditional surrender" had brought Germany to the brink of destruction; and the Soviet Union took its place. Even before the war ended, distance, language, history, ideology, and conflicting conceptions of their interests had already helped to divide America and Russia. Once they were deprived of a common enemy, their new proximity divided them even more.[6]

Between the two giants and partly under their occupation, Europe faced an uncertain future. Only by making a separate peace could either America or Russia disengage herself. This was barely conceivable, although each suspected the other of toying with the idea. It was equally unlikely that both, when the war ended, would return to their former isolation —if only because so much remained to be settled; and unless both did so, neither could afford to retire. Of the two, the United States was the more inclined to withdraw from Europe: but for the Soviet Union this had become unthinkable. Stalin, although fighting for his life and that of Russia, had always made it clear that the prize he expected for his indispensable aid against the Axis powers was a free hand in Eastern Europe. As soon as this demand was even tacitly accepted by the Western Allies, the partition of Europe—at least into spheres of influence—became virtually certain. What was still undecided was the position of the new frontier, its effectiveness as a barrier, and its consequences for those on either side.

The question had arisen as early as December 1941, when enemy tanks had reached the outskirts of Moscow. There, Stalin had urged Anthony Eden, the British Foreign Secretary, to recognize Russian possession of Estonia, Latvia, and Lithuania; he had also pressed his claim to those areas of Poland east of the so-called "Curzon Line" that had remained Russian when the Polish republic had been recreated at Versailles in 1919, but which it had invaded and conquered in the following year. Backed by American prompting, Eden had resisted: when Britain signed a treaty of alliance with Russia six months later, the territorial clauses that Moscow had wanted were left out of the agreement. The result, unforeseen at the time, was that the claims made by Russia in a position of weakness were later restated and augmented in a position of strength.[7]

By the autumn of 1944, the tide of war had turned and the Red Army was sweeping westward. In January it had entered Poland, and begun absorbing or disbanding the national resistance forces; throughout August and September, unable or unwilling to come to the rescue, it had allowed the Warsaw rising to be crushed by the Nazis. In August, Rumania had ended its war against Russia; in September, Soviet troops had entered Belgrade, and were soon to enter Hungary; at about the same time, Marshal Tito of Yugoslavia had quietly slipped off to Moscow for talks with Stalin, and the Communist-dominated EAM (the Ethnikon Apeleftherotikon Metopon or National Liberation Front) was gaining control in Greece. Hopes that an effective world organization—the United Nations—might replace power politics had been dimmed by the disputes over voting rights within it when the United States, the Soviet Union, China, and Great Britain had met to discuss it that autumn at Dumbarton Oaks, near Washington. Churchill, already skeptical, agreed with the South African Prime Minister Field-Marshal Smuts that with Eastern Europe and the Balkans falling under Russian influence, "our position in the Mediterranean and in Western Europe must be strengthened rather than weakened." He therefore "felt acutely the need to see Stalin, with whom I always considered one could talk as one human being to another."[8]

Flying into Moscow with Anthony Eden on the afternoon of Monday, October 9, 1944, he quickly made himself at home in the small but unusually comfortable house that the Russians had provided. The prospect of direct action was exhilarating. "How are you going to begin with Uncle Joe?" asked Eden when he arrived for dinner. "I shall say that the President and I have been like brothers," said Churchill, "but I don't want the USSR to feel it is just an Anglo-Saxon affair. I want them to know it's the three of us. We can settle everything, we three, if we come together."[9]

At ten o'clock that night, Churchill and Eden went round to the Kremlin. Within an hour or two they had concluded with Stalin what in the words of a French writer "can only euphemistically be called a 'gentlemen's agreement.'" It was Churchill who proposed it. "Let us settle about our affairs in the Balkans," he said. "Your armies are in Rumania and Bulgaria. We have interests, missions and agents there. Don't let us get at cross-purposes in small ways. So far as Britain and Russia are concerned, how would it do for you to have ninety per cent predominance in Rumania, for us to have ninety per cent of the say in Greece, and go fifty-fifty about Yugoslavia?" While this was being interpreted, Churchill took a half-sheet of paper and wrote out the percentages, adding further figures for Hungary ("50-50 per cent") and Bulgaria ("Russia 75 per cent, the others 25 per cent"). Stalin looked at it for a moment: then he made a large blue-pencil tick on it and passed it back. There was a long silence. Churchill hesitated. "Might it not be thought rather cynical," he said, "if it seemed we had disposed of these issues, so fateful to millions of people, in such an offhand manner? Let us burn the paper." Stalin had fewer scruples. Perhaps he was pleased to involve Churchill in unholy complicity. "No— you keep it," he replied.[10]

So began the partition of Europe. The bargain indeed seemed cynical in its very rapidity; but it might have seemed no less so if disguised by diplomatic niceties, when in fact it was a recognition of the reality of power. The fate of Poland in 1939, crushed by the Nazis despite the Allied declaration of war against Hitler, had already shown the virtual impossibility of Western intervention to defend Eastern Europe; and if the Balkans now suffered for the same reason, Poland herself was about to do so a second time.

Historically, relations between Poles and Russians had never been happy; now, despite the common struggle against Hitler, they remained tense. The dispute over Poland's eastern territories was still not settled; and the atmosphere was hardly improved by the growing suspicion that Stalin, not Hitler, had been responsible for the slaughter of several thousand Polish officers in the forest of Katyn, near Smolensk. Nevertheless, in February 1944, under pressure from Churchill, the exiled Polish government in London agreed to discuss possible changes in the eastern frontier, and to envisage compensation with further territory in the West. It was the Soviet Union that remained adamant. Not only did Stalin insist on retaining all those regions of eastern Poland which he had recovered in 1939 under the Nazi-Soviet pact; he also set about ensuring a firm Russian grip on the postwar Polish government.[11]

In July 1944, Stanislaw Mikolajczyk, the Peasant Party leader who had succeeded General Wladyslaw Sikorski as head of the London government-in-exile, visited Moscow to discuss the territorial question; but instead of being able to negotiate with Stalin, he found himself obliged to haggle with the Polish Committee of National Liberation, the "provisional executive authority" set up in Lublin, the temporary capital. As Churchill wrote after meeting the Committee's representatives: "It was soon plain that the Lublin Poles were mere pawns of Russia. They had learned and rehearsed their part so carefully that even their masters evidently felt they were overdoing it." Mikolajczyk had the same impression. The Lublin Committee was already planning to dominate the postwar government: its Communist leader, Boleslaw Bierut, hoped to be President. True, he was prepared to offer Mikolajczyk the post of Prime Minister, but with only three other "London" Poles in a cabinet of eighteen. Meanwhile, Warsaw had risen against the Nazis; yet both Bierut and Stalin seemed deaf to appeals for help. Returning to London, Mikolajczyk even now induced his colleagues to propose a further compromise on the frontier question and the shape of the postwar government; but he can hardly have been surprised when Stalin paid no heed.[12]

For a further six weeks the deadlock continued. Then, rather peremptorily, Churchill summoned the leader of the "London" Poles to Moscow. On Friday, October 13, 1944, Mikolajczyk and his colleagues met Churchill, Eden, Stalin and the Soviet Foreign Minister V. M. Molotov; the American Ambassador, W. Averell Harriman, was present as an observer. To Mikolajczyk's dismay, Stalin and Molotov announced that at their Teheran meeting a year before the three Allies had already decided to return Poland's eastern territories to Russia. This was stretching the truth: but Churchill was acquiescent and Harriman, true to his observer's status, said nothing—rather as Roosevelt had done at Teheran. Molotov and Churchill then described how Poland could be compensated by the extension of its western boundaries as far as the Oder. Finally, Churchill put strong pressure on Mikolajczyk to come to an agreement with the Lublin Committee. It seemed to be a case of *force majeure*.[13]

Looking from one calm, stubborn face to another, Mikolajczyk could do nothing—feel nothing but impotent rage and pain. Churchill, despite appearances, was equally powerless. The frontiers that he was proposing seemed to him reasonable: they would nullify the results of Polish aggression against Russia in 1920, yet offer compensation at the expense of the common enemy who had attacked Poland in 1939. As for the postwar government, the very unattractiveness of the Lublin Committee seemed likely to tell against it once free elections were held. Above all, Stalin had shown that he would accept no other solution; and against Soviet intransigence there was little that Churchill alone could do. The London Poles weighed on his conscience; but like all the exiled governments, precariously embodying the ideal of their countries' freedom, they were bound at times to seem needlessly touchy, pretentious poor relations in permanent residence, with no real power to endorse or justify their theoretical claims. Alternately exasperated and conciliatory, he argued for several days in the hope of reaching a compromise. At one bitter moment, Mikolajczyk asked leave to be parachuted into Poland, saying that he preferred to die now "rather than be hanged later by the Russians in full view of your British Ambassador." But the dispute, if acrimonious, was inconclusive: Mikolajczyk returned to his indignant cabinet in London and Churchill to a restive House of Commons. America, meanwhile, was deep in a presidential election, and Polish appeals to Roosevelt produced only tardy and partial assurances. Finally, Mikolajczyk and his Peasant Party colleagues resigned, leaving the government-in-exile in the hands of anti-Soviet Socialists.[14]

Thereupon, preparations began to be made in Poland for the Lublin Committee to become a provisional government; and in January 1945 this was formed. The Soviet Union instantly accorded it diplomatic recognition. A fortnight later, the Red Army entered the ruins of Warsaw, and the Provisional Government was set in place. At the Yalta Conference in February, the United States, the Soviet Union, and Britain made small adjustments to the Polish frontiers proposed by Stalin and Churchill, and agreed that "the Provisional Government which is now functioning in Poland should . . . be reorganized on a broader democratic basis, with the inclusion of democratic leaders from Poland itself and from Poles abroad."[15]

This formula bore every trace of its conflicting origins. Much of the Yalta meeting, as one French diplomat has remarked, turned into a verbal exercise. "The march of events creates difficulties. These take the form of documents. It is necessary to reach agreements, i.e. texts. This is what happens at nearly all such conferences. Never really prepared, they degenerate into drafting committees. Men who are responsible for the destinies of the world get entangled in a mesh of words and phrases, like giants sent back to school."[16] Applied to the "Lublin" government, the word "reorganized" made agreement possible only at the cost of ambiguity. For the Western powers, it meant something like "replaced": for the Soviet Union, it implied minor modifications to a largely puppet government. In the long run, the latter interpretation prevailed.

In all essentials, therefore, the fate of Eastern Europe had been decided in Moscow in the crisp October days of 1944. In Greece, Stalin kept his bargain with Churchill: that winter, the Communist-run EAM's military arm, ELAS (Ethnikos Laikos Apeleftherotikos Stratos or National People's Liberation Army), was defeated in its attempt to seize power. In Yugoslavia, Marshal Tito captured his Serbian rival Draža Mihailović and had him executed for allowing his Četnici to join forces with Germans and Italians against the Communist partisans. Tito's independence of character kept Yugoslavia's status ambiguous; but elsewhere—in Bulgaria, Rumania, Hungary, and Czechoslovakia, as in Poland—non-Communists were finally eliminated from office by various combinations of threats, propaganda, faked elections, purges, deportation, judicial murder, and armed coups. The details differed, but the broad pattern of Soviet policy was everywhere the same. Its purpose was simple and very evident. As Stalin remarked at Yalta, Poland had been throughout history "the corridor through which the enemy has passed into Russia." His aim was to turn that corridor into a barrier, alongside similar barriers in the rest of Eastern Europe. The results, however, were farther-reaching. By annexing part of Poland and establishing a defensive ring of satellites on its own western borders, the Soviet Union merely shifted its problems westward with itself.[17]

In part, this reflected the new world balance. On the world stage, Western Europe now found itself between the United States and the Soviet Union in a position similar to that once occupied by Poland between Germany and Imperial Russia. On the European stage, Poland's traditional role of buffer state was now assumed by Germany, with all the risk of partition which that implied. But whereas Poland had been small and weak, and its people very various, Germany even now was potentially the second greatest power on the continent, with a strong sense of national identity. To divide Germany would be to cut deep into the heart of Europe, inflicting a wound that might dangerously fester if it were left unhealed.[18]

Already during the war this danger had been tacitly acknowledged. In July 1943, for example, the British Foreign Office had suggested to America and Russia a joint organization to administer the future armistice, with a local Allied Commission in each ex-enemy country. At the end of August, Stalin himself proposed a single organization to negotiate with Hitler's allies; and at the Moscow Foreign Ministers' Conference that October, Anthony Eden had put forward a resolution on Allied responsibility in postwar Europe, repudiating separate spheres of influence.[19]

Yet behind this apparent harmony, the realities were more conflicting and confused. Stalin's proposal of August 1943, in particular, had been a response to the current armistice negotiations with Italy, which were concluded on September 3 and announced five days later. As elaborated by Molotov at the Moscow Conference, it would have given the joint Allied organization in Italy control over both the civil and the military activities of the Commander-in-Chief, General Sir Harold Alexander; and this, the Western Allies feared, might hamstring their armies without in return ensuring joint control over Eastern Europe. They therefore successfully insisted that the Allied organization be merely advisory. In practice, this by no means excluded all Russian influence: within six months, the Soviet Union had accredited an independent representative to the Italian government, and Palmiro Togliatti had returned from Moscow to lead the Italian Communist Party. But although such tolerance contrasted sharply with Soviet absolutism in Eastern Europe, the Allies' agreement on Italy further confirmed the emergence of separate spheres of influence, which the Western Allies officially opposed.[20]

In the case of Germany, the question of spheres of influence, or partition, was entangled with that of "dismemberment." If postwar Germany were to have a unified government, partition would be unlikely: if it were to be "dismembered" into separate states or regions, partition might be difficult to avoid. On this subject, each of the three principal Allies had differing opinions; and each shifted its viewpoint during the later stages of the war.

The idea of partition had been broached by Stalin at the end of 1941. Then, he had envisaged independence for Austria, the Rhineland, and perhaps Bavaria, and the transfer of East Prussia to Poland and of the Sudetenland to Czechoslovakia. He felt, as he said two years later at the Teheran Conference, that "if Germany was to be dismembered it should be really dismembered." When his ambitions in Eastern Europe began to be satisfied, however, Stalin seemed ready to listen to other proposals: in February 1945 at Yalta, he asked if dismemberment was still accepted, and whether the whole of Germany should have a single government. By the time of the armistice, on May 9, 1945, he appeared to have swung round completely. "The Soviet Union," he announced in his Proclamation to the Peoples, "celebrates victory but it does not intend to dismember or destroy Germany"—a view he confirmed at the Potsdam Conference in July. To Harry Hopkins, Roosevelt's friend and adviser, Stalin explained this apparent *volte-face* as a concession to British and American feelings; more probably, it was a bid to have some say in administering the Ruhr, from which he hoped for reparations.[21]

British policy was equally changeable and equally consistent. Shifting with events, it yet remained true to diplomatic reflexes conditioned by the balance of power. In 1941, when

Germany was in the ascendant, British diplomatists had assured skeptical Americans that postwar collaboration with Russia would "recreate some reasonable balance of power in Europe, destroyed by the collapse of France, against the possibility of revived Germany." After the Nazi defeat at the battle of Stalingrad two years later, however, Churchill became more cautious. "The prospect of having no strong country on the map between England and Russia," he said, "was not attractive": it was therefore important "to recreate a strong France." He also reverted to his favorite plan for a south German confederation that might include Bavaria, Württemberg, Baden, and even Austria and Hungary. At Teheran, although he repeated that he was "all for" dismemberment, its most important purpose in his eyes was to remove Prussia, "the evil core of German militarism."[22]

American views, finally, were marked by conflict as well as change. Temperamentally, Roosevelt had been inclined toward dismemberment: he had thought of dividing postwar Germany into three or more sovereign states, only economically linked. Sumner Welles, the Under-Secretary of State, had actually drawn up a plan for this purpose when he resigned in September 1943 over policy disputes with the Secretary of State, Cordell Hull. The Welles plan envisaged transferring East Prussia to Poland and splitting the rest of the country into three states, one in the northwest, one in the southwest, and one in the northeast. At Teheran, Roosevelt went even farther, suggesting five self-governing entities: Hanover and northwest Germany; Saxony and the Leipzig area; Hesse-Darmstadt, Hesse-Kassel, and the region south of the Rhine; Bavaria, Baden and Württemberg; and Prussia, "to be rendered as small and as weak as possible." He also proposed internationalizing the Ruhr, the Saar, Hamburg, and the Kiel Canal. Allen Dulles and the State Department, on the other hand, were more in favor of a centralized Germany, provided it were democratically run; and as the war continued, Roosevelt himself grew more reluctant to take decisions in advance. As he wrote to Cordell Hull on October 20, 1944, "In view of the fact that we have not occupied Germany, I cannot agree at this moment as to what kind of a Germany we want in every detail."[23]

At Teheran, Yalta, and Potsdam, the Allies held long, sometimes desultory debates on the subject; but all the time, like a slow fuse unobtrusively burning, the force of events was bringing partition nearer. Any one of a number of circumstances might have prevented it. Had a German government survived the collapse of the Nazis, the country might not have been ruled by the Allies. If "unconditional surrender" ensured that it was, it might yet have been governed as a single unit; failing that, in each zone of occupation a mixed contingent might have exerted joint control. If this in turn were out of the question, the zones might have been designed to converge on Berlin, making it easier for a joint Allied council to supervise their separate administration. Finally, if none of this proved feasible, the Allies might still have gradually lowered the inter-zonal barriers, and free elections might ultimately have been held throughout Germany. At each moment of decision, the issue still seemed open; but one by one the possibilities narrowed. The fuse burned steadily on.

The process began in 1943. In January, the idea of "unconditional surrender" was publicly launched by Roosevelt at the press conference following his Casablanca meeting with Churchill. In the spring it began to take diplomatic form when the British Foreign Office, preparing a visit to Washington by Anthony Eden, proposed that no German government be recognized in the period after the armistice. This same suggestion, still not yet adopted as an Allied policy, was tacitly put to the Russians at the Foreign Ministers' Conference in Moscow that October. There, toward the end of the proceedings, Cordell Hull went up to Molotov and slipped a document into his pocket. It was unofficial, he explained. Molotov showed it to Stalin. Next day, he came back beaming. "This text," he said, "expresses Russian ideas about Germany just as we should have expressed them ourselves."[24]

Cordell Hull's document had been drafted in Moscow on October 23, 1943, by two members of the U.S. delegation. It was based partly on State Department position papers, but partly also on a private study made by the New York Council on Foreign Relations. As such, it reflected the conflicts and uncertainties in American policy, and tried to suggest a suitable compromise. It was divided into three sections. The first dealt with "unconditional surrender," the third with the final peace. The latter raised the possibility of dismemberment, but it also envisaged eventual free elections in Germany as a whole. It was the document's second section, however, that was to prove decisive. Covering the period between the armistice and the peace treaty, it called for disarmament, reparations and the total occupation of Germany by the three main Allies, ruling through a tripartite commission. It thus implied, without actually stipulating, the absence of any central German government until the peace treaty was signed.[25]

Stalin's delight at these proposals is hardly surprising. They made it clear that Germany, unlike Italy, would be a political vacuum; and by confirming the implications of "unconditional surrender," they set the scene for division into zones. The first line of defense against partition had fallen. The second was to follow within a few weeks.

The principle of zoning in Germany had already been put forward that summer. In London, a special Cabinet Committee under the chairmanship of Clement Attlee, then Deputy Prime Minister, had recommended that after the armistice there should be three separate zones of occupation, with only Berlin under joint Allied control. This plan, worked out in agreement with the British Chiefs of Staff, had been transmitted to Washington; but in view of Churchill's changing attitude, it might have remained a dead letter had it not been revived at the Moscow Foreign Ministers' Conference that October and at the November meeting of Allied leaders in Teheran. There, Churchill, Roosevelt, and Stalin agreed "in principle" to a three-zone system, with a fourth inter-Allied zone in Berlin. The details they left to a new tripartite body of senior officials, the European Advisory Commission, set up by the Moscow Conference of Foreign Ministers, and due to meet in London at the end of the year.[26]

The Commission convened, informally, on December 15, 1943, and held its first formal session on the afternoon of January 14, 1944. The setting was Lancaster House, an opulent early nineteenth-century building with giant Corinthian porticoes and a vast marble staircase, overlooking St. James's Park and Green Park at the west end of The Mall, near Buckingham Palace. Before the war it had housed the London Museum; now, it was newly redecorated in white and gold, with red and green fabrics on the walls. The host, as representative of the British government, was Sir William Strang, very much the professional diplomatist, extremely able, sensitive, conscientious, and a little donnish. The Soviet Union and United States had delegated their respective ambassadors—Fedor T. Gusev, whom Strang later described as "a grim and rather wooden person, with, as a saving grace, a touch of sardonic humor and, as a virtue, a somewhat blunt straightforwardness," and John G. Winant, "a self-tortured soul, noble and passionate, inarticulate, deceptively simple, the pattern of honor." Later they were joined by the French Ambassador, René Massigli. Altogether, the negotiations lasted nineteen months, ending in August 1945: in the course of twenty formal and ninety-seven informal meetings, the Commission produced twelve separate agreements for government approval. Except for the allocation of the two western zones between the United States and Britain, the occupation plans for Germany were settled by mid-September, 1944. Seldom can such crucial decisions have been reached in so short a time.[27]

Despite some American second thoughts on the subject, it was too late to contest the principle of zoning. The next possibility—that of mixed Allied contingents in each zone—had already been proposed in Washington by a British Foreign Office official in December 1943. Then the United States had rejected it, chiefly on military advice and for technical reasons rather than because the State Department feared Russian interference in the West. British military opinion shared American misgivings: mixed-manning of the occupation zones, it was said, would be "administratively impracticable." Even so, in the summer of 1944, Strang was instructed to repeat the same suggestion. In his own words, it "was opposed—and I think rightly—by the Americans and soon dropped."[28]

With the zonal division of Germany hardening, the next most important question became the actual demarcation of the zones. On this subject, astonishingly enough, there was as Strang put it "little discussion and early agreement": the greatest difficulty was not between the West and the Soviet Union, but between the United States and the United Kingdom, each anxious to secure the industrialized northwest area that at length became the British Zone. It was on January 15, 1944, that Strang officially proposed zonal boundaries on the broad lines recommended by Attlee's Cabinet Committee; and at the next formal meeting, on February 18, Gusev indicated Russian assent. Such rapid compliance may seem unusual, and it certainly caused euphoria at the time. Yet if Gusev took even as long as five weeks to accept the offer, perhaps it was because he could hardly believe his ears. The proposed Soviet one consisted of Mecklenburg-Pomerania, Brandenburg, Saxony-Anhalt, Thüringia, and areas to the east; it included 40 per cent of Germany's 1937 territory, 36 per cent of her population, and 33 per cent of her productive resources. Berlin lay deep within it, and it brought the Soviet occupation forces to within a hundred miles of the Rhine.[29]

Defending what in retrospect looked ill-considered generosity, Strang pointed out that some of the Eastern Zone was likely to go to Poland. The Western Zones were more fully industrialized, and the military authorities already feared that the administration of a large and populous area might overstretch their manpower. When the zones were delineated, moreover, the Western Allies were still very uncertain how far and how rapidly their armies would advance. A related worry was whether the Soviet armies might not halt on Germany's eastern frontier, leaving Britain and the United States to finish off the war—although this contrasted oddly with the American War Department's prediction that Russia might occupy all of Germany as far as the Rhine. Was the Western offer a bribe to coax the Russians forward, or a sop to keep them at bay? The two explanations were mutually incompatible; but at times of great uncertainty, conflicting hypotheses can often seem to point to the same practical conclusion. A smaller offer, Strang feared, would have caused a deadlock; and although delay might have enabled the Western Allies to claim a larger area once they had reached the Elbe, no one at the time could be sure that they would do so. Even then, there would be no certainty of taking Berlin, and if the Russians reached it first without having signed a zoning agreement, they would no doubt refuse joint control of the capital, and take it over entirely themselves.[30]

Mistaken or not, these arguments seemed plausible; but there was a further question that they failed to answer. Could the Eastern and Western Zones not have met in the German capital, thereby making it easier to govern the country as a single whole? Such a suggestion had in fact been made by Roosevelt. In November 1943, on board USS *Iowa* on the way to Cairo and Teheran, he had penciled across a *National Geographic* map of Germany an East-West boundary running through Berlin. Handed to the U. S. Chief of Staff, General George C. Marshall, and by him to Major General Thomas T. Handy, Chief of the U. S. War Department's Operations Division, this map had been filed away in the Pentagon and was never officially communicated to the State Department. It seems, however, to have inspired a superficially similar proposal made by the U. S. Joint Chiefs of Staff in Cairo two weeks later. The crucial difference was that in this revised version the suggested zonal boundary carefully skirted the German capital, leaving it firmly in the east. A third, more radical variant of Roosevelt's project, mooted informally by some State Department officials, was to redraw the three zones so that they would converge on Berlin like "slices of pie"; and yet a fourth suggestion was circulated later by General Eisenhower, who proposed to ignore the claims of Berlin for the time being and establish what he called "a cantonment capital" in Southern Germany at the *de facto* junction of the American, British and Soviet ones.[31]

None of these ingenious plans, in fact, was feasible. Eisenhower's, in particular, would have weakened still further the occupation authorities' hold on German loyalties, as well as virtually abandoning Berlin to the East. The other three proposals, apart from greatly complicating the work of military government by cutting across German administrative boundaries, would have stood little chance of acceptance by the Soviet Union. Only one of the projects in question was ever transmitted to Winant at the European Advisory Commission in London; this was the memorandum by the Joint Chiefs of Staff. Although drawn up on December 4, 1943, it was not shown to the State Department until late in the following February, through the "Working Security Committee" in which representatives of the Navy, State, and War Departments were responsible for drafting Winant's instructions. After having, at first, refused to take part in the Committee, and then maintained that the European Advisory Commission had no right to deal with zoning, the Civil Affairs Division of the War Department now suddenly produced the Joint Chiefs of Staff proposal, insisting that it be sent to London, but declining to supply any explanation of its principles or aims. The result was what George Kennan, then Winant's assistant, called "a most curious communication." Even the accompanying map, on which the proposed boundary between the British and Russian Zones stopped short of Germany's eastern border, "made no sense at all." Kennan's military colleague in London, a former lawyer, was prepared to be belligerent. "We have to fight for it, my boy," he said. "We have to fight for it." "How does one fight," asked Kennan, "for something which makes no sense and which one does not understand oneself?" After what another official in the State Department described as "frantic queries" from London, Kennan flew to Washington to raise the question with the President. When Roosevelt saw the War Department's bizarre map he laughed. "Why, that's just something I once drew on the back of an envelope," he answered. Shortly afterward, the project was formally abandoned, and the United States accepted the East-West zonal boundary already provisionally agreed on by Britain and the USSR.[32]

There was, however, one further device that might at least have ensured that the Western Allies had land access to Berlin. This had been put forward as early as December 1943 by Professor Philip E. Mosely, then in the State Department's Division of Political Studies and later to replace Kennan in London. Mosely had proposed "that a corridor should be established connecting the prospective Western areas of occupation with Berlin, this to be accomplished by joining certain intervening districts of Saxony-Anhalt and Brandenburg to the Western Zones." "I realized," he said later, "that such a proposal by the United States would probably meet with Soviet objections, but I believed that if it could be presented first, with impressive firmness, it might be taken into account by the Soviet government in framing its own proposals." Mosely's suggestion was incorporated in a State Department memorandum; but when this was put to the Working Security Committee, it was blocked by the War Department's Civil Affairs Division. After some time, Mosely went to see the colonel in charge to make sure that he had received the proposal. "It's right there," said the colonel, opening the bottom drawer of his desk. Then, leaning back, he propped his feet on the open drawer and added: "It's damned well going to stay there, too." The delineation of the future zones, it appeared, was a "military matter" which would be decided "at the proper time" and "at the military level": it was no concern of the European Advisory Commission in London. When the Working Security Committee finally accepted a revised version of the State Department's memorandum, all mention of zoning—and of Mosely's proposal—had been dropped. The question of a land corridor was never officially put to the European Advisory Commission; and although Winant later raised it verbally with the War Department, he was rebuffed. By late June 1944, when Mosely himself was transferred to London, the issue was already closed.[33]

So it came about that the European Advisory Commission abandoned, one by one, the lines of defense against the partition of Germany. Amid uncertainties and illusions, each step seemed logical enough when it was taken. But at least one of the illusions was a little difficult to justify. By the summer of 1944, in view of the Allies' plans to dispense with a German government, it was unrealistic to assume, as at least one member of the Commission did, "that there would be a central German authority competent to sign the terms of surrender and to exercise a measure of jurisdiction over the whole country, subject to the overriding control of the Commander-in-Chief."[34] Roosevelt himself remarked at Yalta that "the permanent treatment of Germany might grow out of the question of the zones of occupation." Nor, as Mosely's suggestion showed, was everyone still optimistic about Soviet intentions. Yet for most of those involved on the Western side, the whole zoning exercise was an interim expedient to be followed by a peace treaty and the formation of a democratic all-German government. It was hard to imagine that the Soviet Union would so soon seal off the Eastern Zone, that a "cold war" would develop so quickly, and that free elections for the whole of Germany would be delayed so long.[35]

To blame the European Advisory Commission for the division of Germany, however, would be to condemn the machinery for the failings of the men at the controls—Edward R. Stettinius, Jr., Under-Secretary of State; the tired, aging Cordell Hull; the State Department officials hamstrung by the military, who, in the words of one participant, "saw the war as a football game you just won and then went home." Moreover, while in practice the European Advisory Commission acted only on government instructions, its decisions were by no means necessarily final. In October 1944, Roosevelt wrote to Cordell Hull: "We must emphasize the fact that the European Advisory Commission is 'advisory,' and that you and I are not bound by its advice. This is something which is sometimes overlooked, and if they do not remember that word 'advisory' they may go ahead and execute some of the advice which, when the times comes, we may not like at all." Churchill felt equally independent. "The proposals of the European Advisory Council [sic] were not thought sufficiently pressing or practical," he wrote, "to be brought before the War Cabinet. Like many praiseworthy efforts to make plans for the future, they lay upon the shelves while the war crashed on."[36]

By the spring of 1945, indeed, peace in Europe seemed likely to be shaped as much by the Allies' armies as by their diplomatists. By ousting the Rumanian government and failing to allow free elections in Poland, Stalin had at least twice strained his Yalta pledges, if he had not technically broken them; and Churchill in particular thought that, whatever zoning agreements might have been drafted for Germany, it was vital to "shake hands with the Russians as far to the east as possible." The question in his mind was whether or not the Western armies could be the first to reach Berlin.[37]

All the Allies agreed that it was important to seize the German capital: but the United States and Britain differed fundamentally as to how important it was, and why. American distrust of the balance-of-power system in Europe, and their hopes for the nascent United Nations Organization, reinforced Roosevelt's "tough" line on Nazi Germany and his faith in the Soviet Union: all discouraged the idea of a united postwar Germany as a counterweight to Russian strength. True, the President's views were changing: on Saturday, March 24, 1945, when he learned from Harriman in Moscow what was happening to Poland, he exploded with anger, pounding the arms of his wheelchair and exclaiming, "Averell is right! We can't do business with Stalin!" But by now he was too near death to reshape United States policy; and in the last month of his life matters tended to drift on the tide of a public opinion understandably reluctant to suspect a valiant ally. With a "policy vacuum" in Washington, it was all the more natural for the American Supreme Commander in Europe, General Eisenhower, not to look beyond his strictly military task of winning the war. Churchill, on the other hand, had the statesman's duty to look further; and his conservative patriotism, together with Britain's balance-of-power psychology, made him privately skeptical of the United Nations Organization and alert to the designs of that rather different nationalist, Joseph Stalin. For Eisenhower, whether or not to capture Berlin was a question of wartime strategy *vis-à-vis* the Nazis: for Churchill, it was one of postwar foreign policy *vis-à-vis* the Soviet Union. Agreement was hardly likely on the price to be paid or the risks taken for an objective they saw so differently. In the last few months of the war in Europe, in fact, this led to sharp friction between the Western Allies, and to mutual recriminations that have sputtered intermittently for the past thirty years.[38]

The dispute first arose between Eisenhower and Field-Marshal Montgomery, the gaunt British hero of El Alamein, now commanding Eisenhower's 21 Army Group. Montgomery was a difficult though loyal subordinate: his flamboyant austerity mixed badly with his Supreme Commander's sometimes irascible doggedness. Their personal relations were made no easier by the fact that Montgomery's position under Eisenhower's order reflected Britain's diminished role in an Alliance increasingly upheld by American money and men. Each at times suspected the other of stealing—and mismanaging—the show.

From August 1944 onward, Montgomery pressed for what he called "one really powerful and full-blooded thrust toward Berlin." This, he thought, "would not only have shortened the war; it would also have held out possibilities of bringing it to an end in Europe with a political balance very much more favorable to an early and stable peace." But Eisenhower feared the strength of enemy reserves, the difficulty of getting supplies across the Rhine, and the danger of borrowing transport from the rest of his armies; he saw Montgomery's project as "a knife-like thrust" or "a pencil-like thrust" doomed to "certain destruction." When after more than a fortnight's delay he at length modified his attitude, it was too late: at Arnhem in Holland, bad luck and bad weather had forced Montgomery's airborne assault troops into a costly withdrawal.[39]

Six months later, Montgomery tried a second time. On Tuesday, March 27, 1945, when he had just crossed the formidable barrier of the Rhine near Wesel, he telegraphed to Field-Marshal Sir Alan Brooke, Chief of the Imperial General Staff: "My tactical HQ moves will be Wesel-Münster-Herford-Hanover—thence via the *autobahn* to Berlin, I hope." Several times he urged Eisenhower to authorize and aid a spearhead drive toward Berlin; but the Supreme Commander was puzzled by the contrast between Montgomery's present eagerness and what he regarded as his previous overcaution: he even suspected, as he told an interviewer many years later, that Montgomery's aim was to "make sure that the Americans—and me, in particular—got no credit." As before, he feared that so long a spearhead would deplete and immobilize the armies on other parts of the front. Instead, he proposed that Montgomery should push toward the lower Elbe, cutting off the Nazis in the north. In the south, by advancing through Regensburg to Linz, Eisenhower hoped to breach the so-called "National Redoubt" in southern Bavaria, western Austria and northern Italy, where the SS, the Gestapo and other hard-core Nazis were said to be preparing for a suicidal last resistance. In the center, meanwhile, Eisenhower planned to make a major attack through Erfurt, Leipzig, and Dresden to meet the Red Army and cut Germany in two. For this purpose, he proposed for the time being to withdraw the American Ninth Army from Montgomery's command, assigning it to the northern flank of the central advance. Berlin, he wrote later, "was politically and psychologically important as the symbol of remaining German power. I decided, however, that it was not the logical or the most desirable objective for the forces of the Western Allies." As he told Montgomery, "that place has become, so far as I am concerned, nothing but a geographical location, and I have never been interested in these. My purpose is to destroy the enemy's forces and his powers to resist."[40]

Montgomery had to acquiesce in this decision; but a tactical error by Eisenhower now gave Churchill one last hope of reversing it. On Wednesday, March 28, 1945, without previously informing either his British Deputy, Air Chief Marshal Sir Arthur Tedder, or the Combined Chiefs of Staff, the Supreme Commander telegraphed his plans to Stalin. This, he thought, was justified by the communication arrangements that the Combined Chiefs of Staff had approved earlier, as well as by the fact that Stalin was Commander-in-Chief of the Red Army; but the British Chiefs of Staff were instantly, and understandably, incensed. When Tedder tried to placate them by suggesting that Eisenhower had acted to forestall a contrary directive issued by Montgomery, Brooke retorted that he was "astonished Ike found it necessary to call on Stalin in order to control Monty." For several days, sizzling telegrams were exchanged between London, Washington, and Eisenhower's and Montgomery's respective headquarters. "Please explain," snapped Churchill in a note to his Chief of Staff, General Sir Hastings Ismay. Brooke complained in his diary of "the nationalistic outlook of allies," and sent his American colleagues a long, barbed enquiry from the British Chiefs of Staff. The U. S. Chiefs of

Staff returned what seemed to Brooke a "rather rude message"; but General George Marshall tartly telegraphed Eisenhower: YOUR COMMENTS ARE REQUESTED AS A MATTER OF URGENCY. Montgomery, meanwhile, was warning Brooke that "we are about to make a terrible mistake": Brooke sympathized but told him, "You should take no further action." Churchill pointed out to Eisenhower that "I should greatly prefer persistence in the plan on which we crossed the Rhine"; and in a message to Roosevelt he repeated: "I say quite frankly that Berlin remains of high strategic importance." But Roosevelt was by now too ill to answer, and Marshall backed Eisenhower. To Churchill, the Supreme Commander replied: "I think you still have some misunderstanding of what I intend to do . . . I have not changed any plan . . . The only difference between your suggestions and my plan is one of timing." With that, Churchill had to be content. He once more stressed "the importance of entering Berlin," but added: "I regard all this business as smoothing itself down quite satisfactorily"; and he told Roosevelt, "I regard the matter as closed."[41]

The final irony of the whole incident was that Stalin could not believe Eisenhower's original telegram to be anything but an attempt to deceive him: he now became convinced that the Western Allies planned to race to Berlin. Determined to meet bluff with bluff, he answered that Eisenhower's proposal "entirely coincides with the plan of the Soviet High Command." "Berlin," he said, "has lost its former strategic importance. The Soviet High Command therefore plans to allot secondary forces in the direction of Berlin." Before sending this answer, he had already made clear to Marshals Koniev and Zhukov that they were to speed up and strengthen their advance on the German capital.[42]

But the Western Allies were to have yet a third opportunity to reach Berlin, if not to capture it. On Wednesday, April 11, 1945, the armored vanguard of the U. S. Ninth Army crossed the Elbe near Magdeburg. When General Bradley reported the news by telephone, Eisenhower asked him what the cost would be of breaking through to Berlin. Bradley answered: "I estimate that it might cost us 100,000 men." For the moment, Eisenhower said nothing; but on the night of Saturday, April 14, when U.S. patrols were within forty-eight miles of the German capital, he cabled to Washington that although "it would also be most desirable to make a thrust to Berlin," this "must take a low priority in point of time unless operations to clear our flanks proceed with unexpected rapidity." If the Ninth Army pressed on, its long supply lines would make it highly vulnerable to the strongpoints it bypassed: nor was he sure what reception a precarious vanguard might meet at its destination—either from a desperate enemy or from a triumphant Red Army. Next morning, therefore, the word came down through Bradley: the Ninth Army was to stop at the Elbe. Once again, Churchill protested to Washington; but Franklin Roosevelt had died on the eve of victory, on Thursday, April 12, 1945, and the new President, Harry S. Truman, gave the stock answer that "the question of tactical deployment of American troops is a military one."[43]

The decision was certainly prudent, and it may have been wise. As Truman reminded Churchill, the occupation zones had been "the subject of long and careful study and negotiation," and "a demand by our governments for modifications of agreed zone boundaries . . . might have serious consequences. The Russians could certainly consider such a bargaining position as a repudiation of our formal agreement." Nevertheless, as Churchill wrote later:

. . . I never suggested going back on our word over the agreed zones provided other agreements were also respected. I became convinced however that before we halted, or still more withdrew, our troops we ought to seek a meeting with Stalin face to face and make sure that an agreement was reached about the whole front. It would indeed be a disaster if we kept all our agreements in strict good faith while the Soviets laid their hands upon all they could get without the slightest regard for the obligations into which they had entered.

In retrospect, in fact, it is hard to avoid the impression that in these weeks the Western Allies lost the last chance to stave off the partition of Germany—although only the last of many.[44]

Retrospective judgments, however, must be treated with caution. Perhaps the British government was to blame for so blithely proposing the zoning arrangements; perhaps Roosevelt, for placing such faith in Stalin; perhaps Eisenhower, for dispersing his military effort; perhaps Montgomery, for exacerbating national jealousies. Yet all of them acted honestly, thoughtfully, and reasonably at the time. Even Stalin no doubt believed that he was serving the cause of future stability and peace. In the last resort, indeed, the partition of Germany was perhaps truly "inevitable" once Adolf Hitler had started the process that brought it about. Whether Hitler and the Nazi regime were inevitable is a separate question; but human history knows no such thing as a "first cause."

Whatever the causes, the results came quickly. By Wednesday, April 25, 1945, the day on which American and Russian troops met at the Elbe, the Red Army had encircled Berlin. It was only a matter of days before the war in Europe was over. Despite more last-minute protests from Churchill, the Western Allies were obliged to withdraw to their zonal boundaries, contenting themselves with four-power control in the capital only, and that imperfect and short-lived. So, in the heart of Germany, Europe's new frontier was established. Not the least of its dangers was that it cut off two-thirds of the German people from their food-growing lands in the east.

SELF-HELP

Salvation lies in taking one step forward. Then another.
It is always the same step that one begins again.
Antoine de Saint-Exupéry[1]

To learn to command is easy: what is hard is learning to
govern. *Johann Wolfgang Goethe*[2]

The spirit of self-help is the root of all genuine growth.
Samuel Smiles[3]

Ruined and divided, Europe in 1945 was soon in some respects to find herself also alone. Some of the generous aid planned by the wartime Allies failed to reach its intended beneficiaries: some was cut off when the fighting ceased. For a time, several European countries were thrown on their own depleted resources. Britain's overseas debts forced her into austerity. Reparations, and the limits at first imposed on industry, helped retard Germany's initial growth. The demands of the Far Eastern war, and the desire to return to normal, hastened the departure of the U.S. armies; America's attention, also, tended to shift elsewhere. Europe's postwar rulers, whether military governments or civil administrations, all faced tasks that were essentially similar: all had to bury the dead, tend the sick and wounded, feed the hungry, house the homeless, clear away rubble and ashes, rebuild, repair and reform. Politically and economically, each of them had what Dwight D. Eisenhower later called a "mandate for change." For two years, each did his best to fulfill it, largely in isolation. Each brought order out of chaos with astonishing speed. But beyond the material damage lay very much deeper problems; and it soon became clear that national self-help, although essential, was not enough.

Early in the war, Winston Churchill had pledged his government's aid in the future relief of continental Europe. On August 21, 1940, at the height of the Battle of Britain, he had told the House of Commons: "We shall do our best to encourage the building up of reserves of food all over the world, so that there will always be held up before the eyes of the peoples of Europe, including—I say it deliberately— the German and Austrian peoples, the certainty that the shattering of the Nazi power will bring to them all immediately food, freedom and peace." This was the seed that three years later produced UNRRA, the United Nations Relief and Rehabilitation Administration, aptly if fulsomely described by one historian as "tantamount to a declaration of the moral solidarity of the whole human race."[4]

In all, UNRRA distributed some 3.7 billion dollars' worth of food, clothing, medical supplies, manufactures, raw materials, farm equipment, and machinery. In many places, it prevented widespread famine. Food accounted for half of its deliveries to Italy, nearly half of those to Poland, and 60 per cent of those to Greece. It was equally vital in China, where in the words of its official history, "two to three million destitute people were rescued from starvation"; while Austria, according to the head of its Mission there, "owes its survival to UNRRA aid." Of the organization's operating funds, 94 per cent were provided by America, Britain, and Canada. Nearly three-quarters came from the United States, including gifts by private citizens amounting to almost one dollar per head of the population. Canada supplied over seventeen million dollars' worth of private gifts of clothing, Australia nearly five million, New Zealand nearly one and a half million. At its peak, UNRRA employed some 25,000 people; but its administrative expenses were only 1.18 per cent of its total costs. Its aid was offered without discrimination by race, religion, or political allegiance: its multinational field staff, isolated, overworked, short of supplies and often inexperienced, trod precarious tightropes between rival factions. Some UNRRA employees were ineffectual; a few were extravagant; one or two may have been corrupt. But the vast majority, courageous lonely figures in khaki battledress with special distinctive shoulder-flashes, distributing dried milk and chemical fertilizer, teaching new methods to doctors or to peasants, organizing construction gangs, or trying to turn barracks into something like home for smudge-eyed orphan children, well earned their charges' frequent tribute, "Oonra—OK."[5]

Really effective altruism is seldom wholly unselfish; and this was true, in 1940, of Churchill's promise of aid. It had accompanied the announcement that Britain was extending her blockade of Germany to all the occupied countries. One of its aims had been to quell the misgivings of exiled European governments and servicemen—especially Norwegian seamen—unwilling to penalize their countrymen: another had been to offer future outlets for any overseas food surpluses caused by the blockade. Equally hardheaded, later, were the long negotiations that preceded and followed the formal establishment of UNRRA on November 9, 1943. To provide "relief" was indispensable and urgent; but United States negotiators, in particular, feared that Congress might frown on "rehabilitation" if this were to include long-term assistance to future industrial competitors. UNRRA's scope was therefore limited to immediate reconstruction. The range of its beneficiaries, moreover, was restricted in two ways.[6]

Under the UNRRA Agreement of 1943, aid was to go to "the population of any area liberated by the armed forces of the United Nations"—the wartime Allies; but despite Churchill's original promise, this was held to exclude ex-enemy countries. In practice, Austria and Italy came to be admitted, as to a lesser degree were Hungary and Finland: but UNRRA's work in Germany had to be confined to the relief and rehabilitation of refugees. Secondly, moreover, UNRRA's governing Council curtailed its freedom further by imposing a "means test" on the recipients of aid. To avoid the vicious circle of war debts that had paralyzed international finance after World War I, it had been agreed that "acceptance of relief should not result in a burden of indebtedness." As a reasonable counterpart of this enlightened generosity, aid was debarred to any area "the government of which is in a position to pay with suitable means of foreign exchange." The unforeseen practical result of these

two restrictions was to exclude from UNRRA assistance the
greater part of Western Europe.[7]

The largest sum spent by UNRRA in any one country—
nearly 518 million dollars—went to China. Next came Poland, with 478 million; then Italy, with 418 million; then
Yugoslavia, with 416 million; then Greece, with 347 million.
The next biggest beneficiaries, in order, were Czechoslovakia,
the Ukraine, Austria, Byelorussia, Albania, the Philippines,
Hungary, the Dodecanese, Finland, Korea, Ethiopia, and San
Marino—and that was all. In other words, except for Italy,
Austria, and Greece, the bulk of UNRRA funds in Europe
went not to the Western European recipients originally envisaged, but to the countries of Eastern Europe that were
already becoming known as "satellites" of the Soviet Union.[8]

Britain, which might have sought UNRRA relief, if only
for air-raid victims, had already decided not to do so. The
former occupied countries of Western Europe had a still more
obvious claim to assistance; but the "means test" discouraged them from pressing it. All of them still had overseas
assets that had been "frozen" during the war to prevent
their exploitation by the Nazis: all might technically be held
capable of paying "with suitable means of foreign exchange."
For the most part, the assets in question would have proved
too small to pay for all the imports needed: but their owners
were reluctant to have them scrutinized by UNRRA, and
very unwilling to sell them in order to qualify for aid. It
has always made better sense to borrow than to liquidate
sound investments—even in the hope of future gifts. So it
came about that France, Belgium, the Netherlands, Luxembourg, Norway, and Denmark followed the British example
and made no claims on UNRRA: all they received were
small liaison missions to advise on health and welfare and on
the problems of "displaced persons." Their overseas imports
they paid for, dealing directly and unilaterally with the Combined Boards that had handled the Allies' wartime supplies.[9]

Receiving no aid from UNRRA, these countries naturally
turned to other forms of overseas assistance, and in particular to the existing machinery of "Lend-Lease." This, like

UNRRA, had been conceived early on in the war. On December 8, 1940, Churchill had written to Roosevelt asking whether American ships might not be allowed to carry some of Britain's vital imports: he had added that before long it would become impossible to pay for the armaments ordered from the United States. Roosevelt's response was the press conference of December 17, 1940, in which he explained the situation with the homely metaphor of the garden hose. If a neighbor's house caught fire, he argued, a man who owned a hose would not demand payment for the use of it, but would lend the hose, help put the fire out, and then take the hose back. In a radio "fireside chat" a few days later, Roosevelt announced that America was to become the "great arsenal of democracy"; and on January 7, 1941, he proposed the "Lend-Lease" bill to Congress. Two months later, on March 11, it went on the Statute Book under the memorable designation of HR 1776.[10]

Essentially, the "Lend-Lease" Act empowered the President to authorize the production or procurement of any defense article for the government of any country whose defense he deemed vital to that of the United States. It enabled him to test, inspect, prove, repair, outfit, recondition or otherwise place in good order any such article, to exchange information about it, and to "sell, transfer title to, exchange, lease, lend, or otherwise dispose of" it on whatever terms and conditions he thought fit. "The benefit to the United States" might be "payment or repayment in kind or property, or any other direct or indirect benefit which the President deems satisfactory." No cash was to be transferred to the beneficiaries; but in practice no cash was demanded in return: the only requirement, beyond that of fighting the Nazis, was the promise made by Britain in the "Lend-Lease" Mutual Aid Agreement of February 23, 1942, to reduce trade barriers and eliminate trade discrimination after the war. Between March 1941 and October 1945, "Lend-Lease" cost the United States more than 46 billion dollars. As President Truman remarked later, "We may never get the money back, but the lives we saved are right here in America."[11]

In Roosevelt's eyes, the possible uses of "Lend-Lease" procedure were not confined to the supply of materials for war.

On December 11, 1942, in his Seventh Lend-Lease Report, he told Congress: "Where commercial channels of supply have been cut off, lend-lease can be the instrument for renewing them. Where relief distribution is necessary, lend-lease can supply the materials of relief." Whether or not such aid should cease at the end of hostilities was another question. "Success in restoring the countries we free," Roosevelt's message continued, "will be a powerful factor in shortening the war and giving the liberated peoples their chance to share in the victory." But could Lend-Lease be continued long enough to give them a reasonable share in the peace?[12]

The question was partly juridical. Some of the President's advisers believed that Lend-Lease would still be legal when the war was over; but Roosevelt himself was uncertain. His Chief of Staff, Admiral Leahy, told him quite bluntly: "Mr. President, I know almost nothing about lend-lease and I don't want to go to jail when they begin, after the war is over, to investigate what has been done with the money." Roosevelt smiled. "If you go to jail," he answered, "I'll be going along too, and we will have good company." Many others, however, including the American Joint Chiefs of Staff, were convinced that Lend-Lease could only be used for war.[13]

Behind the legal dispute, moreover, there were political issues. A vociferous minority had always opposed Lend-Lease on principle. Others wished to keep it within strict limits; some were unhappy about its going to Communist Russia; and a further group, including the Secretary of State, Cordell Hull, was anxious to use it as a "bait" to secure from the British something "they were trying to run away from"—a diminution of Commonwealth preference. All this amounted to a sizable opposition, which reinforced the natural tendency of Treasury officials to hold the purse-strings tight.[14]

Such was already the climate when the future of Lend-Lease came up for discussion at the second Quebec Conference between Churchill and Roosevelt in September 1944. Churchill asked for an assurance that Lend-Lease would at least continue beyond the end of the war in Europe. Roosevelt was about to give in, when Henry Morgenthau, U. S. Secretary of the Treasury, interposed. The problems involved were complex, he argued; they required further study. At his suggestion, Churchill and Roosevelt agreed to refer the future of Lend-Lease to an American Committee consisting of Morgenthau himself, the Under-Secretary of State Edward Stettinius, and the Irish-American Leo Crowley, head of the Foreign Economic Administration. They were to consult with a corresponding British Treasury team led by Lord Keynes and Sir Robert Sinclair.[15]

After several months of hard discussion with the British, the Morgenthau committee reached what seemed reasonable compromise arrangements: it then considered itself dissolved. But the problem itself did not dissolve so easily. On Tuesday, May 8, 1945, the day after the Nazi surrender in Rheims and the day before the formal armistice in Berlin, Leo Crowley and the Acting Secretary of State Joseph C. Grew came into the office of Harry S. Truman, who had been President for less than a month. With them they brought a draft order cutting back Lend-Lease supplies, which Roosevelt, they explained, had approved but not signed. Would Truman sign it? Without reading the document, he reached for his pen, and it was done.[16]

In Truman's own words, "The storm broke almost at once." Crowley put an immediate embargo on all shipments to Europe, and even had some of the ships turned round and brought back to be unloaded. Instantly, protests began flooding into Washington, and they continued for some weeks. On Sunday, May 27, in Moscow, Stalin expressed bitter indignation to Harry Hopkins about the unloading of ships bound for Russia; and on the next day, Churchill sent a personal telegram to Truman complaining that the U. S. War Department was trying to cut down on the supply arrangements made after Quebec.[17]

Truman quickly rescinded the order of May 8, and in a press and radio conference on May 23 he explained that his intention had been to honor existing commitments, and not to cancel shipments but to make, as he put it, "a gradual readjustment to conditions following the collapse of Germany." The studied vagueness of these words reflected his embarrassing position, immobilized under crossfire from several directions at once. When he had been Vice-President, presiding over the Senate, he had given a personal promise that

Lend-Lease would lapse at the end of the war. He was convinced, as he wrote on June 15 to five complaining Congressmen, "that the Lend-Lease Act does not authorize aid for the purposes of postwar relief, postwar rehabilitation, or postwar reconstruction." But this left open the question of how far it could continue to apply in Europe during the remainder of the war in the Far East. The American Joint Chiefs of Staff had told the British on June 7 that "there was no legal authority for further assignment of any Lend-Lease materials except for use in the war against Japan." Leo Crowley agreed with them, and wanted Truman to give an order to this effect: but the State Department and the Army wanted to continue giving Lend-Lease aid to Europe, especially for use by the French occupation forces in Germany. Truman continued to hesitate; but when the British asked point-blank at the Potsdam Conference for Lend-Lease aid to be used in the occupation of Germany and Austria, he told Churchill that in his opinion this was "very definitely a part of the war." "After all," he added, "we technically still are at war with them."[18]

Here matters might have rested, had the war against Japan not been brought so rapidly to its bitter end. Thereupon, quite suddenly, the whole issue of Lend-Lease was re-opened. The Far Eastern war ended on Thursday, August 14, 1945. Five days later, on Sunday, August 19, the radio made an unexpected announcement. Lend-Lease had been canceled: henceforth all overseas supplies would have to be paid for—including those already ordered and on their way.[19]

Will Clayton, the Assistant Secretary of State, was in England when the news came. Hurrying back to the American Embassy, he exploded with rage over the transatlantic telephone. "It was good," noted one observer, "to see the whole six-foot-six of him reinforcing the vehemence of his rebukes." All he could secure, however, was a promise that the question of payment for goods already in transit would be held over for negotiation; and in the end, even so, 650 million dollars had to be paid. On the following Tuesday, Washington made the formal announcement: "The President has directed the Foreign Economic Administrator to take steps immediately to discontinue all Lend-Lease operations and to notify foreign governments receiving Lend-Lease of this action. The President directs that all outstanding contracts for Lend-Lease are canceled."[20]

The burly and pugnacious Hugh Dalton, Chancellor of the Exchequer in Britain's 1945 Labour government, believed that the decision was chiefly the work of Leo Crowley, whom he accused of showing "no sign of either hesitation or regret." In London, it was tempting to look for scapegoats and alternatives. If only Roosevelt had still been living—if Truman had been longer in office—if Dean Acheson, the new Secretary of State, had not been on holiday in Canada—if Clayton had not been away in England—if Fred Vinson had not so recently succeeded Morgenthau at the U. S. Treasury . . . then, surely Britain might have had a reprieve. As it was, wrote Dalton, "this heavy blow was struck at us without warning and without discussion. We had expected at least some tapering off of Lend-Lease over the first few years of peace. But now we faced, not war any more, only total economic ruin."[21]

In reality, speculation was largely beside the point. The legal and political pressure to stop Lend-Lease when the war ended was nothing new. Truman himself had already made his views clear; and it was the collapse of Japan, rather than anti-British malice in Washington, that was responsible for the shock. Even tapering Lend-Lease off, moreover, would hardly have changed the basic situation: the end could not have been postponed for long. Although Truman subsequently authorized further shipments to China "on the grounds of that country's grave economic and political difficulties"—galloping inflation, famine and the threat of renewed civil war—all Lend-Lease operations virtually ceased on October 1, 1945.[22]

With characteristic restraint, Clement Attlee told the House of Commons on Friday, August 24, 1945, that the termination of Lend-Lease placed Great Britain in "a very serious financial position." Before the passing of the Lend-Lease Act in March 1941, the country had undertaken a determined export drive to earn foreign exchange; but since American exporters would have objected to being undercut by an economy that their own government was subsidizing, this had had to be abandoned. By the end of the war, there was in any case little to export, and Britain was overspending her income by about £2.1 billion a year. With strict control of imports, a successful export drive, drastic cuts in overseas expenditure, and a great deal of luck, Treasury experts believed that it might be just possible for Britain to pay her way by 1949; but by then, even on the most optimistic reckoning, she would have incurred an additional deficit of at least £1.7 billion. Her gold and dollar reserves at the end of 1945 were expected to stand at about £500 million; but they could not, it was thought, be run down below half that sum. £200 million might be raised in loans from the sterling area, finally, leaving an over-all deficit of £1,250,000,000, or 5 billion dollars.[23]

Such was the stark prospect that faced Attlee's government in the summer of 1945. There was clearly no alternative but to seek further help from America; and Lord Keynes was sent to Washington to begin talks on Tuesday, September 11. Before he left, he was optimistic: he hoped, indeed, to secure a free gift or "grant in aid" of 6 billion dollars. But when he reached Washington he found the atmosphere very different from that of wartime. The Americans, he reported, were now interested in the future, not the past; and an old soldier showing his medals was not a persuasive advocate. Gradually, Keynes had to retreat from the idea of a gift to that of an interest-free loan, then to a loan bearing interest; from a larger sum to a smaller; from the prospect of credit with few strings attached, to that of precise conditions. The contrast between Keynes's Old Etonian urbanity and Fred Vinson's frontier manners only served to emphasize Britain's reduced status in the world.[24]

But Britain's was only an extreme example of a general European plight. In the early years of the peace, many countries of Western Europe were seeking North American credit. France borrowed 550 million dollars from the U. S. Export-Import Bank in December 1945, and 650 million five months later; the Netherlands obtained 300 million, the Netherlands East Indies 100 million; and a further 100 million went to Belgium. France was lent a further 720 million dollars to

buy up remaining Lend-Lease and other American equipment, while the Soviet Union received 360 million, and other
countries smaller amounts. Canada, likewise, not only loaned
$1,250,000,000 to Britain, but also advanced 100 million to
Belgium, 140 million to the Netherlands East Indies, and
240 million to France.[25]

By comparison with most of these arrangements, the terms
that Keynes finally secured for Britain on Thursday, December 6, 1945, were fairly favorable—a loan of $3,750,000,000
repayable from December 1951 onward in fifty annual installments, at an interest rate of 2 per cent, to be waived in any
year when Britain earned insufficient foreign exchange. At
the same time, she was to receive all the Lend-Lease material
ordered or about to be ordered when the war with Japan
ended, together with stocks of American goods in the United
Kingdom and Colonies. The wartime costs of Lend-Lease
were written off; and to pay for postwar deliveries of goods
"in the pipeline," Britain received an additional credit of 650
million dollars on the same terms as the larger loan.[26]

Two major drawbacks, however, marred the American
credit agreement. One was the United States' insistence that
sterling be made convertible against the dollar within fifteen
months. This was in line with the "non-discrimination" principles that the Allies had accepted at the Bretton Woods
Conference and that were now to be embodied in the International Monetary Fund and the World Bank; but the
deadline for applying it soon proved to be absurdly unrealistic. The agreement's other weakness was its failure to solve
the problem of the sterling balances—Britain's largely wartime debts to other members of the sterling area, and particularly at that time to India. For a while, Keynes envisaged
joint Anglo-American pressure to persuade Britain's sterling
creditors to write off some of their claims. Politically, this
might have been unwise as well as rather unreasonable; and
the American loan agreement merely recorded Britain's intention to approach each of her creditors herself. Friendly
persuasion, in fact, produced gifts of £10 million from New
Zealand and £20 million from Australia: but with these
"shining exceptions," as Dalton said, "no creditor was willing
to write off a cent." Worse still, the American agreement

forbade Britain to use any part of the dollar loan to reduce her sterling area debts. In both these ways, trouble was laid up for the future. The problem of the sterling balances, in particular, was to remain unsolved for more than twenty years. In this respect, if other European countries were physically devastated in the struggle against Hitler, the economic wounds that Britain suffered were no less deep and enduring.[27]

More immediately, the British were dismayed to find that life in the early years of peace was in some ways more austere than in wartime. This led to anomalies. UNRRA clothing standards, for example, had been based on the 1944 British ration; but when they came to be applied, the British ration had dropped to below the UNRRA minimum. One regular item in Britain's wartime diet had been imported dried egg: in February 1946, while the American loan agreement was still before Congress, supplies abruptly vanished from the shops. When they were restored in response to public protests, there began to be a shortage of bread. For a time, campaigns were waged against waste; then, in April, the Ministry of Food reduced the weight of standard loaves. The bakers had advised putting more air in the dough, so that the bread would look no smaller; but the Ministry preferred a reduction in size. The result was easily predictable: housewives bought more loaves, and bread consumption remained the same. Three months later the government announced that bread was to be rationed, something that had never happened during the war.[28]

Most of Britain's postwar privations were due to her shortage of dollars; but bread was rationed on account of the world shortage of food. At the beginning of 1946, Attlee had held a long telegraphed correspondence on the subject with Truman, and had sent the British Minister of Food, Sir Ben Smith, to Washington to discuss it with the American administration. At that time, world food production was 12 per cent below normal, and European production 25 per cent down. North America had just brought in a record wheat crop; but war damage and severe drought had greatly reduced output in Europe and North Africa, and wheat supplies in the first half of the year threatened to be seven million tons short of what the importing countries had already asked for. In Asia, moreover, the rice crop was 15 per cent below normal; and if famine was to be prevented, one to two million tons of wheat would have to be diverted to India and the Far East. As Truman wrote later, "More people faced starvation and even death for want of food during the year following the war than during all the war years combined."[29]

Spurred by Attlee's urgings, Truman appointed a Famine Emergency Committee under ex-President Herbert Hoover, to recommend a detailed program of relief. In conjunction with most of the producing countries, steps were taken to save wheat, to increase acreage, to speed and regularize distribution, to co-ordinate buying and to conserve food. The United States and Britain both raised their flour extraction rate, to 80 per cent and 85 per cent respectively—thereby incidentally narrowing the residue used as feed grain and reducing the supply of pigmeat, poultry, and eggs. By these measures the worst was avoided: but the danger of famine came very close. Even the United States suffered twice from meat shortages; and in Europe, as elsewhere, many people still went hungry.[30]

At the heart of Europe's problem, as so often, was Germany, the origin, exemplar, and principal victim of the general distress. "Germany," said Attlee in a conversation years later, "was down to her last potato almost." At the time he wrote, more formally, to Truman: "The ration there is already very low and substantial further cuts will bring starvation and unrest, which, apart altogether from humanitarian considerations, will increase our military commitments and retard Europe's economic recovery by reducing the export of essential supplies from Germany, particularly the coal which is so urgently needed."[31]

Germany's plight, moreover, was worsened by East-West divisions. Poland now held what had once been part of the country's food-growing area, and much of the rest was under Soviet control. As Churchill had written to Truman on April 18, 1945, "The Russian occupational zone has the smallest proportion of people and grows by far the largest proportion of food, the Americans have a not very satisfactory proportion of food to conquered population, and we poor British are to take over all the ruined Ruhr and large manufacturing districts, which are, like ourselves, in normal times large importers of food." For this reason it had seemed essential to pool all German food resources and divide them equitably between the zones; but when the question was raised with Stalin at the Potsdam Conference it was without success. Now, the population of the Western zones was swollen by at least four million refugees. In the spring of 1946, rations in the American zone had to be cut to 1,275 calories, and in the British zone to 1,040. In April, Herbert Hoover was told that even these meager allowances might have to be reduced, perhaps to 915 calories a day. It was little wonder, despite the unpopularity of austerity measures in Britain, that Attlee felt obliged to furnish no less than 400,000 tons of foodstuffs to the British zone.[32]

This was a far cry from some of the ideas about Germany's future that had been current in Britain and America during the war. In August 1944, Roosevelt had written in an angry mood to Cordell Hull:

> . . . It is of the utmost importance that every person in Germany should realize that this time Germany is a defeated nation. I do not want them to starve to death, but, as an example, if they need food to keep body and soul together beyond what they have, they should be fed three times a day with soup from Army soup kitchens.

"If I had my way," he was further reported as saying, "I would keep Germany on a breadline for the next twenty-five years."[33]

It was in this frame of mind that Roosevelt had accepted the "Morgenthau Plan" drawn up by the U. S. Secretary of the Treasury, Henry Morgenthau, and by his assistant Harry Dexter White, who was later accused of being an undercover Communist—"not Dexter White," as someone remarked, "but sinister Red." Gleefully exploited by Goebbels's Nazi propagandists, the Morgenthau Plan became notorious as a handbook of repression: but its basic premise, paradoxically, was that the rebirth of nationalism could not be prevented by repressive measures such as those applied by the Allies after World War I, however sternly they were imposed.

Reparations in kind, as favored by the British, would strengthen German industry, Morgenthau argued, at the expense of its competitors. The destruction of existing armaments, merchant ships, and industrial plant would merely remove what would soon become obsolete, leaving room for brand-new replacements. The distinction between wartime and peacetime industries was in any case hazy: the latter could quickly be converted in time of war. The suppression of Nazism would simply drive it into hiding; forced re-education would prove impossible; and Allied occupation, however permanent in theory, would in practice sooner or later come to an end.

Much of this was sensible; but instead of concluding that repression was self-defeating, Morgenthau wished to carry it to extremes. Germany, he said, should be dismembered, its large estates broken up, and all but its lightest industries dismantled. Even perfume factories should be eliminated, since they could be converted for the production of poison gas. At first, Morgenthau suggested the closure of the Ruhr's mines and industries: later he proposed their internationalization. Himself an enthusiastic agronomist and owner of a model farm near New York, he intended that Germany be "pastoralized." The resultant mass unemployment, he said, would provide labor battalions to rebuild the rest of Europe.[34]

Looking back, it is hard to see the Morgenthau Plan as anything but an index of the insane atmosphere of war. Its proposals, however, were contested even at the time. Henry L. Stimson, U. S. Secretary of War, was particularly outspoken: "The question," he told Roosevelt, "is whether over the years a group of seventy million educated, efficient, and imaginative people can be kept within bounds on such a low level of subsistence as the Treasury proposals contemplate . . . It would be just such a crime as the Germans themselves hoped to perpetuate upon their victims—it would be a crime against civilization itself." When Roosevelt put the project to the British at the second Quebec Conference, in September 1944, Churchill was equally hostile. At a men's dinner party for the Allied leaders on September 13, Morgenthau argued that the closure of the Ruhr would help

British steel exports; but Churchill answered, "England would be chained to a dead body." "I'm all for disarming Germany," he said, "but we ought not to prevent her living decently. There are bonds between the working classes of all countries, and the English people will not stand for the policy you are advocating." He paused, and added: "I agree with Burke. You cannot indict a whole nation."[35]

Unfortunately, the matter did not end there. It was well known that Churchill could sometimes be influenced through his friend Lord Cherwell, formerly F. A. Lindemann, commonly nicknamed "the Prof." Harry Dexter White therefore approached Cherwell, and hinted that acceptance of the Morgenthau Plan might make it easier for Britain to obtain postwar American aid. "The Prof" went to Churchill. "I explained to Winston," he said later, "that the plan would save Britain from bankruptcy by eliminating a dangerous competitor. Somebody must suffer for the war, and it was surely right that Germany and not Britain should foot the bill." Within forty-eight hours, Churchill had swung round to supporting the project. When someone suggested that it might not work—"why shouldn't it?" he demanded. "I've no patience with people who are always raising difficulties." So, on September 15, 1944, Roosevelt and Churchill both initialed a memorandum embodying Morgenthau's proposals for the "metallurgical, chemical and electric industries in Germany." "The industries referred to in the Ruhr and in the Saar would . . . be put out of action and closed down," it stated. "This program for eliminating the war-making industries in the Ruhr and in the Saar is looking forward to converting Germany into a country primarily agricultural and pastoral in its character . . ."[36]

Churchill soon returned to the more generous principle embodied in the epigraph of his war memoirs—"In Victory: Magnanimity." He acknowledged, however, that the tide of feeling was strong. In January 1945 he wrote to the Foreign Secretary, Anthony Eden:

I have been struck at every point where I have sounded opinion at the depth of the feeling that would be aroused by a policy of 'putting Germany on her legs again'. I am also well aware of the arguments about 'not having a poisoned community in the heart of Europe'. I do suggest that, with all the work we have on our hands at the present moment, we should not anticipate these very grievous discussions and schisms, as they may become. . . .

It is a mistake to try to write out on little pieces of paper what the vast emotions of an outraged and quivering world will be either immediately after the struggle is over or when the inevitable cold fit follows the hot.[37]

In Washington, likewise, cooler counsel prevailed. Widespread opposition, especially from Stimson, Cordell Hull, and James V. Forrestal, induced Roosevelt to abandon the Morgenthau Plan, at least as public policy. But its influence lingered; and it strongly marked the directive JCS/1067 drawn up by the U. S. Joint Chiefs of Staff to guide their occupation authorities. When President Truman issued it on May 14, 1945, Stimson thought this a "fairly good paper": later, more accurately, he called it "a painfully negative document." In the words of General Lucius D. Clay, Eisenhower's Deputy Military Governor in charge of the American zone, it prescribed that:

Germany was to be occupied as a defeated nation under a just, firm, and aloof administration which would discourage any fraternization. . . . It specifically prohibited us from taking any steps to rehabilitate or maintain the German economy except to maximize agricultural production. . . . Patents and trade processes were declared subject to seizure. Production in war plants was to be stopped and plants equipped for such production were to be removed without awaiting action by the Allied Control Council. Until agreement was reached in the Council, there was to be no production of iron, steel, chemicals, machine tools, radio and electrical equipment, automobiles or heavy machinery. Only the production of light consumer goods and the mining of coal were to be encouraged.

A broadly similar policy was to be followed in the whole of western Germany, including the French zone established after the Yalta Conference. As a plan, it was almost entirely arbitrary. Before Clay left the United States to take up his appointment in Germany, no one suggested that he pay a call on the State Department: future long-term peace arrangements still seemed very far away. One consequence was that when the occupation forces came to apply official Allied policy, they found that for the most part it denied their genuine needs and ignored their practical problems. If Berlin had looked remote from Washington, Washington seemed even more remote when looked at from Berlin. In this way, at a time when U.S. troops were withdrawing from other countries in Western Europe, the military government in Germany found itself likewise on its own.[38]

Initially, the occupation involved severe restraint of German industry. At Yalta, Stalin had demanded that Germany pay 20 billion dollars' worth of reparations in the form of plant, goods, and labor—half of this sum to go to the Soviet Union. This had been accepted as "a basis for discussion." At Potsdam, the Allies agreed on a formula allowing reparations from resources "unnecessary to the German peace economy"; later, with some difficulty, they fixed on a "level of industry" as the basis for pooling the spoils they hoped to divide. This assumed that the economy of all Germany would be treated as a single whole; but in practice it was not. Without even waiting for the inter-Allied Reparations Commission to report to the Potsdam Conference, the Russians had begun removing a large variety of goods and capital equipment from the Soviet zone. An observer in Berlin described some of their exotic booty—a truck containing "a mountain of brass: tubas, trumpets and trombones, covered by heavy Bokhara rugs," and another filled with "thousands of naked typewriters." More systematically, they collected miles of rail track and stripped a number of steelworks, plywood factories and hydrogen processing installations. At the same time, however, while the British were blowing up the Blohm and Voss shipyard in Hamburg and finding it hard to get even half their target output from hungry and exhausted steelworkers in the Ruhr, the Russians successfully boosted industrial production in the East. By 1946 it had reached 70 per cent of its prewar level, the highest figure for any of the Allied zones. Since the Soviet authorities refused to account for either the equipment they removed or the manufactures they received without payment, it began to look as if the Western Allies, by handing over material from their own zones, into which they were pouring food and money, were paying much of the reparations bill themselves. To many, this was reminiscent of the economic absurdities that had followed World War I. At length, in the spring of 1946, Clay stopped reparations deliveries from the American zone, thereby formally acknowledging the economic cleavage between east and west Germany, and paving the way for the later amalgamation of the Western zones that led to the formation of the German Federal Republic.[39]

As it turned out, the effect of reparations was paradoxical. In all, about 500 million dollars' worth of equipment and machinery was dismantled. This caused much resentment among the Germans: but its benefit to the Allies and its harm to the German economy were both much less than had been expected. The Russians, in particular, failed to profit from much of their plunder. It took time and skill to reconstruct dismantled material: intelligence reports and photographs revealed many sidings in eastern Germany and the Soviet Union crowded with freight cars full of machine tools uselessly rusting. Moreover, as Morgenthau had predicted, the removal of existing plant made way for later innovations, and when the time came helped put Germany ahead in the competitive race.[40]

A more serious handicap for Germany's immediate recovery was the inflation and demoralization that most of all affected the Western zones. Anyone who went there in the first two years after the war had the strange, unnerving experience of entering a barter economy. The basic and very simple reason was that, amid so much destruction, war financing had increased the supply of money by more than 400 per cent. The results, although predictable, were grim. Cigarettes, and in a lesser degree coffee and chocolate, had almost replaced normal currency. Such business as there was had to be conducted by composite bilateral exchanges of goods. Nominal incomes were largely meaningless. The usual incentives to work were lacking: so were health and strength. Everyone was poor and shabby, and almost everyone was hungry. The mood was one of tired exasperation and bewilderment; only those who were exceptionally determined, or lucky, or agile managed to resist.[41]

In a world so much awry, the occupation authorities

performed wonders: but since their power was virtually absolute, mistakes and lapses were inevitable. The most celebrated blunder was that of the unfortunate Brigadier Barraclough, who, on October 6, 1945, dismissed Konrad Adenauer as Oberbürgermeister of Cologne and forbade him "to indulge either directly or indirectly in any political activity whatever" for his lack of "proper supervision and energy" in "the general task of preparing for the coming winter," "the repair of buildings and the clearance of the streets." At a lower level, temptations abounded. The official historian of the American zone admitted that "looting was all too frequent"; and black-market trading of PX and NAAFI supplies was notoriously common. In July 1945 U.S. troops sent home a million dollars more than they received in pay; one man sent back a complete motorcycle, in three separate shipments. In these ways, as in others, the occupation proved the difficulty of applying in practice stern and high-minded precepts worked out so far away. Of all of them, however, the earliest casualty was the ban on fraternization. On June 12, 1945, Field-Marshal Montgomery relaxed it to allow British soldiers to speak to, and play with, German children. "They were, of course, doing it already," he said. Soon, the ban was lifted entirely—a necessary concession to human nature in a situation where hunger, desire, and compassion were often quite literally bedfellows.[42]

In a gray universe of shortages, undernourishment, corruption, and disorder, the occupation authorities faced the same twin tasks as all Europe's postwar governments. One was the indispensable mundane duty of administration; this was headache enough. The other was more inspiring, but also far more challenging—the overriding need to build society anew.

"Denazification" was to Germany what "*épuration*" had been to France, southern Belgium, and Luxembourg, "*epurazione*" to Italy, and "*zuivering*" to Flanders and the Netherlands: the attempt to identify, expel from office, punish and perhaps reform or re-educate those who had willingly served the dictators. As elsewhere, it made for very rough justice, and it created as much resentment as it appeased. More constructive were the Allies' positive efforts to reintroduce democracy, fostering free speech and discussion, spreading information, counteracting the years of lies and half-truths, using authority to fight the long habit of yielding to it, and gradually building up, with the aid of the liberated Germans, new political institutions that would make occupation unnecessary. It was an uphill struggle against conditioning and prejudice—on both sides. Rightly or not, some Allied officers could not but believe that the German people was subservient by nature: even anti-Nazi Germans, for their part, grew tired of being lectured on their nation's collective guilt, although many were prepared to acknowledge it. A few on both sides had unshakeable faith in the rightness of their own methods and institutions, from newspaper layout to proportional representation: often it took close personal contact between occupied and occupier, working together on the same job, to reveal that what was unfamiliar in either Anglo-American or pre-Nazi German tradition was not necessarily inferior, but in most cases merely different.[43]

Slowly and imperfectly, the task was accomplished. The press, the radio, the cinema, publishing, education and political life were gradually overhauled. Nazi newspapers were at first replaced by Allied bulletins; then, on July 31, 1945, the Americans licensed a new German paper, the *Frankfurter Rundschau,* to be followed by forty-four others during the next two years. The British were slower to begin, with the *Braunschweiger Zeitung,* inaugurated on January 8, 1946; but by midsummer they had licensed thirty-four others. Parallel with them, to provide competitive stimulus and a standard of comparison, the Allies maintained their own semi-official organs—*Die Neue Zeitung* in the American zone, *Die Welt* in the British. In both zones, the occupation authorities did their best to lighten the traditionally heavy makeup of German newspapers and to remodel their contents: in particular, they sought to establish a clear distinction between comment and news. Radio was handled separately. In Berlin, the Russians had taken over both the transmitter and the studios, although all were located in the western sectors of the city. The British and Americans therefore set up regional networks in their own zones. At first, unlike most of the newspapers, these were staffed by the Allies; gradually, later, they were transferred to German control. Cinemas, which had initially been closed altogether, were reopened to show purely escapist productions from the Nazi epoch and dubbed or subtitled versions of British and American films. The old UFA studios in Neu-Babelsberg were now in the Soviet zone: under a new company, DEFA, they reopened in 1946 to produce Wolfgang Staudte's powerful, guilty, slightly evasive *Die Mörder sind unter uns*—a first attempt to scrutinize "the murderers in our midst." In the western zones, film production revived a little later, and the shortage of capital, stock, and equipment ensured the predominance of foreign films for several years. A similar pattern at first emerged in publishing, where translations of authors long forbidden by the Nazis—from H. G. Wells and Upton Sinclair to Proust and Emile Zola—were quickly released for eager German readers, sometimes under special copyright arrangements. Meanwhile, in the summer of 1945, universities began to reopen, followed by elementary schools in October, and by secondary schools in the spring. Finally, German public life began to be liberalized on the lines laid down at the Potsdam Conference, which had called for "the decentralization of the political structure and the development of local responsibility." The Americans allowed parties to be formed on a district basis in August 1945, on a Land basis in November, and on a zonal basis in February 1946; the British sanctioned party activity from September 1945 onward. But already, in fact, the trade unions had begun to turn their own gatherings into political rallies. As one British official put it:

Each meeting had the same pattern: after a few words of thanks for their liberation (we were still liberators in those days) the speakers launched a tirade against their former bosses, many of whom had been Nazis and had by then disappeared. They were not, however, after their blood, nor did they even want to see them sent to prison. They merely wanted to see them take their coats and collars off and do some real work by which they apparently meant manual labour. I always knew when a speech was veering round to an attack on the bosses, as the passage invariably started with the words: 'Let them take a pick and shovel. . . .' and the rest was usually drowned in applause.[44]

Crudely, this expressed a feeling that was general in Germany and in Europe—the urge to transform the old political, economic, and social structure, which many believed had been largely responsible for Europe's present ills. "From Resistance to Revolution" was the masthead motto of *Combat*, the underground newspaper founded by Albert Camus and his friends in January 1941, which first appeared openly just after the liberation of France in 1944. "Politics is no longer something remote from the individual," wrote Camus at the beginning of September; "it is now a matter of man speaking to man." Many of those who had fought against Hitler, including the German Resistance, had fought not only for their countries but for a new kind of democratic comradeship, something of which they had experienced either as rankers in the services, as colleagues in the underground, or as victims of the air raids. In time of danger, it had been easy to feel that all men were fundamentally equal, differentiated only by their courage or their skill. Now, it seemed, was the time to take in hand the old structure of society, to make it and the state no longer hierarchical and alien, but a true and direct expression of human kinship.[45]

In Italy, at the end of March 1944, the political committee of the Action Party partisans in one section of Cuneo province issued a characteristic circular. They were far from being Communists; but they wrote in rousing terms:

The soldiers of this army are not so much, or at least are not only, the champions of a general patriotism, aiming simply at 'driving the foreigner off the sacred soil of the mother country', but rather the armed force and the resolute advance-guard of a movement of renewal, of a revolutionary process that is at work on the country's whole political and social structure, to give to Italy, disgraced and degraded by the Fascist tyranny that was backed and upheld by well-known accomplices, the new aspect of a free, democratic, and civic nation.

In Holland, the Christian-inspired Volksbeweging or People's Movement similarly called for help in "the common task: the necessary radical renovation of our people's life—economically, socially, politically, spiritually." It was a cry that was echoed by the many Christian-Democrat parties that now came into prominence, seeking to apply firm moral standards to political and social life. Its eloquence was perhaps greatest in Germany. In Berlin, in June 1945, the Christian Democratic Union issued a resounding appeal:

> From the chaos of guilt and shame into which the idolization of a criminal adventurer threw us, an order of democratic freedom can grow only if we return to the cultural, moral and intellectual forces of Christianity and open up this source of strength more and more for our people. . . .
>
> Great is the guilt of wide circles of our people who lowered themselves all too willingly to being the tools and help-mates of Hitler. All guilt calls for atonement. . . . Fighters of truly democratic faith, Protestant and Catholic Christians, countless Jewish fellow-citizens, men and women from all classes of the people suffered and died. In the spirit of their legacy, united by the same love of our people, we recognize our duty of going with this people the way of atonement, the way of rebirth.

From all parties, but especially from the left and center, the call was similar. In Britain, when the Labour party won its sweeping 1945 victory, one of its ministers wrote:

> That first sensation, tingling and triumphant, was of a new society to be built; and we had the power to build it. There was exhilaration among us, joy and hope, determination and confidence. We felt exalted, dedicated, walking on air, walking with destiny.

It was in Britain, indeed, that inept slogan-makers called the new world they wanted "the century of the common man." For many, the phrase conjured up visions of caricatured proletarians in cloth caps and mufflers, following each other sheeplike through the turnstiles of a giant bureaucracy. But for its originators it signified a vision, and one they were determined to fulfill.[46]

In France and Britain, in particular, this new impulse led to a broad extension of public welfare and public ownership. General de Gaulle's first postwar government introduced a fairly comprehensive system of social security; Britain inaugurated the National Health Service to provide medical care free. In both countries, the railways, gas and electricity, and cables and wireless were nationalized; in France, government ownership or control was extended in the oil industry, to air transport, to the Renault motor works, and to several important banks, while Britain nationalized coal and steel and long-range road transport. Similar movements took place on a lesser scale elsewhere. In Austria, government control ranged over large segments of heavy industry; in Italy, the Istituto di Ricostruzione Industriale extended and strengthened its already firm grip. In these ways, the state was directly involved in many of Europe's first postwar measures of reconstruction, whether through new nationalization, through existing corporate holding companies, or through the cognate controls established by the Allies in Germany.[47]

For a while, such efforts succeeded remarkably. Transport was rapidly re-established: by the end of 1946, 90 per cent of all France's railway bridges had been rebuilt, and 300,000 tons of shipping had been salvaged. Despite war damage and reparations, Germany emerged from the war with increased industrial capacity: soon, it was to be brought back more and more into production. Belgium successfully fought off inflation with a new note issue; Norway, later, did the same. For roughly eighteen months, in fact, European governments struggled to return to normal; and it seemed as if their self-help would suffice. Yet all the time, new dangers were looming, and old weaknesses were about to be revealed. By 1947, the immediate hopes of the postwar period had begun to dim again; politically and economically, the countries of Europe were now abruptly reminded that war, among other things, had cut them down to size.[48]

THE RELUCTANT ST. GEORGE

If 1946 was Annus Mirabilis, 1947 was Annus Horrendus.   Hugh Dalton[1]

The best public measures are . . . seldom adopted from previous wisdom, but forced by the occasion.
                                                                  Benjamin Franklin[2]

America was thus clearly top nation, and History came to a .   *W. C. Sellar and R. J. Yeatman[3]*

In the gray late afternoon of Friday, February 21, 1947, the U. S. State Department took an urgent telephone call from the private secretary to the British Ambassador in Washington, Lord Inverchapel. Could the Ambassador come round at once to see General George C. Marshall, the newly appointed Secretary of State? As it happened, Marshall was already on his way to Princeton, New Jersey, to attend the university's bicentennial celebrations, make a speech and receive an honorary degree. An appointment was arranged for the following Monday; but Dean Acheson, the Under-Secretary, asked whether the notes that Lord Inverchapel wished to deliver could be brought round unofficially and studied over the weekend. It was a wise precaution, for their message was momentous. Britain was serving notice that from the end of March 1947, in less than six weeks' time, she could no longer be responsible for economic aid to Greece and Turkey. As Joseph C. Harsch, the CBS radio commentator, put it a few days later, "London might just as well have dropped an atomic bomb on Washington; the impact could have been no more startling."[4]

The immediate implications of the British move were serious enough. Although the largely Communist EAM had failed in its bid for power in Athens, its guerrilla fighters were still active in the Pindus Mountains and the Peloponnese; only

British aid, and the presence of a British division, enabled the Greek army to hold them in check. Sir Clifford Norton, Britain's astute and affable ambassador, had warned the Foreign Office that the Greek government would fall if there were "even a whisper" of British withdrawal. The country's economy was near collapse: with only 14 million dollars of free foreign exchange in the Treasury, it would need a further 240 to 280 million dollars during 1947 alone. Turkey's economic situation was less alarming; but her strategic position was extremely vulnerable, and she had been continually subject to political pressure from the Soviet Union. If Britain were now to leave the Balkans and if nothing were done to fill the resultant power vacuum, the outcome would at best be further instability in an area traditionally dangerous, at worst the extension of Soviet control to the shores and harbors of the Aegean and a direct threat, from a new direction, to the oilfields of the Middle East.[5]

Rumors that Britain was about to reduce her Balkan commitments had long been circulating, and urgent warnings had reached the State Department by early February 1947. Few in Washington, however, had expected so drastic a cutback to be announced so soon. What had happened was that Hugh Dalton, the British Chancellor of the Exchequer, had finally and abruptly won the running battle for economy that he had been fighting all winter against the Foreign Secretary, Ernest Bevin.[6]

It had been a hard winter in more senses than one. Several British Ministers were ill, including the bulky and energetic Bevin, whose heart was showing signs of strain. The Prime Minister, Clement Attlee, was thought by his colleagues to be in need of a holiday; both Herbert Morrison, the Deputy Premier, and James Chuter Ede, the Home Secretary, were suffering from thrombosis; Ellen Wilkinson, the Minister of Education, was near to death. To make matters worse, the weather suddenly became Siberian. For three days at the end of January 1947, Britain suffered her biggest blizzard since 1894. Snow fell continuously almost everywhere: in places it was twenty feet deep, burying trees and hedgerows in an undulating white waste. Even in the densely populated industrial Midlands, many villages were isolated, and food supplies had to be dropped to them by parachute. When the thaw came, it lasted twenty-four hours. Then the thermometer fell again, and the partly melted snowdrifts turned to ice. Roads were blocked, railways immobilized, dock gates frozen solid, helping to cause a fuel shortage that aggravated the cold. Coal could still be produced wherever miners could dig their way to the pits; but some pithead machinery was frozen, and many stocks could not be moved. Overloaded power stations were forced to reduce their output: industry in London, the South-East, the Midlands, and the North-West was largely paralyzed. Some 80 per cent of the country, it was estimated, was once more plunged into the gloom of the wartime blackout. Severe restrictions were placed on electric heating, and domestic supplies were cut off altogether from 9 A.M. to noon and from 2 to 4 P.M. every day.[7]

The fuel crisis dramatized and helped decide the Chancellor's battle with the Foreign Secretary. As Dalton confided to his diary,

Bevin, very short of breath because he had had to walk up two flights of stairs to a Committee in Great George Street [the site of the Treasury] since, with electricity cut off, the lifts were not working . . . wanted me to come round to the Foreign Office and pore over a lot of papers. I said that I did not think I need trouble him with all this detail. I wanted firm instructions sent both to Norton and to Inverchapel, but I was quite prepared to do a deal and was willing that Norton should be allowed to hold his hand, provided we sent Inverchapel into action at Washington. Bevin said, not perhaps quite realizing what he was agreeing to, 'Well, that's quite fair.'

With that, Dalton acted, and "a stiff Treasury draft" was sent off.[8]

The real dispute, however, went far deeper than the clash of personalities or government departments. In fact, it was the beginning of a struggle between Britain's traditional world responsibilities and her newly reduced economic resources; and it was to continue for the next twenty years.

In December 1945, Britain had met her early postwar difficulties by negotiating the $3,750,000,000 United States loan. Since then, American wholesale prices had risen by more than 40 per cent, reducing the loan's effective value by nearly one-third. The first credits became available in July 1946; by the end of the year, 600 million dollars had already been spent. At that rate, the British Treasury reckoned, the loan would be exhausted by September 1949. In the New Year, however, the rate of expenditure rose alarmingly: now, it was feared, the money might run out as early as February 1948. Still worse was to come. On July 15, 1947, in accordance with the loan agreement, the pound was declared convertible: holders of sterling were now at liberty to change it into dollars. The result was a flight of capital from London—and the still more rapid exhaustion of the loan. In July, the drain on Britain's reserves was 115 million dollars a week; in August it increased to 150 million dollars, and it rose to 237 million dollars in the third week of the month. On Wednesday, August 6, the Prime Minister estimated that the American loan would all be drawn by the end of 1947. The next day, Dalton corrected this to October, just two months ahead. Finally, on Wednesday, August 20, 1947, convertibility was suspended, five weeks after it had begun.[9]

Living on rapidly dwindling credit, Britain was at the same time bearing heavy overseas burdens. Not only Greece and Turkey, but a number of other countries, were dependent on her aid. In 1946, she had spent 60 million dollars on feeding the German people, however inadequately; in the first quarter of 1947 she was to spend 60 million dollars more. Around the globe, moreover, rightly or wrongly, British soldiers were still acting as policemen—against Communists in Greece, against the Zionist Irgun Zvei Leumi in Palestine, between Hindus and Muslims in India. Nearly two years after the end of World War II there were still a million-and-a-half men in the Services, while at home the available manpower was 630,000 short of Britain's needs.[10]

In this situation, clearly, something had to give. The question of Palestine was referred to the United Nations in February 1947; but Britain's inglorious involvement was to continue until the State of Israel was proclaimed on Friday, May 14, 1948. The withdrawal from India was more precipitate. In May 1946 a Cabinet mission had proposed a federal union of the Indian provinces, which had been accepted both by the mainly Hindu Congress Party and by Mohammed Ali Jinnah's Muslim League. But mistrust and hostility between the two was soon redoubled by a tactless press conference given by the Congress President, Jawaharlal Nehru; and when Lord Wavell, the British Viceroy, invited Nehru to form a government, Jinnah refused to join it, calling for "Direct Action"—which led to a four-day riot in Calcutta, with 5,000 dead and 15,000 wounded. Only the personal intervention of Mahatma Gandhi prevented violence spreading throughout the country. Although the Muslim League joined Nehru's Executive Council in October 1946, this was only, in practice, to hinder its work. With civil war once more threatening, the British government called Nehru, Jinnah, and the Sikh leader Sardar Baldev Singh to a conference in London. When this, too, proved inconclusive, Attlee decided to replace the long-suffering Wavell by Lord Mountbatten; but Mountbatten insisted that if he became Viceroy it could only be "to wind up the show." On Thursday, February 20, therefore—on the day before the withdrawal from Greece was announced in Washington—Attlee told the House of Commons that Britain would leave India "by a date not later than 1948." In the event, she was to quit by the middle of August 1947.[11]

Thus, within the span of a few months and by a few crucial decisions, the British government tacitly acknowledged the closing of an epoch. *Pax Britannica* was coming to an end. Harried by economic necessity, Britain was embarking on a long, painful, and halting process of readjustment: very gradually, she was becoming one European country among many, each no longer strong enough to play a decisive world role by itself.

The reality of the change was not always dramatic. In many places, British garrisons were to linger for two more decades. Elsewhere, despite the military withdrawal, administrators and technicians remained behind—as did, in some cases, a sprinkling of Service personnel. When British troops withdrew from Cairo early in 1947, for example, they at first fell back only to Suez and the Canal Zone; and the British Embassy's powerful radio continued to be serviced, *sub rosa*,

by army signalmen in civilian clothes, driven to and from
the Egyptian capital in disguised military trucks.[12] At home,
moreover, the significance of the British withdrawal was
masked by the very emergencies that prompted it. Unde-
feated and uninvaded, Britain still felt undiminished. Her
economic plight was so acute as to seem temporary, not
structural; and the dismantling of the Empire, although permanent, was camouflaged by its metamorphosis into the Commonwealth.

From across the Atlantic, however, the situation looked
very different. As one State Department official put it:

Each day's cables, each day's newspapers and broadcasts, brought
the story: From the Mediterranean eastward to the Sea of Japan
nationalism was successfully asserting itself. In the very heart of the
British Empire six independent states were emerging: India, Pakistan, Burma, Ceylon, Nepal and Afghanistan. Revolutionary movements were challenging French and Dutch control in Indochina and
Indonesia, with good prospects of success. The Philippines had
achieved independence; Thailand had thrown off British influence.
Victorious China had freed herself of Western controls. In the
Middle East, colonies were moving toward self-government, man-
dated countries toward independence, all toward nationalistic self-
assertion that weakened alliances. . . . What was clearly happening
was the sudden disappearance of the imperial system and the rise of
independent, weak, nationalist states. This had happened in Europe
hundreds of years earlier—and had led to centuries of bloody, nationalistic strife.[13]

In this context, Britain's announcement that she was to end
her aid to Greece and Turkey became a symbol and a por-
tent: it triggered off a process of rethinking in Washington
that was all the more radical for being so long overdue.

Already for eighteen months, in fact, America had manifestly been the greatest power on earth. During World War
II, her total production had doubled, from 90 billion to 180
billion dollars. Less spectacularly in the face of wartime restrictions, her standard of living had also risen: her annual
meat consumption, for instance, had increased from 125 to
163 pounds a head. But most striking of all was her new
preponderance in the military field, where she now enjoyed
the equivocal privilege of seemingly absolute power. If one

precise moment may be quoted as a turning-point, it was shortly before noon on Monday, August 6, 1945. Sailing home after Potsdam Conference, in the USS *Augusta,* President Truman was eating lunch with the crew when Captain Frank H. Graham, watch officer of the White House Map Room, hurried in with a top-priority signal: "Big bomb dropped on Hiroshima." Truman, in the laconic words of Admiral Leahy, "was excited over the news." As he himself put it, "I was greatly moved." Shaking Captain Graham by the hand, he said: "This is the greatest thing in history."[14]

It would have been understandable if, from that moment onward, *hubris* had begun to dominate American policy. Reared in optimism, conditioned to feel that most things are possible if given a big enough effort, Americans might have been expected to want to start running the world. "Dominance" might have been far from their intentions, but "leadership" has always been a seductive euphemism. Yet during the months that followed Hiroshima, the United States in some respects retreated from world responsibilities. The termination of Lend-Lease, the resumption of business-as-usual, the concern to bring the troops home—all seemed to echo the universal tendency to model the future on the past. The Republican party, traditionally isolationist, in November 1946 won a majority in both Houses of Congress for the first time in fourteen years; quickly calling for cuts in taxes and military expenditure, it sought to reduce by half the sums requested for food and emergency relief in ex-enemy countries. For a while, some Americans seemed to have forgotten that whereas once—until the Battle of Midway—they had sheltered behind the British navy, Britain and other countries now had to rely on the military and economic strength of the United States. Perhaps America's nuclear monopoly encouraged comfortable unconcern. At all events, Britain, in those early days, was still counted on for a leading contribution to world order. Typical of the climate of opinion was the title of a thoughtful essay published by the Yale University Press in 1945—*The Big Three.* Two of the three, quite naturally, were the United States and the Soviet Union. Twenty years later, the third might well have been China, or—just possibly—Europe; at

that time, it was Great Britain. Not until the cruel spring of
1947 was it fully obvious how anachronistic this notion had
become. Then, over the cold weekend of February 22–23,
1947, the "big three" were revealed as only two. Britain's
postwar weakness was suddenly made manifest: America had
to take her place. If not a reluctant dragon, the United States
now had to become a reluctant St. George.[15]

By comparison with prewar American attitudes, the change
was profound; and subsequent publicity made it spectacular.
But most such political turning-points are somewhat ficti-
tious; and President Truman's response to Britain's impending
withdrawal from the Balkans was certainly no exception. On
several occasions since the end of World War II the Administration had affirmed, as the then Secretary of State
James F. Byrnes had put it in a crucial speech in Stuttgart
on September 6, 1945, America's intention "to continue our
interest in the affairs of Europe and of the world." On February 28, 1946, in particular, Byrnes had told the New York
Overseas Press Club that while "there is no reason for war
between any of the great powers, we will not and we cannot
stand aloof if force or threat of force is used contrary to the
purposes and principles of the [United Nations] Charter."
Exactly one year later, in February 1947, Truman was given
the chance to dramatize and make concrete this conception
of America's role. "This was the time," he wrote in retrospect,
"to align the United States of America clearly on the side,
and at the head, of the free world." It was an ambition that
he had cherished ever since succeeding to the presidency on
Franklin Roosevelt's death. In private letters—later published
—he played, as in a Frank Capra movie, the small-town hero
catapulted into power; but in fact he had long held firm
and downright views on foreign as well as domestic policy.
On Thursday, April 19, 1945, just a week after taking office,
he had told Averell Harriman, U. S. Ambassador to the Soviet
Union, that in negotiating with the Russians, whom Harriman
saw as bent on a "barbarian invasion of Europe," "I would
not expect 100 per cent of what we proposed. But I felt
we should be able to get 85 per cent." When he saw the
Soviet Foreign Minister, V. M. Molotov, a few days later,
Truman spoke so "sharply"—his own adverb—that Molotov

protested: "I have never been talked to like that in my life."
"I told him," Truman wrote afterward, "'Carry out your
agreements and you won't get talked to like that.'" This was
the same truculent Middle-Westerner who later claimed to
have told James Byrnes "I'm tired of babying the Soviets"—
although Byrnes denied that the letter containing these words
was ever sent or read to him. Now, as a Democratic President
facing a Republican Congress, Truman saw in the British
Notes of February 1947 an opportunity to assert America's
newly realized world role.[16]

If Truman was eager to seize this opportunity, the same
was true of the State Department. For years, its officials had
suffered from continual frustration. Under Roosevelt American foreign policy had been constantly and often capriciously
remade in the White House; of successive Secretaries of
State, Cordell Hull had been tired and had seemed uninter-
ested in the future, while Edward R. Stettinius was crisply
described by one of his former colleagues as "a disaster."[17]
During the early months of Truman's Administration, Byrnes
had conducted a somewhat personal foreign policy, and relations with the White House had become severely strained,
culminating in the Secretary's resignation. Now, under General Marshall, the atmosphere changed. One of his first decisions as Secretary of State was to move the Department
from its old Washington headquarters at 17th Street and
Pennsylvania Avenue into a new and bigger air-conditioned
building at 21st Street and Virginia Avenue—a material symbol of its altered status. In headily modern surroundings,
its officials found themselves once more in effective teamwork
with the White House, although physically farther away from
it. With a new sense of power and purpose, they reacted
swiftly to the two British Notes they received on Friday,
February 21, 1947.[18]

That same afternoon, Under-Secretary of State Dean Acheson called for an urgent study of the Greek and Turkish
problems, and arranged for close consultation with the War
and Navy Departments in Washington. In the evening, a
senior staff meeting discussed practical proposals for aid; one
of those present went home late that night "with the stimu-

lating impression of having participated prominently in a historic decision of American foreign policy." Drafting and further discussion continued throughout the weekend. On Monday morning, February 24, at ten, Marshall officially received Lord Inverchapel, bearing the British government's formal message; he at once conferred with the President, as well as with James V. Forrestal, Secretary of the Navy, and Robert P. Patterson, Secretary of War. On Tuesday, after a further staff meeting, State Department officials worked late to produce a final version of their detailed "Position and Recommendations," proposing loan legislation, military supplies, administrative aid, consultation with Britain, and a program of public information. On Wednesday, February 26, Forrestal and Patterson endorsed this document, and at 3:00 P.M. Marshall and Acheson presented it to the President. At ten the next morning Truman received Congressional leaders in his office, together with Marshall and Acheson, who in turn explained the situation and, despite initial suspicion, convinced their audience of the need to act. The Republican Senator, Arthur H. Vandenberg, who had previously been isolationist, admitted that he was "greatly impressed" by Acheson's presentation in particular, and urged that any presidential request for funds be accompanied by a similar message to Congress and to the American people. That night, Acheson gave a first background briefing to selected newspapermen; and on the following morning, Friday, February 28, a full information campaign was roughed out. At the same time, with the aid of officials from the War and Navy Departments, and in liaison with Clark M. Clifford at the White House, the State Department began drafting what later came to be known as "the Truman Doctrine."[19]

During most of the week that followed, Truman himself was absent, on a state visit to Mexico. He was not on hand, therefore, to receive the formal request for aid that the Greek government submitted on Monday, March 3, 1947; but this hardly mattered, since its text was a State Department draft. Returning to Washington late on Thursday, March 6, Truman held a full Cabinet meeting on the following day; and on Monday, March 10, he again saw a Congressional delegation, this time including the formidable Republican Senator, Robert A. Taft. Finally, after last-minute drafting changes, the message to Congress was ready. At 1:00 P.M. on Wednesday, March 12, 1947, in a House of Representatives crowded to overflowing for this joint session with the Senate, the President spoke to the nation and to the world. "His voice," as one of the audience noted, "was flat and not impressive, but this day he spoke with a newly acquired forcefulness." He was asking Congress for 400 million dollars in aid to Greece and Turkey because, in his own words, "it must be the policy of the United States to support free peoples who are resisting attempted subjugation by armed minorities or by outside pressures." He himself had insisted on the word "must" in place of his speechwriters' "should." This was "the Truman Doctrine." It was the beginning of America's systematic contribution to the recovery of Europe.[20]

Applause greeted Truman's words that sunny March afternoon on Capitol Hill; but the audience was subdued and, to one participant, it seemed bewildered. One reason was the gravity of the President's message; another was the scale of the proposed expenditure. But the Truman Doctrine was also criticized more fundamentally—on the one hand because it seemed to ignore the United Nations, and on the other because it made an issue of principle out of two not identical cases.

On the subject of the UN, Truman's message to Congress was pungently brief. "We have considered how the United Nations might assist in this crisis. But the situation is an urgent one requiring immediate action, and the United Nations and its related organizations are not in a position to extend help of the kind that is required." A further paragraph, proposing the study of means whereby the UN "might undertake financial and economic responsibilities in such areas," had been inserted in the original draft at the suggestion of Dean Rusk, then Director of the State Department's Office of Special Political Affairs; but it had been dropped by the White House, and at least one member of the drafting committee had not even noticed. This, it seemed, was no time for pious aspirations. Experience had shown how the UN could be paralyzed by the veto in the Security Council, which by December 1946 had already been used so often that the General Assembly had called for the voting rules to be changed.[21]

More serious, however, was the objection that the Truman Doctrine linked two dissimilar cases under a general principle that was debatable and ill-defined. On the afternoon of Thursday, March 6, 1947, a late draft of Truman's message to Congress had been handed to George Kennan, who was soon to inaugurate the State Department's Policy Planning Staff. Reading it, he became "extremely unhappy." Economic aid for Greece was one thing: military aid for Turkey was quite another. "I suspected," he wrote later, "that what was intended primarily was military aid, and that what had really happened was that the Pentagon had exploited a favorable set of circumstances in order to infiltrate a military aid program for Turkey into what was supposed to be primarily a political and economic program for Greece." Whether or not the Pentagon was responsible, Kennan was probably right. Even the State Department's semi-official historian, himself involved in shaping the Truman Doctrine, admitted that "there was a grain of truth" in the Washington gibe that "when the new dish was being prepared for American consumption, Turkey was slipped into the oven with Greece because that seemed to be the surest way to cook a tough bird."[22]

Kennan's uneasiness had also a more general cause. "On many occasions, both before and after this Greek-Turkish episode, I have been struck by the congenital aversion of Americans to taking specific decisions on specific problems, and by their persistent urge to seek universal formulae or doctrines in which to clothe and justify particular actions." The "sweeping language" of Truman's message, he thought, "might be subject to misinterpretation": "it implied that what we had decided to do in the case of Greece was something we would be prepared to do in the case of any other country."[23]

Kennan was not alone in scenting danger. On Monday, March 24, 1947, Dean Acheson was careful to assure the Senate Committee on Foreign Relations that "any requests of foreign countries for aid will have to be considered accord-

ing to the circumstances in each individual case." It was perhaps as well, at that moment, that Congress had not yet been
called upon to authorize economic aid to the whole of Western Europe.[24]

Yet this was precisely what Truman's advisers were soon
to propose. The problems of Greece and Turkey, they now
saw, were not exceptions but symptoms. It was Britain's economic weakness that had thrust them on America's attention;
but although Britain's plight had some unique features, most
European countries were in similar or worse distress. Its underlying reasons had the cruel logic of a trap.

Before World War II, Western Europe had imported much
of its food and raw materials, and had paid for them largely
by exporting industrial goods. Now, the terms of this rough
equation were drastically altered. Crippled by war and by
underinvestment between the wars, Europe's industrial production in 1947 was still only a fraction of the peacetime
norm—less than two-thirds in Austria, Greece, and Italy, less
than one-third in Western Germany. Output per man-hour
was even lower, partly on account of undernourishment. The
population had increased by twenty million, but it now had
only four-fifths the prewar supply of food. Farm yields had
fallen, and traditional supplies of food and raw materials were
no longer coming from Eastern Europe and the Far East.
The only alternative was to buy them from America, together
with urgently needed capital goods and manufactures: but
this required vast sums of money that European countries
were no longer able to pay. Their currencies were often
monstrously inflated; their overseas assets were shrunken or
rapidly shrinking. With exchange rates unstable, and without
multilateral clearing arrangements, even their trade with each
other had to be mainly bilateral—reduced to a quasi-barter
system that in turn stifled production. Both France and Italy,
for instance, had unused capacity for making ball-bearings;
but in 1947 it remained idle because neither had kronor to
buy enough chrome steel from Sweden. In trade with the
rest of the world, Europe was equally handicapped. Its annual exports to non-European countries were now worth only
5.4 billion dollars as compared with 8 billion dollars in 1938;

its current-account deficit with the dollar area—seven-tenths of it with the United States—was 7 billion dollars.[25]

Even the elements seemed to conspire against Europe. Britain's hard winter of 1946–47 was no less severe on the Continent. Coal production was partly paralyzed, and when the snow at last melted, many pits were flooded. Already in 1946 Western Europe had had to import seventeen million tons of coal from America at eleven dollars a ton—twice the domestic price; now it needed even more. In Western Germany, with steel plants starved for energy, coal output in 1947 reached only 144 million tons as compared with 221 million before the war: steel production stood at less than four million tons, not even a quarter of the prewar figure. France's coal production, it was true, had risen above the 1938 level; but her output of crude steel and pig-iron was well below it. In Norway, the production of finished steel had dropped from 82,000 to 53,000 tons.[26]

The winter, moreover, was preceded and followed by two torrid summers. In January, Europeans shivered in flats, offices, farms, and factories, or trundled through a white landscape in unheated trains with ill-fitting boards for windows; in August, for two years in succession, they saw drought shrivel the crops. In France, the 1947 harvest turned out to be only 50 per cent of what it had been a year earlier, and the bread ration had to be cut below its wartime level to only 200 grams a day. In Norway, the daily food ration fell from 2,500 calories to 2,200; for a time in Germany it was little more than 1,000. Finally, to add to Europe's difficulties, the cycle of hardship, unemployment and inflation helped to touch off widespread disruptive strikes.[27]

With gloomy reports and forecasts beginning to pile up in Washington, it gradually became obvious that Europe's postwar problems had been seriously misjudged. As Dean Acheson admitted to a later interviewer, "We had operated on a theory of dealing with hunger, disease, and unrest until one or two good crops could come in. But the problems were more far-reaching, and it grew upon us toward the end of 1946 that we were heading for very bad trouble." Partly through self-help, partly through emergency assistance, Europe had survived for two years since the end of hostilities.

Now, with the blood-transfusion ending, radical action was needed to prevent a relapse.[28]

That action, when it came, marked America's decisive assumption of world responsibilities. The form it took was the European Recovery Program, better known as the Marshall Plan. Not surprisingly, its pedigree was more complex than its name.

Fundamentally, it sprang from American generosity; but this was spiced with a saving grain of self-interest. The United States had long been pressing for the reduction of trade barriers, and in December 1945 had made formal "Proposals for Expansion of World Trade and Employment," calling for a liberal, non-discriminatory and multilateral trading system, with an International Trade Organization (ITO) as an offshoot of the UN. Many of these ideas were to reappear in the Havana Charter agreed by fifty-four nations during the winter of 1947–48; and although the U. S. Congress at length refused to ratify the Charter, some of its content was salvaged by perpetuating the General Agreement on Tariffs and Trade (GATT), a looser interim arrangement made in the previous summer. America's sponsorships of these efforts reflected her new economic role. Since the war, she had become more deeply involved in international commerce: in 1946 her total exports of goods and services were nearly four times the pre-war average of 4 billion dollars a year. Early in 1947, the President's Council of Economic Advisers was expecting a slight domestic recession; and if this coincided with a fall in exports, the results at home could be serious. Here was a subsidiary reason—and a useful political argument—for helping to save Europe from economic collapse. More pertinent still, as time went by, was the fear of further Soviet expansion. A poverty-stricken Western Europe looked a likely breeding-ground for Communism and a prey too tempting for Stalin to ignore. In this respect, the Truman Doctrine and the Marshall Plan, as Truman himself put it, were "two halves of the same walnut."[29]

Motifs and motives intertwined as the U. S. Administration labored at the double task of planning aid for Europe and persuading Congress to support it. In doing so, the planners gradually arrived at two basic principles, both apparently

simple. The first was that recipient nations should be dealt
with *en bloc* as a collective entity; the second, that Europeans themselves should take the initiative and be encouraged
to stand on their own feet. In the circumstances, both notions
seemed natural: but in fact they were very novel. Together,
they were the negation of the maxim "Divide and conquer"
that previous world powers had taken as their watchword;
together, they contained in embryo the twin concepts of European unity and equal transatlantic partnership. In this way,
almost without realizing it, a handful of officials in Washington helped to make possible a gradual revolution in international affairs.

The question of further aid to Europe had already been
informally discussed in the later months of 1946; but it was
in the following spring that a number of separate and little-
publicized efforts, overlapping and sometimes contrasting,
began to dovetail into a coherent plan. The first step was
taken on Tuesday, March 11, 1947, when at Dean Acheson's
suggestion the State, War, and Navy Departments' Co-
ordinating Committee set up joint machinery to study foreign
aid requirements. To prepare its formal position in these interdepartmental palavers, the State Department appointed its
own Foreign Aid Committee. This included in particular three
young officials from the staff of Will Clayton, Under-
Secretary for Economic Affairs: the acute economist Charles
Kindleberger, fresh from active service in Germany with the
G-2 Section of 12th Army Group; Harold Van Buren Cleveland, distinguished member of a well-known political and
civil-service family; and the shrewd, burly, gravel-voiced Ben
T. Moore. All three had long been concerned at the plight
of Europe; and in the early meetings of the Foreign Aid
Committee they strongly urged that it be tackled not on a
national basis, but as a coherent whole. Later, dismayed by
the slow workings of the administrative labyrinth, they produced a crisp and authoritative paper of their own. Its final
version was not completed until June 12, 1947; but preliminary drafts were circulating early in May. America, they
argued, should if possible induce the Soviet Union to negotiate a global settlement in Europe restoring the former pat-

tern of intracontinental trade. "Europe's three hundred and fifty million people must be allowed to play a positive international role by helping to blunt the sharpness of the antithesis between the United States and the Soviet Union." For this purpose, aid should ideally be channelled through the Economic Commission for Europe (ECE) recently set up by the United Nations. However, in case the East European members of ECE should refuse to co-operate, the United States must show that it was able and willing "to go ahead with a consistent and adequate recovery program for non-Communist Europe with or without the USSR." This part of their recommendations they summarized in one half-sentence: "Solidarity for ever if at all possible, but a well-protected flank if not."[30]

The case for a global approach, meanwhile, was being put more publicly. On Thursday, March 20, 1947, Walter Lippmann wrote one of a series of articles on the need for foreign aid, urging that it go to Europe as a whole rather than to individual European nations. His argument was reinforced on the following Sunday, March 23, when the veteran engineer, businessman, statesman, and former President of the United States, Herbert Hoover, released a report on economic conditions in Germany and Austria that he had recently completed for President Truman. In the previous year, as honorary chairman of Truman's Famine Emergency Committee, Hoover had made a country-by-country report on the food needs of twenty-two nations. Now he insisted that Europe—including Germany—be treated as a single economic unit:

There is only one path to recovery in Europe. That is production. The whole economy of Europe is interlinked with the German economy through the exchange of raw materials and manufactured goods. The productivity of Europe cannot be restored without the restoration of Germany as a contributor to that productivity.[31]

This was partly what the U. S. Secretary of State, George C. Marshall, was just then trying to negotiate in Moscow. The meeting was a crucial installment in the series of Foreign Ministers' Conferences—in Paris, London, and Moscow—which have been aptly called a "constitutional struggle" over the future of Europe and of Germany.[32] Resisting British and American calls for German economic unity, as well as French appeals for the internationalization of the Ruhr, Stalin's Foreign Minister V. M. Molotov had long since taught Western diplomatists and newspaper readers at least one word of Russian—his harsh and monotonous *nyet*. Now, in Moscow, as the wrangle continued evening after evening, often into the small hours, hopes of a settlement grew more and more distant. Stalin's terms for a unified German economy were a strong central government—especially unacceptable to France—and a further 10 billion dollars in reparations. He refused either to account for previous pickings or to allow the Western zones of Germany to resume their prewar imports from the East. Even if the Soviet Union no longer hoped to conquer the whole of Germany, it clearly planned to exploit her, virtually siphoning off the aid with which its wartime Allies were keeping the Western Germans just above starvation. By the time that Marshall returned to Washington on Saturday, April 26, 1947, he was deeply disillusioned. Was Stalin's aim to delay a German settlement while awaiting Western Europe's economic ruin? At all events, there was no more time to be wasted. As Marshall said in a broadcast on the following Monday, April 28, Europeans were crying out "for help, for coal, for food, for most of the necessities of life . . . The patient is sinking while the doctors deliberate."[33]

Next morning, he summoned George Kennan to his office. The State Department's Policy Planning Staff, which Kennan was to head, must be recruited and must start work without delay. Its top priority would be aid to Europe. "Avoid trivia" was Marshall's final, characteristic advice.[34]

Within a week, by Monday, May 5, 1947, Kennan had gathered round him a small, close-knit team. He himself at that time was still acting as "deputy for foreign affairs" at the recently established National War College; and it was here that on the following day, Tuesday, May 6, he set out in a lecture some of his ideas on Europe. The Soviet Union, he said, thought that America would not "be able to muster, as a nation, the leadership, the imagination, the political skill, the material resources, and above all the national self-discipline necessary to bring material stability, confidence, and hope for the future to those areas of Western Europe which have been brought low by the effects of the war." Yet "it may be fairly stated, as a working rule for dealing with the Russians, that only those people are able to get along with them who have proven their ability to get along without them." "Today," he concluded, "we find ourselves before the recognition that the economic rehabilitation of Western Europe is of urgent and primary importance. The restoration of German productivity, if only in a part of Germany, is essential to that rehabilitation. We cannot wait for Russian agreement to achieve that restoration."[35]

While Kennan and his staff were working out what this conclusion implied in practice, other officials were looking at the problem in its broader context. A month earlier, Truman had asked Dean Acheson to take over a speaking engagement that he himself had had to cancel, a talk to be given to the Delta Council in Cleveland, Mississippi, on Thursday, May 8, 1947. One of the officials called in to prepare a draft text suggested that he base it on preliminary papers from the State Department's Foreign Aid Committee. Acheson agreed. The result, as the speechwriter put it, was to "elaborate the economic intent of the Truman Doctrine into a comprehensive statement of our foreign reconstruction policy." After recalling the extent of wartime devastation in Europe and Asia, the postwar restraints imposed on German and Japanese production, and the "acts of God" that had destroyed most of Europe's food and fuel supplies, Acheson pointed out that "the accumulation of these grim developments has produced a disparity between production in the United States and production in the rest of the world that is staggering in its proportions." America had already done something to redress the balance:

We have contributed nearly 3 billion dollars to foreign relief. We have taken the lead in the organization of the International Bank for Reconstruction and Development and the International Monetary Fund, and have subscribed to these two institutions to the extent of almost 6 billion dollars. We have increased the capacity of the Export-Import Bank to make loans abroad by almost 3 billion dollars. We have made a direct loan of 3¾ billion dollars to Great Britain. We are proposing this year to contribute a half billion dollars for relief and reconstruction in the Philippines, and a billion dollars to relief in occupied areas. The President's recommendations for aid to Greece and Turkey to the extent of 400 million dollars and for post-UNRRA relief to the extent of 350 million dollars are still under consideration by Congress. And there are a few other smaller items. . . .

[But] great as is our supply of commodities and services to the world during the current year, it is still far short of what people of the world need. . . .

What do these facts of international life mean for the United States and for United States foreign policy?

They mean first that we in the United States must take as large a volume of imports as possible from abroad in order that the financial gap between what the world needs and what it can pay for can be narrowed. . . .

[They] also mean that the United States is going to have to undertake further emergency financing of foreign purchases. . . .

Since world demand exceeds our ability to supply, we are going to have to concentrate our emergency assistance in areas where it will be most effective in building world political and economic stability, in promoting human freedom and democratic institutions, in fostering liberal trading policies, and in strengthening the authority of the United Nations. . . .

The fourth thing we must do in the present situation is to push ahead with the reconstruction of those two great workshops of Europe and Asia—Germany and Japan—upon which the ultimate recovery of the two continents so largely depends. . . .

Quoting Marshall's broadcast, Acheson added:

European recovery cannot be complete until the various parts of Europe's economy are working together in a harmonious whole. And the achievement of a co-ordinated European economy remains a fundamental objective of our foreign policy.[36]

Two weeks later, on Friday, May 23, 1947, George Kennan's Policy Planning Staff produced a thirteen-page paper of recommendations to this end. "The ideas by which it was inspired," wrote Kennan later, "came from many sources; the drafting was largely my own." To sharpen its impact, the memorandum distinguished between the present emergency, which called for immediate action to raise Europe's coal output, and the need for a longer-term aid program, "directed not to the combatting of Communism as such but to the restoration of the economic health and vigor of European society."

It would be neither fitting nor efficacious for this government to undertake to draw up unilaterally and to promulgate formally on its own initiative a program designed to place Western Europe on its feet economically. This is the business of the Europeans. The formal initiative must come from Europe; and Europeans must bear the basic responsibility for it. The role of this country should consist of friendly aid in the drafting of a European program and of later support of such a program, by financial and other means, at European request. . . .

The program which this country is asked to support must be a joint one, agreed to by several European nations. . . . It must, for psychological and political, as well as economic reasons, be an internationally agreed program. The request for our support must come as a joint request from a group of friendly nations, not as a series of isolated and individual appeals. . . .

This European program must envisage bringing Western Europe to a point where it will be able to maintain a tolerable standard of living on a financially self-supporting basis. It must give promise of doing the whole job. . . .

It was no accident that the Policy Planning Staff's memorandum twice spoke of "Western Europe" rather than just "Europe," although in one instance the Marshall Plan's semi-official historian later omitted the adjective. Kennan and his colleagues agreed with the State Department Foreign Aid Committee that the forum for action should ideally be the Europe-wide ECE. However, forewarned by hearing of Soviet tactics at the ECE's first meeting, they added a sharper proviso: the United States, they suggested, should ensure that the Eastern European countries "either exclude themselves by an unwillingness to accept the proposed conditions or agree to abandon the exclusive orientation of their economies." Finally, the Planning Staff proposed "the despatch of instructions to certain European missions designed to obtain a uniform digest of the views of the respective chiefs. It is also proposed that secret discussions with the British be undertaken at once . . ."[37]

By now, the essentials of what was to be the Marshall Plan had taken shape in Washington. But the final impulse had still to be given; and it came just four days after the Policy Planning Staff memorandum. For the past week Will Clayton, Under-Secretary of State for Economic Affairs, had been back in Washington from a six weeks' tour in Europe. He had cut it short chiefly to advise the President to veto a Congressional attempt to raise the wool tariff—a question that kept him busy for several days. No sooner was it settled than he fell ill with a heavy cold; and not until Tuesday, May 27, 1947, was he able to send to Marshall, via Dean Acheson, his urgent report on the situation in Europe. Clayton's firsthand impressions revealed more vividly than bare statistics just what Europe was suffering; but even more forceful than what he wrote was what he said. In a voice still not quite recovered from fever, he described with homely logic:

. . . the peasant who would not produce more than he and his family and his cattle could eat because with the money he might get from selling his surplus produce in the market he could not buy buttons or thread or cloth or farm tools; the manufacturer of buttons and thread and cloth who could not produce for want of materials and fuel and because workers, being unable to satisfy their wants with money, were refusing to work; the middleman, and everyone else for that matter, who was hoarding supplies because of mounting inflation.

In the present crisis, Clayton's paper concluded, it would be "necessary for the President and Secretary of State to make a strong spiritual appeal to the American people to sacrifice a little themselves, to draw in their own belts just a little in order to save Europe from starvation and chaos (not from the Russians) and, at the same time, to preserve for ourselves and our children the glorious heritage of a free America."[38]

On the morning after receiving Clayton's memorandum, Marshall called a meeting in his office. One by one, at his request, the officials present gave their views on aid to Europe—Acheson, Clayton, Kennan, Charles Bohlen, Benjamin Cohen. Marshall listened gravely, thanked the group, and dismissed it. As usual, it was hard to tell exactly what he himself thought. Late that afternoon, one of his senior assistants brought in a pile of documents for signature. While there, he asked whether the Secretary could now confirm his tentative acceptance of an invitation to the Harvard Commencement Exercises in a week's time. Marshall thought that he would; presumably, he added, his hosts would expect him to make a speech. His assistant remarked that this might be a good opportunity to launch the appeal for aid to Europe that had been discussed that morning. When Marshall put this idea to Acheson, he advised against it for fear of inadequate news coverage; but next day, after further thought and consultation, Marshall sent a telegram agreeing to speak at Harvard, and he asked Charles Bohlen to draft him a text. Working chiefly on the basis of Clayton's and Kennan's memoranda, Bohlen produced his draft early in the following week. When Clayton and Acheson had gone over it, Marshall himself made some alterations, the last of them on the flight to Boston, Massachusetts, on the afternoon of Wednesday, June 4. He stayed the night with the Harvard President, James B. Conant; and on Thursday, June 5, in company which included General Omar N. Bradley, T. S. Eliot, and J. Robert Oppenheimer, he duly received an honorary degree. Then, after luncheon, he addressed the Harvard Alumni—and the Marshall Plan was launched.[39]

What Europeans faced, Marshall told his Harvard audience, was nothing less than "the dislocation of the entire fabric of European economy": "the modern system of division of labor upon which the exchange of products is based is in danger of breaking down."

The truth of the matter is that Europe's requirements for the next three or four years of foreign food and other essential products—principally from America—are so much greater than her present ability to pay that she must have substantial additional help or face economic, social, and political deterioration of a very grave character.

The remedy lies in breaking the vicious circle and restoring the confidence of the European people in the economic future of their own countries and of Europe as a whole. The manufacturer and the farmer throughout wide areas must be able and willing to exchange their product for currencies the continuing value of which is not open to question. . . .

It is logical that the United States should do whatever it is able to do to assist in the return of normal economic health in the world, without which there can be no political stability and no assured peace. Our policy is directed not against any country or doctrine but against hunger, poverty, desperation and chaos. Its purpose should be the revival of a working economy in the world so as to permit the emergence of political and social conditions in which free institutions can exist. Such assistance, I am convinced, must not be on a piecemeal basis as various crises develop. Any assistance that this Government may render in the future should provide a cure rather than a mere palliative. Any government that is willing to assist in the task of recovery will find full co-operation, I am sure, on the part of the United States Government. Any government which maneuvers to block the recovery of other countries cannot expect help from us. Furthermore, governments, political parties, or groups which seek to perpetuate human misery in order to profit therefrom politically or otherwise will encounter the opposition of the United States.

It is already evident that, before the United States Government can proceed much further in its efforts to alleviate the situation and help start the European world on its way to recovery, there must be some agreement among the countries of Europe as to the requirements of the situation and the part those countries themselves will take in order to give proper effect to whatever action might be undertaken by this Government. It would be neither fitting nor efficacious for this Government to undertake to draw up unilaterally a program designed to place *Europe* on its feet economically. This is the business of the Europeans. *The initiative*, I think, must come *from Europe*. The role of this country should consist of friendly aid in the drafting of a European program and of later support of such a program *so far as it may be practical for us to do so*. The program should be a joint one, agreed to by *a number, if not all*, European nations.[40]

It was this paragraph that Marshall had still been revising on the way up to Harvard. Although closely modeled on Kennan's Policy Planning Staff memorandum, it revealed one important change and one shift of emphasis, italicized above. Where Kennan had written "Western Europe," Marshall's text read "Europe," and it replaced "several European nations" with the awkward but comprehensive "a number, if not all." Marshall, in other words, was anxious to keep the offer open to the East. At the same time, he qualified American "aid in the drafting" and "later support" with the proviso "so far as it may be practical for us to do so"; and he stressed more firmly the "initiative from Europe" that Kennan had described as merely "formal."

This point, indeed, was crucial. "I have always wondered," said a British official afterward, "if Mr Marshall expected the reaction that his speech received." His apparently casual approach to it seemed to suggest that he did not; but he himself, in retrospect or hindsight, claimed that he had wanted it to break with "explosive force"—and without premature leakage: his nonchalance may have been a smoke screen. Good luck, good timing, and some degree of conspiracy or subterfuge are usually needed to make the march of history change step. "It is easy to propose a great plan," wrote Marshall, "but exceedingly difficult to manage the form and procedure so that it has a fair chance of political survival." And whatever his intentions, his Harvard speech might have been no more than a further persuasive argument if Dean Acheson had not helped to engineer a response.[41]

Already, before making his Delta Council speech a month earlier, Acheson had had a private lunch with three British reporters—Stewart McCall of the *News Chronicle*, Leonard Miall of the BBC, and Malcolm Muggeridge, then of the *Daily Express*. Now, on Wednesday, June 4, 1947, while Marshall was leaving for Harvard, they lunched together again. During the meal, Acheson explained the importance of the next day's speech, and the need for a swift and decisive European reaction. As a result, Miall made an eloquent broadcast on the following afternoon, while McCall and Muggeridge, at Acheson's request, telephoned their editors to urge that the full text of Marshall's remarks be sent round at once to Ernest Bevin, the British Foreign Secretary.[42]

Bevin was at home in bed when the private message reached him. The rumor ran that to save cable costs the British Embassy in Washington had delayed the official version by entrusting it to the diplomatic bag. If so, Bevin scarcely waited for it: that same night he sent out an urgent call to his senior advisers. "It was astonishing," said one of them, "the way in which he, with his elephantine frame, sprang into action." Sir William Strang, his Permanent Under-Secretary, suggested that a query be sent to the Embassy asking if Marshall's speech really meant what it seemed to imply. "No," said Bevin, "I don't want to ask Marshall that question. I don't want to take any chances that it wasn't meant. I want to go on the assumption that it was fully meant, and give an answer myself." As he afterward told the House of Commons, "When the Marshall proposals were announced, I grabbed them with both hands."[43]

As it happened, the first quasi-official reaction to Marshall's speech was a communiqué issued on Saturday, June 7, 1947, by Agence France Presse. This, while recalling previous French actions and proposals, welcomed "an appeal to the peoples of Europe that will be heard in France with especial sympathy because it corresponds to a concern for international organization and economic recovery that France has always shared." A week later, on Friday, June 13, Bevin made the first public and official response in a talk to the Foreign Press Association; and on the same day the French Foreign Minister, Georges Bidault, invited him to discuss the Marshall proposals in Paris. There, on Tuesday, June 17, they agreed to suggest a "European Economic Commission" to study the needs of Europe; and on the following day they issued a communiqué expressing "the greatest satisfaction" at Marshall's statement and inviting Molotov to a three-power meeting during the week of June 23. Less than two weeks after its launching, the Marshall Plan was already under way.[44]

EUROPE OF THE STATES

So we grew together . . .
But yet an union in partition.
William Shakespeare[1]

To quicken the Memory of past Kindness thou hast done
to any one, is a very nice Point to manage.
Thomas Fuller[2]

When great revolutions are successful, they eradicate
the causes that produced them; their very achievements
make them inexplicable.   *Alexis de Tocqueville*[3]

Welcome, Mr. Marshall (¡Bien venido, Mister Marshall!) was
a film made in 1952 by the Spanish director Luis Berlanga,
then thirty-one years old. Its title was paradoxical, since
American aid to Spain was not included in the Marshall
Plan; but this is immaterial to the plot. The setting is a
small Castilian village due for a visit from fund-distributing
officials. The mayor, already gloating over the prospect of
riches, plans to impress the visitors with a display of local
color; but the village, unfortunately, is far from picturesque.
All it can offer are priests, ruined aristocrats, and rascally
peasants. So the mayor hires an impresario to supply some
instant tradition, complete with shawls, mantillas, castanets,
and inept toreros. At last, when rehearsals are more or less
over, the officials appear—and drive straight through without
stopping. The only American who finally lingers is a nuclear
physicist who would rather make fireworks than bombs.

Written by its director and his friend Juan Antonio Bardem,
who later made *Death of a Cyclist* and *Calle Mayor*, this
mild, ironic, rather ingratiating fable hinged on the uneasiness felt in transatlantic relations between individual European countries and the American giant. The mayor was a

characteristic figure. For him, Americans were wealthy inno-
cents hungry for "folklore," easy prey for the ruthless, sad-
eyed Europe of Machiavelli and Talleyrand. His scorn was
a poor disguise for the indignity of his own position, part
huckster, part sutler, part beggar; and it misjudged the seriousness of the visitors, too briskly altruistic to notice local
antics, although no doubt willing to pay for any spectacle
they enjoyed. The physicist, finally, embodied the hope that
not all Americans were happy with their nuclear-backed
omnipotence, and that old-world picturesquerie, however
corrupted, still expressed something important in human life.

Uneasiness of this sort, born of inequality, has haunted
and somewhat muffled discussion of the Marshall Plan. Initially, some Americans may have felt that their generosity
and idealism entitled them to give more commanding advice
than was always welcome; later, they may well have resented
some Europeans' grandiloquent ingratitude. In Europe, while
knowing and even stating that Marshall Aid was a precondition of all later "affluence" and "economic miracles," as well
as of moves toward European unity, some have tended to
take it for granted, like a successful man making light of the
legacy that set him up in business. Orthodoxies, moreover,
usually provoke reactions; and attempts to correct—or over-
correct—the excesses of "cold war" rhetoric have sometimes
unjustly impugned the Marshall Plan's origins or one-sidedly
criticized its results. Impatience, propaganda, clichés, grati-
tude, guilt, boredom, resentment and counter-propaganda
have all in turn combined to confuse a central episode in
Europe's postwar history.

At the vantage point of twenty years' distance, it seems
fair to say that the Marshall Plan was Europe's "great leap
forward," marred by one big and two smaller steps back.
With food and raw materials, it saved Europeans from im-
minent economic ruin. With investment aid, fertilizers,
machines and machine tools, productivity programs and
planned growth, it laid the real foundations of later prosperity. With America's insistence on a co-ordinated approach
to European recovery, it supplied the incentive and the institutional machinery for permanent mutual consultation; and

it led to the gradual reduction of quantitative and monetary barriers to intra-European trade. But it suffered from three weaknesses. In the first place, most obviously and crucially, it was rejected and later opposed by the Soviet Union and the other countries of Eastern Europe. Secondly, it failed to involve America in a fully reciprocal economic "dialogue"; and thirdly, its European participants, while agreeing to co-operate, refused at this stage the degree of economic unity that such a dialogue would have required.

The restriction of Marshall Aid to Western Europe was by no means a foregone conclusion. Most Washington officials, certainly, had divided minds on the subject; but Marshall, in the final text of his Harvard speech, had been careful to extend the American offer to the whole of Europe—a point he repeated formally a week later, on Thursday, June 12, 1947. The next day, Ernest Bevin told the Foreign Press Association in London that "when the United States throws a bridge to link east and west, it would be disastrous for ideological or other reasons to frustrate the United States in this great endeavor." At their meeting in Paris on Tuesday and Wednesday, June 17 and 18, Bevin and Georges Bidault were quick to invite their Soviet colleague V. M. Molotov to join them during the following week. True, on Thursday, June 19, Bevin warned the House of Commons that Britain would go ahead with or without the Soviet Union; but twenty-four hours later, in a speech to the French National Assembly, Bidault stressed that the invitation to Molotov was genuine, not merely formal: it had emphasized, in fact, that Marshall had not officially approached the French and British Governments, and that the aim of the three-power meeting would be to begin working out a joint European program in close liaison with the United Nations. Two days later, on Sunday, June 22, came a Note from the Soviet Union accepting the invitation and proposing to meet on the following Friday.[4]

Bevin and Bidault agreed; and at 4:00 P.M. on Friday, June 27, 1947, the three Foreign Ministers met at the Quai d'Orsay. All were accompanied by advisers and assistants, but Molotov had brought with him no fewer than eighty-nine—

a fact that to some Western observers seemed encouraging. As representative of the host Government, Bidault opened the proceedings with a long statement that was to prove crucial in the subsequent debate:

The Government and Congress of the United States must quickly be given a document as precise and complete as possible explaining the effort made by Europe itself, its needs and the conditions that would result from a more marked deterioration of its economy. On this basis the American authorities will be able to take their decisions.

This document, which must be our first objective, should be completed by the beginning of September.

What is meant by Europe? In our view, it should include all countries of Europe, allies, ex-enemies, or neutrals, with the provisional exception of Spain.

All these European countries, in different degrees, are suffering from the same ills. . . .

At a European level, every country faces the same task.

In essential economic fields, European states must make a balance-sheet of the efforts that each is undertaking and the results that they promise. They will find that they lack large quantities of supplies and equipment. As far as possible, this deficit should be made up by inter-European action, and only for the remainder should we seek outside help. . . .

To call a vast conference to evaluate Europe's needs and resources does not seem an efficacious method. A good way to proceed would be to arrange as quickly as possible to set up a number of *ad hoc* committees, each for a different branch of economic activity, with a steering committee to co-ordinate their work.

These committees might be composed solely of representatives of the three powers [France, Great Britain and the Soviet Union] or, preferably, of their representatives assisted by those of the European States most concerned in the activities under consideration. . . .

Two sorts of studies should be made:

(a) A study of ways of increasing production in essential sectors of the economy, i.e. agriculture (fertilizers, farm machinery, seeds); energy (equipment for mines, refineries and hydro-electric power stations); transport (equipment for railways, sea and river transport, and ports); and the iron and steel industry.

(b) The steering committee and *ad hoc* committees, taking account of the result they expect from this development of Europe's means of production, would draw up the balance-sheet of Europe's resources. In this way it would be possible to work out the tonnage of food (grains, fats) and essential raw materials (coal, steel, textiles, petroleum, etc.) that Europe lacks. . . .

Six *ad hoc* sub-committees should be set up: (a) agriculture; (b) energy; (c) transport; (d) iron and steel; (e) raw materials; and (f) balance of payments.

But if we wish to get the job done quickly, we must ask them to concentrate their efforts on a few products only, those that I have enumerated and that are indispensable in national life. What is more, it will be advisable to be very precise about the questions—which should be kept as simple as possible—to be submitted by the steering committee to each of the nations concerned. To this end, each country should present to the steering committee a balance-sheet of its own situation, its production targets, and its needs, on a uniform model; the *ad hoc* sub-committees would discuss the particular programmes on the basis of the overall programme thus drawn up by each country.

The European countries must be able to make known their observations and to say whether or not they accept the methods suggested.

The simplest procedure would be to submit joint proposals to the Economic Commission for Europe, which will be meeting in Geneva on 5 July. The Economic Commission for Europe could not draw up these documents because it so far scarcely exists, because its statutes are not yet complete, and because questions about voting and about the composition of its various constituent bodies are still under discussion. This does not mean that we should exclude the Economic Commission for Europe: it will make its observations on the machinery as a whole. The closest contacts will be maintained with the ECE Secretariat-General; finally, when it is definitively established, we must study how to transfer to it the whole of this heavy task.

Clearly, it is impossible to imagine an overall European programme not including Germany. It may be objected that the reconstruction of Germany raises all those questions on which agreement has yet to be reached in the Council of Foreign Ministers—the level of German industry, reparations, the Ruhr, etc. This is undeniably a difficulty. But the first 'European report' to be drawn up should not prejudice future decisions about the ultimate status of Germany. On the one hand, because it would essentially be a study of how to increase certain types of production that everyone agrees should be developed in Germany—agriculture and coal. On the other hand, because as regards other types of production, such as iron and steel and the electrical industry, the projects are not required to cover more than one or two years. German production is still far below the levels set by the Control Council on 15 March

1946. Whatever efforts are made over one year or two, these levels will not be exceeded. If, in the meantime, it is agreed to increase the figures fixed by the Control Council's decision of 15 March 1946, account will be taken of this in drawing up the European report.[5]

Bevin seconded these proposals; but Molotov, from the start, was more reserved. Already, ten days earlier, *Pravda* had attacked the Marshall offer as a further installment of Truman's "plan for political pressures with dollars and a program for interference in the internal affairs of other states," and on June 25 had alleged that its real aim was to prolong America's postwar boom. Now, on Saturday, June 28, the second day of the three-power conference, the Tass news agency in Moscow carried a message from its Paris correspondent denouncing the Franco-British proposals as "foreign interference." "Obviously," it said, "the internal economic problems of a State are a matter of its own sovereignty, and no other country can concern itself with them." At that day's meeting, Molotov made the same point:

Hitherto [he declared] it was established that every country should decide for itself what were the best means of reinstating and developing its economy. It seemed perfectly clear that questions of internal economy were a matter concerning the sovereignty of the peoples themselves, and that other countries should not interfere in such questions. Only on this basis can relations between countries develop normally. Attempts made from without to intervene in the economic life of various countries have not had nor can they have any positive results. If this is the case the attempts made to force the Conference to draw up a general economic programme for the European nations—which would inevitably involve the intervention of certain States—could not serve as a basis for collaboration between the countries of Europe.[6]

He proposed instead that each country submit its own list of requirements to the United States; he added that a distinction must be made between allied, neutral, and ex-enemy countries, and that Germany must be dealt with only by the four-power Conference of Foreign Ministers.[7]

Bevin pointed out at once that "it has never been our intention that anything in connection with this work which we have to undertake should interfere with the sovereignty of participating Governments, and if it were to do such a thing I should not wish to be a party to it . . . It is, however, necessary that we should undertake work in collaboration with each other and that our demands should be co-ordinated." For this purpose, the British delegation formally proposed that "a steering Committee should be set up forthwith to draft, for the consideration of the Governments of Europe, a program of reconstruction co-ordinating the needs of European countries over the next four years for presentation to the United States."[8]

But Molotov remained unconvinced. When the Conference met again on Monday, June 30, he made a counter-proposal restating his previous objections. "The Conference believes," his draft read, "that it is not its function to draw up an all-embracing programme for the European countries, since the drawing up of such an economic programme for the whole of Europe, even with the participation of certain other countries, would inevitably result in the imposition of the will of strong European Powers upon other European countries, and would constitute intervention in the domestic affairs of those States and a violation of their sovereignty."[9]

To Bidault, these fears seemed quite unjustified; and at the next day's meeting, on Tuesday, July 1, he set out his arguments in detail:

The idea of co-operation embodied in the French proposal, I must state, not only with firmness but with the greatest insistence, does not imply any interference in the internal affairs of the European States, nor any infringement of their sovereignty. The aim of our proposal is to collect and to co-ordinate the statistics, the economic data which will be provided voluntarily by those European States which declare themselves ready to associate themselves with our action. On the one hand we are not dreaming of constraining anyone to join in against his will; and on the other hand, we impose no sort of modification on national economic policies, no change in existing economic plans, which can only be modified in the exercise of national sovereignty. We do wish, naturally, to harmonize the efforts of everyone, with a view to obtaining the maximum development of production, but this can only be accomplished by the consent, freely given, of all the interested parties, who are at all times in a position to refuse it.

I would like, to make myself clearer, to recall the example of the co-operation which was obtained during and after the war, in a certain number of international bodies, whose existence has never been considered as being an infringement of the independence of the member States. Now this is a kind of war which we have to win, not war against the invader, fascism, and criminal violence, but against poverty and penury, and ruin. This war must be won by the same means as the other, that is, by the co-operation of the nations. During the war there existed what were called 'combined boards', organisms whose duty it was to distribute raw materials. More recently, in important European bodies like E.C.O. [the European Coal Organization], which distributes coal, a useful collaboration has been established. We have never considered, either yesterday or to-day, that the sovereignty of the States could be involved in this way. It is this same spirit which the French delegation wishes to see presiding over the working out of the common programme for Europe which we have in mind.

At the end of this statement, Bidault read a revised version of the French proposal, which now explicitly stressed that its aim was to collect and collate information, not to interfere in national affairs.[10]

By this time, however, there was little hope of avoiding a breach. At the next day's meeting, on Wednesday, July 2, as if he had not heard or understood Bidault's explanation, Molotov once more attacked the idea of "a new organization standing over and above the countries of Europe and interfering in their internal affairs down to determining the line of development to be followed by the main branches of industry in these countries." If the French and British proposals were adopted, he said, "the European countries would find themselves placed under control and would lose their former economic and national independence because it so pleases certain strong powers." Poland, for example, might be pressed into producing more coal while neglecting other industries; Czechoslovakia might be required "to increase her agricultural production and to reduce her engineering industry." In this way, "American credits would serve not to facilitate the economic rehabilitation of Europe, but to make use of some European countries against other European countries in whatever way certain strong powers seeking to establish their dominion should find it profitable to do so."[11]

Bidault answered that he was disappointed, but he added:

France solemnly declines all responsibility for the consequences that may arise from a decision that she has done all in her power to prevent. . . France is determined, and the French Government feels obliged, to continue studying the prospects opened up by Mr Marshall's suggestions. This task will be undertaken with all those who would like to co-operate in it. I express the hope here and now that no refusal is definitive and that, as a result, the labours ahead of us will not be the work of only a part of Europe.

Thereupon, Molotov and his huge delegation withdrew.[12]

On the following day, Thursday, July 3, after a further meeting between Bevin and Bidault, the French Foreign Ministry issued a brief communiqué:

The French and British Governments have reached the following decision with a view to giving rapid effect to the suggestion made by Mr Marshall in his speech on 5 June at Harvard University, according to which Europe should take the initiative in the work of reconstruction.

It is essential to draw up as rapidly as possible a programme covering Europe's resources as well as her needs. A temporary organization must be set up to collect the data on which such a programme will be based.

The French and British Governments have therefore decided to invite all European States, with the provisional exception of Spain, that wish to take part in working out a response to Mr Marshall's suggestions, to collaborate with them in order to establish this organization. The task to be undertaken will be to draw up a European reconstruction programme in which the resources and the needs of each State will be co-ordinated as each of the European countries freely decides.

This invitation to take part in the organization will remain open to all European countries.[13]

In the event, only one East European country accepted the invitation to the forthcoming conference, which began in Paris on July 12, 1947. This was Czechoslovakia. But her acceptance was short-lived. On July 9, the Czech Premier Klement Gottwald and his Foreign Minister Jan Masaryk visited Moscow. By the time that they returned to Prague they had changed their minds. The Marshall Plan was to be confined to Western Europe.[14]

Challenging the pieties of much official history, some recent writers have questioned whether Bidault and, especially, Bevin were sincere in discussing the Marshall Plan with Molotov.[15] "Bevin and the British Foreign Office," it has been said, "were fearful that Stalin would agree and took no pains to create a hospitable atmosphere at Paris."[15] Certainly, they went there with mixed feelings, and they may well have feared that Soviet acceptance might alienate the U. S. Congress. Chilled by recent experience, moreover, they may have been privately relieved to escape the delays, exhaustion, and exasperation of trying to collaborate with Stalin. But there is no proof that they or Bidault deliberately alienated Molotov, and little likelihood that diplomatic cordiality could reverse a Soviet decision.

It is just conceivable, as some have suggested, that Molotov had instructions to accept or at least explore the Marshall proposal, and that he misplayed his hand. But although a few Soviet officials—including, perhaps, Anastas Mikoyan—may have favored the Marshall Plan, *Pravda* had already condemned it as early as June 16; and at least one Western observer was convinced that the final decision came from Moscow. "It seems," he told an interviewer, "that Molotov has a bump on his forehead which swells when he is under emotional strain. The matter was being debated, and Molotov had raised relatively minor questions or objections at various points, when a telegram was handed to him. He turned pale and the bump on his forehead swelled. After that, his attitude suddenly changed and he became much more harsh." During the last twelve hours of the conference, moreover, he had a telephone line through to Moscow all the time.[16]

In Soviet terms, indeed, the decision to withdraw was understandable. The Marshall proposal, although partly distinct from the Truman Doctrine, looked from a distance like an extension of it. Impressed by the fighting speeches made by all and sundry since Churchill's denunciation of the "Iron Curtain" at Fulton, Missouri, on March 5, 1946, officials in Moscow were not to know how scrupulously their counterparts in Washington—not least Marshall himself—had kept open the door to the East. To the men in the Kremlin, the mere idea of having Soviet needs, resources, and production targets discussed internationally was highly suspicious. Conditioned by "realism" as much as by Marxist mistrust of capitalist imperialism, they could hardly imagine that America, if not France or Britain, would refrain from interfering in the economic plans she was invited to see. Equally extraordinary, in their eyes, was the proposal to stop penalizing ex-enemy countries. Most fundamentally of all, perhaps, they suspected that the program described by Bidault and Bevin would encourage East European countries to turn their economies westward, expanding farm production to feed Western Europe in exchange for imported manufactures—a form of "economic colonialism" well understood in Moscow.

Was the East-West clash over the Marshall proposals, then, merely another decisive instance of mutual incomprehension, for which both sides were equally responsible? The conclusion looks temptingly impartial: but in fact it shirks a necessary judgment. To assess Soviet behavior on its own terms would be to accept as normative Moscow's habits of proselytism, Realpolitik, and secretive suspiciousness: and the Western proposals, however mixed their motives, were undoubtedly more intelligent, humane, and adult than the Soviet reaction. To that extent, the main responsibility for deepening the division of Europe in 1947 must surely rest with Joseph Stalin.

The Soviet withdrawal from the Marshall Plan deferred all hope of restoring prewar trade between Eastern and Western Europe. At the same time, however, it cleared a path for action in the West. As one official put it, "When the cat was away the mice could work."[17] Thrown together by common necessity, freed for the moment from haggling with the stone-faced Molotov, and fired by the prospect of being able at last to get things done, Western statesmen and civil servants rediscovered a wartime vigor and adaptability.

Responding to Bevin's and Bidault's invitation, representatives of sixteen countries—Austria, Belgium, Denmark, France, Greece, Iceland, Ireland, Italy, Luxembourg, the Netherlands, Norway, Portugal, Sweden, Switzerland, Turkey, and the United Kingdom—met in Paris on Saturday, July 12,

1947. On Wednesday, July 16, they set up a Committee of European Economic Co-operation (CEEC) under the chairmanship of the British delegate Sir Oliver Franks, to produce a rough four-year recovery program. By September 22—in less than ten weeks—it was completed. Only two months later, on November 18, France, Italy, and the Benelux countries made the first halting move toward multilateral payments clearance, followed at some distance by a number of their colleagues. In Washington, meanwhile, President Truman had already endorsed Marshall's proposals on June 11; eleven days later, he called for three separate reports on Europe's needs and America's potential assistance. Shortly afterward, he and Marshall began a series of consultations with Congressional leaders from both political parties. On July 29, the House of Representatives set up a nineteen-man study committee, whose members toured Europe in August and September under the leadership of Christian A. Herter. They returned in the same ship that was taking Franks and a group from the CEEC to help the United States Government present the European case to Congress. Now, at short intervals, successive reports arrived to back it: on September 25, the Anderson report on world food problems; on October 19, the Krug report on "National Resources and Foreign Aid"; on October 28, the Nourse report on "The Impact of Foreign Aid upon the Domestic Economy"; on November 7, the highly influential Harriman report on "European Recovery and American Aid." But on October 23, long before the scheduled hearings, Truman called a special session of Congress to propose emergency measures: the result was interim aid of 522 million dollars for France, Italy, and Austria, raised to 577 million dollars by a further grant on March 31, 1948. By this time, on December 19, 1947, Truman had submitted to Congress "A Program for United States Support to European Recovery"; and on January 8, 1948, the Senate Foreign Relations Committee and the House Committee on Foreign Affairs had begun their public hearings. Altogether, they took oral or written testimony from 350-odd witnesses, filling five volumes and 3,735 pages: the documentation available, it was estimated, would have taken four or five months to read.[18]

At last, worked over day and night in committee, the Economic Co-operation Act drafted by a Democratic Administration was ready for presentation to a predominantly Republican Congress. Supporting it before the Senate, in a speech that he had himself rewritten half a dozen times, the white-haired Arthur H. Vandenberg, once known as an isolationist, admitted that:

It would be a far happier circumstance if we could close our eyes to reality, comfortably retire within our bastions, and dream of an isolated and prosperous peace. But that which was once our luxury would now become our folly. This is too plain to be persuasively denied in a foreshortened, atomic world. We must take things as they are. . . .

Within the purview of this plan are 270,000,000 people of the stock which has largely made America. These are 26 percent of all the literate of the earth. Before the war they operated 68 percent of all the ships that sailed the sea. They grew 27 percent of all the world's cereals. They produced 37 percent of the world's steel. They sold 24 percent of the world's exports and bought 39 percent of the world's imports. They are struggling, against great and ominous odds, to regain their feet. They must not be allowed to fail.[19]

On Saturday, April 3, 1948, after large majority votes in both the House and the Senate, the Economic Co-operation Act became law. One week later, its initials changed their meaning, adding a new ingredient to Washington's alphabet soup, when the Economic Co-operation Administration (ECA) came into being to direct the European Recovery Program (ERP).[20]

Like most creative ventures, the ECA had few precedents to smooth its path. Truman initially thought of appointing Dean Acheson to run it. Both Acheson and Senator Vandenberg, however, advised him that the fifty-six-year-old Paul Hoffman, president of the Studebaker Corporation, would be more congenial to Congress. Truman took the point. "It seems," said Hoffman in private afterward, "that I was the least obnoxious of the Republicans." Even so, although he had helped to prepare the Harriman report, he was reluctant to take the ECA post; and he only agreed, finally, when Truman had forced his hand with a purposely premature rumor of his acceptance. He was sworn in on Friday,

April 9, 1948; but at first he had no proper Washington headquarters, and the ECA began its official existence in Room
W-900 of the Hotel Statler. Within two weeks, the freighter
John H. Quick was sailing from Galveston, Texas, with 9,000
tons of wheat for Europe, although Hoffman himself had
originally opposed large food shipments. "I had not myself
been up against the kind of situation in which chronic undernourishment cut down people's working energy," he confessed.[21]

If the ECA's policy had to be flexible, so did its staffing
arrangements. For the first two weeks, all appointments were
provisional; and most of the 400 people ultimately engaged—
many of them from outside public administration—were hand-
picked by co-optation rather than selected from lists of ap-
plicants. When Averell Harriman was persuaded to head
the ECA's Office of the Special Representative (OSR) in
Europe, this was thought of as a roving embassy; but by the
time he had crossed the Atlantic it had been decided to settle
the OSR in Paris—first in two borrowed offices on the second
floor of the United States Embassy, later in the rue St. Flor-
entin on the northeast corner of the Place de la Concorde,
in the eighteenth-century mansion where Talleyrand had
lived with the last of his mistresses. The European recipients of Marshall Aid, meanwhile, set up their staff headquarters in Passy, on the site of the former sixteenth-century
Château de la Muette, itself touched with scandal by the
Duchesse de Berry, the lively daughter of the Regent.[22]

Making mistakes, changing their minds, trying out new
procedures, arguing and often wrangling, the men and
women who put the Marshall Plan into practice accomplished
more than was sometimes recognized a few years later, when
improvisation had given way to institutions and routine. Between 1948 and 1952, in addition to the 9.5 billion dollars
that the United States had already made available to Western
Europe since World War II, the ERP supplied grants and
credits totaling $13,150,000,000. The largest sums went to
the United Kingdom and her dependencies ($3,176,000,000),
France ($2,706,000,000), Italy ($1,474,000,000) and Western Germany ($1,389,000,000). On top of this, helped by

a 22-million-dollar mail subsidy, American citizens sent private relief parcels valued at more than 500 million dollars—an average of over 3 dollars a head. In the first year, half of all Marshall Aid imports into Europe consisted of food; by 1951, only a quarter. During the whole four-year program, nearly two-thirds of the total aid was spent on food, feed, fertilizers, raw materials, and semi-finished products. Fuel accounted for 16 per cent, machinery and vehicles for 17 per cent. More than two-thirds of all these imports came from America; but one-sixth of the aid was used to finance trade within Western Europe itself. Between 1947 and 1950, this trade more than doubled, reaching its prewar level in the last quarter of 1949, two years ahead of expectations. By the summer of 1951, Western Europe's industrial production was 43 per cent, and farm production was 10 per cent above their respective prewar totals. Progress was far from uniform; but by then European recovery had ceased to be only a program: it was well on the way to being achieved.[23]

Psychologically as well as financially, dollar aid was what made this progress possible. The Europeans certainly matched America's drive and imagination with their own skill and hard work. It was only under American pressure, however, that they set up a permanent body to concert their efforts. In the decade that followed, European economic co-operation was taken for granted, if not actually belittled; but in the 1940s its novelty was as striking—and, to some, as disconcerting—as the "supranational" projects launched later by the Europe of the Six. Originally, some governments had intended to deal with Marshall Aid on a purely temporary basis. When Ernest Bevin spoke at the sixteen-nation Paris Conference on July 12, 1947, he stressed that "We have no idea of setting up a permanent organization to rival the United Nations. It is a piece of *ad hoc* machinery to grapple with this special problem." The CEEC report of September 12, likewise, spoke of an "organization . . . of a temporary character . . . [which] will cease to exist when the special assistance necessary for the recovery of Europe comes to an end." It took repeated efforts by Under-Secretary Will Clayton and his colleagues, culminating on January 5, 1948, in a simultaneous *démarche* by all the U.S. embassies in Western Europe, to persuade the recipients of Marshall Aid to negotiate and at length establish, on April 16 of that year, the Organization for European Economic Co-operation (OEEC). A senior British civil servant, Sir Hugh Ellis-Rees, later Chairman of the OEEC Council, revealingly described it as "a perpetual international conference." But in 1948 even this was something quite new to Europe; and under its first Secretary-General, the thirty-seven-year-old Robert Marjolin, an acute French economist with an American wife and a partly American education, it performed at least three outstanding and difficult tasks.[24]

The first was thrust upon it. On Saturday, June 5, 1948, Averell Harriman announced to the OEEC Council that it must itself take charge of allocating Marshall Aid. His audience was dumfounded. Some, like the British, had hoped to profit by dealing direct with Washington; others had been less optimistic; but none had expected this sudden responsibility, and all foresaw trouble—especially when the funds made available by Congress for 1948–49 proved to be 500 million dollars short of Europe's requests. To cut up the cake would be difficult: to cut down the portions would be harder still. In a sixteen-nation gathering it was out of the question. On Friday, July 16, therefore, after what one participant described as "much backstage fighting," the Council appointed a group of four national civil servants—from Britain, France, Italy, and the Netherlands—to propose how the aid should be divided. Each country in turn brought them its program for vetting; a member of one delegation has recalled how he and his colleagues "entered the examination room with the special feeling of tension well known to anyone who has gone through examinations in private life." The four experts then left Paris for an undisclosed address in Chantilly, twenty-five miles away, to work out their proposals in peace. When they presented them to the Council, as an eyewitness put it, "pandemonium broke loose": for two hours, an argument raged about the merits of discussing them at all. But at length, after weeks of recrimination, a much amended version of the experts' work was accepted. The so-called "restricted committee" method had proved its worth; and a year later, in an even graver crisis, it was used again. The following years' allocations were made more simply, by using the 1949–50 percentages; but by now the OEEC had established two of its characteristic procedures—the mutual confrontation of national programs, and their scrutiny by a small committee acting "extranationally" on behalf of the whole group. Necessity in the face of Congress had been the mother of the OEEC's invention.[25]

Co-operation is hard to quantify; but the OEEC's second main achievement—the liberalization of trade—is easier to measure. At the outset, trade in Western Europe was clogged by national import controls, relics of the '30s depression maintained and multiplied during and after World War II. Individually intended to boost home production and improve the balance of payments, the restrictions were collectively self-defeating; but few governments would risk removing their own unless their competitors did likewise. It was not until November 2, 1949, that the OEEC countries formally committed themselves "to remove before December 15, 1949, quantitative restrictions on at least 50 per cent of their total imports on private account [i.e. all but state trading] from the other Member countries as a group." All but six were able to keep their promise. On August 18, 1950, the OEEC agreed on a "Code of Liberalization" to ensure greater equity; and by the end of the year all member states but two had achieved a 50 per cent liberalization, all but three had reached 60 per cent, two had topped 70 per cent, and one had attained 86 per cent. The years that followed saw some steps backward; but, in January 1955, the minimum liberalization of private trade was raised to 90 per cent, and by the end of 1956 the average level for all imports was 89 per cent. Five years later, when the OEEC was formally superseded by the Organization for Economic Co-operation and Development (OECD), liberalization had reached 95 per cent. By this time, the OECD method of removing restrictions from one group of products after another, instead of gradually relaxing all of them, had met a "hard core" of difficult cases; but these were mainly agricultural, and controls on industrial imports had almost disappeared.[26]

Imports must obviously be paid for; and there would have been little point in removing restrictions on trade if nothing had been done to free intra-European payments from exchange controls. Here, too, Western Europe had been caught in a net of contradictions. Lacking gold and dollars, each country had wanted to earn them with its exports, yet none had been eager to spend them on imports. The situation was too absurd to last; but the immediate remedies found for it were purely bilateral. Pairs of trading partners agreed to meet each other's deficits with limited credits: only beyond these margins—and seldom in practice even then—would they seek payment in hard currency or cash. By 1947, nearly two-thirds of the trade within Western Europe was bound by such agreements; without a central clearinghouse, it was almost a barter system. On November 18, 1947, Belgium, France, Italy, Luxembourg and the Netherlands made the first agreement on Multilateral Monetary Compensation; but this was extremely cautious. Even when extended to all the OEEC countries, its total turnover was only 10 million dollars a month. Beginning on October 16, 1948, the United States supplemented these sums by making part of Marshall Aid "conditional" on its recipients' granting equivalent credits— "drawing rights"—to their European debtors. At first, drawing rights were strictly national; then, a year later, debtors were allowed to transfer 25 per cent of them to other countries. Even this extra liquidity, however, reduced net deficits and surpluses by less than 800 million dollars, and the scramble for gold and dollars went on. Not until July 7, 1950, did the OEEC countries agree on a real multilateral clearance system, the European Payments Union (EPU). That day a triumphant press release, known to its sponsors as "The Child's Guide to the EPU," gave a layman's—or a clubman's —explanation:

If four people play bridge during an evening, they may settle their debts at the end of each rubber. But if they change partners continually, they may prefer to keep the score on a piece of paper and only settle at the end of the evening. Only the players who are net losers will pay; only the net winners will receive.

"I see," said a reporter: "Now they're playing bridge instead of demon patience." Whatever the game, it moved briskly. The EPU was formally established on September 19, 1950. Soon it was handling 250 million dollars a month.[27]

However, despite these achievements, the OEEC had more success with immediate problems than with longer-term questions of investment and balanced growth. It suffered, in particular, from two related handicaps. One was Europe's inability to deal as an equal with America. The other was the lack of real unity among Europeans themselves.

The very existence of the Marshall Plan implied that Western Europe's postwar difficulties were more than merely European. Had they not been dealt with, their effects could have been very widespread; their causes, too, lay partly elsewhere. Europe's dollar deficit largely reflected North America's surplus; and a better balance in the world economy ideally required a joint policy, worked out together by both sides. As it was, America supplied advice and dollars; but in return the European countries concerted their policies only with each other. While far from one-sided, this was certainly asymmetrical. To plan their investments and overseas exports, the Europeans needed to know something of America's intentions; but American apostles of planning in Europe were disciples of *laissez-faire* in their own country: there was no United States "plan" to act as a guide. Nor, with or without a plan, could the Europeans have much say in American policy, notwithstanding America's impact on their own. Dependent on United States dollars, they were in no position, psychologically or politically, to talk on equal terms with their powerful patron. At times, this was unpalatably obvious: when the aid requests for 1948–49 were cut, the U.S. military representative from the British and American zones of Germany—by then merged into the "Bizone"—caused deep resentment by insisting on its privileged status. But for the most part, the ECA combined firmness with tact and wisdom. American leadership was simply a fact of life. Paying the piper, the United States felt entitled to suggest at least some of the tunes, all the more because Congress held the purse-

strings. Some Administrations, no doubt, have been glad to
use Congress as a pretext for pressing their own policies;
but Congressional control of Marshall Aid was genuine and
thorough, and it helped to kill any real hope of joint transatlantic planning, which Europe and America could only
have tackled as equals.[28]

It was here, by a strange paradox, that American leadership failed. To achieve greater influence in Washington,
European countries would have had to unite; and this was
what America repeatedly urged them to do. Far from feeling
at ease in her lonely pre-eminence, she constantly tried to
share it, reverting only fitfully to the impatient use of power.
Western Europe was her obvious potential partner—another
industrial society, mainly of the same stock, with a similar
civilization, a comparable way of life, and analogous forms
of government. Often, no doubt, there was ambivalence in
Americans' views of that Old World from which so many of
their ancestors had been religious, political, or economic
refugees. Like some exotic widow, veiled, sloe-eyed, and
musky, Europe had always exerted equivocal fascination;
now, her charms were stale and she had been too often conquered. In the wake of two world wars, the European countries seemed so small, so backward, so disputatious, stiff with
tradition and hierarchy. There was a great temptation to as-
cribe their troubles to defects of character, or to preach
them zealous lessons from America's experience of unity.
Transatlantic bluntness, real or supposed, caused as much
amusement as annoyance. It was curious, one night in a garden in New Delhi, to watch the French Ambassador's face
as Professor Walter Hallstein, then president of the Common
Market Commission, told the story of the American businessman flying over Europe for the first time. "That's France
down below," said his assistant. "Don't bother me with details," was the reply. This was no doubt apocryphal; but at
least one American tourist has been known to complain: "You
come to so many frontiers when you cross Europe—why don't
they all get together?" Nor have such thoughts been confined to private visitors. One day during World War II John
Foster Dulles, later Secretary of State under President Eisenhower, pointed to a map of Europe and said: "After the war

all that will have to be united, otherwise nothing lasting can be built."[29]

In the State Department, interest in European unity went back at least as far as 1942, when George Kennan unsuccessfully urged that some of the technical centralization imposed by Hitler be retained and entrusted to "a new European federal authority." In the same year, the Department commissioned a study group from the Council on Foreign Relations to examine "American Interests in the Economic Unification of Europe with Respect to Trade Barriers"; but its report, which was carefully qualified, aroused little response.[30]

For several years, in fact, American official thinking on this subject was tinged with suspicion. President Truman was said to favor a United States of Europe; but it was only gradually, as hopes of "Big Three" collaboration dwindled, that opinion in Washington began to follow suit. The first pressures came from outside the State Department. As early as 1946, Paul Hoffman became convinced of the need to apply in Europe the production techniques made possible by America's mass market; and in January 1947, in his testimony before the Senate Committee on Foreign Relations, he elaborated his ideas for "greater unity in the European economy." On January 17, with the backing of Governor Thomas E. Dewey and Senator Vandenberg, John Foster Dulles made a speech before the National Publishers' Association in New York urging the United States to take the lead in reconstructing Europe on federal lines. On March 22, resolutions calling for a United States of Europe were introduced into both Houses of Congress. On April 5, in the New York *Herald Tribune*, Walter Lippmann proposed "not less than an economic union" in Europe.[31]

The most fully argued appeal, however, came from the State Department itself, in the memorandum by Charles Kindleberger, Harold Van Buren Cleveland, and Ben T. Moore, drawn up in its final form on June 12, 1947:

There appears to be no alternative equally effective for present-day Europe. The symbols of nationalism in France and Italy and in Germany are essentially bankrupt and in danger of being captured by reactionary and neo-fascist political elements which we do not wish to support. There is a possibility of developing tremendous emotional drive in Western Europe behind the supranational idea of European unity. . . .

To avoid injuring sensitive feelings of nationalism, our appeal should be couched in terms of a European recovery plan which stresses the raising of European production and consumption through the economic and 'functional' unification of Europe. In our propaganda and our diplomacy it will be necessary to stress (even exaggerate) the immediate economic benefits which will flow from the joint making of national economic policies and decisions.[32]

Under-Secretary Will Clayton had been even more specific in the paper he had handed to General Marshall on May 27, 1947:

This three-year grant to Europe should be based on a European plan which the principal European nations, headed by the United Kingdom, France and Italy, should work out. Such a plan should be based on a European economic federation on the order of the Belgium-Netherlands-Luxembourg Customs Union.[33]

On July 23, George Kennan's Policy Planning Staff recommended as "a long-term objective" what it called "the eventual formation of a European Customs Union." The aim, wrote Kennan later, was "to force the Europeans to begin to think like Europeans, and not like nationalists, in their approach to the economic problems of the continent." When the Harriman Committee at length reported, on November 7, 1947, it more tactfully made a similar point. For twenty years, Averell Harriman himself had believed that Europe needed economic unity in order to share America's advantages; now, his Committee's Report firmly underlined the benefits of removing trade barriers. The Herter Report, published on May 1, 1948, went even further, and called for a "European federation." Paul Hoffman and the ECA were more cautious; but time and again, in the months and years that followed, they urged the Europeans toward what Hoffman called, in a memorable homily, "nothing less than an integration of the Western European economy." "The substance of such integration," he added, "would be the formation of a single large market within which quantitative restrictions on the movement of goods, monetary barriers to the flow of payments, and eventually, all tariffs are permanently swept away."[34]

The early history of the Marshall Plan can be read as a struggle between this American vision and the stubborn, untidy realities of Western Europe.

It began in the dry, cloudless summer of 1947, at the Paris meetings of the CEEC. On Tuesday, July 15, Count Carlo Sforza, the Italian Foreign Minister, announced to what he later described as "that frigid gathering of statesmen and economists": "We must look for more than technical agreements; we must be willing to destroy the myths of self-sufficiency, we must limit national sovereignty; to the dogma of national independence we must add the dogma of European independence." He went on to propose a customs union, initially between Italy and France.[35]

Before very long, the idea was broadened to include all Western Europe. Will Clayton, who had already proposed this in Washington, came to Paris at the end of the month; and the Europeans soon realized, in the words of a Dutch delegate, that "a customs union would be one of the projects which would vitalize and catch American public opinion and imagination." In mid-August, the CEEC's Executive Committee—the Ministers' deputies—began to discuss it: but at first their progress was slow. When Clayton remarked on this to Sir Oliver Franks, their British Chairman, Franks asked him whether a European customs union was a precondition for American aid. No, said Clayton, it was not; but he added that it would greatly improve the chances of Congressional approval. He repeated the point less bluntly at a formal meeting with all European Heads of Delegation, on Saturday, August 30, 1947, when he argued that "definite steps should be taken to diminish trade barriers, leading to an eventual abolition of all impediments to trade."[36]

The Report that the CEEC finally produced on September 22, 1947, however, was very much more cautious. "The advantages which the United States has enjoyed through the existence of a large domestic market with no internal trade barriers," it declared, "are manifest." But from this it merely concluded that "the idea of a Customs Union including as many European countries as possible is one which contains important possibilities for the economic future of Europe and it is in the general interest that the problems involved should receive careful and detailed study by governments." For this purpose, on September 13, 1947, all of them except Iceland, Norway, Sweden, and Switzerland formed, and all except Iceland eventually joined, a Customs Union Study Group, which began work two months later in Brussels. Out of it arose two further bodies—a Tariff Committee, later known as the Customs Committee, which labored to collate definitions and rates of duty; and an Economic Committee to study the industrial and other problems that a customs union would involve. Thanks to the Customs Committee, nomenclature was at length partially standardized, and a permanent Customs Co-operation Council was set up; but although the Economic Committee concluded that there were "fewer difficulties in the way of the formation of a Customs Union than might have been expected," its detailed findings were far from comprehensive. Few Governments answered its questionnaires fully; three—Ireland, Switzerland, and Turkey—supplied no answers at all. Equally academic, as it turned out, was the work of the parent Study Group, whose Report of March 1948 was characteristically inconclusive:

It is not practicable at this stage to pronounce definitely on the merits and disadvantages of a Customs Union. There is a presumption, however, that such a Union would in the long run make for the greater prosperity of the countries composing it. How far it would do so would depend on the proper solution of a great many problems and the nature of the compromise reached. . . .

In the end, after further pronouncements in a similar vein, the customs union project was abandoned. What was clearly lacking was a firm political will.[37]

By no means all of the OEEC countries were opposed to economic integration. Belgium, the Netherlands, and Luxembourg had already accepted it in principle when they signed the Benelux Convention of September 5, 1944. In April 1946 they agreed to aim at an economic union, with harmonized economic policies; and its first element, the Benelux customs union, began to take effect on January 1, 1948. Italy and France, responding to Sforza's suggestion of July 15, 1947, devised a bilateral customs union known as "Francita," whose Treaty they signed on March 26, 1949. Later in the same year, with the Treaty still unratified, they considered merging it with Benelux under the daunting name of "Fritalux" or "Finebel." Denmark, Norway, and Sweden, meanwhile, spent two years discussing a Scandinavian customs union; and there was also talk—but nothing further—of similar unions between Italy and Austria and between Turkey and Greece.[38]

All these projects met with serious obstacles, and only Benelux ultimately reached its goal. The specific problems were manifold: but the basic issue in each case was very much the same. By removing the customs barriers between them and establishing a common tariff against the rest of the world, governments would give their economies the stimulus of mutual competition and the benefits of a larger home market. At the same time, however, they would surrender to the resultant union part of their national autonomy. *Vis-à-vis* its partners, each government would have lost one of the weapons of economic policy; *vis-à-vis* the rest of the world, that same weapon could now be wielded only jointly. The removal of mutual protection, moreover, would mean economic changes, some of them painful; but it would also mean a smaller range of purely national measures with which to meet them. To recover control of their economy, the members of the union would increasingly have to work together, not only on tariffs but also on other matters; tax policy, freight rates, capital movements, rates of exchange. In any but a *laissez-faire* system of devil-take-the-hindmost, the customs union would require some measure of economic union as well.[39]

No wonder that some governments were hesitant to start on what looked like a slippery slope of economic interdependence: no wonder that, once embarked, they found it a tricky run. If even tiny Benelux faced complications, an OEEC-wide customs union would have been more complicated still. Its member states would have included ex-allies, ex-neutrals, and ex-enemies; former great powers and much smaller nations; imperial, ex-imperial, and non-imperial countries; devotees of planning and of economic liberalism; countries nearly starving and others—the neutrals—replete with steaks and butter; some with uncontrolled inflation and at least three with strong, stable currencies; those that were members of the United Nations and one that was not; even, for that matter, republics and monarchies. To weld them all together would have been a perplexing task.[40]

It would be unjust, therefore, to blame only Great Britain, as some have done, for the failure of American plans for European economic union. Ernest Bevin responded promptly to the Marshall Plan; and British administrative expertise was invaluable in the OEEC, as was the work of devoted and skillful civil servants like Sir Oliver Franks and Eric Roll. Nor, at the outset, was Britain alone in stressing national independence. When Bevin and Bidault tried to negotiate with Molotov, both assured him that they planned no abandonment of sovereignty; and if, at the opening of the sixteen-nation CEEC conference, Bidault proclaimed that "the hour has come to construct a Europe," his words were vague and perhaps intended chiefly to impress the U. S. Congress.[41]

Britain, nevertheless, was in a key position. At that time, as the Herter Committee insisted, she alone possessed "the past experience and the present economic resources and political stability necessary for bold and imaginative leadership"; yet while France, for whatever motive, was soon prepared to move toward economic union, Britain repeatedly shied away. In August 1947, after conceding that "some or all of the participating countries might form a customs union or unions," Sir Oliver Franks sounded a note that was to become familiar: for Britain, a customs union involved special difficulties. "These difficulties arise," he said, "from our links both economic and political, outside Europe, and especially with the Commonwealth," which had "the effect of making the U.K. an extra-European as well as an intra-European power." Throughout the subsequent work of the Customs Union Study Group, Britain maintained the same stand. In March 1948, when France urged that the future OEEC should have majority voting, a strong executive board, and an independent Secretary-General with real powers of decision, it was Britain in particular that insisted on weaker institutions. In the following year, during the talks that finally led to the European Payments Union, Britain likewise resisted continual American pressure for "really effective machinery" and "a central authority possessing adequate supranational powers." At the end of 1949, again, Paul Hoffman and the ECA urged that the OEEC Council meet often, perhaps always, at ministerial instead of official level, and that it be headed by a political Secretary-General. About the first proposal, Britain remained skeptical: against the second she was adamant.[42]

The memory of these disputes was not effaced easily. For many Americans and continental Europeans, it entered the mythology of recent history; and it led to a lasting suspicion of Britain's actions and aims. Her insular aloofness from European union seemed all the greater because some had expected its opposite.

Just two years before the Marshall Plan, by a strange irony, the U. S. State Department had even suspected Britain of something like what it now urged her to do. In a Briefing Book paper prepared for the Potsdam Conference in July 1945, it had warned the United States Government against a supposed "British Plan" to establish a West European "bloc." "As a 'hedge' against the possible failure of Big Three collaboration in the postwar world," it had reported, "the British are following the policy recommended by General Smuts of strengthening their position by drawing the nations of Western Europe into closer association with the Commonwealth." The "plan," as proposed by Smuts to the Empire Parliamentary Association on November 25, 1943, had been to offer Belgium, Denmark, France, the Netherlands, and Norway something akin to Dominion status in the Commonwealth, with "a common foreign policy, co-ordination of military strategy, combined boards for finance, transport, production, supplies, resources, and raw materials, a customs union, currency arrangements, and a joint approach to civil aviation and colonial problems." According to the Briefing Book, all this had been made clear by the British Foreign Secretary, Anthony Eden, in the House of Commons on September 29, 1944. In reality, all that he had said was: "We have had certain informal discussions about our future relations, and these will be pursued further in due course." "It will give us," he had added, "more authority with the other great Powers if we speak for the Commonwealth and for our near neighbours in Western Europe." His argument, as it happened, was refuted by another of the Potsdam briefing papers, aptly classified Top Secret. "At meetings of the 'Big Three,'" it noted, "Mr Churchill may occasionally, without due reflection, give the impression that he is the spokesman for the whole British Commonwealth. He is, on the contrary, only the representative of the United Kingdom."[43]

Anthony Eden's alleged "plan," which if anything had been tentative, was certainly short-lived; but his successor Ernest Bevin had also toyed in the past with similar notions. Visiting America in 1926, he had found, as he said later, "130,000,000 people within one economic entity, with no tariffs, with an ability among the people to move about without the boundary handicaps that apply to Europe." On the second day of his visit he had written in his notebook:

I came to the conclusion that the road my mind has been travelling is a correct one:
  a. That Britain must have a customs union within the Empire, and
  b. With Europe as well, if possible.
  c. Or, if Colonies will not join then with Europe without colonies. . . .

He told an American reporter that within fifty years there would be a United States of Europe; and at the 1927 Trades Union Congress in Edinburgh he argued that "If we are to deal with the problems of Europe, we have got to try to teach the people of Europe that their economic interests, their economic development have to transcend merely national boundaries." He therefore proposed a European customs union "to inculcate the spirit of a United States of Europe—at least on an economic basis, even if we cannot on a totally political basis." "We want," he declared, "an indivisible united nation spreading from the borders of Russia right to the borders of France." At the 1939 Labour Party Congress, again, Bevin proposed—"even though it may in-

volve a limitation of our sovereignty"—to "invite countries like
Scandinavia, Holland, Belgium, Russia, France, and the
U.S.A. who are willing to co-operate to come within our
[Commonwealth] preference system" in order to achieve "a
real pooling of the whole of the colonial empires and their
resources."[44]

The ambiguities in these ideas were evident. Did "the
people of Europe" include the British? Which "borders of
Russia" were intended—East or West? Why mention "the
borders of France" and not those of Great Britain? What likeness was there among the proposed recruits to the Commonwealth preference system? Were only the "colonial empires"
to be pooled? Clearly, Bevin was never doctrinaire. Already
in 1930 he had helped to draw up a report by the Trades
Union Congress Economic Committee which advised against
British membership of "a European block" in favor of "as full
a development as possible of the economic relations between
the constituent parts of the British Commonwealth." Now, as
Foreign Secretary, he spoke from a similar brief. Events had
overtaken two of the traditional axioms of British foreign
policy—naval supremacy, and a balance of power in Europe
with no permanent commitment to either side. In Europe, in
particular, as a State Department memorandum put it, there
was "no longer any power to balance." The real power lay
with the United States and the Soviet Union, both far beyond
Britain's weight. This might have been an incentive for her to
match them by pooling her resources with her neighbors;
but although Bevin still at times talked of a United States of
Europe, he evidently thought of it as something for export
only. History, geography, language, traditional policy, the
fortunes of war and the habits of the wartime alliance—all
made it seem more natural and necessary to cleave not only
to the Commonwealth, but also to the "special relationship"
with the United States. Some Americans did their best to
discourage what they saw as an illusion: at one Anglo-
American conference held in the late '40s, a paper prepared by the British with the title "U.S.-U.K. Special Relationship" was withdrawn and then destroyed at the U.S.
delegation's request. The Commonwealth countries, likewise,
gradually disabused Britain of some lingering "imperial" as-

sumptions. For the time being, however, British policy was slow to respond. Economically, Commonwealth preference complicated links with the continent; politically, Britain's sense of still leading her former empire and being a privileged partner of America delayed the realization that she was no more than equal to other European countries of comparable size.[45]

One incident may serve to show the strength of Britain's arguments against joining in an economic union of Europe—as well as the weakness of their underlying premise. In June 1949 the Americans were trying hard to persuade European countries to free themselves from their tight bilateral payments system and make transferable at least some of the "drawing rights" that creditors granted to debtors as a condition for receiving part of their Marshall Aid. Maurice Petsche, the French Finance Minister, proposed that 40 per cent of "drawing rights" should be made transferable. Britain, however, feared that this would saddle her with dollar debts, since Belgium and Switzerland would only hold a limited amount of sterling without converting it into dollars or gold. Transferability, in other words, threatened the British with convertibility—and they had vivid memories of the drain on sterling that this had caused two years earlier. Sir Stafford Cripps, the austere and astringent Chancellor of the Exchequer, put the argument persuasively to the OEEC Council on June 29, 1949, using the example of the "drawing rights" that Britain had granted to Germany:

I take the case of a country to whom the United Kingdom has granted a credit of, let me say, 50 million dollars in sterling, that is the valuation of it. During the course of the year, owing to the United Kingdom purchasing more goods from that country, and owing to other countries outside the O.E.E.C. spending more sterling in the country, the credit on the United Kingdom is no longer required. Under the existing scheme that credit is carried forward and will be utilized in cases of necessity in future years. Under M. Petsche's scheme, 40% of that credit would become usable in some other countries, and could be used for any other purpose, necessity or non-necessity, and if so used the United Kingdom would lose 40%, that would be 20 million dollars of the conditional aid, and this, Mr Chairman, because the United Kingdom have taken every step, as they are bound to do, to liberalize their trade with that country, and to increase it. That apparently desirable action is, therefore, penalized by the loss of 20 million dollars, regardless of the requirements of the United Kingdom in dollars for her Recovery Programme. Now the only reaction which can be taken to that risk by any creditor country is to see that fewer purchases are made so that it is quite certain that the debtor country, who receives the credit, spends all the credit with the creditor country, and therefore the creditor country cannot lose dollars. The whole of the impetus, therefore, is to restrict in order not to lose dollars.

Answering Cripps shortly afterward, Petsche pointed out that "the United Kingdom might, by the interplay of transferability, equally well earn dollars as lose them." As the biggest net debtor and recipient of "drawing rights," France had an interest in her own argument: but she also had a point. Transferability meant not only risks, but opportunities; what was more, it pointed the way toward a multilateral system. Each country by itself might well be afraid to remove national controls, but if all did so together their general prosperity would increase. The British position, as Averell Harriman had already remarked, was "unacceptable because it failed to provide, in any effective form, the stimulation to the liberalization of intra-European trade which would result from increased competition . . . It would tend to make Europe a high cost area." Indeed, understandable as was Britain's concern with her own national problems, it seemed to reveal an uncharacteristic pessimism and lack of imagination. At the time, her fears were well-founded: within less than three months, on September 19, 1949, she was obliged to devalue sterling by 30 per cent. But she seemed not to see—or, if she saw, she rejected—one sure way to enjoy the collective benefits of multilateral payments while minimizing their national risks. This would have been to accept the strong central monetary institutions proposed for Europe by Paul Hoffman and the ECA. But that was "supranationalism," and Britain would have none of it. Even when the European Payments Union was finally established, she and the Scandinavian countries made sure that its Managing Board was subordinate in practice to the OEEC Council, and not an independent body with real power over national policies.[46]

As incidents of this type multiplied, it grew hard to avoid the conclusion that Britain's technical arguments concealed a deep-rooted feeling that somehow she was different from her continental neighbors—not merely as they all differed from each other, but in a quite special and ineradicable way. Was it pride? Was it self-absorption? Was it the concern to build a more just society at home, and a better world in general, that made continental Western Europe seem irrelevant or remote? All these there may have been; but they seemed to be reinforced by the innocent, self-protective obtuseness with which, in the early postwar era, Britain made crucial policy decisions by default, almost viscerally, without appearing to suspect that alternatives existed. By doing so, she delayed both the unification of Europe and her own chance to share in it. Where was the adventurous inventiveness that she had shown during World War II? Reassuringly, the challenge of events was soon to prove that neither she nor her Western allies had lost it.

THE AGE OF ANXIETY

For indeed it is a most lying thing that same Past Tense always: so beautiful, sad, almost Elysian-sacred, 'in the moonlight of Memory', it seems; and *seems* only. For observe: always, one most important element is surreptitiously (we not noticing it) withdrawn from the Past Time: the haggard element of Fear!   *Thomas Carlyle*[1]

I confess that I have no comprehension of the Russian character.   *Joseph Conrad*[2]

Underneath all the solid and magnificent virtues of the German race there lies a layer of nervous uncertainty.   *Harold Nicolson*[3]

All international meetings look rather alike. The baize-covered table with a delegation's name-card at each place, the sharpened pencils, the pads of paper, the carafes and water glasses, the microphones, the interpreters' glass-fronted cabins—all these are more or less standard. Fairly standard, too, are the aides, the civil servants, discreet ingenious men in sober suits, holding files of documents like shields. Even the ministers or heads of delegation seldom seem colorful: an ebullient Bevin or an implacable Molotov is rare. The fly on the wall, or the spy beneath the table, would have a hard time deciphering requests "to replace Paragraph Roman two figure one little c of Conference Document seventeen by Revised Draft capital B one little f, circulated this morning by the Secretariat." Even the active participants, drafting, expounding, arguing, bargaining, and drafting again, sometimes feel lost in a timeless bureaucratic frenzy. The long hours of committee and council meetings at the Paris headquarters of the ECA and OEEC were no exception. It was not always easy, there, to picture the bulldozers, dams, giant transformers, dredgers, looms, or steel plants behind the texts, graphs, and statistics. Nor was it easy, later, to remember that in these early years of recovery, Western Europe felt increasingly under siege from the East.

Molotov and the Soviet delegation had walked out of their Paris meeting with Bevin and Bidault on Wednesday, July 2, 1947. By the end of the following week, the Soviet Union had begun to draw the East European countries into a tighter network of trade agreements—with Bulgaria on Thursday, July 10; with Czechoslovakia on July 11; with Hungary on July 14; with Yugoslavia on July 25; with Poland on August 4; with Rumania on August 26. On September 22, at Russian bidding, Communist Party representatives from Bulgaria, Czechoslovakia, Hungary, Yugoslavia, Poland, Rumania, and the Soviet Union—as well as from France and Italy—met at Wilcza Gora, the country house of Wladyslaw Gomulka, Polish Deputy Premier, to set up the Cominform, or Communist Information Bureau. This, despite its name, was a partial revival of the 1919 Comintern, the Third or Communist International, which had been dissolved in May 1943 as a gesture of goodwill toward the West. It was formally established, with headquarters in Belgrade, on October 5, 1947.[4]

These moves, clearly, were in part a riposte to the Truman Doctrine and the Marshall Plan, which Stalin's emissary at the September meeting, A. A. Zhdanov, denounced as "an embodiment of the American design to enslave Europe" and "an attack on the principle of national sovereignty"; "the imperialists," he added, sought "to unleash a new war." His language had the characteristic shrill violence with which Communist orators seemed to outbid each other; but given Soviet beliefs about the nature of "bourgeois" society, it was no doubt sincere. Although the East-West confrontation could be seen as the co-existence of two mutually suspicious power centers, it was never in reality free of ideological content. Each side believed that its own society was superior to the other's; each was committed in principle to converting the rest of the world. Each saw most clearly the other's imperfections; but because "bourgeois" decadence, corruption, and economic injustice were in practice less revolting than the drab, cynical ruthlessness of Stalinist dictatorship, the West might have been expected to be even more Messianic or "imperialist" than the East. In the first postwar years, however, ideology had seemed secondary to traditional power politics: both the Soviet Union and the United States had tacitly respected, for the most part, each other's sphere of influence. Only now did each begin to take the other's slogans literally; and the combined effect was as if both had been bent on expansion all along. "The Soviet Union," Zhdanov told his audience at Wilcza Gora, ". . . will bend every effort in order that [the Marshall Plan] be doomed to failure . . . The Communist parties of France, Italy, Great Britain and other countries . . . must take up the standard in defense of the national independence and sovereignty of their countries." Their first effort was to help foment, in the winter of 1947–48, a series of industrial strikes. To this extent the Marshall Plan—and more especially the Truman Doctrine—contributed to what the Cominform itself called the consolidation of "two opposite political lines." They were not, however, the only factors; they were also a response to moves by the USSR.[5]

Long before the Truman Doctrine was enunciated, the East European countries had made many economic agreements with each other and with the Soviet Union; and the idea of something like the Cominform had already been mooted in the spring of 1946. By the time of the Marshall Plan, moreover, Stalin had two further reasons for tightening the reins. One was growing restiveness among the neighboring Communist parties; the other was the natural development of what had been happening in Eastern Europe since the defeat of the Nazis.[6]

For some time the files in Moscow had grown fat with evidence of what has been called "the revolt of the First Secretaries." In Rumania, Stalin was being warned against the ambitions of Gheorghe Gheorghiu-Dej, while his colleague Lucretiu Patrascanu, an intellectual of middle-class origins, was becoming what his accusers later described as "an exponent of bourgeois ideology." In Poland, Wladyslaw Gomulka was openly criticizing Soviet policy. In Hungary, Mátyás Rákosi was said to be reliable, but was making accusations against László Rajk. In Czechoslovakia, President Edvard Beneš had said as recently as May 6, 1947, that his country sought a middle way between the American and the Soviet systems. But the worst offender was Marshal Tito of Yugoslavia, later to be expelled from the Cominform. Since 1944 he had been trying to form a federation with Bulgaria; and in June 1947 he told Western newspapermen that "the free Balkan peoples" should build "a strong monolithic entity." Tito's potential partner was Georgi Dimitrov, the victim and hero of Nazi persecution after the Reichstag fire of 1933, who had recently returned from exile in the Soviet Union and resumed his Bulgarian citizenship. Called upon to explain in Moscow Bulgaria's plans for alliance with Yugoslavia and a customs union with Rumania, Dimitrov faced a memorable, revealing tirade:

'Yes, but you didn't consult with us,' Stalin shouted. 'We learn about your doings in the newspapers. You chatter like women from the housetops whatever occurs to you, and then the newspapermen get hold of it.' . . .

Dimitrov remonstrated, 'There are essentially no difference between the foreign policies of Bulgaria and the Soviet Union.'

Stalin, decidedly and firmly: 'There are serious differences. Why hide it? It was Lenin's practice always to recognize errors and to remove them as quickly as possible.'

Dimitrov, placatingly, almost submissively: 'True, we erred. But through errors we are learning our way in foreign politics.'

Stalin harshly and tauntingly: 'Learning! You have been in politics fifty years—and now you are correcting errors. Your trouble is not errors, but that you are taking a line different from ours.'[7]

Differences were only to be expected, since in many ways the East European countries were as various as those of the West. In language and tradition, all except Albania, Hungary, and Rumania were predominantly Slav; but Czechoslovakia and Yugoslavia were each made up of at least two separate peoples. In religion, Czechoslovakia, Hungary, and Poland had in the past been mainly Catholic, Bulgaria and Rumania mainly Orthodox; Yugoslavia had been mixed, and Albania 70 per cent Muslim. Politically, Czechoslovakia and Poland had been republics, the remainder monarchies. In World War II, finally, Bulgaria, Hungary, and Rumania, willingly or not, had been on the side of the Axis, the others on that of the Allies. And yet, despite their differences, all had two features in common. All were in the Soviet sphere of influence: when hostilities ended, it was natural for them to enter her tutelage. But all had largely agrarian economies, which from a Marxist point of view required nursing before their backward peasantry and weak proletariat would be fully ripe for Communism. It was equally natural, therefore, that initially most of them should be governed by "bourgeois democratic" left-wing coalitions. Even without the Truman Doctrine and the Marshall Plan, this phase would have been part of what Marx and Lenin had called "a political transition period." Sooner or later, the East European countries would have been expected to move toward the dictatorship of the proletariat in one-party Soviet-type regimes. The process had begun, indeed, soon after the end of hostilities. It took different forms in different countries; but in anxious Western eyes its main elements were ominously uniform.

In Poland, as has been seen, the struggle had begun while the war still continued; it merely became more open in 1945. On January 4, the Communist-controlled "Lublin Committee" declared itself to be "The Provisional National Government of the Polish Republic." Western attempts to have it reorganized on a broader basis, with democratic leaders from exile and from Poland itself, remained fruitless for several months. Meanwhile, at the end of March 1945, the Russians arrested sixteen Polish underground leaders who had been unwise enough to reveal themselves, and flew them to Moscow, to the Lubianka Prison, where they awaited trial— and all but four of them, imprisonment—for alleged "diversionist" sabotage in the rear of the Red Army. In May, however, Stalin seemed to relent. He assured Harry Hopkins, the late President Roosevelt's Special Assistant, that Poland would have a system of parliamentary government similar to that of Belgium or Holland; and in June a number of Polish leaders—including Stanislaw Mikolajczyk from London—were invited to Moscow for consultations. On June 23 they agreed on a "re-organized" Provisional Government, to include representatives of the Peasant, Socialist, Democratic, and Christian Labour parties. Of its twenty-one members, six-teen had been in the previous Provisional Government, three came from London, and two from Poland itself. Mikolajczyk was Second Deputy Premier and Minister of Agriculture and Land Reform; but much of his authority, he later complained, was usurped by the Communist Minister of Forestry. The Communists, moreover, held the key ministries, including that of Public Security; and when Mikolajczyk tried to reorganize the Peasant Party, which from a left-wing agrarian group was turning into a center of miscellaneous opposition to Communism, they attacked his supporters with censorship, suppression, threats and even murder. In June 1946, the Government held a referendum on three separate issues, the first of which was the abolition of the Senate; and although this was popular, Mikolajczyk urged his followers to vote against it in order to test their electoral strength. Where the Peasant Party could check the results, more than 80 per cent were in its favor; elsewhere, the Government suppressed them. When Britain and the United States reminded Poland of the definition of free elections agreed upon at Yalta, the only response was a protest against foreign inter-ference. Police pressure against the Peasant Party continued, with arrests and raids on its headquarters. An election was at last fixed for January 19, 1947; but already in the previous September the Polish Socialists and Communists had agreed with Stalin and Molotov on the composition of the new Gov-ernment. During the election campaign, Mikolajczyk and his party faced a reign of terror: many of his supporters were arrested, and in ten out of fifty-two constituencies his can-didates were disqualified. Again the United States and Brit-ain protested; again they were told that their information was false, and that they should mind their own business. The election result was a landslide, prearranged in flagrant contradiction of the Yalta and Potsdam agreements. The American Ambassador, Arthur Bliss Lane, resigned in pro-test; and Mikolajczyk, in the end, escaped to the West.[8]

In Bulgaria, the "Fatherland Front" had seized power on the night of September 8, 1944, just as the Russians were liberating the country at the cost of more than 20,000 ci-

vilian lives. It set up a coalition government in which the
Communists, the Agrarian Party, and the Zveno military
partisans were equally represented, together with Social-
Democrats and Independents; the Communists, however,
held the key posts of Minister of the Interior and Minister
of Justice. Shortly afterward, the Agrarian leader Dr. G. M.
Dimitrov, namesake of his Communist rival, returned from
war work with the British in Cairo to reorganize the party
as its Secretary-General. British intervention in the Greek
civil war, however, made him suspect to the Communists;
and on January 18, 1945, he was forced to cede his office to
Nikola Petkov. By now, the Agrarian Party was splitting;
and, in May 1945, Petkov himself was replaced by Alexander Obbov, from its pro-Communist wing. The Social-
Democrats were likewise divided into three conflicting
groups. On June 18, the Fatherland Front Government announced an election for August 26; but only the Government itself was to present lists of candidates. Six ministers
demanded that opposition parties be allowed to do likewise.
When they got no satisfaction, the Agrarian and Social-
Democrat dissidents, Petkov and Grigor Cheshmedjiev, resigned from the Government. After Western warnings that
any rigged election would indefinitely delay the peace treaty,
the Government made some concessions. It even allowed the
opposition to publish newspapers—which quickly reached ten
times the circulation of the official press. It refused, however, to appoint non-Communist Ministers of the Interior
and of Justice; and the opposition parties therefore decided
to boycott the election. After some delay, it was held on November 18 with only one list of candidates; there was also
some evidence of violence and threats. The Fatherland Front
won three-quarters of the seats, and supplied all the members of the new Government; but as a result of further diplomatic skirmishes among the Allies, the Soviet Union "advised"
Bulgaria to appoint two opposition ministers, Petkov and the
moderate Socialist Kosta Lulchev. They in turn demanded,
without success, that the Ministries of the Interior and of
Justice be freed from control by Communists: the dispute
dragged on for nearly twelve months. Meanwhile, the Communist Party was extending its grip on the country. In the

summer of 1946 it purged the Bulgarian army of its Zveno
leaders; at a referendum on September 8, 92 per cent of
the population voted to abolish the monarchy; and on October 27 an election was held for the Great National Assembly
of the new Republic. Through the Allied Control Commission, Britain and the United States tried hard to ensure free
voting in accordance with the Yalta Declaration on Liberated Europe; but intimidation, delays in the issue of voting
cards, and the imprisonment of some opposition leaders and
supporters made the poll something of a travesty. Many
would-be electors were held up by road blocks—one of which
stopped the British Control Commission representative, General Oxley. Even so, Petkov later claimed that the Agrarian
and Social-Democratic opposition had won 60 per cent of the
votes. The official returns gave them 22 per cent,
with 101 seats in the Assembly. The Fatherland Front won
364 seats. Of these, 277 were held by Communists; and
when Georgi Dimitrov became Premier, his Cabinet included
nine Communist ministers, making the coalition a mere
façade.[9]

In Rumania, King Michael had broken with the Nazis in
the last week of August 1944, arresting Marshal Ion An-
tonescu and appointing a coalition Government under General Sanatescu which included all four political parties—the
National Liberals, the National Peasants, the Socialists, and
the Communists. The Red Army, meanwhile, entered and
occupied Bucharest. An armistice was signed in Moscow on
September 12, 1944, fixing reparations to the Soviet Union
at 300 million dollars to be paid in kind over a period of six
years. As a start, the Russians seized 50 per cent of Rumania's
rolling stock, its whole navy, most of its merchant fleet, and
much oil equipment. According to Anna Pauker, the Communist leader who was later to be Foreign Minister, there
were barely a thousand Communists in the country before
the Red Army arrived; and they had only one post in Sanatescu's Government. With their allies from the "Ploughmen's Front" and left-wing splinter groups, however, they
quickly formed a "National Democratic Front"; and in November, when Sanatescu reshuffled his Cabinet after clashes

with the Russians, the National Democratic Front secured more Government places. On December 2 Sanatescu resigned, to be replaced by the seventy-year-old General Radescu; but he in turn was not to last long. His main offense was to delay the land reform pressed by the Communists, which produced farm holdings so small as to be unworkable without collectivization. When the censored press attacked him, Radescu hit back with bitterly anti-Communist broadcasts and public speeches; and in January 1945 Anna Pauker and her colleague Gheorghe Gheorghiu-Dej, then on a visit to Moscow, were told to mobilize the National Democratic Front in a countercampaign of demonstrations and strikes. Radescu, who was his own Minister of the Interior, did his best to crush them; but with help from the Red Army, the demonstrators disarmed the few Rumanian troops left in the capital, and the disorders continued. On Tuesday, February 27, 1945, the Soviet Deputy Foreign Minister Andrei Vyshinsky arrived in Bucharest and asked to see King Michael, who received him that evening with his Foreign Minister Constantine Visoianu. Radescu's Government, said Vyshinsky, was incapable of keeping order: it should be replaced by one that represented "the truly democratic forces of the country." Next day, Vyshinsky was back again. What was the decision? The King explained that he had notified Radescu and had begun consulting party leaders with a view to replacing him. This, said Vyshinsky, was not enough. Looking at his watch, he told King Michael that he had just two hours and five minutes to announce Radescu's dismissal. By eight o'clock, a new Prime Minister must be named. Visoianu pointed out that Rumania was a constitutional monarchy, and that the King was obliged to respect its rules. Vyshinsky accused Radescu of "protecting fascists": a royal decree of the previous day, retiring ten Rumanian officers, had been "an unfriendly act," and must be annulled. The King agreed to rescind it, and Vyshinsky left. According to the American political representative in Bucharest, "he slammed the door so hard that the plaster around the door frame was cracked badly." The King went on consulting party leaders, but on the following day, Thursday, March 1, 1945, Vyshinsky announced that the Soviet Union's choice for Prime Minister was Dr. Petru Groza, a landowner and former member of the pro-Communist Ploughmen's Front. The King could only acquiesce. When Groza formed his Government on Tuesday, March 6, he appointed Communists to the Ministries of the Interior, of Justice, and of Public Works. The Foreign Ministry went to Gheorghe Tatarescu, a former Liberal; the remaining posts were divided among the Ploughmen's Front, the left wing of the Social-Democrats, and other splinter groups from the National Democratic Front, while the Peasant, Liberal, and right-wing Socialist parties refused to join. The American and British representatives on the Allied Control Commission declared that the new Cabinet was unacceptable to their Governments; but when the King asked Groza to resign, he simply refused. The King then withdrew to his palace at Sinaia, and himself refused to sign governmental decrees. For several months, Groza carried on without him. Royalist demonstrations were broken up with violence, including some deaths. After further Western pressure, the Cabinet was enlarged to include one representative of the National Peasant Party and one of the National Liberals; and at length, on February 4, 1946, the Government was officially recognized by Britain and the United States. In preparation for the election, first to be held in May, then postponed till November, Groza's Government broke up meetings by the rival parties, threatened, injured and even killed some of their militants, stopped them from broadcasting, limited the circulation of their newspapers, and hindered the registration of their electors. The printers' union refused to work on anti-Government material, and some two hundred opposition leaders were imprisoned. At the polls on November 19, 1946, the Government coalition won 348 out of 414 seats. The Western Governments once again protested; but they felt powerless to do more.[10]

Events in Hungary followed a similar pattern. A Nazi coup on October 16, 1944 cut short a bid by the Regent, Admiral Horthy, for a separate peace; and fighting dragged on, devastating the country, until April 1945. Already in December 1944, however, a Provisional National Assembly had been formed at Debrecen near the Rumanian border, and on December 22 it approved by acclamation a Provisional National Government. In this the Communists, the Smallholders, and the Social-Democrats had two portfolios each; the remainder went to smaller groups and individuals, including a few ministers and generals from the Horthy regime. The Communists held only the Ministries of Agriculture and Trade; but Communist deputy ministers and officials were influential elsewhere, especially in the Ministry of the Interior. Despite the Allied Control Commission, the Russians were the country's ultimate rulers. Under the armistice agreement signed in Moscow on January 20, 1945, Hungary had to pay 300 million dollars' worth of reparations, and a further 200 million dollars in ex-German property. When the Ministry of Finance tried to stem inflation by restricting the number of roubles in circulation, Red Army men staged a virtual armed robbery of the National Bank. The first test of popular feeling was the land reform carried out quickly and successfully in March 1945; a second took place on October 2, when a municipal election was held in Budapest. In a capital recently freed from the rule of Nazi collaborators, the Communists and their Social-Democrat allies seemed confident of victory, and certainly played fair. To their surprise, however, the Smallholders' Party, a moderately liberal group with some recent right-wing support, won 51 per cent of the votes and 121 of the total of 240 seats. Marshal Voroshilov, the Russian chairman of the Control Commission, thereupon pressed the Smallholders' leaders to present at next month's general election a single list of candidates drawn up jointly with the other Government coalition parties. When they refused, the Communists agreed to separate lists, but insisted that the coalition continue whatever the results at the polls. In the event, on November 4, 1945, the Smallholders won 59.9 per cent of the votes, the Communists 17.1 per cent, the Social-Democrats 16.9 per cent and the National Peasant Party 5.6 per cent. Zoltán Tildy, a Smallholder, became Premier with nine other ministers from his own party, four from the Communists, four Social-Democrats and one from the National Peasant group. The Communists, however, threatened to leave the Government unless they obtained the Ministry of the Interior. Tildy consented, and it went to Imre Nagy. On February 1, 1946, when the National Assembly declared Hungary a republic, Tildy became its first President. Desider Sulyok, the Small-holders' original candidate to succeed him as Premier, was ousted from the party under Communist pressure, and the post went to his colleague Ferenc Nagy, who had pre-viously been President of the Assembly. While rifts among the Smallholders deepened, the Communists organized a left-wing bloc with the Social-Democrats, the National Peasant Party, and the trade unions; and when Sulyok criticized their economic policies and their control of the police, they coun-terattacked him fiercely, staging demonstrations in the capital and demanding that twenty-two other members of the Smallholders' Party be dismissed. The Communist Min-ister of the Interior, Imre Nagy, was now replaced by the formidable László Rajk, and Communist control was also extended to the Ministry of Defense. With the Communist Mátyás Rákosi as Deputy Premier, with the trade unions controlled by the Soviet-trained Stephen Kossa, with another Communist, Zoltán Vas, running the Supreme Economic Council, and with a deluge of unwanted advice pouring daily from Radio Moscow, Ferenc Nagy began to find his position untenable. By October 1946, when Sulyok's dissident Small-holders, renamed the "Freedom Party," were officially recog-nized, even Nagy's wing of the party had virtually become an opposition minority. In December 1946, the Ministries of the Interior and of Defense began making a series of arrests without even informing the Premier. They claimed to have uncovered a vast conspiracy organized by the prewar na-tionalist group "Hungarian Community" (Magyar Közöségg), which allegedly planned to reinstate the former regime. The charges against it implicated many Smallholder leaders, in-cluding Ferenc Nagy's friend and colleague Béla Kovács, who despite his parliamentary immunity was seized by the Russians on February 26, 1947, and subsequently disap-peared. Three months later, while on a mission to Switzer-land, Nagy himself was forced to resign under threats to his son, who had remained in Hungary. In a highly suspect election held that August, 35 per cent of Hungarians still voted for the opposition; but the remaining resistance, now centered in the Catholic Church, was steadily eroded. In the following year, the militant Cardinal Mindszenty was arrested and sentenced to life imprisonment. Not long afterward the Assembly was dissolved, and a one-party election gave the Communist-dominated Government a majority of 90 per cent.[11]

If developments in Poland, Bulgaria, Rumania, and Hungary were broadly similar, Finland, Albania, and Yugoslavia pursued separate courses; only the prevailing winds were the same.

In Finland, once the Nazis were driven out, a new Government was formed under Juho Kusti Paasikivi, a former Conservative now Independent. His Cabinet included representatives of the extreme left, one of whom was a Communist; and his policy, dictated by the facts of geography, was to seek "the best possible understanding" with the Soviet Union. At the elections of March 17 and 18, 1945, after Paasikivi had asked voters to give Parliament "a new face," the Communist and Social-Democrat People's Democratic League won an overwhelming victory and took key posts in the new Government; the Communist Yrjoe Leino became Minister of the Interior. So great was the revulsion against the wartime past that the Soviet Union felt little need to intervene directly. Stalin, who had himself proclaimed Finland's independence at Helsinki in 1917, and who had taken the measure of Finnish toughness during the Winter War of 1939–40, decided that moderation, as he put it, was "not kindness but common sense." Only nine months later, at the "War Guilt" trials, did Soviet pressure become marked. In March 1946 the seventy-nine-year-old President Carl von Mannerheim, who had been Commander-in-Chief in the Winter War, resigned for health reasons, and Paasikivi became President. The new Prime Minister, Mauno Pekkala, brought three Communists into the Cabinet, and in May of the same year began a further purge of right-wing organizations, staff officers, and civil servants. There was some friction with Russia over the terms imposed by the Peace Treaty; but on February 10, 1947, the Finnish Government signed it, and settled down in watchful semi-independence.[12]

In Albania, economically the most backward of the East European countries, the Communists seized power at once through their control of the Liberation Front, later renamed the "Democratic Front." Essentially, this was an alliance between the peasants and partisans from the intelligentsia. Its leader was the French-educated Communist Enver Hoxha, whose Government was recognized by the Allies in November 1945. In the election held on December 2, 86 per cent of the population voted for it: there were no opposition candidates at all. In January 1946, King Zog was formally deposed; and from then onward Hoxha ruled almost unchallenged as a military dictator, first under the patronage of Yugoslavia, until Tito's expulsion from the Cominform in 1948, then—until 1961—more directly under Moscow. A semblance of popular consent was supplied by referenda: but the ballot was hardly secret. Owing to the high rate of illiteracy, voters were given a ball to drop into a box with two openings marked respectively "Yes" and "No." Through the "Yes" slot, the ball fell silently into a sack; through the "No" slot, it rattled into a tin can.[13]

In Yugoslavia, when the war ended, effective power lay with the People's Liberation Front, which now became the People's Front. This included prewar political parties, two of which—the Croatian Peasant Party and the Serbian People's Peasant Party—retained apparent autonomy; the controlling organization was that of Marshal Tito's Communist partisans. In March 1945, a coalition Government was formed. Stalin described the Yugoslav regime as "something between de Gaulle's France and the Soviet Union"; but although the cabinet included politicians back from wartime exile, and although King Peter remained technically in office, there was no question at this time of establishing a Western-style democracy or constitutional monarchy. Opposition leaders were arrested or otherwise harassed; and when a general election was held on November 11, 1945, there were no opposition lists of candidates, but merely a separate ballot-box in which to express dissent. 88.6 per cent of the electorate voted, 90.5 of it for the People's Front. On November 29 the new Assembly declared Yugoslavia a republic; and on January 31, 1946, it approved a constitution closely modeled on the Soviet Constitution of 1936. That summer, Tito eliminated the remaining opposition leaders. General Draža Mihailović, the Serb patriot whose forces had fought during the war against Tito's partisans as well as against the enemy, was tried for treason and shot on July 17, 1946. Dr. Dragoljub Jovanović, leader of the People's Peasant Party, who criticized the People's Front on whose ticket he had been elected, was violently attacked and threatened, removed from his university chair and from the Serbian regional Parliament, expelled by the Communists from his own party, and later arrested and tried. A similar fate befell Archbishop Stepinac, the Croatian Primate, who had failed to protest during the war when individual Croatian priests had been involved in the persecution and forcible conversion of Serbs. In October 1946 the Archbishop was sentenced to imprisonment for sixteen years.[14]

Before long, Yugoslavian nationalism was to lead to a breach with the Soviet Union: Tito was expelled from the Cominform on June 28, 1948. But if this seemed to modify the stereotype of a monolithic East European bloc, any comfort that it might have given Western observers was far outweighed by the fate of Czechoslovakia.

Here, the first postwar President was the veteran statesman Edvard Beneš, who had been Foreign Minister under Thomas Masaryk and had succeeded him in 1935. Three years later he had resigned, bitterly disillusioned at the Munich agreement by which Britain and France had truncated his country under threats from Hitler and Mussolini. It was a betrayal that he never forgot. In 1941, when he became President of the exiled Czechoslovak Government in London, he decided that his country was too vulnerable to rely on distant Western allies, and resolved to secure the support and friendship of the Soviet Union. His diagnosis was accurate; his prescription was tragically mistaken.

In April 1945, coming from London via Moscow, Beneš set up a Provisional Government at Košice, in the liberated area of Slovakia. On May 5, Resistance workers in Prague rose against the Nazi occupation; and fearing what they had heard about Red Army behavior, they urged the Americans —then fifty-six miles away—to come to their aid. But when General Eisenhower told the Russian Chief of Staff, General Antonov, that he was willing to do so, Antonov said no. One result was a mass slaughter among the Czech Resistance; another was the undisputed Russian occupation of Prague. It was shortly after this that the Provisional Government moved there.[15]

The Prime Minister was the left-wing Socialist Zdeněk Fierlinger; with him in the Cabinet were two other Socialists, three Czech "National Socialists" (left-wing Liberals), three Populists, three Slovak Democrats and seven Communists, three of them Slovaks. All these were members of the so-called "National Front." The Agrarian and other right-wing parties from the London Government were excluded; but Jan Masaryk, the son of Thomas, and like Beneš close to the "National Socialists," continued to be Foreign Minister as he had been in London; and the independent General Ludvik Svoboda became Minister of Defense. The Communists, however, were put in charge of the Ministries of the Interior, of Education, of Agriculture, and of Information. Their strategy, as described later by their leader Klement Gottwald, now a Deputy Premier, was to exploit the "national and democratic revolution" to attract a majority into the party. No elections were held for a full year; meanwhile, Beneš and the National Front pushed through a series of drastic reforms, expelling German minorities, redistributing farmland, and nationalizing much of Czechoslovakian industry.[16]

At length, on May 26, 1946, the country went to the polls to elect a Constituent Assembly. Some 250,000 to 300,000 alleged wartime collaborators had meanwhile been struck off the voting lists, and the land reform had helped local Communists at the expense of the Agrarian Party, which was now dissolved; but on polling day itself there was little or no malpractice. The Communists won 38 per cent of the vote, and their Social-Democrat allies 13 per cent, giving them together 153 seats in the Assembly, against 147 held by the other parties. The new government was headed by

Gottwald himself; it contained two more Communists and two fewer Slovaks than before. There followed a period of comparative calm and progress. Production rose and trade developed, especially with the countries of the West. It was no doubt this that encouraged Gottwald to respond, at first, to the offer of the Marshall Plan in July 1947—a move quickly checked by Stalin, who also forestalled a new treaty of alliance with France. The resultant ill-feeling was increased by the foundation of the Cominform that October: even the Social-Democrats grew restive, and in November they ousted their former leader Fierlinger. With an election due to be held in March 1948, the Communist Party began to fear that it might not win a majority of the ballot; and it made preparations for victory by other means—campaigning for new recruits and working to extend its hold on the trade unions, the army, and the police.[17]

Its hour struck in early February 1948, when the Communist Minister of the Interior Václav Nosek dismissed eight non-Communist police commanders in Prague and replaced them with his own men. Led by the Czech "National Socialists," a majority of the Cabinet demanded that Gottwald rescind the order. He refused. Thereupon, on Friday, February 20, 1948, the twelve non-Marxist Ministers resigned from the Cabinet. They hoped to overthrow the Government: but the Social-Democrats, who had originally joined in the protest, now remained in office, leaving Gottwald a quorum of thirteen. "Believe me," he told Masaryk afterward, "we have spent months thinking how to carry out the *putsch*, what excuse to use, how to do it, then those ex-Ministers handed it to us on a plate. They gave us a perfect excuse, and all that was needed was to stand there and kick them in the behind, and that is what we did." Already, in fact, the Communists had put out feelers to Moscow: "Our friends," said one party official, "have given us guarantees against any eventuality." On Thursday, February 19, Valerian Zorin, former Soviet Ambassador in Czechoslovakia and now a Vice-Minister of Foreign Affairs, had arrived in Prague unexpectedly, and extra contingents of the Red Army had entered the Soviet Zone of Austria near to the Czechoslovak frontier. With these assurances, Gottwald now asked President Beneš to accept a new Cabinet purged of "reactionaries." At first, Beneš hesitated. The dissenting Ministers tried to see him, to argue with Nosek, to negotiate their way back into the Cabinet: but they found the way blocked and their offices taken over. On Saturday, February 21, the Communists formed workers' militia and staged a rally of 200,000 people in the ice-bound capital. On Sunday, February 22, at a vast Congress of Workers' Councils from all over the country, they announced a governmental program; the Congress threatened a general strike unless Gottwald formed a Cabinet to carry it out. Meanwhile, with the army confined to barracks, Communist-controlled gendarmes and security police patrolled the Prague streets. For two days, Czechoslovak students gathered in counterdemonstrations; but on Monday, February 23, they were finally crushed: the Minister of the Interior claimed to have put down a reactionary plot. On Tuesday, February 24, Gottwald announced his ultimatum: on the following morning, for the last time, he would submit his new Cabinet list to Beneš. Meanwhile, the Communist Party shut down opposition newspapers; huge crowds of workers filled Wenceslas Square, carrying red flags, shouting slogans and singing the *Internationale*. Five truckloads of armed workers seized the Social-Democrat headquarters. That same evening, the non-Communist parties threw in their hand. Next day, while workers armed with brand-new rifles marched through the streets, Beneš accepted Gottwald's conditions, and the *putsch* was complete. Two days later, the Socialist Minister of Justice Prokop Drtina tried to kill himself; and at dawn on Wednesday, March 10, 1948, the pajama-clad body of Jan Masaryk was found on the pavement under the window of his apartment in the Czernin Palace, headquarters of the Foreign Ministry. Was it suicide, as his private secretary thought, or murder? The answer remained uncertain; but the question itself was eloquent. In May, new elections were held with a single list of candidates. On June 8, Beneš resigned. When he died in September, vast crowds attended his funeral. Their silence was more eloquent still.[18]

Western spectators of all these events, largely unable to affect them, were both indignant and alarmed. In one country after another, they saw non-Marxist parties squeezed out of office, seldom democratically, sometimes by subterfuge, most often by a combination of fraud, intimidation, and force. The first step, it seemed, was for the Communists to enter left-wing coalition Governments, sooner or later securing the key ministries, including that of the Interior, and packing them with a number of their own supporters. Gradually, these bridgeheads would be enlarged. Public information would be controlled; non-Marxist newspapers would be harassed, censored, or abolished; non-Communist political meetings would be shouted down or broken up; party headquarters would be sacked and party militants arrested. Industrial action—strikes, demonstrations, marches—would redouble the political pressure. Finally, at the right moment, a crisis would be stage-managed. The non-Communist parties would be routed, their electors tricked and their leaders imprisoned. From then onward, only Soviet-type "democracy" would be allowed.

If this could happen in Eastern Europe, there seemed some chance of its being repeated in the West, and especially in Belgium, France, and Italy, where the Communists were relatively strong. Armed insurrection by Communist Resistance fighters seemed the most immediate danger—although in all three cases it was precluded by the facts of power. In Belgium, the Communist-led Front de l'Indépendance refused to surrender its weapons at the liberation, but eventually obeyed a Government order to do so, backed by the presence of British troops. In France, sporadic uprisings by the similar Francs-Tireurs et Partisans were discouraged by Moscow and easily defeated. Even in Italy, where both Communist and right-wing partisans maintained private arsenals, and where many old scores were settled by violence, there was no real attempt at revolution. No less an authority than the Central Committee of the Soviet Communist Party gave the revealing explanation. "Unfortunately," it admitted, "the Soviet Army could not render . . . assistance to the French and Italian Communist Parties."[19]

It was no wonder that the news from Eastern Europe made the "bourgeois" parties in Belgium, France, and Italy wary of their Communist colleagues. In each case, the Communist

Party's Resistance record had helped it to win a larger show-ing in Parliament. In the Belgian election of February 17, 1946, it had secured 23 seats in the Chamber—more than twice its prewar representation. In France, in the first Con-stituent Assembly elected on October 21, 1945, it held 151 seats as against 150 for the Catholic Mouvement Républi-cain Populaire (MRP) and 139 for the Socialists; in the sec-ond Constituent Assembly elected on June 2, 1946, it dropped two seats; but in the election for the National Assembly on November 10 of that year it obtained a total of 171, against 162 MRP and 102 Socialists. In the Italian Constituent As-sembly, elected on June 2, 1946, the Communists won 104 seats, coming third after the Christian-Democrats with 207 and the Socialists with 115. In all three countries, the Party was a power to be reckoned with; and in all of them it se-cured ministerial posts. Each of Belgium's first two post-Liberation Governments contained two Communist ministers, and on March 31, 1946, this number was doubled. In France, the Party held two portfolios in General de Gaulle's 1944 Provisional Government, and five in his first regular Cabinet, formed on November 21, 1945. When the General resigned in January 1946, the next two Governments each had six Communist ministers; and although these were followed in December 1946 by an all-Socialist caretaker Cabinet under Léon Blum, the Government formed by Paul Ramadier on January 22, 1947, once more contained a five-man quota of Communists. In Italy, likewise, Communists had been mem-bers of the two successive Governments headed by Ivanoe Bonomi after the liberation of Rome, of Ferruccio Parri's Government, set up in June 1945, and of the first three cabi-nets formed by the Christian-Democrat leader Alcide De Gasperi as tripartite coalitions of Communists, Christian-Democrats, and Socialists.[20]

Would the Communists use their new position in parlia-ments and governments to weaken constitutional authority, infiltrate the administration, and ultimately seize power? In Italy, Palmiro Togliatti might claim that his party had "al-ways declared that it does not conceive of the republican Constitution as an expedient for using the institutions of bour-geois democracy until the moment of insurrection in order to conquer the State and transform it into a Socialist State, but as a unitary pact freely concluded by the great majority of the Italian people and a basis for the organic development of national life." However orotund and abstract, this was an echo of the Resistance hope of renovating Western society; but if it was opposed—as it was—by many vested interests, it was also vitiated by Communist actions elsewhere. Not everyone saw the danger, or agreed that there was one. Many very able or idealistic Westerners continued to vote Communist as a protest, in ignorance, out of loyalty, or in stubborn hope of change. More and more, as time went on, they seemed to be sealed off in a private system of politics. Perhaps this dramatized their grievances, and the need for greater justice and equality: "bourgeois" fear of Communism was often an incentive to reform. But it was also an excuse for disdain or repression; and those who supported the Party for years without criticism, despite Prague, despite Budapest, inevitably came to seem illogical, malevolent, venal, or blind to what was happening in the other half of Europe. Even Togliatti, moreover, had qualified this promise of moderation by saying that it applied "for a whole historical period." What might follow remained unstated.[21]

It was without great regret, therefore, that the governments of Belgium, France and Italy now lost their Communist ministers. It might seem that this was the mirror-image of events in Eastern Europe; but the likeness was merely superficial. In the West there was little of the chicanery, and virtually none of the terror and violence, that were used against non-Communists in the East. In at least two of the three cases, moreover, the Communists virtually excluded themselves.

In Belgium, in March 1947, the Communist ministers resigned in a dispute over coal prices and subsidies to coalmines; and on March 12 the Socialist Paul-Henri Spaak formed a new government without them. In France, at the end of April, after several clashes on defense, economic, and foreign policy, Communist ministers attacked the Ramadier Government's wage freeze—partly to placate more militant strikers at the Renault car works. On May 4, when a vote of confidence was taken in the National Assembly, the Party voted against it; but the Communist ministers refused to leave the Government, hoping that this would force Ramadier himself to resign. Instead, he dismissed all but one of them that same evening; the other, a non-member of the Assembly, resigned next day. In Italy, finally, it was De Gasperi himself who at length dropped the Communists from his Cabinet. Even before the Marshall Plan, they had denounced the "economic imperialism" of American aid to Italy—although De Gasperi's Foreign Minister, the Socialist leader Pietro Nenni, was their chief working ally. When tension rose to breaking point, it first split the Socialist Party: in January 1947, the moderate leader Giuseppe Saragat walked out of its Rome Congress, taking with him a group of distinguished militants. Both he and Nenni now left the Cabinet; and De Gasperi himself resigned on January 20, to form a new tripartite Government two weeks later, but with the "Atlanticist" Count Carlo Sforza as Foreign Minister. At last, on May 30, 1947, after further quarrels and crises, De Gasperi felt strong enough to form a further Cabinet, this time without either Communists or Nenni Socialists. This ensured stability until the election of the first postwar parliament, due on April 18, 1948. The Czechoslovakian coup of February 1948 turned the campaign into a suspense drama: would the Prague *putsch* be repeated in Rome? Many quite sober observers feared that it might. Both the United States and the Vatican put their weight behind De Gasperi, the former threatening to cut off aid if the Communists and Socialists won the election, the latter encouraging priests to refuse the sacraments to godless pro-Soviet voters. As it turned out, the Christian-Democrats won 48.5 per cent of the poll, compared with 35.2 per cent in the 1946 election for the Constituent Assembly. The joint Socialist-Communist ticket received 31 per cent—which, even together with the 7.1 per cent won by the Saragat Socialists, still totalled less than the 39.7 per cent obtained by Socialists and Communists in 1946. With more than 300 Christian-Democrat seats out of 574 in the Chamber, De Gasperi was urged by the Vatican to form a one-party Catholic Government. Wisely, he refused, and put together the center coalition of Christian-Democrats, Liberals, Republicans, and Saragat Social-

Democrats that was to become a classical pattern in postwar Italian politics. Italy, like France and Belgium, had rounded the cape.[22]

The fear of internal subversion was exorcized; but throughout these same months events in Eastern Europe had cast still darker shadows. Was Soviet Communism inherently expansionist? Was Stalin determined to spread it westward by the use of armed force? In his *Problems of Leninism,* he had stated the orthodox doctrine: the capitalist system included "as an inevitable element imperialist wars." As Lenin had written:

. . . The existence of the Soviet Republic side by side with imperialist states for a long time is unthinkable. One or the other must triumph in the end. And before that end supervenes a series of frightful collisions between the Soviet Republic and the bourgeois states will be inevitable.

"The bourgeois states," added Stalin, ". . . send spies, assassins and wreckers into our country and are waiting for a favorable opportunity to attack it by armed force." "We must remember that we are surrounded by people, classes, and governments who openly express their intense hatred for us. We must remember that we are at all times but a hair's breadth from every manner of invasion." To defend itself, the Communist Party must forestall attack and overthrow non-Communist governments, beginning with the weaker countries, such as former colonial dependencies.[23]

In context, these words seemed to refer to "the successful seizure of power" in the class struggle—to the pattern, that is, being followed in Eastern Europe. John Foster Dulles, later to be President Eisenhower's Secretary of State, himself admitted that:

Class war, rather than *national* war, is taught as the preferred method of achieving Soviet Communist encirclement. That explains why Stalin can say, as he not infrequently does, that the Soviet Union and the United States, as nations, can coexist peacefully, i.e., without national war.

But the violent rhetoric of Stalin and his associates blurred the distinction. "Many feel," said Dulles, "that because Soviet

Communist leaders treat us as 'enemies,' and because their
nation has a great military establishment, it necessarily follows that the Soviet Union will fight a national war against
us, and that we should concentrate on military things." Despite his later reputation as a "Cold Warrior," Dulles
preached caution. "Whether Soviet leaders do plan a fighting
war," he added ". . . is by no means certain, and if we treat
it as certain and make our dispositions accordingly, we may
fall victim to a fatal trick play."[24]

Western fears, then, may possibly have misread Soviet intentions: but what was significant on both sides was the
climate of fear. World War II was not long over; its violent
sequels were still being enacted in the "satellite" countries;
the landscape of Europe, and the minds of men, still bore its
scars. Dulles, even when he spoke of peace, used the language of war. "It is time," he said, "to think less of fission
bombs and more of establishing justice and ending terrorism
in the world." But this very sentence was preceded by another: "It is time to think in terms of taking the offensive in
the world struggle for freedom and of rolling back the en-
gulfing tide of despotism." Such words confirmed the worst of
Soviet suspicions, as Communist rhetoric confirmed those of
the West; and mutual distrust, rightly or wrongly, was deepened by the military situation of each side. To be prepared
is the duty of all military planners: unless they are themselves
distrustful, they betray their trust. And the relative military
strength of the West and the Soviet Union in the late '40s
inevitably increased the political tension. Since 1945, the
United States had possessed the atomic bomb; they had also
withdrawn many of their troops from Western Europe. The
Soviet situation was precisely the opposite. Stalin's technolo-
gists had not yet produced a nuclear weapon; in compensation, the Soviet Union maintained and was developing
conventional forces far greater than those of the West. Being
asymmetrical, the balance of power was highly dangerous:
each side's weakness faced the other's strength. The ensuing
arms race was therefore run, as it were, on two separate
tracks. The Soviet Union made immense efforts to build an
atomic device, which it finally tested in 1949. The West,

meanwhile, felt obliged to strengthen its conventional defense.[25]

In Western Europe, the first move was made by Ernest Bevin, the British Foreign Secretary. On January 13, 1948, he told General Marshall, U. S. Secretary of State, that Britain planned to propose to France and the three Benelux countries a series of bilateral defense agreements. With President Truman's backing, Marshall answered that the United States agreed with Britain on "the urgent need for concerted measures by the nations of Europe." On January 22, Bevin explained his plan to the House of Commons. After reminding his audience how the original postwar hope of a united world had come to grief, he declared that the free nations of Europe must now draw closely together. It was not, he was quick to add, a formal political union that he had in mind, but "the closest possible relations." "We have then to go beyond the circle of our immediate neighbours . . . and consider the question of associating other historic members of European civilization, including the new Italy, with this great conception." Bevin put his proposal formally at the end of January. In the third week of February the Benelux countries, and particularly Paul-Henri Spaak, the Belgian Foreign Minister, urged that it be a collective regional arrangement, economic, social, and cultural as well as military, rather than a series of bilateral defense pacts. Meanwhile, Czechoslovakia was in turmoil—and the ominous news from Prague helped speed the work of the diplomats. On Thursday, March 4, one week after Klement Gottwald's *putsch*, a negotiating conference met in Brussels. On Wednesday, March 17, one week after Jan Masaryk's death, Britain, France, and the Benelux countries signed a brief, crisp treaty eleven articles long. Concluded for fifty years, it set up a Consultative Council of Foreign Ministers, a Military Committee, and other permanent bodies to deal with economic, social, and cultural matters: one of their products was to be a Cultural Identity Card. More important was the multilateral defense commitment, pledging its signatories to aid each other against armed aggression—automatically if it occurred in Europe, after consultation if elsewhere. Unlike the Treaty of Dunkirk signed by

Britain and France a year earlier, on March 4, 1947, the Brussels Treaty was not limited to defense against Germany; in this way it was the first postwar treaty implicitly to recognize a potential Soviet threat. Largely on French insistence, however, it mentioned possible aggression by Germany. The ambivalence was characteristic of the changing times.[26]

Victors and vanquished are always mutually suspicious. Which of the defeated can their conquerors trust? The openly hostile, sturdy in their defiance—or the eager, the efficient, the compliant? Are the victors themselves to be trusted? Is there arrogance in their good intentions, or a saving grace of honesty in their lapses? Can either side speak plainly? How long will it be before memories and misgivings are effaced?

After World War II, this process was slower than usual. More than most others, it had been a "people's war." As in World War I, conscripts had formed vast citizen armies, and bombing had brought civilians under fire. Occupation, first of Allied countries, then of the Axis, had involved whole populations; millions had been deported or imprisoned; millions had become refugees. Yet, paradoxically, some of those who had known occupation proved more tolerant than those who had escaped it: if their sufferings were greater, they at least saw the enemy at close quarters, and could distinguish between the bad and the worse.

Of all the Axis leaders, it was Hitler who had left the deepest mark on Europe. For many of the Allies, it had been the second war against Germany in two generations; for France, it had been the third. The war in the Far East had most directly affected the United States, Australia, and New Zealand. Mussolini's legions had proved imperfectly martial. But the Nazis had largely lived up to their legend; and their death camps had given human evil unimagined new dimensions. Caught in collective guilt, the most conscientious Germans now wound their way through labyrinths of tortured logic to recover a necessary minimum of self-respect. Political leaders quoted Karl Jaspers; journalists wrote anguished books to explain German unpopularity, lacerating their readers only less than themselves. Yet at the same time they resented the lordly airs of their new conquerors, few of whom had had to face such appalling ethical dilemmas. To many among the Allies, in fact, the ordinary apolitical German, living his life as best he could in the interstices of disaster, seemed to have been feckless and irresponsible; his defeated democratic leaders, rightly or not, looked ineffectual and out of touch. Only after searching, frank, and painful—almost psychoanalytical—discussion of the Nazi era could real mutual trust between Germans and others again become possible. Failing that, horror at Nazi atrocities all too easily led to an understandable but still ugly form of race hatred: as anti-Semitism was defeated, anti-Germanism grew.[27]

To a generation that grew up fearing and then fighting Hitler, much that was German now had a suspect fascination. Films from the Weimar epoch were seen by one influential critic—himself of German origin—as revealing "deep psychological dispositions": they helped, he thought, "in the understanding of Hitler's ascent and ascendancy."[28] Propaganda, abetted by national habit, had established some unattractive stereotypes. The stout, beer-drinking, cigar-smoking Bavarian, at home the embodiment of robust, jovial prosperity, was often seen abroad as boorish and self-indulgent: the lean, aristocratic captain of industry seemed to many non-Germans a vulpine capitalist, if not a "Prussian militarist" in civilian clothes. German seriousness seemed heavy, German scholarship pedantic, German romanticism sentimental, German realism cruel. Wagner, like imperial architecture, spelled glory at home, but abroad was sometimes accused of bombast. The "Deutsches Eck" at Koblenz, recommended to foreigners in search of "the German character," to Germans meant sobriety, solidity, hard work, and the mighty Rhine: to too many others, it held all the gray menace of the Reich's somber factories, the overcast powerhouses of the Ruhr. Even the uniforms worn by postwar German railway porters sent chills down middle-aged foreign spines. The German peaked cap recalled the Wehrmacht; a German accent in English, French, or Italian revived unwelcome emotions; and even the German language risked seeming pompous, ambiguous, abstract, and back-to-front.

Amid the marsh of speculation and prejudice there were a few rocks of fact. Germany, like almost every European country, had long had a hierarchical society; but whereas in most others industrialization had thrown up a new middle class of managers, here there had been no real social revolution before 1933. Discipline and hierarchy had reinforced German industriousness, making the country a great—and rival—economic power, but with a social fabric ready to split at the seams. At the same time, Germany had long been in an exposed position. For centuries—from the Counter-Reformation until after the French Revolution—its internal divisions and lack of firm natural frontiers had made it the victim of others' quarrels, an object of diplomacy and one of the spoils of war. Now, once more divided, this time between East and West, it lay across Europe like a crippled giant. Both Eastern and Western Allies were anxious to exorcize its past and potential menace; but they differed as to how it should be done.[29]

The Potsdam Conference had stipulated that "during the occupation period, Germany shall be treated as a single economic entity," and that "so far as is practicable there shall be uniformity of treatment of the German population throughout Germany." The four Commanders-in-Chief who made up the Allied Control Council in Berlin were to rule "jointly, in matters affecting Germany as a whole." Their decisions, however, were subject to the rule of unanimity; and each of them, on instructions from his government, was to exercise "supreme authority" in his own zone of occupation. If unity was a political aspiration, division thus became an administrative fact. France, in particular, was hostile to the establishment of a central German administration; and although the Soviet Union ostensibly agreed with the United States and Britain on the need to treat Germany as a unit, in practice it followed its own familiar policy in the Eastern zones, as it did in the Eastern sector of Berlin.[30]

Fighting in the capital had ended on Wednesday, May 2, 1945. When the Americans arrived on Sunday, July 1, they found a complete apparatus of government already in place. Prominent positions had been assigned to non-Communists, but Party members were safely in control of key posts, including education and the police. Even the clocks had been set to Moscow time: dazed Berliners found that it was still dark at 7:00 A.M. during the summer, while at midnight it was still light. Meanwhile, in the Eastern zone as a whole, Sovietization proceeded rapidly. Early in the occupation, the Soviet Union drew from Germany some 500 million dollars a year—a striking contrast with the 700 million dollars that the United States and Britain were paying in. But not content with official reparations, the Soviet authorities amalgamated two hundred firms into large state corporations, *Sowjetische Aktiengesellschaften*, whose output they could freely exploit since they held 51 per cent of the shares. By mid-1946, in these and other ways, they expropriated 7,000 factories. In a drastic land reform, East Germany's large estates were broken up, and 400,000 peasants became smallholders with farms of seventeen to twenty-two acres each. At the same time, party politics in the Eastern zone began to acquire a decisive Soviet stamp. The first order issued by the Soviet Military Administration, on June 10, 1945, authorized four political parties—the Communist KPD, or Kommunistische Partei Deutschlands; the Socialist SPD, or Sozialdemokratische Partei Deutschlands; the Christian Democrat CDU, or Christlich-Demokratische Union; and the Liberal LDP, or Liberal-Demokratische Partei. In the West, permission was similarly granted by the Americans, the British, and the French; and in the following winter and spring the SPD, CDU and LDP held their first interzonal conferences. The KPD, however, was small; and from the autumn of 1945 onward, partly at Soviet prompting, it began to press for amalgamation with the SPD. A number of German Socialists, including the concentration camp victim Kurt Schumacher, were suspicious of the proposed merger; and on March 1, 1946, a mass meeting in Berlin came out against it. But Otto Grotewohl, the SPD's Berlin leader, had already persuaded his colleagues on the Executive to approve it; and although other Berlin Socialists organized a plebiscite which overwhelmingly opposed it—by 82 per cent of the votes—their protest was limited to the Western sectors, since the Russians forbade it in the East. Accordingly, on April 21–22, 1946, the East German SPD merged with the Communist Party in the new Socialist Unity Party, or SED (Sozialistische

Einheitspartei Deutschlands), with Grotewohl and the Communist Wilhelm Pieck at its head. It was never recognized in the West. For a time, the two groups within it struggled for supremacy; but the Communists, with strong Soviet backing, maintained effective control. They made no pretense of excluding former followers of Hitler: one militant coined the appealing slogan, "The SED—the great friend of the little Nazi." Alongside it, paradoxically, the Soviet authorities encouraged the formation of "anti-Fascist democratic mass organizations" of farmers, youth clubs, trade unions, women, and cultural groups. These were openly political. The statutes of the trade union organization, the Freier Deutscher Gewerkschaftsbund (FDGB), declared as its aim "a Socialist structure of society"; but its officials, far from being freely elected, were appointed by the Soviet authorities, then confirmed in office by the bodies that they themselves had set up.[31]

Local elections were held in the Eastern zone in September 1946—eight months after the first vote in the American zone. The SED was allowed to put up candidates in all the 11,623 local communities involved; but the CDU, which was registered in 4,200 of them, was allowed to do so in only 2,082, and the LDP, although registered in 2,200, in only 1,121. Heavy pressure was exerted on CDU leaders, three of whom were forced out of office; and in several areas, non-Marxist meetings were broken up. Partly by these means, the SED won 52.4 per cent of the votes, and the "mass organizations" 3.3 per cent. Similar tactics were used at the provincial elections held on October 20, 1946: the SED was allotted 900 tons of newsprint for its electoral manifestos, compared with nine tons for the CDU and LDP. Even so, out of the 520 seats in the Land assemblies, the SED secured only 249, or 47.6 per cent; votes for the mass organizations brought the Marxist total to 265, or just over 50 per cent, against 133 for the CDU and 122 for the LDP. The precariousness of this qualified victory was made more obvious by the election results in Berlin, where inhabitants of all four sectors voted, under Allied supervision, and where the SPD was still able to put up candidates: here the SED won only 20 per cent of the votes, against 48.7 per cent for the SPD.

In the Eastern zone as a whole, the SED now had an absolute majority in two of the five Länder–Saxony and Saxony-Anhalt; in Thüringia it had half the votes, and just under half in Brandenburg and Mecklenburg. On this basis, it took five out of nine cabinet posts in Saxony, three out of six in Saxony-Anhalt, six out of nine in Thüringia, three out of six in Brandenburg, and four out of eight in Mecklenburg. In four of the five Länder, moreover, it secured the Ministry of the Interior, and thereby controlled the police.[32]

In the West, meanwhile, it had become increasingly clear that the Soviet authorities were not applying the "all-German" provisions of the Potsdam Agreement. Far from treating Germany as an economic unit, the Soviet Union had been stripping the Eastern zone of resources that should have helped Germany's recovery as a whole. Early in April 1946, General Lucius D. Clay, U. S. Deputy Military Governor, came to the conclusion that so long as each zone was treated as a separate economic entity, the Americans "were being placed in the position not only of financing reparations to the Soviet Union but also of agreeing to strip our own zone (which had insufficient industrial capacity for self-support) without getting the benefits which would come from the amalgamation of all zones." As a second-best solution, he began to envisage economic unity among the Western zones alone. On Friday, May 3, 1946, after further arguments, he stopped reparations payments to the East; and shortly afterward he recommended to Secretary of State James Byrnes that, failing French and Soviet agreement, "the British be approached to determine their willingness to combine their zone of occupation with ours. If the British are willing for this merger to be accomplished, the French and Russian representatives should be advised that it is our proposal to effect this merger before winter, even though we would much prefer to obtain Allied unity in the treatment of Germany as a whole." Two months later, on Thursday, July 11, 1946, Byrnes announced to the Paris four-power Conference that "pending agreement among the four powers to implement the Potsdam agreement requiring the administration of Germany as an economic unit, the United States will join with any other occupying government or governments in Germany for the treatment of our respective zones as an economic unit." On the following morning, the British Foreign Secretary, Ernest Bevin, announced his government's agreement in principle; and after much hard bargaining over relative occupation costs, Britain and the United States concluded a final settlement on Monday, December 2, 1946. The "Bizone" —"Bizonia" to those unafraid of Ruritanian echoes—came into being on New Year's Day, 1947.[33]

In these ways, both the Soviet Union and the Western powers were beginning to take steps, on either side of the East-West border, that ultimately led to the establishment of two rival German Governments. Formally, each step could be seen as a riposte. Thus, on Thursday, February 27, 1947, the Soviet Union lodged a protest against the formation of the Bizone; on Thursday, May 29, 1947, after Soviet intransigence at the four-power Moscow Conference in March and April, the British and Americans set up the Bizone's Economic Council of fifty-two delegates from the Land assemblies, together with an Executive Committee representing the Land governments; in June, the Soviet Union established an East German Permanent Economic Commission (Ständige Wirtschaftskommission) of twenty-five members, a majority of them appointed by the Soviet administration, the remainder representing the trade unions and farmers' organizations. In July, the Western powers decided to extend Marshall Aid to their occupation zones of Germany. In December, while a further four-power Conference was still deadlocked in London, the Soviet authorities held the first of a series of German People's Congresses (Volkskongresse), composed of 2,215 delegates theoretically representing the whole of Germany— although the Western parties declined the invitation, and the non-Marxist parties in the Eastern zone were outnumbered and outmaneuvered by the SED.[34]

It was 1948, the year of the Czechoslovak crisis, that saw the most decisive moves. Early in February, the British and Americans proposed that they meet in London with the French to discuss the future of the Bizone. On Monday, February 9, however, without waiting for French agreement, they enlarged its Economic Council to 104 members, and added an upper house, or Länderrat, consisting of two governmental delegates from each Land; at the same time, they remodeled the Executive Committee, which now grouped the heads of the various administrative agencies. This, as General Clay remarked:

. . . was a realistic political structure of the federal type even though it had no sovereign powers, was limited in its authority to fiscal and economic measures, and its acts were subject to Military Government approval. There was a legislature, with broad authority in fiscal and economic fields, composed of a lower house, whose members were elected by the state parliaments and were at least indirectly responsible to the people, and an upper house representing the states. There was a chairman of the Executive Committee (roughly, the chairman corresponded to a Prime Minister and the Committee to a Cabinet) responsible to the legislature. . . . We had the machinery for government, if not a government.

It was completed on the same day by a High Court, and on Monday, March 1, 1948, by a central bank, the Bank Deutscher Länder, serving all three Western zones. Meanwhile, on Monday, February 23, while the Prague crisis was at its height, the French, British, and Americans had begun their meeting in London, behind closed doors at India House at the bottom of Kingsway, where they invited the three Benelux countries to join them. On Saturday, March 6, they announced their agreement to establish international control of the Ruhr, "to guarantee that its economic resources are not used again for aggressive ends, and that satisfactory access to its coal, coke, and steel is ensured in the interest of a large part of the European community, including Germany." They added that they favored "a federal form of Government" as "the most appropriate to make possible the ultimate re-establishment of German unity."[35]

The response from the East came quickly. That same day, a Soviet Note of protest was delivered to the British Government; and on Tuesday, March 9, it was published by the Tass news agency. Next day, the Soviet Union increased the powers of the East German Economic Commission; and on Wednesday and Thursday of the following week, on March 17 and 18, it held a second People's Congress. This promptly elected a 400-member "People's Council," which in turn appointed a committee to draft a formal "All-German" Constitution. Finally, on Saturday, March 20, 1948, the previously affable Soviet member of the four-power Control Council in Berlin, Marshal Vassily Sokolovsky, read a long aggrieved statement to his colleagues, interrupted the British representative who began to reply to it, and declared: "I see no sense in continuing this meeting." He and the whole Soviet delegation then walked out of the room. There now seemed little hope of an all-German settlement. In practical terms, as General Clay put it, "the Allied Control Council was dead."[36]

In London, the Western powers continued their "semi-official" talks. At length, on Tuesday, June 1, 1948, the conference ended; and on the following Monday, June 7, its conclusions were published. They recommended not only the establishment of an International Authority for the Ruhr, but also the formation of a German Constituent Assembly, whose members were to be elected by each of the Western Länder according to whatever procedure its legislative body chose. The Constituent Assembly was to draw up a Constitution which, in the words of the Allied communiqué:

. . . should contain such provisions as will enable the Germans to contribute to putting an end to the present division of Germany, not by the reconstruction of a centralized *Reich* but by the adoption of a federal form of government which satisfactorily ensures the protection of the different States' rights while providing for sufficient central authority and guaranteeing individual rights and liberties.

The Constitution was to be submitted to the Commanders-in-Chief, who would verify its conformity to these principles; it was then to go to the various Länder for ratification. On June 20, moreover, the Western Allies issued a new West German currency, the Deutsche Mark, which was exchanged at the rate of one DM for ten old Reichsmark—later reduced to 6.5 DM for 100 RM. Everyone was allowed, however, to exchange forty of his RM for forty DM, with the promise of a further twenty DM for twenty RM two months later. The instant result was a brief orgy of spending, and a renewed faith in paper money after years of quasi-barter in which cigarettes had been the hardest currency. Ludwig Erhard, the heavily-built Bavarian who as the Bizone's Director for Economic Administration had played a large part in the currency reform, shortly afterward removed a number of price restrictions—rather startling the Allies. "It was strictly laid down by the British and American control authorities," he confessed later, "that permission had to be obtained before any definite price changes could be made. The Allies never seemed to have thought it possible that someone could have the idea, not to alter price controls, but simply to remove them." Helped by Allied appropriations and by already increasing production, these measures triggered off rapid economic growth. In 1946, the Western zones of Germany had produced 33 per cent of their 1936 total: by mid-1949 the proportion had risen to 90 per cent.[37]

When currency reform had first been mooted, the Soviet Union had toyed with the notion of using the new Deutsche Mark, and had asked the Americans for a set of printing plates. Warned by a previous experience, when the Russians had failed to account for the Allied "military Marks" that they had printed from duplicate plates, General Clay refused their request. He proposed instead that the printing works, in the American sector of Berlin, be placed in an enclave under four-power control; but this, in turn, was rejected by the Russians. Instead, they responded with a separate currency reform in East Germany, a walk-out from the four-power Kommandatura, and a land blockade of the city of Berlin.[38]

Berlin had felt pinpricks earlier. On December 15, 1947, the Soviet Military Administration had begun to require permits for motorized travel into the city; on January 18, 1948, the Soviet Commandant had prohibited the transfer of property between the sectors; on February 23, the Soviet authorities had cut by one-fifth the number of permits for goods trucks between Berlin and the West. On March 29, they announced that from April 1 onward permits would be required for Allied troop movements, and that private baggage would be checked. In May, the formalities were made more complex; on June 10, civilian traffic between Berlin and the West was suspended for two days. Now, at 6:00 A.M. on Thursday, June 24, 1948, all rail traffic was stopped. Shortly, the ban was extended to canal and highway traffic. By August 4, Berlin was in a state of siege.[39]

When the blockade began, the two-and-a-half million

civilians in West Berlin had food stocks for thirty-six days and coal stocks for forty-five days. Any new supplies would now have to come by air. To withstand the siege, it was estimated, Berlin would need a daily airlift of at least 4,500 tons. The United States had on hand just over one hundred twin-engined transport and troop-carrying aircraft of 2½ tons capacity each, some of them already elderly; the British had fewer; the French had none. To meet the target with existing resources, every aircraft would have had to make the impossible total of a dozen flights a day. Nevertheless, hopeless as it seemed, the airlift began on Friday, June 25, the day after the rail blockade. By Thursday, July 22, when Clay reported to President Truman in Washington on the progress of operations, fifty-two C-54 and eighty C-47 aircraft were making two round trips daily; but they could carry only 2,400–2,500 tons a day. Truman asked Clay what risks might be involved in sending in armed land convoys. The Russians' initial reaction, Clay answered, would be to put up road blocks; and if these were dismantled, they might then resort to force. They would not, he thought, attack Allied planes with fighters; but when he asked for additional aircraft, the President's Air Force advisers hesitated: they were anxious not to weaken Allied air strength if the Soviet Union were really bent on war. Wisely, Truman agreed with Clay in thinking that the blockade was not, as many imagined, the prelude to hostilities. He gave orders for continuing talks with the Russians and for rapid expansion of the airlift. By August 20, 1948, it was carrying 3,300 tons a day, with 4,575 tons as its biggest daily load. By September 9, the average was 4,000 tons; by December it had reached 4,500 tons; by February 1949 it had risen to 5,500 tons; and by the spring, it had attained 8,000 tons—as much as had previously been brought in by rail and water. On one record day, the airlift delivered nearly 13,000 tons of food, fuel, goods, and raw materials.[40]

It was during these anxious months that the United States took a further decisive step in its progressive involvement with Western Europe, following the Truman Doctrine and the Marshall Plan. On Wednesday, March 17, 1948, shortly after the Czechoslovakia crisis, on the same day that Britain,

France, and the Benelux countries signed the Brussels Treaty, President Truman hailed their newly created "Western Union" as "a notable step in the direction of unity in Europe for protection and preservation of its civilization." "This development," he added, "deserves our full support . . . I am sure that the determination of the free countries of Europe to protect themselves will be matched by an equal determination on our part to help them to protect themselves." He therefore urged Congress to provide for universal military training and a restoration of selective service. A few weeks later, on Friday, April 23, Ernest Bevin sent to Washington a top-secret telegram in effect proposing a North Atlantic security system; and on Tuesday, July 6, his hand strengthened by Arthur H. Vandenberg's Senate Resolution in favor of regional arrangements "based on continuous and effective self-help and mutual aid," Truman's Under-Secretary of State Robert A. Lovett began secret talks with the Washington Ambassadors of Canada and the Brussels Treaty powers. In February 1949 these talks became formal negotiations and on Monday, April 4, 1949, the North Atlantic Treaty was signed by the United States, Canada, Belgium, Denmark, France, Iceland, Italy, Luxembourg, the Netherlands, Norway, Portugal, and the United Kingdom. Its essential provision was that all its signatories agreed "that an armed attack against one or more of them shall be considered an attack against them all." Its essential significance was that the United States had turned its back on the concept of "Fortress America." As Paul-Henri Spaak, later to be NATO Secretary-General, put it, "the Monroe Doctrine was abandoned; American isolationism was dead."[41]

The almost immediate sequel to the Atlantic Pact, if not necessarily its consequence was that the Soviet Union called off the Berlin blockade. Firmness and moderation, backed by the airlift's display of wealth and resources, had worked. On Wednesday, May 4, 1949, the four occupying powers announced that it would end on Thursday, May 12. Until the last moment of the long negotiations preceding this agreement, the Soviet Union had insisted that the Western powers cease their efforts to establish a West German Government; now, it no longer made this a prior condition. Stalin recognized, no doubt, that on both sides of the East-West border the State-making process had passed the point of no return.

On Sunday, May 8, 1949, in fact, the West German Constituent Assembly—renamed the "Parliamentary Council"—adopted the Constitution, renamed the "Grundgesetz" or "Basic Law"; on Thursday, May 12, the Allied Military Governors provisionally approved it; and in the following week it was ratified by all the Länder Assemblies with the exception of Bavaria, which would have preferred a looser confederation, but agreed to abide by the majority's decision.[42]

Almost simultaneously, on Sunday and Monday, May 15 and 16, the third East German People's Congress approved the draft Constitution submitted to it by the People's Council on the previous March 19. This particular Congress had been voted in by what were described as "universal, secret, and direct elections"; but these had been held on the basis of a single joint list of candidates put up by the SED, the mass organizations, and the East-zone CDU and LDP. It was impossible to choose between parties, and even between candidates. In fact, 37.2 per cent of the electorate rejected the joint list; but the SED was assigned 90 seats, the mass organizations 126, and the CDU and LDP 45 each, while 15 each went to two new groups, the National Democratic Party and the Agrarian Party. Thus assembled, the Congress approved the draft Constitution, and appointed a new People's Council, seventy of whose members were deemed to represent West Germany.[43]

On Monday, May 23, 1949, the West German Parliamentary Council held its last meeting, and proclaimed the adoption of the Basic Law. While the Western occupying powers made their final arrangements, drawing up an Occupation Statute to regulate their remaining duties and amalgamating the three zones under an Allied High Commission, the West Germans themselves prepared for their first postwar election. This was held on Sunday, August 14, 1949, and 78.5 per cent of those eligible actually voted: of the 402 seats in the lower house, the Bundestag, the CDU won 139, the SDP 131, the Free Democratic Party 52, and the Communists and regional parties 80. On September 12, the Parliament elected Theodor Heuss of the FDP as Federal President, and he in turn proposed as Chancellor Konrad Adenauer, former Mayor of Cologne, who was elected by a one-vote majority, having characteristically voted for himself.[44]

On Friday, October 7, 1949, without any pretense of elections, the East German People's Council set itself up as a "Provisional People's Chamber" (Volkskammer) and promulgated the new Constitution. Three days later, the Eastern Land Assemblies selected delegates to a second legislative chamber, the Länderkammer; and on October 11, at a joint meeting, the two houses elected as President of the Republic the Communist leader Wilhelm Pieck.[45]

In this way, by a fatal leapfrog process, the Eastern and Western parts of Germany moved toward separate statehood. Both the Soviet Union and the Western powers claimed that the administrative apparatus which they were respectively assembling would be suitable for the whole of Germany; but each reflected the political conceptions of its sponsors, and each move inevitably hardened the East-West division. Neither side was necessarily insincere: but what was at issue was a question of ideology, confused with a problem of power politics. The Soviet Union was primarily anxious to impose its own Marxist order on Germany, as on the rest of Eastern Europe; it was also concerned to build a buffer between itself and the West, and perhaps to recruit the resources of Germany as a whole. The Western powers hoped to install and instill Western concepts of democracy; but they also hoped to build a bulwark against the East, and to have Germany make her essential contribution to Western Europe's well-being, as later to its defense. As so often in the past, Germany was still thought of—by both sides—as part-threat, part-ally and part-prey. Which side the Germans themselves preferred was suggested by the 1½ million refugees who crossed from the East zone to the West between 1945 and September 1950;[46] but during all this time, despite the very real differences between the Eastern system of centralized, bureaucratic and pitiless "People's Democracy" and the federal, liberal, democratic organization of West German capitalism, there remained one feature in common between East and West. The Germans, on both sides of the border, were still an object of policy; they had not yet recovered full political stature. As time went on, and as West Germany in particular grew richer, this situation became too paradoxical to last.

EUROPE AND THE ISLANDS

> The Summer holds: upon its glittering lake
> Lie Europe and the islands . . .
> *W. H. Auden*[1]

> The waters of the Channel have run for too many years
> in our blood. *William Golding*[2]

> The Sage is full of anxiety and indecision in undertaking
> anything, and so he is always successful. *Chuang-tzu*[3]

> It is easier to induce nations to discuss problems than to
> discuss politics . . . The only way to promote unity is to
> induce people to concentrate on problems with which
> they are economically confronted. *Ernest Bevin*[4]

The Preamble to the "Basic Law" of the German Federal Republic declared that the West German people was resolved not only "to preserve its national and political unity," but also "to serve the peace of the world as an equal partner in a united Europe."[5]

This statement was less simple than it seemed. For many, a "united Europe" no doubt meant a Europe including the countries of the East. If all of Europe were to achieve "unity," this would help restore the "unity" of the German people—although in the two contexts the same word meant different things. For others, "Europe" in 1948 and 1949 already meant "Western Europe." Some, perhaps, saw Western European unity as a substitute ideal to placate the Germans, robbed of national unity; some as a means of strengthening the West with German resources, and anchoring to it the newborn Federal Republic; some as a means of taming Germany, dissolving in a broader unit the renascent national identity already implicit in the Basic Law's reference to "an equal partner."

Most of these unstated interpretations, however, were open to question; and none of them adequately conveyed the emotional force of "the European idea." "Europe"—if only as a hope of transcending narrow national frontiers—had especial appeal to the Germans, who had so recently explored the dark excesses of Hitler's nationalism; but others had shared very similar or worse experiences. They had seen the misery, destruction, chaos, poverty, and weakness to which unbridled national sovereignty could lead. Many were determined, in varying degrees and sometimes inexplicitly, to introduce into the relations between their countries some civilizing influence like that exerted by laws and institutions within the nation-state itself. They also realized, however obscurely, that only by acting together—and perhaps only by uniting—could European countries ever recover that influence in the world that had passed, now, to the super-powers, the United States and the Soviet Union, with the People's Republic of China, still distant, just visible on the horizon. It was no coincidence that the postwar constitutions of both France and Italy also envisaged the limitation of national sovereignty. "On conditions of reciprocity," said the Preamble to the Constitution of the Fourth Republic, "France will accept the limitations of sovereignty necessary to the organization and defence of peace." "Italy," stated Article 11 of her 1947 Constitution, ". . . agrees, in conditions of parity with other States, to the limitations of sovereignty necessary to an order that will ensure peace and justice among Nations." And if such pledges of principle could be made by written constitutions, practical plans and projects abounded elsewhere.[6]

"The European idea" had a venerable history, and had acquired many meanings at different times. The classical world had left on the notion of Europe the twin imprints of Greek philosophy and Roman law; Christianity had sanctified it; the medieval Empire and the Papacy had endowed it with largely misleading analogies; the Crusades had stiffened its pride and solidarity; post-medieval nostalgia and the search for perpetual peace had spawned some premature utopias; cosmopolitan culture had colored it; the United States' example had inspired it, and Napoleon partly perverted it; Romanticism, nationalism, international Socialism and trade unionism, nineteenth-century federalism—all had contributed to the shades of meaning and connotation that the word "Europe" inspired. There had been innumerable proposals, some harebrained, for Europe-wide States, Republics, Federations, Assemblies, Senates, Councils, Diets, Tribunals, Armies: the panoply of the *ancien régime* had been invoked to build a new international order. With the exception of the Memorandum put forward in 1930 by Aristide Briand, the French Prime Minister, it was only during and after World War II that European unity potentially became a matter of practical politics. Statesmen like Winston Churchill, Charles de Gaulle, Pope Pius XII, Paul-Henri Spaak, Alcide De Gasperi, Robert Schuman, Johan Willem Beyen, Konrad Adenauer, Joseph Bech; Resistance leaders like Ernesto Rossi, Altiero Spinelli, Henri Frenay, Eugen Kogón, Hendrik Brugmans, Alfred Mozer; writers like Albert Camus, George Orwell, Denis de Rougemont; tireless publicists like Count Coudenhove-Kalergi—all urged, and many helped to organize, efforts to establish what Churchill memorably called, in a speech at the University of Zurich on Thursday, September 19, 1946, "a kind of United States of Europe." Support for the idea came from many countries and most parts of the political spectrum. "Europe," like "unity," covered a multitude of senses; and Churchill himself was badly misunderstood by those who imagined that he proposed to include Great Britain in his European United States. At the time, however, action seemed more important than exegesis. In the winter of 1947, a number of separate organizations together set up an International Committee of the Movements for European Unity, led by Joseph Retinger, who had been right-hand man to the London Polish leader General Wladyslaw Sikorski. The Committee proceeded to organize a full-scale "Congress of Europe" in The Hague from May 7 to 10, 1948. This brought together more than 750 statesmen, who called for political and economic union in Europe, a European Assembly and a European Court of Human Rights. There followed some weeks of frenzied backstage lobbying, during which Retinger and the national delegations pressed their governments for action on the Resolutions. France and Belgium, in particular, expressed interest; Clement Attlee, the British Prime Minister, was reluctant to commit himself at this stage. Eventually, on Tuesday, July 20, the French Foreign Minister Georges Bidault, who had attended the Hague Congress, put forward some of its proposals officially at the second session of the Consultative Council of the five-nation Brussels Treaty.[7]

What Bidault proposed was a customs and economic union among the Brussels Treaty powers and any others that wished to join them, together with a consultative European Assembly to advise the Governments on this task. Initially, the proposal made no headway, especially with Ernest Bevin, the British Foreign Secretary, who said that he was anxious about likely Communist members of such an Assembly, and would therefore prefer it to be unofficial—a club that could blackball whomever it wished. On the following day, the organizers of the Hague Congress asked each of the five Brussels powers to receive a small delegation to discuss the question. Ten days later, Bevin answered that pending further study he saw no point in an interview at the present time.

The French, however, kept up the pressure. On July 28, 1948, the Foreign Affairs Committee of the National Assembly called on the Government to convene the European Assembly proposed by the Hague Congress, so that it might among other things prepare a draft federal constitution for Europe. On August 18, a new French cabinet quickly gave its backing, not to this suggestion, but to a further Memorandum from the Hague Congress organizers. While admitting that "until such time as the nations should decide to transfer some part of their sovereign rights to an international European authority, the Assembly could have no legislative or executive powers," this Memorandum distantly envisaged such an authority, and called for the Assembly to be established with all possible speed. But despite French acquiescence, the British still hung back. On September 2, they circulated an eleven-point questionnaire whose tone was cold, skeptical and scathing: it asked, for example,

Are the [Assembly] delegates to represent the views of the Parliaments or the Governments? If the former (as the memorandum suggests) in what sense are they delegates, since the Parliaments have no corporate views on the issue nor any machinery for giving instructions to delegates? Moreover, if the delegates cannot speak for the Governments, what is expected of the Preparatory Conference and why indeed are Governments being consulted?

Reading such words more than twenty years later, one can hardly wonder at the now outmoded stereotype of the British as both insular and arrogant.[8]

On September 30, 1948, the French Government essayed some answers to the British queries; and it reaffirmed that while the proposed Assembly might ultimately become a legislature, for the present it would have a purely consultative role. If this principle were accepted now, some of the points of detail raised by the British—on whether or not overseas dependencies should be governed nationally or jointly, or whether European states should still be represented nationally at the United Nations—could reasonably be dealt with later. On October 7, the British complained that their questions had still not been precisely answered; but at length, in the last week of October, they at least agreed to set up a committee to study further steps. There were, said Bevin, three major problems: first, "a feeling of hesitation at the prospect of being united with the Continent without taking the Commonwealth into account"; secondly, "the question of sovereignty" which "seemed to his Government a particularly delicate one"; and thirdly, the "differences between the political systems of the five countries." Robert Schuman, the French Foreign Minister, was quick to reassure him that the French had similar anxieties, and he once more stressed the proposed Assembly's consultative status.[9]

The Study Committee accordingly met in Paris from November 24, 1948, to December 15, when it presented several alternative proposals. The French and Belgians, in particular, favored a Consultative Assembly of parliamentarians alongside a Committee of Ministers: but on Tuesday, January 18, 1949, having asked for a twelve-day postponement of the Committee's New Year meeting, the British delegation, led by Hugh Dalton, abruptly proposed that "the Committee of Ministers already suggested be supplemented not by an assembly but by an intergovernmental conference of delegates at which all the delegates from one country should be nominated by its government and should cast a single bloc vote." Amid general consternation, the discussions broke down; the whole question, it was agreed, must be referred to the Council of the Brussels Treaty powers, due to meet in London at the end of the month.[10]

Opening the London meeting, Bevin did his best to explain the British proposal. What Whitehall feared were "conflicts of competence . . . between an Assembly adopting resolutions which might endanger the work of responsible bodies with well-defined tasks." "A free Assembly," as he aptly called it, might tread on the toes of OEEC and thereby risk "conflicting with the concrete work of the Governments." Unless there were bloc voting, finally, might not the votes in the Assembly run counter to national policy? To meet the first of these points, Schuman suggested that governments should control the Assembly's agenda; on the question of voting he pleaded for a flexible, pragmatic approach. After further discussion, the procedure for appointing delegates was left to each individual government; with the Ministerial Committee enjoying the right of veto on the Assembly's agenda, the proposal for bloc voting was dropped. On Monday, March 7, 1949, the Brussels Treaty powers convened a conference to which they also invited Denmark, Norway, Ireland, Italy, and Sweden. On Tuesday, May 3, the Foreign Ministers of the ten countries met at St. James's Palace, London, and two days later they formally agreed on "The Statute of the Council of Europe." Its main feature, they declared, was:

. . . the establishment of a Committee of Ministers and of a Consultative Assembly, which together will form from the Council of Europe. Of these two bodies, the Committee of Ministers will provide for the development of co-operation between Governments, while the Consultative Assembly will provide a means through which the aspirations of the European peoples may be formulated and expressed, the governments thus being kept continually in touch with European public opinion.[11]

The fanfare was encouraging; and for a while its promise seemed to be kept. The Assembly met in Strasbourg on Wednesday, August 10, 1949, and elected as President the eloquent, sometimes ebullient Paul-Henri Spaak. At the end of the session he declared: "I came to Strasbourg convinced of the need for a United States of Europe. I leave with the certainty that union is possible." Yet two years later Spaak was to resign from the presidency in disillusion and disgust. "If a quarter of the energy spent here in saying No," he thundered at the Assembly, "were used to say Yes to something positive, we should not be in the state we are in today." Nearly two decades afterward, looking back on his experience in the Committee of Ministers, he wrote: "Of all the international bodies I have known, I have never found any more timorous or more impotent."[12]

Spaak's strictures were not entirely fair. The Council of Europe was the first European organization to be avowedly political. Its Assembly's members were, in the end, appointed by parliaments; they sat in the Chamber not by national delegations, but in alphabetical order of their surnames; they were not obliged to vote in blocs. With the help of a dedicated permanent Secretariat, the Council performed—and still performs—many valuable, unsung technical tasks. The European Convention for the Protection of Human Rights, and its European Court, form a lasting monument to one of its political aims. Yet, all the same, the corridors of the Maison de l'Europe were paved with good intentions as much as with brown linoleum: essentially, it was to be a house of disappointed hopes. Emasculated even before the negotiations that established it, the Assembly never acquired the legislative status that the French had ultimately promised and the British immediately feared; the Committee of Ministers, empowered only to make recommendations to the member governments, was further hamstrung by its practice of taking decisions unanimously even in those few cases where this was not the rule. It was hardly surprising, with such a structure, that the Council of Europe failed to achieve the European political union that had been the goal of the Hague Congress. The truly effective thrust in this direction had to come indirectly; and it came, not from Strasbourg, but from the opposite side of France.[13]

Cognac is not only a brandy: it is also a town of some 21,000 inhabitants on the Charente river, roughly halfway between Angoulême and the Atlantic estuary of the Gironde. For centuries it has lived on brandy and the salt trade: near the stills and warehouses, especially along the river front, the walls are black with microscopic fungus caused by the alcohol fumes. It is a solid, hard-working French provincial town, quiet and modest, but well-to-do and fundamentally self-assured. It rather resembles its most distinguished citizen—Jean Omer Marie Gabriel Monnet.

Jean Monnet was born in Cognac on Friday, November 9, 1888. His grandfather was a farmer who became Mayor and lived to the age of 102; his father, Jean Gabriel Monnet, founded the brandy firm that bears his name. Monnet, like his brother Gaston, was trained for the family business; at the local *lycée* he took only the first part of his *bachot*, and never went on to a university. Instead, he set out at eighteen as a brandy salesman in the Canadian backwoods, along the Vancouver railroad in boom towns like Calgary, Moose Jaw, and Medicine Hat. It was there that he learned his clipped, North American English; he learned also to appreciate transatlantic informality. One day in Calgary, when he was looking for a horse and buggy to hire, he asked a stranger for the nearest livery stable. "Can you ride?" asked the stranger. "Then take my horse. When you're through just hitch it up here." This, said Monnet later, was his first lesson in the international pooling of resources.[14]

He began to apply it early in World War I. Returning to France via London, he discovered from friends in the City that Britain and France, although allies, were bidding against each other for scarce raw materials. Back in Cognac, he persuaded an influential local lawyer to introduce him to the Prime Minister of France, René Viviani. With all the assurance of his twenty-six years, Monnet urged that the Allies should set up a joint procurements system. Viviani agreed, and asked Monnet to help with the job. Already refused for military service on account of kidney trouble, he leaped at the offer, and became an official of the French Board of Trade. After two years of persistent argument, France and Britain at last set up a joint supply commission, on which Monnet himself served. By the end of the war he had made his reputation. In 1919, at the age of thirty-one, he was asked by the two Governments to become Deputy Secretary-General of the newborn League of Nations.[15]

At the League, he learned a further lesson. Raymond Poincaré, the new French Premier, believed that the only way to prevent a further war was to keep the defeated enemy under Allied domination. Monnet disagreed fundamentally, and said so. Only as equals, he thought, could nations learn to trust one another; there must be rules to guarantee their equality and institutions to see that the rules were kept. The League, as he saw it, was only a "switchboard" keeping nations in touch with each other; and it was hampered by the unanimity rule. In 1923, Monnet resigned and went back to the family business, which was now in low water. Within two years its affairs were once more prospering.[16]

From then on, Monnet pursued a very varied international career. For a while, he worked as an associate of the Blair Foreign Corporation in New York; on its behalf he went to Warsaw to advise the Polish Government and to Bucharest to help in the stabilization of the Rumanian currency. He also became Vice-President of the Transamerica holding company, which owned the Bank of America. He made a fortune on Wall Street, then lost it in the 1929 crash. Next, the Swedish Government asked him to wind up the Kreuger match empire. It was at this time that he met and eloped with Silvia de Bondini, the painter wife of an Italian diplomat; later, he married her after a lightning Moscow divorce. In 1933 and 1934 he spent two years in China as a financial adviser, helping to reorganize the railways: to recruit nervous capital, he set up the China Finance Development Corporation, in which London, New York, Paris, and Shanghai financiers were willing to stake money together and on an equal footing—whereas none would have done so on a majority basis or, less still, alone.[17]

In March, October, and December 1938, and again in January 1939, Monnet went to the United States on confidential missions for the French Government, which was anxious to buy American military aircraft. When World War II broke out on September 3, 1939, he remembered his World War I experience; on that same day he sent a note to Premier Edouard Daladier proposing that France and Britain pool their supplies from the outset. Within three months, his efforts succeeded; and he himself was appointed Chairman of the Franco-British Committee for Economic Co-ordination. As R. A. Butler, then Under-Secretary of State for Foreign Affairs, told the House of Commons on November 30, 1939, Monnet had become "the first inter-Allied official." In this role, he ironed out many anomalies: at one point, French agents were found to have been bidding for Australian tallow against the British Ministry of Food, which itself had been bidding on behalf of France. At the same time, he went on asking questions. How many aircraft did the Allies need to match the Luftwaffe? How many could they build? How many should they buy in the United States? The questions were simple; but nobody knew the answers. So Monnet set out to supply them, and on that basis to have planes and engines ordered in the United States. This was the key that unlocked the American arsenal—and it had one unexpected result. At 3:00 A.M. on June 17, 1940, just before the fall of France, her representative in Washington signed over to Britain, for the token sum of one dollar, the whole French share of these American contracts. They proved invaluable later in helping Britain to withstand the Blitz.[18]

Meanwhile, during the anxious days of May and early June, 1940, Monnet had proposed to Winston Churchill and General de Gaulle an even more radical form of international pooling—political union and joint citizenship between Britain and France. It came within a few hours of succeeding; and even when failure seemed inevitable, Monnet made a last-minute effort to persuade France to agree. Borrowing a British aircraft, he flew to Bordeaux, where the Government had taken refuge. His plane—the Sunderland flyingboat *Claire*—was big enough to carry the French Cabinet to London or North Africa; but for fear of being branded as cowardly *émigrés* or even dupes of Churchill, its members refused to leave under a British flag. Looking back three years later, in Washington, Monnet said: "Think what it would have meant if the political offer of union had succeeded. There would have been no way of going back on it. The course of the war, the course of the world, might have been very different. We should have had the beginnings of a union of Europe."[19]

As it was, Monnet returned to London with his flyingboat full of refugee families. He might at this point have joined General de Gaulle's Free French movement; but since Britain and America were now the essential bastions of the Allied cause, he preferred to work directly with them. With a French passport personally endorsed by Churchill, Monnet went to Washington as a British civil servant, a member of the British Supply Council. There, he played an important part in devising Roosevelt's "Victory Program" of aircraft production, and was credited with the invention both of the slogan "the arsenal of democracy" and of Lend-Lease. After Washington, he went to Algiers. There, he helped to reconcile General de Gaulle and General Giraud; he also became a member of the French National Liberation Committee. It was at this time that he first proposed to de Gaulle the project with which many Frenchmen still most closely associate him—the "Monnet Plan" for the postwar modernization of France. Hitherto, much of his work had been international, trying to persuade governments to see their problems as common problems, to pool their resources and tackle together tasks that none of them could accomplish alone. Now, he hoped to apply the same principle on a national scale, bringing employers, workpeople, and government officials together round the table to work out joint targets for French recovery and growth.[20]

In 1946, appointed as France's first Commissaire au Plan, with modest offices in the rue Martignac administratively attached to the Prime Minister and to no one else, Monnet became for the first time rather more than a gray eminence. His small group of colleagues and assistants—men like the engineer Etienne Hirsch, the economist Pierre Uri, the rising civil servant Paul Delouvrier—formed a close-knit and mutually complementary team: many of them were to follow him in later European ventures; almost all became personal friends. All were more "brilliant" than Monnet: but it was he who left the most lasting impression—and it was he who got things done. As a young man, he had looked unmistakably Latin, a short, rather stocky, well-dressed figure with a dark, slightly saturnine mustache. Now, at fifty-eight, the mustache was grayer; his face was ruddy, and his watchful, hooded eyes twinkled readily under eyebrows that seemed always to be impassively raised. Chiang Kai-shek had once said that there was something Chinese about Monnet; and he had certainly learned something from his days in China. A friend who lived there had advised him: "Stop trying to understand these people—you never will. Just stick to what you want, and make your actions conform with your words." Monnet did. He was also, still, something of a French peasant: wherever he worked, he preferred to live in the country. Outside Paris, he had bought an L-shaped converted farmhouse with a thatched roof; but the property was marred by an intrusive adjoining field. Monnet's predecessor had tried to buy the field from its peasant owner—but in vain. Monnet was rebuffed also, until he bought a better field elsewhere in the village, and offered it in exchange. His offer was instantly accepted: like had dealt with like.[21]

With it all, Monnet still had something of the international entrepreneur, and a merchant banker's feel and flair. As an orator, he was undistinguished: in large gatherings his small dry voice was lost. But in private he could be immensely persuasive, arguing, cajoling, asking Socratically simple questions, breaking now and then into a sharp staccato chuckle, tirelessly repeating his homely maxims. Clear as water, they had the deceptive strength of pure spirit: "there is no choice" —"we must go on"—"these are common problems"—"conditions must be changed." "Must"—"indispensable"—"rapid"— "concrete"—"immediate": his whole vocabulary breathed action. Action was preceded, invariably, by painstaking inquiry, long hesitation, and discussion with friends and colleagues; but it was marked by a willingness to seize every opportunity as soon as it came. Persistent, optimistic, and restless, Monnet was unlikely to be content for long to deal only, and in isolation, with the affairs of France.[22]

Already in the later years of World War II he had concluded that the United Nations, like the League of Nations, would also be only a "switchboard": it would involve no real abandonment of sovereignty. "This," he said, "is not going to happen on a world scale . . . and let us not blind ourselves this time, by the picture of impressive machinery, to the really tough things that need to be done if we are to have peace." The journalist who reported these reflections added: "What are those tough things? For Monnet, as for most Europeans, the toughest questions of all are Germany and European unity. Monnet would like to see . . . the great Rhine coal and iron fields run by a European authority for the benefit of all participating nations . . . But this in turn implies a Europe far more unified than before the war. Here he would like to see not merely a 'switchboard' association, but a true yielding of sovereignty by European nations to some kind of central union—a union that could cut down tariffs, create a great internal European market and prevent that race of nationalism 'which is the curse of the modern world.' But where to begin? And how far to go? And could England be brought in?"[23]

Monnet went on developing these themes in the years immediately after the war. In private notes and in letters to friends in the French cabinet, he pointed out that Europe could not rely indefinitely on Marshall Aid, nor remain forever dependent on America: She must learn to stand on her own feet. This required a form of collective effort in which Germany's contribution could safely be included. To expect it of OEEC, with sixteen separate and sovereign nations, was an illusion. Only a federation, and one that included Great Britain, could ensure Europe's rapid recovery and, in the long run, prevent war. It was an ambitious project; but a start might be made, Monnet thought, if Britain and France could be induced to act together. Why not begin by applying in the economic field the idea of cross-Channel union that he had proposed in 1940?[24]

Already in January 1947, when the British and French Governments were preparing the Dunkirk Treaty that they eventually signed on March 4, they had set up a permanent joint Economic Committee "to study . . . the respective reconstruction and modernization plans with a view to preventing their conflicting with each other." It had held its first meeting in Paris on January 18–20, 1947, under the chairmanship of Hervé Alphand from the French Foreign Office, with Sir Edmund Hall-Patch at the head of the British delegation. A few days later, Monnet visited London to talk with British officials; and at the end of April 1947, he was invited by Sir Stafford Cripps, the Chancellor of the Exchequer, to a further series of meetings. Afterward he told Agence France Presse: "I did not come to London to discuss ways of harmonizing the French and British economies, because I think that for the moment there is only the broadest of notions [*il y a une simple vue de l'esprit*], given present economic circumstances and the impossibility of forecasting now what the economic situation will be in the next few years. Moreover, the French Plan is a plan for the future, aiming at an effective increase of our resources, whereas Britain's Plan is so far limited to the allocation of her resources for 1947."[25]

Nevertheless, close contacts continued, and Monnet did his best to encourage them. On January 16 and 17, 1948, when the French Finance Minister René Mayer met Cripps in London, they issued a joint communiqué announcing that in addition to reviewing the events of the past year they had "examined together the problems facing them in 1948 with a view to co-ordinating as far as possible their respective policies." These prospects were dimmed, however, by disagreement over the French devaluation on Saturday, January 24; and although talks were held at intervals on specific points of detail, more ambitious hopes lay dormant until early in 1949. Then, on February 20, Sir Stafford Cripps visited Paris for discussions with Maurice Petsche, who was now French Finance Minister. Monnet seized the opportunity. On his suggestion, Petsche proposed that the French and British planning authorities jointly examine their respective economic plans. With Petsche's blessing, Monnet went to London to explain his proposal; and by March 3, when Cripps was again in Paris, it had been accepted. Monnet then invited Sir Edwin Plowden, head of the U. K. Economic Planning Staff, to come out to Houjarray, the small village forty minutes' drive to the southwest of Paris where he had his country home.[26]

Plowden arrived on the morning of Thursday, April 21, 1949, accompanied by his deputy and by Robert Hall, the Head of the Economic Section of the Cabinet Office. With Monnet were Etienne Hirsch, already familiar in wartime

London as "le Commandant Bernard," and the mercurial Pierre Uri. The advantage of the meeting, as Monnet saw it, was its total informality. Gathered in the long, low, stone-floored drawing-room with its family *bibelots*, its paintings by Madame Monnet, and its tall french windows overlooking the fields toward Rambouillet, it was possible to discuss ideas frankly rather than negotiate from prearranged positions. On this friendly basis, Monnet and Plowden reviewed and compared the economic situation in Britain and France, and the plans and problems both governments had before them. Then Monnet turned to the crucial question. What would happen if the French and the British, instead of planning separately, were to draw up a joint plan? How far, in particular, would it be possible to pool the resources of the two countries for the benefit of both?[27]

To do so, Monnet knew, would mean economic as well as psychological change. Trade in Europe was still subject to heavy national controls and restrictions; and while these could hardly yet be dismantled entirely, owing to the dollar shortage, those between Britain and France would have to go if the two were to combine their resources. If they did, they might establish between them an economic union which other European countries could later join.

At this point, at first almost imperceptibly, a basic mis-understanding began to take shape. Perhaps Monnet was at fault in not making his project clear enough; perhaps his visitors found it hard to grasp its radical implications. Whatever the explanation, while Monnet was proposing a general objective and a principle, the British characteristically began discussing details and facts. Britain lacked food; France lacked coal. Could each not help to supply the other's needs?

The idea was reasonable and practical. It might well have formed part of an overall joint plan for the two economies, such as Monnet had in mind. He agreed with Plowden that they should exchange information, and study what could be done. The results, however, were disappointing. Without joint action on economic policy generally, trade by itself ran into difficulties. On September 18, 1949, Britain devalued the pound by 30.5 per cent; and although France followed suit on September 19, the franc's parity dropped by only 22.4

per cent. The resultant discrepancy between the two currencies inflated the price of French exports to Britain, while reducing that of British exports to France. Both sides felt aggrieved, although for formally opposite reasons; the episode not only hampered the proposed exchange of food and fuel, but also weakened mutual trust. By the end of the year it had become obvious, as Etienne Hirsch wrote later, that "the British Government was not interested in drawing up a joint plan for France and Britain, but only in a more extensive exchange of goods along traditional lines."[28]

World events, meanwhile, were giving a new urgency to the need to unify Europe. On September 23, 1949, President Truman revealed that American experts had detected a nuclear explosion in the USSR; and next day the Soviet Union publicly acknowledged that it now possessed the atomic bomb. The "cold war" had turned into the "balance of terror." Dismayed, resentful, and increasingly nervous, both East and West appeared to be growing resigned to the prospect of real war: instead of preparing for a more hopeful future, both seemed to be hypnotized by precautions against disaster. Central to their fears was divided Germany. For the time being, German reunification was impossible, since there was no prospect of agreement between the Soviet Union and the United States; in October 1949 the four occupying powers had once more failed to agree. In this situation, Germans themselves were increasingly restive: in the West, shortly after the August 1949 elections, Chancellor Adenauer had startled a press conference by announcing that the Federal Republic hoped to join not only the Council of Europe but also the Atlantic Alliance. Under the three-power Occupation Statute, which came into force on September 21, 1949, a number of central questions—including armaments, reparations, decartelization, and foreign policy—were reserved to the Allied High Commissioners; but it was becoming clear that this could hardly last. Already there had been disagreements among the Americans, the French, and the British on the International Ruhr Authority: the Americans found it too stringent, the French too lax; the British tried to placate all parties. By the spring of 1950, moreover, the Americans were pressing hard for a greater German contribution not only to Western Europe's economy, but also to her defense. In mid-April, U. S. Secretary of State Dean Acheson proposed to Britain and France a conference of experts in London to prepare a meeting of ministers to be held there on May 12 and 13. No one knew what might be its outcome; but many feared that the prospect of a rearmed independent West Germany would alarm and provoke the Russians no less than it disquieted the French.[29]

In this uncertain, uneasy, and rapidly shifting situation Monnet saw both danger and opportunity. The danger was a further stiffening of "cold war" attitudes; the opportunity might be to sublimate the German question, as it were, in the beginnings of a united Europe. A small step in this direction could lead to others, at length transforming the whole context of relations between East and West. What was essential was to change the course of events—to stop the drift. Words and plans alone would be ineffective without "real, immediate, and dramatic action" to replace fear by hope. As usual, Monnet put his thoughts on paper, for himself and for the French Government. In late April 1950, he sent a memorandum to the Prime Minister, Georges Bidault. Then he waited, to give Bidault time to react.[30]

What Monnet urged was "action on one limited but decisive point"—that the French Government propose "to place the whole of Franco-German coal and steel production under a common High Authority, in an organization open to the participation of the other countries of Europe." By this means, five years after the end of the war, Germany would again be treated as an equal; the pooling of basic resources would make war between France and Germany "not only unthinkable but materially impossible"; the problem of controlling the Ruhr would be dissolved into that of supervising international heavy industry; and the fusion of interests thus achieved could lead to the establishment of "an economic community," leading toward "the European federation which is indispensable to the maintenance of peace." Gradually, one step would lead to another, changing the whole context of the question. At each successive stage, problems that had

previously seemed forever insoluble would be seen to have
solutions. The essential thing was to start.[31]

This project, like most of Monnet's proposals, was the result of long reflection, debate, and repeated collective drafting; the small circle of those who helped to write it included
Hirsch, Uri and Paul Reuter, Professor of Law at Aix and
legal adviser to the French Foreign Office. Nor, contrary to
common belief, was it entirely novel—even when Monnet
himself had broached it in wartime Washington. None other
than Leon Trotsky had once suggested that "the question
of the Ruhr, that is of European fuel and metal . . . may
perfectly well be settled in the framework of a United
States of Europe." And if Monnet had not read Trotsky, he
certainly knew of the rather similar ideas put forward by
Konrad Adenauer. As long ago as the '20s, the future German
Chancellor had said that "a lasting peace between France
and Germany can only be attained through the establishment
of a community of economic interests between the two countries," and he had drawn up a plan for the integration of
German, French, and Belgian industry. On New Year's Day,
1949, the Minister-President of North-Rhine/Westphalia,
Karl Arnold, had likewise proposed, with CDU backing, "an
association with an international legal status" into which "Germany would bring the Ruhr, France the ore resources of
Lorraine, both of them the Saar, Belgium, and Luxembourg
their heavy industries." Adenauer had revived this notion in
January 1950 in a conversation with John J. McCloy, the
American High Commissioner. Unhappy about the controls
still unilaterally imposed on the Ruhr, and about France's
intention to continue running the mines in the Saar, he suggested that the produce of both areas be internationalized.
On March 7, four days after the Franco-Saar Conventions
which satisfied French demands at the expense of annoying
Germany, Adenauer went further. In an interview with Kingsbury Smith of the American International News Service he
proposed a political union between Germany and France,
to be open also to Britain, Italy, and the three Benelux countries; and he repeated the idea in further interviews and
speeches on March 23, April 2, and April 18.[32]

The response, however, had proved disappointing. General

de Gaulle, then in opposition and President of the Rassemble-
ment du Peuple Français, had certainly hailed the proposal
in a press conference on March 16. "For thirty years," he declared, "I have followed with interest and appreciation the
words and deeds of Konrad Adenauer. I see in what this
good German says a kind of echo of the appeal of Europe."
But the French Government, perhaps piqued by the fact
that Adenauer's suggestions seemed chiefly to be made to
Americans, had merely declared its willingness to listen to
any "concrete proposals."[33]

What was required was action; and this was what Monnet
proposed. If his project itself was not new or wholly original,
his sense of timing, persuasiveness, and persistence were all
his own. Now, they were certainly needed. Days passed, and
no news came from Bidault. Monnet decided to try another
tack. One of his close associates was Bernard Clappier, at
that time Directeur de cabinet to Robert Schuman, the
French Foreign Minister. Schuman, a quiet, shrewd, stooping,
rather bookish bachelor two years older than Monnet, came
from Lorraine, on the disputed Eastern frontier; he had studied in Germany, and still spoke German fluently; his personal
experience, his firm religious faith, and his present responsibilities, all made him likely to be sympathetic to a practical
proposal for reconciling Germany and France. Monnet invited Clappier to lunch, and showed him the memorandum
to Bidault. Clappier promised to take it to the minister, with
a covering note in Monnet's own hand.[34]

Now once again Monnet waited. Schuman had taken the
memorandum with him over the weekend of April 29–30 to
his rather austere country house—not unlike a very large cottage—at Scy-Chazelles, near Metz. There, in the peace of
his study, he read it and reflected. That Sunday, April 30,
1950, he made up his mind. Next day, back in Paris, he
telephoned Monnet. "I accept," he said. "For me, it's decided."[35]

Throughout that week, in consultation with Schuman, Monnet and his colleagues went on putting the finishing touches
to the draft text. They also sent a further copy to Bidault,
but still he gave no answer; afterward, the document was
found lying in a drawer in his assistant's office. Schuman,

meanwhile, wrote a brief introduction, and discussed the plan with other "Europeans" in the Cabinet, including René Mayer, Minister of Justice, and René Pleven, Minister of Defense. Then, on the morning of Tuesday, May 9, 1950, he presented it formally to the Cabinet, which authorized him to proceed. Rather to his colleagues' surprise, he did so rapidly and publicly. That same afternoon, in the gilded Salon de l'Horloge of the French Foreign Office building on the Quai d'Orsay, he read to the press what had now become "the Schuman Declaration," proposing in effect the European Coal and Steel Community (ECSC), forerunner of the Common Market.[36]

As one of Monnet's staff confessed later, the launching of the Schuman Plan had been something like a conspiracy. Only a few people had been involved in it; and on the evening before Schuman's press conference, most of the preliminary drafts were burned. Stealth and surprise, in Monnet's view, were essential to the project; but it was equally important to ensure its instant acceptance by Germany and support by the United States. To secure Adenauer's agreement, Schuman had sent to him in Bonn, with the utmost secrecy, a private envoy who was also a close personal associate. Not until the morning of May 9, while the French Cabinet was already in session, did he telephone Schuman to report that his mission was accomplished. Monnet, meanwhile, had kept in close touch with his friends in the American Embassy—David Bruce, the Ambassador, and William Tomlinson, a brilliant young U. S. Treasury official, later to meet a sadly early death.[37]

The British Government, however, had not been let into the secret. Only when the French Cabinet had approved Schuman's proposal was an urgent message sent to London via the French Ambassador, René Massigli, announcing the statement to be made to the press later that day. This caused both embarrassment and annoyance—the former to U. S. Secretary of State Dean Acheson, the latter to Ernest Bevin, the British Foreign Secretary. By a pure coincidence, Acheson had chosen to stop off in Paris on Sunday, May 7, 1950, on his way to the London Foreign Ministers' Conference due to begin on the following Thursday, May 11. Both Schuman and Monnet seized the chance to explain their project to him; and before the French Cabinet had approved it on the morning of May 9, he sent an "eyes only" telegram to President Truman urging that he be authorized to express United States support. Then he left for London, where he was lunching with Ernest Bevin. When he arrived, the news had still not reached Whitehall, so he said nothing to his host. During lunch at Bevin's house, a message arrived from Massigli asking for an appointment with the Foreign Secretary that afternoon. As Acheson realized, it was to announce the Schuman Plan; but he still felt bound to keep the secret. At 4:00 P.M., when they met again, this time at the Foreign Office, Bevin was furious at having been kept in the dark. What was more, in Acheson's words, "he bristled with hostility to Schuman's whole idea."[38]

It can be argued that France's—and Monnet's—tactics were partly to blame. Conceivably, had Bevin been consulted earlier, it might have been just possible to launch the Schuman Plan with Britain as a full participant, laying the foundations of the future Common Market on a broader basis than that of its six founder-members. There can be no doubt that the abruptness of the French announcement irritated Whitehall. But fundamental decisions of foreign policy grow from deeper roots than passing irritation; and in the words of Kenneth Younger, who at that time was Minister of State at the Foreign Office, "the pique was slight and faded quickly." More important was the suspicion in London that a proposal made so suddenly could hardly be serious. More important still was what Younger himself described as "a nation-wide attitude which could not be doubted"—a deep British unwillingness to limit national sovereignty by pooling it with that of other countries, especially in continental Europe, at a time when the Atlantic Alliance naturally seemed paramount and the Commonwealth still seemed to preclude any move by Britain toward a European union. Many times in the recent past this attitude had shown itself; and in the light of experience Monnet feared that if Britain had the chance she would automatically, almost innocently, transform the project into something quite different—a traditional, unambitious system of co-operation between independent sovereign states. Robert Schuman was especially skeptical: answering questions at his May 9 press conference, he explained that Britain, like Italy and the Benelux countries, would be invited to join in the project, but that he realized the difficulties, both technical and psychological. He had no idea, he said, what the British reply would be.[39]

The first comments in the British press, on Wednesday, May 10, 1950, were very largely favorable. Only the *Daily Express* and the *Daily Worker* dissented—a conjunction of Right-wing and extreme-Left opposition that later grew familiar. But except for *The Economist*, most papers treated the Schuman Plan as economic rather than potentially political, and few called for Britain to take part. Speaking for many, the weekly *Statist* urged that she "wait and see." This seemed broadly to be the Government's policy: on May 11, in the House of Commons, Prime Minister Clement Attlee declared that:

. . . the proposals . . . have far-reaching implications for the future economic structure of participating countries; and this aspect will require very careful study by His Majesty's Government and the other Governments concerned. His Majesty's Government will approach the problem in a sympathetic spirit and desire to make it clear at the outset that they welcome this French initiative to end the age-long feud with Germany and so bring unity and peace to Europe.

Next day, the London *Times* published a collective letter urging acceptance of Schuman's proposal. Its signatories were members of the British Committee of the European League for Economic Co-operation (ELEC), which had been founded in 1946 by Paul Van Zeeland, former Prime Minister of Belgium: they included Julian Amery, Edward Beddington-Behrens, David Eccles, Bob Edwards, Harry Hynd, Lord Layton, Harold Macmillan and Peter Thorneycroft.[40]

There was some reason for optimism, therefore, when Monnet arrived in London on Sunday, May 14, 1950, to talk over the project with Plowden and other British officials. Schuman, meanwhile, had been discussing it with Bevin in the intervals of the three-power Foreign Ministers' Conference. In all these conversations, the British asked a number of technical questions. What would be the position of cartels? Might the Schuman Plan lower the standard of living? How would it affect French planning? Would it affect the ownership of industry? What form would the proposed High Authority take?[41]

To the British, such questions seemed natural: they were astonished at how little concrete detail the Schuman Plan then contained. To Monnet, on the other hand, questions of detail were secondary. He made it clear, in the words of a U. K. Minute, "that the French Government felt it desirable that the acceptance by other Governments of the principles set out in the French communiqué of May 9 should precede any working out of the practical application of their proposals."[42]

Superficially, this looked like continental dogmatism *versus* British pragmatism; but in fact it was an insistence that immediate practical problems should not be allowed to compromise the Schuman Plan's aims and structure. For Monnet, the essential objective was to establish, in a limited field, European rules and institutions binding equally all the participating governments. In the past, Great Britain had resisted all such "supranationality"; now, it was all the more important to commit her to the common objective lest in discussing the means she lead others—including Germany—to desert the ends. And if she refused that commitment? There had been a time when British refusal might have blocked such projects; but by now that time was past. On Monday, May 15, 1950, at an Anglo-French press luncheon, Schuman had declared that France would "pursue the project with only one other country if necessary." Sir Stafford Cripps now put the same question to Monnet. He answered that Cripps knew his feelings toward Britain and could not doubt them, but that he himself was convinced that, always a realist, she would adjust to the facts once she saw that the plan was a success. Despite suggestions to the contrary, there can be no doubt that Monnet was sincere.[43]

Monnet left London on Friday, May 19. On the following Tuesday, May 23, 1950, he went with Clappier to Bonn. His first call was on the Allied Control Commission, where he explained the Schuman proposals and announced his intention of going to see Chancellor Adenauer with a view to opening negotiations. The Commission was broadly in agreement; but some of its members were anxious that they should be represented at the talks. This Monnet refused. The reason, as he said afterward, was very simple: "one cannot build Europe except on absolute equality and total liberty." "There will be a negotiation," he told the Commission, "if France and Germany sit as equals round the table without supervision of any kind." Finally, the Commission relented, and that afternoon Monnet went to see Adenauer. After explaining the project, and securing the Chancellor's formal support for it, Monnet described his visit to London, and repeated the substance of what he had said to Cripps. Although the British had proved rather hesitant, they had the great virtue of being realists. Adenauer agreed that they were people who needed to be given a little time.[44]

Two days later, on Thursday, May 25, 1950, Monnet wrote a long explanatory letter to his British friends in the hope of dispelling their anxieties. But time, for Britain, was already running out. That day, the French Government sent London a Memorandum announcing that the Federal German Government had agreed to negotiate on the Schuman Plan and had accepted the terms of a draft communiqué to be published in about a week's time. This declared:

> The Governments of . . . are resolved to carry out a common action aiming at peace, European solidarity and economic and social progress by pooling their coal and steel production and by the institution of a new High Authority whose decisions will bind . . . and the countries which will adhere to it in the future.
>
> Negotiations, on the basis of the principles and essential undertakings contained in the French proposals of 9 May last, will open on a date which will be proposed shortly by the French Government, with a view to drawing up a Treaty which will be submitted for ratification to the respective Parliaments.

The draft text, the Memorandum added, had been transmitted to the Belgian, Netherlands, Luxembourg, and Italian Governments: the French Government hoped that Britain would also be able "to participate on the same conditions in these negotiations from the outset."[45]

By an unlucky coincidence, this message crossed with one from London sent on the same day. In this, Bevin rejected the whole idea of an international conference based on a prior commitment of principle: he proposed instead "direct conversations between France and Germany" in which the British would like "to participate from the outset, with the hope that, by obtaining a clearer picture of how the proposals would operate in detail, they would be able to join the scheme."[46]

When Sir Oliver Harvey, the British Ambassador in Paris, delivered this message to the French Foreign Office, it undoubtedly caused perplexity. Britain's desire to take part in the "conversations" and her hope of joining the "scheme" certainly appeared encouraging; but she made no mention of the basic principle and failed, in the words of a probably inspired comment by Agence France Presse, "to take account of a whole series of clarifications on the part of the French." For the moment, Monnet advised patience. He hoped that his own letter and the French Government's message might in the meantime modify the British stand. They did—but only to harden it. On Saturday, May 27, 1950, came a fresh Memorandum from Bevin. "His Majesty's Government," it declared:

. . . wish to reiterate their desire to participate in any discussion which takes place in the manner suggested in my message, and generally to adopt a positive attitude towards the French proposals. It should, however, be realized that if the French Government intend to insist on a commitment to pool resources and set up an authority with certain sovereign powers as a prior condition to joining in the talks, His Majesty's Government would reluctantly be unable to accept such a condition. His Majesty's Government would greatly regret such an outcome.

His Majesty's Government appreciate that it would not now be possible to confine the conversations to a purely Franco-German basis if some of the Governments which have been approached wished to participate on the same basis as the German Federal Government, and, further, that it might be necessary to consult such Governments before agreeing to participation in the discussions of other Governments on a different basis.[47]

The refusal, the tone and the suggestion seemed clear enough. Britain was now categorically rejecting the "prior condition"; she seemed to resent the speed with which France had approached the other governments; and she still hoped to join the talks "on a different basis." And yet, even so, it remained just possible that the breach now widening between Paris and London was due to a simple mistake.

From the French point of view, the "prior condition" was that those taking part in the talks should agree on what they were about. But this did not mean that every participant would thereby be committing itself, in advance, to pooling resources under the proposed High Authority: only the acceptance of the eventual treaty could pledge it to that. What was at stake was a commitment of principle, not the signature of a blank check. Were the British afraid even to try negotiating such a treaty, for fear of being drawn into entanglements which at present they shunned? Were they overscrupulously anxious to avoid raising false expectations? Or might they, after further explanation, agree to negotiate on the basis proposed by Monnet and Schuman, and find later that what they had feared was not so formidable after all?

It was a slim hope; but it seemed worth investigating. Next day, although it was a Sunday, René Massigli called on Kenneth Younger at the Foreign Office. "He asked me," Younger reported:

> . . . if he was right in thinking that, while we are not prepared to commit ourselves now to the principle of pooling resources under an international authority possessing certain sovereign powers, we are not taking up an attitude of opposition to this principle but are prepared to enter into discussions with the object of finding a practical method of applying the principle.
>
> I told him that I thought that roughly expressed the difference between us. We were certainly not proposing to go to these discussions with our minds set against the principles referred to, but equally we were not prepared to commit ourselves to the principle without a much clearer idea than we have at present about the way in which it is to be carried into effect. The Ambassador said that he had always felt sure that this was our attitude but had thought it better to get it confirmed by me before passing this interpretation to his Government.

He said he found my explanation reassuring since it seemed to him that our reservations would not in any way limit our effective participation in the discussions.

Younger himself, as he afterward recalled, "pressed hard for Britain to join the Schuman Plan Conference before finally recognizing that hardly anyone thought the conditions of participation could be accepted." Bevin's reaction to this advice, according to one story, was: "Splash about, young man, you'll learn to swim in time." But even the conversation with Massigli left ambiguities unresolved. When the Ambassador tried then and there to redraft the proposed French communiqué, "he succeeded in producing something which seemed to me to be on the whole unobjectionable," said Younger; "but I told him that if there was to be a single communiqué it would have to explain clearly the attitude of the different Governments." The gap, therefore, remained.[48]

Prompted by Monnet, the French Government now made one last attempt to close it. On Tuesday, May 30, Schuman handed to Sir Oliver Harvey an 830-word exegesis of his proposals, pointing out that previous British Notes seemed to have misunderstood the commitment of principle stipulated by the French. This was no mere debating point: at that moment, it was still conceivable that semantics, not policy, divided the two governments. For this reason, the new French Memorandum took great pains to be clear:

The special position in these negotiations which the British Government wishes to preserve is justified in their Memorandum by the intention, said to be held by the French Government, of asking as a prior condition for full participation in the discussions, for an undertaking to pool coal and steel resources, and to set up an authority with certain sovereign powers.

As their representatives have informed the British representatives orally, the French Government wish particularly to confirm once more that these are not their intentions. As has already been made clear in the French Memorandum of 9th May, there will be no commitment except by the signature of a treaty between the States concerned and its parliamentary ratification.

In fact the aim which the French Government proposes is quite different. Knowing the practical difficulties which the discussion will have to surmount, it seems essential that they should constantly be guided by common principles. Only if the negotiations are clearly directed by agreement between participating Governments on the fundamental objectives to be reached, will it be possible to work out quickly the ways and means and the supplementary arrangements necessary for giving effect to M. Schuman's plan of 9 May. That is the meaning which should be given to the word 'undertaking' [engagement] in the second paragraph of the draft communiqué. . . .

To carry out its task, the [High] Authority will act—within the limits of its mandate and subject to possible appeal by Governments —by virtue of a statute which will have been considered by sovereign states and ratified by Parliaments. One of the objects of the negotiations will be to lay down precisely by treaty the conditions under which the Authority shall act, the nature of its powers, and the machinery for appeal. But in order that its work may serve to develop a European community, it is essential that such an Authority should be independent both of Governments and of individual interests. This partial fusion of sovereignty is the contribution which the French proposal makes to the solution of European problems. Public opinion has recognized its importance and its novelty.

The French Government consider that the above explanations will clear up any misunderstanding about the scope of the proposed basis for negotiation. They do not think that there can be any difference of view between them and the British Government on the objectives put forward. They hope now that the British Government will consider it possible to take part in the projected negotiations on the same basis as the other Governments.[49]

All day on Wednesday, May 31, 1950, Monnet and Schuman waited to hear how the British Government had reacted to these careful explanations. While they waited, the Dutch Government sent to the French Foreign Office a *note verbale* which cast further light on the point at issue. Basically, it accepted the Schuman Plan and the French draft communiqué as a basis for negotiation. "Nevertheless," it added, "since this text implies the acceptance of certain principles which form the basis of the French Government's Memorandum, the Dutch Government is obliged to reserve the right to retract, during the course of the negotiations, its acceptance of these principles if their application were to prove impossible in practice."[50]

Superficially, this appeared to confirm and justify British reservations. In reality it did the reverse. On the one hand, it made clear that the Netherlands initially accepted the Schu-

man Plan's basic principles; on the other, it merely spelled
out more explicitly the normal right of withdrawal which, as
the latest French Note had made plain, was available to any
participant in the talks. Would Britain, now, take a similar
line?

At ten that evening, Wednesday, May 31, 1950, the answer came. It was as if the British Government had not received, or not understood, the French Note.

> . . . It remains the view of His Majesty's Government that to
> subscribe to the terms of the draft communiqué enclosed in the
> French Government's Memorandum of 25 May would involve enter-
> ing into an advance commitment to pool coal and steel resources and
> to set up an authority, with certain supreme powers, before there
> had been full opportunity of considering how these important and
> far-reaching proposals would work in practice. His Majesty's Gov-
> ernment are most anxious that these proposals should be discussed
> and pursued but they feel unable to associate themselves with a
> communiqué which appears to take decisions prior to, rather than
> as a result of, intergovernmental discussions.

The Government therefore proposed an addition to the draft
communiqué, announcing that:

> . . . the Government of the United Kingdom will participate in
> the proposed conversation in a constructive spirit and in the hope
> that, as a result of the discussions, there will emerge a scheme which
> they will be able to join. But they cannot at this stage enter into
> more precise commitment.[51]

Monnet's disappointment on reading these words can easily
be imagined. Not only had the forthcoming negotiations become a mere "conversation" in the British draft, but Britain's
refusal to accept their basis was now to be stated in a public
communiqué as well as in intergovernmental memoranda.
What Britain was asking, once again, was to take part in
the negotiations, but "on a different basis" from that accepted
by others. This implicitly denied the principle of equality
underlying the Schuman Plan; it also had manifest dangers.
"It is obvious," wrote Monnet in a confidential note to the
French Government:

> that if Great Britain takes part in the negotiations in such a way
> that she is able not to propose but to dispute the principles them-

selves, other countries, and particularly Germany, will do the same.
. . . To accept British participation on these terms is therefore to
resign oneself in advance to the replacement of the French proposal
by a conception which would be only a travesty of it, and from
which all the essential notions would have disappeared.[52]

Even so, Monnet persuaded the French Government to
make one more effort. On Thursday, June 1, 1950, it proposed to Britain a final revised version of the draft communiqué. Now, instead of stating that "governments . . . *are resolved* to carry out a common action . . . *by* pooling their
coal and steel production and by the institution of a new
High Authority," the draft declared that "Governments . . .
in their determination to pursue a common action . . . *have
assigned to themselves as their immediate objective*" the
pooling of coal and steel and the establishment of the High
Authority. An objective was less binding than a "resolve,"
and better expressed the distinction made in the French
Note of May 30. By this time, however, Monnet suspected
that this verbal change too might well be lost on its British
readers. At all events, the French Government was now explicitly prepared to proceed if necessary without waiting for
Britain. For the first time, it now set a firm time-limit to further discussion: when Schuman handed the new Note to Sir
Oliver Harvey, he asked that Britain's answer should reach
Paris by 8:00 P.M. on the following day, Friday, June 2,
1950.[53]

When intergovernmental talks are visibly leading nowhere,
there comes a point at which each party begins to think less
about the problems at issue than about its own public image.
This stage may well have been reached earlier in London
than in Paris. Its beginnings can be sensed in the stiff British
Memorandum of May 31, and are also discernible in the
French Note of June 1, with its virtual ultimatum. By Friday, June 2, 1950, there was little doubt left: both governments were now seeking to justify themselves rather than
to convince each other.

That day, the British Government met the French deadline with a counterproposition—"a meeting of Ministers of
the countries interested at which the question of the most
effective and expeditious method of discussing the problems

at issue could be examined and settled." In retrospect, it is hard to take the suggestion seriously. What it implied was just such a discussion as Monnet and Schuman feared—calling into question the basic principles which other countries had by this time accepted. First orally, in talks with Sir Oliver Harvey that same Friday, June 2, 1950, then in a written Note on the following morning, the French Government restated its position. The meeting proposed by the British, it argued, "would have the effect of delaying the opening of the negotiations without offering any real possibility of reconciling divergent points." With that, there was nothing to do but agree to disagree.[54]

That same day, Saturday, June 3, 1950, three separate communiqués were issued. The first was from the governments of France, Germany, Italy, and the three Benelux countries, announcing their intention to negotiate on the basis of Robert Schuman's proposals. The second, from the British Government, repeated its refusal to accept that basis for negotiation, recalled its latest counterproposition, and announced that it was preparing its own "proposals inspired by the French initiative"—although these, as it turned out, were never to be officially published. The third communiqué came from the French Government: it promised to keep in touch with the British Government, both to inform it of the progress made and to "take into account to the greatest possible extent" Britain's point of view, so that Britain might "have the chance to join or associate itself with the common effort at the time when it judged this to be possible."[55]

Appearances had been saved; but feelings were undoubtedly ruffled. At one point during the last tense hours of discussion, the British Embassy in Paris had produced a draft communiqué which spoke scornfully of "international organizations set up with fanfares of trumpets." Accident, too, had contributed to the difficulties. The weekend of May 28 had been Whitsun; Parliament was in recess; many ministers were out of London; Attlee and Cripps were on holiday—in France; Bevin was ill; and the Deputy Prime Minister was Herbert Morrison, no outstanding expert on foreign affairs. Had circumstances been different, Britain might perhaps have joined

in the Schuman negotiations on the basis proposed by France.
But had she done so, it is hard to believe that she would have
stayed to the end—unless the negotiations had failed in their
essential object of setting up rules and institutions which, at
that time, Britain found too much to accept. Monnet's and
Schuman's insistence on the commitment of principle was a
gamble; but it would have been an even greater gamble to
accept Great Britain's proposals, since in that case the foundations of the European Community might never have been
laid at all.

As it was, these few weeks in the spring of 1950 witnessed
momentous decisions, some taken by default. Significantly,
the first of the three communiqués issued on June 3, 1950,
when subsequently published in a British White Paper, bore
the heading "Six-Power communiqué." It was the first official
appearance of "the Six"—those six continental countries that
were later to form the Common Market. Europe was on the
point of being built. For the first time since World War II,
an important European initiative was being taken without
Britain. Her new isolation was to last for another twenty
years.

THE ECHTERNACH DANCE

All other Errors but disturb a State,
But Innovation is the Blow of Fate.
John Dryden[1]

It is in the nature of progress to appear much greater
than it really is. *Johann Nestroy*[2]

Politics is the slow public application of reason to the
governing of mass emotion. *Theodore H. White*[3]

One of the attractions of the Grand Duchy of Luxembourg
—apart from its tiny size (1,000 square miles and 350,000
round inhabitants), its forests and castles and its *truite au
bleu*—is an annual procession held at Echternach near the
eastern corner of the country. Here, on Whit Tuesday, pil-
grims gather with brass bands playing to make their way to
the tomb of St. Willibrord. Their progress is halting: they
move in a dance rhythm, repeatedly taking five steps forward
and three steps back. It was appropriate that Luxembourg,
the home of this sixteenth-century survival, should become
the headquarters of the Schuman Plan, the first practical
move in Europe's equally fitful progress toward unity. Perhaps
it was also appropriate that St. Willibrord was British.

Six countries—Belgium, France, Germany, Italy, Luxembourg, and the Netherlands—had accepted the Schuman proposal; and on Tuesday, June 20, 1950, their delegations met
in Paris to work out its details, in the same Salon de l'Horloge
where Schuman had made the Declaration of May 9. Although the trappings were traditional, this was not in the
ordinary sense a negotiation. In the words of the French delegation's official report: "It was a joint constructive effort whose
aim was not to eliminate disagreements but to solve the

multitude of problems . . . For the first time, the participating Governments did not seek a provisional compromise between their respective interests: they took a common view of their common interests, and their representatives together sought ways of reaching the goal that they had recognized as valid for all of them." As Robert Schuman himself put it, "the six delegations were in some sense allies, pooling their knowledge and their skill."[4]

It was Jean Monnet, leader of the French delegation and chairman of the Schuman Plan Conference, who made this approach possible. Instead of presenting a merely French point of view, he did his best constantly to identify and defend the common interest. In this respect he foreshadowed the "supranational" or "extranational" role to be played later by the High Authority of the Schuman Plan and the Commission of the European Common Market. "During the nine months that it took to turn the Schuman declaration into a treaty of one hundred articles and a number of annexes," a Dutch delegate recalled:

he saw to it that neither the central objective, a European Community, nor the proposed method, delegation of powers to common institutions, got lost in the mass of details about coal, steel, scrap, transport, wages, cartels, distortions and discriminations. More than that, he never allowed the negotiations to become negotiations in the traditional sense. Apart from the basic objective and the method laid down in the Schuman declaration and accepted by each of the Six before negotiations began, he showed great flexibility. The delegations were not confronted with French positions, but were invited to discuss, to contribute, to help find common answers to common problems. Monnet never defended a merely national and therefore of necessity a partial view, but tried to define the general interest of the community the negotiations were establishing together. Some of the delegates, formed in the tug-of-war of economic negotiations of the 'Schachtian' decade, at first believed that they were simply being tricked when, during meetings, they saw the little group of Frenchmen around Monnet disagreeing among themselves just as much as with other delegations. How could one negotiate one nation's special interest in orderly fashion against another's, if the inviting delegation seemed to have no clear view of the national interests it wanted to defend? But Monnet's method was so contagious, the attempt to find solutions for common problems instead of defending simply one's own national interests was so liberating and exhilarating, that none of the chief delegates resisted this new approach for very long.[5]

The Schuman Plan Conference had been at work for less than a week when events on the far side of the globe gave new urgency to its underlying purpose. At dawn on Sunday, June 25, 1950, North Korean troops crossed the 38th parallel dividing the north from the south of the country. Next day, the United States called a meeting of the United Nations Security Council, which at once ordered a cease-fire—but in vain. The invading forces included almost all the North Korean army, which comprised four divisions and three brigades of armed police; within twenty-four hours their tanks were in the suburbs of Seoul, the Southern capital; by the following day it was encircled; by Wednesday, June 28, it was occupied. On June 26, President Truman had promised aid and supplies to South Korea, and next day he had ordered General Douglas MacArthur to give naval and air support. The Security Council meanwhile condemned North Korea for its breach of the peace, and recommended that "the members of the United Nations supply to the Republic of Korea the assistance which may be necessary to repulse armed attack and re-establish peace and international security in this area." Before long, America and her allies were engaged in a real if limited war.[6]

From Europe, this looked doubly ominous. The Security Council's resolution had been passed—no doubt could only have been passed—in the absence of the Soviet delegation. Now, the Soviet Union rejected it, protesting against its "illegality." But despite this refusal to "interfere in the affairs of other peoples," North Korea's forces were known to be using Soviet arms and equipment. Rightly or wrongly, they were also suspected of having obeyed Soviet prompting. The United States had refrained from intervening in China's Communist revolution; and on January 12, 1950, Secretary of State Dean Acheson had told the National Press Club in Washington that America's "defensive perimeter" stretched from the Aleutians off the coast of Alaska to Japan and from there to the Ryukyu Islands east of Formosa—a ring that clearly excluded Korea. This, it was thought, had encouraged the Soviet Union to engineer the invasion from the North, although in April 1950 the U. S. National Security Council had in fact revised its strategic doctrine and raised the military estimates from thirteen to thirty billion dollars so as to be able to parry any attack. Nervously uncertain of each other's intentions, the two giant powers seemed in danger of unleashing a third world war. Weak and divided, the countries of Europe could neither deter the Soviet Union nor restrain the United States. So real and widespread was the fear of war that continental housewives began hoarding sugar, rice, soap, and canned goods; in France the gold napoleon, index of the small speculator's sense of insecurity, rose from 3,140 to 3,500 francs in two days.[7]

But European uneasiness was specific as well as general. Korea resembled Germany. Formerly on the side of the wartime Axis, it had been divided in 1945 between the Soviet Union and the United States, who had agreed to exercise joint trusteeship and to help the inhabitants establish democratic institutions. For two years, from 1946 to 1948, the Russian and American authorities on the spot had failed to agree on the country's future, largely because the Soviet Union had resisted efforts to reunite it. In 1948, tension had grown to breaking-point, and each side had established in its own zone a government that claimed authority over both. Now, the Communist Government had gone to war with its rival. Could the same thing happen in Germany?

Optimists pointed to some crucial differences. The South Korean Government of Syngman Rhee was at once belligerent and weak: in the elections of May 1950 it had been shown to be widely unpopular. What was more, except for a 500-man military mission, the United States had withdrawn its troops from the South. But if South Korea was militarily ill-prepared, Western Germany was totally unarmed; without American troops, it would be defenseless. In Eastern Germany, there were 300,000 highly mechanized Soviet forces, backed by 54,000 German Bereitschaften, or armed barracks police, many of them recruited from the former Wehrmacht. In Western Germany, there were only 200,000 Allied men, poorly equipped and badly organized: the French First Army in Cologne, for example, depended as a NATO unit on the

U. S. Army Group in Heidelberg, but as a French unit took its orders from the High Command in Paris. In Western Europe as a whole, the Allies had only fourteen divisions and a thousand aircraft, compared with 175 or more Soviet divisions and 20,000 Soviet planes.[8]

Of the European countries, Britain and the Netherlands were already spending on defense a higher proportion of their national incomes than the United States. France's contribution was only slightly less. It was natural, therefore, for some Europeans to look to America for further military assistance. But America was now involved in the Korean War, and just as naturally she pressed for greater efforts from Europe. In July 1950, the five members of the Brussels Treaty agreed to increase their armaments and prolong military service; but there were obvious limits to what they could do. Britain was still policing the sizable remnants of Empire; France had much of her army in Indochina, Belgium was still committed to the Congo, and the Netherlands to West Irian; Luxembourg was sturdy but small. Europe's greatest reserve of potential military strength was the German Federal Republic; and American pressure to use it, which had already been felt earlier, now grew very rapidly. In a speech in New York on May 7, 1950, the former U. S. Military Governor in Germany, General Lucius Clay, had first openly suggested a German contribution to Europe's defense. On July 25, it was proposed by John J. McCloy, now American High Commissioner in Germany. On August 5, President Truman asked his European Allies how Europe could improve its military arrangements; and although he avoided mentioning Germany, several susceptible Frenchmen—including the new Government's Defense Minister, Jules Moch—even began to wonder whether the Pentagon might not have welcomed the Korean War as a pretext for prodding Europe, and Germany, toward rearmament. Moch had lost a son in World War II, and was understandably mistrustful; yet such suspicions showed not only the deep fear of Germany, but also the uneasiness of relations between middle-sized European countries and their powerful, distant American ally. Fear and uneasiness grew, moreover, when later in August Chancellor Adenauer—who himself opposed the restoration of a German national army—requested permission to raise two to three divisions of armed police as a counterpart to the East German Bereitschaften. On Saturday, September 9, 1950, Truman promised to send more U.S. troops; but three days later, on Tuesday, September 12, when Dean Acheson met his colleagues Ernest Bevin and Robert Schuman in Washington, he formally proposed that NATO forces should include German divisions.[9]

Schuman's reaction was frankly hostile; so, initially, was Bevin's. Acheson made it clear, however, that if there were no German defense contribution America might oppose the establishment in Europe of General Eisenhower's inter-Allied High Command. When the other members of the Alliance met a few days later, most of them gave way before American pressure; and on September 16 Bevin himself threw in his hand. France was now in what Maurice Schumann, then a leader of the Catholic MRP called later "an infernal situation": her Government was unstable, she had heavy transatlantic debts, and she was in danger of being isolated from her allies. Sooner or later, it was clear, she would have to acquiesce. As Hubert Beuve-Méry, editor of *Le Monde,* had written when the Alliance was concluded, "the Atlantic Pact contains the rearmament of Germany, like the embryo in an egg."[10]

But if there had to be German rearmament, need there be a German national army? Could German units, or even German individuals, not safely serve under an Allied command? The Americans proposed that this command should be NATO. Could it not be Europe? Why not form a European army? Why not set up, alongside the Schuman Plan's European Coal and Steel Community, a European Defense Community of which Germans—but not a German army—could form a part?

Such was the reasoning that led to the project for a European Defense Community (EDC). As a practical proposal, it was put forward by Jean Monnet; but as in the case of the Schuman Plan, the idea was not new. Konrad Adenauer had suggested it in an interview with the Cleveland *Plain Dealer* as early as the previous December; and in France it had been publicized in March 1950, in a book by General Pierre Billotte. In the first week of August, the French Socialist André Philip proposed it in the Consultative Assembly of the Council of Europe, followed on August 11 by Winston Churchill in a motion carried by eighty-five votes to five. Later, on October 8, 1950, Arthur Koestler revived the idea in an article in the New York *Times,* suggesting a kind of European Foreign Legion with multinational platoons. But once again it was Monnet—as much a man of collective action as a man of individual ideas—who put the project to the right person at the right time. Even he, moreover, had to make two attempts before he succeeded.[11]

Characteristically, Monnet's first approach to defense was from the viewpoint of pooling resources and supplies. In August 1950, he began to discuss with his friends a joint European procurements fund. As Commissaire au Plan, he was anxious for France to make the best use of scarce manpower and materials; as instigator and chairman of the Schuman Plan Conference, he saw the scope for avoiding reduplication within a European Community. By September, his thoughts had crystallized further: he now envisaged a "European" solution to the problem of rearmament. When Acheson made his proposal to rearm Germany, on September 12, 1950, Monnet grasped both the danger and the opportunity. Although slightly unwell at the time, he quickly sent a memorandum to his former assistant René Pleven, who was now French Prime Minister, and to Robert Schuman, who was negotiating in New York. What Monnet proposed was that Europe's defense should be organized collectively on the lines of the Schuman Plan for coal and steel.[12]

Schuman was all for action; but the French Government was divided, and on September 22 the delegates in New York adjourned without reaching a conclusion on the American proposal or hearing any counterproposal from France. A further meeting was fixed, however, for October 28, 1950. Then, it seemed certain, the United States would redouble its pressure. Meanwhile, the military situation itself had begun to strengthen America's hand. General MacArthur had launched an offensive on September 15 which gave U.S. troops their first major success in Korea; in Indochina, the

French army's weakness was emphasized by a serious defeat at Cao-Bang on October 8. It was harder, now, for Jules Moch to maintain his intransigence—especially since talks with General George C. Marshall had convinced him that the United States would welcome a "European" defense proposal from France.[13]

This was Monnet's second opportunity, and he seized it. In a much-redrafted memorandum to Pleven, he proposed that before meeting again with her allies on October 28, France should make a public statement refusing German rearmament on a national basis, but suggesting the formation of a European army, in a European Defense Community, in which the Germans would participate with other European nations.[14]

This time, Monnet was successful. On Tuesday, October 24, 1950, Pleven presented to the French National Assembly the project for a European Defense Community that came to be known as "the Pleven Plan." It provided for a European army, jointly equipped and financed, with national contingents incorporated at the level of the smallest practicable unit, which was then thought to be the battalion. At the same time, member States would be able to retain their national armies, and might be authorized to supplement them at time of need by withdrawing some of their "European" units. In charge of the European army would be a European Defense Minister, appointed by the member governments and responsible both to them and to a European Assembly. Policy directives would be laid down by a Council of Ministers from the respective member States.[15]

Bold as this seemed, the National Assembly approved it by 343 votes to 225. That night, Jules Moch called in his closest assistants and told them to produce, at top speed, a paper for the NATO meeting in four days' time. Working against the clock, they did so; but the result, as one of them confessed afterward, was "a disaster." As it at length turned out, he might have said the same of the EDC project itself.[16]

For the time being, all seemed hopeful. The United States welcomed the French proposal; so did a number of her European allies. On Thursday, February 15, 1951, less than four months after Pleven's speech to the National Assembly, a treaty-making conference met in Paris under the chairmanship of Hervé Alphand from the French Foreign Office; and although at first only five countries—Belgium, France, Germany, Italy, and Luxembourg—were members of it, the Netherlands joined them in the following October, making the full complement of the Schuman Plan Six. Meanwhile, on April 18, 1951, the Schuman Plan Conference itself ended with the signature of the Treaty establishing the European Coal and Steel Community (ECSC). Symbolically, the document signed was printed in French by the National Printing Office, in German ink on Dutch vellum; the parchment of the cover came from Belgium, the ribbon from Italy and the glue from Luxembourg. The text provided for a common market in coal, coke, steel, iron ore, and scrap, to be run by an independent nine-man High Authority, a Council of national Ministers, a seventy-eight-member Common Assembly chosen by and from the national Parliaments, and a supreme Court of Justice with seven judges and two advocates-general. Just over a year later, the Pleven Plan Conference produced the EDC Treaty, initialed on May 9, 1952—the second anniversary of the Schuman Declaration—and formally signed on May 27, also in the Salon de l'Horloge. Instead of a European Defense Minister, the EDC was now to have a nine-man executive Commissariat similar to the ECSC High Authority, a Council of Ministers, a Court of Justice to be shared with the ECSC and a European Assembly—that of the ECSC slightly enlarged—which was to prepare further steps toward political unity. A month later, in mid-June 1952, the last of the six national parliaments ratified the ECSC Treaty. In August, after the Six had failed to agree on a site for its headquarters, the High Authority began work in Luxembourg with Monnet as its first President; and in September, without waiting for EDC to come into force, the Council of Ministers of the ECSC asked its Common Assembly to co-opt eight additional members into an "Ad hoc Assembly" to draft the Treaty for a European Political Community. Within six months, by March 10, 1953, the draft was ready. It provided for a European Executive Council, to be known as the "Ministers of the European Community"; a Council of national Ministers; a Court of Justice; and a Parliament consisting of a Senate whose members were to be chosen by the national parliaments, and a People's Chamber directly elected by the citizens of the Community as a whole. If blueprints were buildings, Europe was built.[17]

Unfortunately, even on paper, the construction had serious flaws. Within two years, the institutions of the Political Community were intended to inherit the tasks of the ECSC and EDC; but they also had an even broader mandate—to coordinate foreign policies, prepare a general common market for all goods, and guarantee constitutional order and democratic institutions within any member country, either at its own request or on a unanimous vote of the Council. Had the Political Community come into existence, this last provision might have been tested in France in May 1968: but in all probability it would have been found wanting. The draft Treaty contained more good intentions than specific provisions: on the proposed common market, in particular, it was even less explicit than the later Rome Treaty—itself an outline treaty—establishing the European Economic Community. It was hardly surprising that when the Foreign Ministers of the Six examined it, in the summer and autumn of 1953, they felt obliged to start again from the beginning. In part, this was due to the natural conservatism of governments, in part to the waning of momentum as time passed and the "cold war" began to thaw. On Thursday, March 5, 1953, just five days before the Ad hoc Assembly published its draft political treaty, Joseph Stalin died; a little over four months later, the Korean War came to an end. In a new and seemingly hopeful international climate, those who had seen the unity of Western Europe only as "a bulwark against aggression" began to question whether it was still needed. Their doubts, and their hostility, crystallized around EDC.[18]

It had taken a year to ratify the ECSC Treaty; in all six national parliaments the debate had been heated and long. EDC was even more controversial—so much so that the German Bundestag, the first national assembly to approve it, did so only on March 19, 1953, ten months after the signing of the Treaty. The Bundesrat followed suit on May 15; the lower house of the Dutch Parliament on July 23; the Belgian Chamber of Deputies on November 26; the Dutch Senate on January 20, 1954; the Belgian Senate on March 12; and the Luxembourg Chamber of Deputies on April 17, 1954.[19]

From this slow roll-call there were two crucial absentees—Italy and France. In both countries, the delay was partly the result of government instability; but this in turn was increased by fierce opposition to EDC from the extremes of Left and Right. Even in Germany, the Social-Democrat SPD had fought it, as they had fought the Schuman Plan. They argued that to integrate the Federal Republic with the rest of Western Europe might block German reunification; but their opposition was sharpened by the antagonism that existed between Adenauer and the SPD leader Kurt Schumacher, mutilated and embittered by twelve years in Nazi concentration camps, and deeply fearful of giving his compatriots guns. In Italy and France, as in other countries, many felt the same fear: they tended to forget that EDC had been devised precisely to forestall the creation of a new German army. Communists made much of these feelings: so did Right-wing nationalists, who in addition to the German bogey disliked the prospect of committing a part of the services to a motley European army of fourteen divisions, all in some soulless European uniform. It was a strange mixture of motives—pacificism, jingoism, internationalism, fear, pride and nostalgia—that brought together in the opposition camp German Social-Democrats and Italian Neo-Fascists, Communists and Gaullists, Pietro Nenni and Marshal Alphonse Juin, the Comte de Paris and Kurt Schumacher. In the long run, they might have been defeated—but for one further absentee.[20]

This, once again, was Great Britain. If Britain had joined without reservations in the Schuman Plan and the project for a European Defense Community, much of the opposition would have been weakened. The weight of Germany, which so obsessed EDC's French opponents, would have been balanced by that of another well-established democracy. France's sacrifice of sovereignty would have been matched by a colleague and rival no less proud. True, Britain's presence might have weakened the institutional structure: she might have sought to limit its "supranational" powers. Once in, however, she would have wanted it to be efficient and democratic; she therefore might well have favored a strong decision-making body responsible to a real European Parliament. But as it was, Britain remained aloof. Not for the last time, her absence proved embarrassing.

The original exchange of Notes between Paris and London in May and early June 1950 had seemed to hinge on the question of "prior commitment"—whether or not to accept, as a condition for taking part in the Schuman Plan Conference, the objective of a European Community and the method of delegating power to common institutions. The real stumbling-block for the British, however, was not "prior commitment" as such, but the proposed pooling of sovereignty. As early as Tuesday, March 28, 1950, Ernest Bevin had told the House of Commons that Britain could never agree to the creation of an executive organ in Europe whose mandate it would be to impose decisions on any State. The Conservatives, although they now pressed for Britain to take part in the Schuman Plan Conference, fundamentally agreed with their Labour opponents. Britain, said Winston Churchill, "could not be an ordinary member of a federal union limited to Europe in any period which at present can be foreseen." But it was the Labour Party Executive that took the most openly hostile stand. On Monday, June 12, 1950, ten days after the Franco-British exchange of Notes and a week before the Schuman Plan delegates met in Paris, Hugh Dalton—who had recently resigned as Chancellor of the Exchequer after a "Budget leak"—presented to the press a pamphlet that he had personally steered through to approval. "Bevin, Cripps and I," he wrote in his memoirs, "were all definitely anti-Federal." His pamphlet, misleadingly entitled *European Unity*, was no less so. Expressly rejecting "supranationality," it recommended instead "co-operation between responsible Governments on the basis of mutual consent." "No Socialist Party," it proclaimed, ". . . could accept a system by which important fields of national policy were surrendered to a supra-national representative authority."[21]

European Unity soon became notorious. Its chocolate-colored cover inspired Winston Churchill to call it "Dalton's Brown Paper." The American press dismissed it as "a ridiculous manifesto"; the French press was predictably incensed. Two days later the British Prime Minister, Clement Attlee, drew a careful distinction between the Party's pamphlet and the Government's policy; but the main difference seemed only to be that the Government recognized the value of the Schuman Plan for others, provided that Britain remained outside. As Jean Monnet remarked at the second session of the Schuman Plan Conference, the British attitude was on the whole sympathetic to the project, but hostile to the delegation of sovereignty to the proposed High Authority. For obvious reasons, France and the other participants were anxious to see Britain join. The British authorities would be kept fully informed of the Conference's progress; but its economic, political and moral aims would be compromised if it were to abandon the principle of a supranational authority. However, Monnet added, the British had one great virtue: they recognized facts. To act was the best way of securing their eventual support.[22]

By an irony that might have confirmed Monnet's refusal to temporize, the British Government had already instructed its senior civil servants to work out an alternative to the Schuman Plan. By a further irony, the chairman of the interdepartmental committee set up to prepare it was Monnet's friend Sir Edwin Plowden. It was he, together with Sir Edward Bridges, Sir William Strang, and Sir Roger Makins, who had been responsible for drafting the British side of the recent exchange of Notes with France. The counterproposals that he was now asked to draw up had first been announced in the British communiqué of June 3, 1950. Two days later, Agence France Presse had reported from London that they would be submitted at or after the opening of the Schuman Plan Conference, where Britain, it was said, hoped to maintain "an invisible presence." She may also have hoped to recover the initiative if—as many in London expected—the Conference failed. Since it at length succeeded, Britain's counterproposals came to nothing, and were never officially divulged. They were, however, radically different from the Schuman Plan. Technical rather than political, they provided for the sharing of European markets, the reduction of transport costs, the rationalization of machine-tools capacity, and the adjustment of tariffs. They envisaged the establishment of regional, national and international boards to deal with European heavy industry; but the members were to be national representatives, not independent persons responsible to the group as a whole. There would have been, in other words, no supranational authority.[23]

This was the obstacle at which the British, however well-disposed in theory, in practice repeatedly balked. Ernest Bevin and Hugh Dalton had been two notable examples: another, now, was Harold Macmillan, who eleven years later was to lead Britain to the threshold of the Common Market. Like his colleagues in the Conservative Party, he had attacked the Labour Government for its reaction to the Schuman Declaration: it had been, said Macmillan, "a black week for Britain, for the Empire, for Europe and for the peace of the world." Two years earlier, on September 17, 1948, he had told the House of Commons: "Europe needs a common currency, a free movement of goods with due regard to existing obligations and preferential arrangements of the participating countries." On August 17, 1949, he had proposed in the Council of Europe that "the Committee of Ministers shall be an executive authority with supranational powers." Now, however, he appeared to change his mind. In June 1950, in a private minute to Churchill, he urged that Britain should enter the Schuman negotiations. "Then," he said, "we can mould the plan to our own pattern." On Tuesday, August 8, 1950, he and David Eccles submitted to the Council of Europe a bulky memorandum which indicated what in their view that pattern should be. It proposed that any member countries wishing to do so should form a Ministerial Committee, which in turn would appoint an Authority for coal and steel. The Authority's members would be chosen from representatives of employers, trade unions, and consumers; they would have votes proportional to their respective countries' coal and steel output—an arrangement advantageous to Britain. The supranational principle was to be abandoned: each country was to have the right of veto and the right to withdraw. "One thing is certain," said Macmillan, "and we may as well face it. Our people are not going to hand

over to any supranational authority the right to close down
our pits or steelworks." This, as it happened, was a caricature
of the powers eventually granted to the ECSC's High Authority, which were far less drastic; and—as Monnet pointed out
in a personal letter to Macmillan on August 8, 1950—the
line of thought completely missed the point.[24]

The ensuing debate in the Council of Europe's Consultative Assembly illuminated the contrast between what Macmillan called "Anglo-Saxon" and Continental habits:

> The difference [he declared] is temperamental and intellectual.
> It is based on a long divergence of two states of mind and methods
> of argumentation. The continental tradition likes to reason *a priori*
> from the top downwards, from the general principles to the practical
> application. It is the tradition of St Thomas of Aquinas [*sic*], of the
> schoolmen, and of the great continental scholars and thinkers. The
> Anglo-Saxon likes to argue *a posteriori* from the bottom upwards,
> from practical experience. It is the tradition of Bacon and Newton.

It might be retorted that even Bacon and Newton based their
thought on assumptions: the real difference was that these
were too inexplicit to be recognized as principles. The assumption underlying British attitudes seemed to be the in-
alienable nature of the nation-state. But Macmillan was more
subtle than his own oversimplifications. "Of course," he added,
"the Scottish people, who are the intellectuals of Britain,
know that there is nothing to be frightened of: one should
accept everything *en principe*, get around the table and start
the talks." In time of crisis, Britain would "certainly be prepared to accept merger of sovereignty in practice if not in
principle": she might join in the unification of Europe "in a
fit of absence of mind or by a series of improvisations which
would be particularly gratifying to my countrymen." Macmillan's words hinted at the crabwise stealth with which he was
later to coax Britain toward the Common Market. They
also suggested that if continental Europeans could recruit
Britain as an associate of the Schuman Plan, she might end
up as a full member.[25]

The notion that Britain might be "associated" with the
Schuman Plan was first voiced in London in May 1950 by

Robert Schuman himself. Speaking on Monday, May 15, at a luncheon given by the Anglo-French press, he said:

We shall pursue the project with only one other country [à deux] if necessary. Besides, one can imagine varying degrees of participation and, for example as regards Great Britain, if there is not one-hundred-per-cent participation, there can be association compatible with her economic ideas and structure.

Six weeks later, on Tuesday, July 25, 1950, he declared that "if we do not manage to get the British to share our views we are determined to seek a form of association between the Authority and the United Kingdom."[26]

"Association," although still undefined, was also mooted on the British side. On Friday, August 11, 1950, speaking to the same session of the Council of Europe's Consultative Assembly that had just heard Winston Churchill's proposal for a European Army, Hugh Dalton announced that:

. . . if agreement is reached between these six nations, we British will be most ready to consider how, and how far, Britain could be associated with any new organization which the Governments and Parliaments of these six continental countries might have approved for this most important problem of the better organization of their heavy industries.

The pledge was repeated in the House of Commons on Tuesday, November 7, 1950, when Ernest Davies, Under-Secretary of State at the Foreign Office, told a questioner that Britain was prepared, if invited, to discuss with the Six the practical means whereby she could associate herself with the proposed High Authority. Much depended, it was clear, on the content of the Schuman Plan Treaty. When at last this was signed, on April 18, 1951, the road seemed open. Speaking in Paddington on Labour Day, Tuesday, May 1, 1951, the Minister of State at the Foreign Office, Kenneth Younger, revealed that the Government was studying the provisions of the Treaty to see how far Britain could become an associate. A few weeks later, on Saturday, June 9, 1951, the British Ambassador in Paris, Sir Oliver Harvey, presented to Robert Schuman an official British Note to the same effect, indicating that the Government would be glad to discuss the question when the time was ripe.[27]

Still more categorical was the joint communiqué issued on Friday, September 14, 1951, after three-power talks in Washington between Dean Acheson, Robert Schuman, and Herbert Morrison, who had become Britain's Foreign Secretary on March 9, just five weeks before Ernest Bevin's death from a heart attack on April 14, 1951:

The three Ministers recognize that the initiative taken by the French Government, concerning the creation of a European Coal and Steel Community and a European Defence Community, is a step towards European unity. They welcome the Schuman Plan as a means of strengthening the economy of Western Europe and look forward to its early realization. . . . The Government of the United Kingdom desire to establish the closest possible association with the European continental Community at all stages of its development.

The significance of this statement was threefold. First, it made clear that America welcomed the integration of Europe, and that her welcome was acknowledged and seconded by Great Britain. British skeptics could no longer plausibly argue that the emerging European Community was incompatible with the Atlantic Alliance. Secondly, Britain now recognized the Schuman Plan as part of a political movement, not merely concerned, in Dalton's phrase, with "the better organization of . . . heavy industries." Finally, the British Government were now pledged to "the closest possible association" not only with the ECSC but also with EDC. Potentially, this might mean a great deal.[28]

The hope that Britain might join in the effort to unite Europe seemed to be confirmed six weeks later, on Thursday, October 25, 1951, when Attlee's ailing Labour Government was replaced by a Conservative administration under Winston Churchill. Continental Europeans were encouraged by reports from London that the new government planned to set up a permanent mission to the European Coal and Steel Community. They recalled—and misremembered—Churchill's celebrated speech at the University of Zurich on September 19, 1946, urging "a kind of United States of Europe"; they reread—and misinterpreted—his words in the Council of Europe on August 11, 1950. "We should make," he had said, "a gesture of practical and constructive guidance by declaring ourselves in favour of the immediate creation of a European army under a unified command, and in which, we should bear a worthy and honourable part." But, as in so many political speeches, the word "we" turned out to be misleading. In Zurich, Churchill had made it clear that Britain would support but not join a united Europe; now, her "honourable part" was to be with but not in EDC. On Wednesday, November 28, 1951, Sir David Maxwell Fyfe, the new Home Secretary, told the Council of Europe: "I cannot promise that our eventual association with the European Defence Community will amount to full and unconditional participation because this is a matter which must be left for intergovernmental discussion elsewhere." This sounded hopeful; at a press conference afterward he added, "It is quite wrong to suggest that what I said was any closing of the door." But in Rome on the same day the new Foreign Secretary, Anthony Eden, slammed the door shut. He had asked himself, he wrote later, "whether in practice we could join an army forming part of a European federation; I agreed with our predecessors that we could not." To join a federation on the continent of Europe, he explained in a lecture at Columbia University in New York on the following January 11, 1952, "is something which we know, in our bones, we cannot do."[29]

Even in his bones, however, Eden could hardly fail to notice that Britain's absence hindered the progress of EDC. As he wrote in a personal minute to Churchill on Saturday, December 1, 1951, "Now that the Plevin Plan is running into trouble in the countries that put it forward, we are being made the whipping boy." It was partly for this reason that on Tuesday, December 18, after talks with the French Government in Paris, Britain promised that "the United Kingdom Forces under the direction of the Supreme Allied Commander in Europe will be linked with those of the European Defence Community for training, supply and operations by land, sea and air." Meeting Robert Schuman again on February 1, 1952, Eden spelled this out in more detail. The proposed "link" would be "particularly profitable" between the respective air forces; arrangements could be made for the exchange and loan of individuals, units and formations; and Britain would maintain troops on the continent "for as long as is necessary." However, when Schuman pressed for a formal treaty promising mutual aid against aggression, Eden replied that "it was doubtful whether we could accept this. We already had the NATO commitment and I was not convinced that a further engagement was necessary." At length, after consultation with Acheson on February 13, he proposed instead a joint Anglo-American declaration of support if any European country threatened the peace.[30]

Shortly afterward, the EDC Conference ran into further trouble, once more aggravated by Britain's aloofness. Germany, as the country most exposed to any attack from the East, was anxious that the European army should respond automatically to aggression against any member of the future Defense Community; but the Dutch, in particular, were reluctant to give this undertaking without a similar commitment from Britain. On Friday, March 14, 1952, in the hope of solving the dilemma, the EDC Conference formally asked the British Government to conclude a mutual assistance treaty. France and the Netherlands suggested that this might be done by extending the Brussels Treaty which already linked Britain with France and the three Benelux countries, to the whole of EDC.[31]

Again, however, Eden demurred. "This," he told Dirk Stikker, the Dutch Foreign Minister, "was a difficult business for us. It was natural that we should conclude the Brussels Treaty with our closest European friends and allies. To extend it to Italy and Germany, because they were members of EDC and for the forty-five years which the treaty had to run, was quite a different proposition." He said the same to Robert Schuman. "Once again," he reported wearily, "I heard the cry that for parliamentary reasons, it was necessary for Her Majesty's Government to enter into some form of treaty commitment with the European Defence Community . . . Was there a danger that we should be asked to go further and join EDC?"[32]

To forestall it, Eden finally gave way. On Saturday, April 5, 1952, after a further meeting of the Cabinet, the British Ambassador in Paris, Sir Oliver Harvey, announced to Schuman that the British Government would indeed conclude a formal treaty; and a first draft was put to the EDC Conference on the following Tuesday, April 8, 1952.[33]

It had been a long and tiresome task to secure even this undertaking. Ultimately it turned out to be too little, too late. Meanwhile, Eden and his staff had taken another step which, however well-meant, suggested that they scarcely realized what continental "Europeans" were trying to achieve. On Wednesday, March 19, 1952, at a meeting of the Council of Europe's Committee of Ministers in the Salon de l'Horloge at the French Foreign Office, Eden presented an Aidemémoire largely drafted by Anthony Nutting, his Parliamentary Under-Secretary. The paper, which came to be known as "the Eden Plan," proposed an institutional merger between the Council of Europe and the future Community of the Six. "The essence of the plan," wrote Nutting, ". . . was to make the Council of Europe the parent body . . . The Committee of Ministers, the Assembly and the Secretariat of the Council of Europe would become the Committee of Ministers [sic] of the Coal and Steel Pool and the EDC."[34]

The idea itself was not entirely novel. Something like it had been suggested by Harold Macmillan and David Eccles in 1950, in their counterproposals to the Schuman Plan, and had been echoed by the Council of Europe's Committee of Ministers in October of that year. Now, the first reactions seemed favorable. "As the Foreign Secretary read through his typescript giving an outline of his plan to his European colleagues," said Nutting:

I could feel a deep sense of relief and thankfulness filling the room. Only the impassive features of the Chairman, Osten Unden of Sweden, showed no signs of emotion. He was no doubt busy trying to work out in his mind how he could square his neutral conscience with sitting in on a Committee of Ministers charged with overseeing the E.D.C. M. Bech, Luxembourg's doyen among the Foreign Ministers of Europe, beamed like a contented seal through a forest of snow white moustaches, his jubilant rotundity bearing happy witness to the delights of combining the not always arduous duties of Foreign Minister of Luxembourg with the ever pleasurable activities of the Minister for Winegrowing. Even the sphinx-like features of Dr Adenauer could not conceal a smile as he sat like a Grand Inquisitor slowly twiddling his thumbs in his lap. As for Robert Schuman, he made no attempt to hide his joy and summed up the reactions of his fellow ministers by saying that, apart from the intrinsic merits of the plan, by far the most important and encouraging aspect of it was that it represented a British initiative.[35]

Despite the ministers' smiles, it soon became clear that the Eden Plan had a number of drawbacks. Some were technical. The Council of Europe's Ministerial Committee consisted of Foreign Ministers: the Council of the ECSC comprised those concerned with economic questions, and the Council of EDC would no doubt include Ministers of Defense—a subject specifically excluded from the Council of Europe. Some of the delegates in the Council of Europe's Consultative Assembly were nominated by governments, and did not have to be members of parliament: those in the Community Assembly were to be chosen by and from their national legislatures. It might be difficult, finally, for the Council of Europe's Secretariat, with staff from all the member countries, to handle confidential subjects for the Six.

More serious were the political problems that underlay the technical difficulties. What the Six were hoping to achieve was not just an intensified version of the Council of Europe's co-operation between separate sovereign States: it was a pooling of resources and a fusion of material interests within a Community that might gradually become a United States of Europe. This distinction the Eden Plan seemed to ignore. Under it, as Nutting himself said, "Great Britain could play a part without being committed to the obligations of membership of any supranational agencies." Without, that is, accepting the duties of Community membership, she and other countries would acquire the right to scrutinize, if no more, the internal affairs of the new entity that the Six were forming. For Jean Monnet and his colleagues, in Nutting's words, it would be "like some nagging mother-in-law moving in on the newlyweds."[36]

Although, therefore, both the Committee of Ministers and the Consultative Assembly of the Council of Europe approved the Eden Plan in principle, the Assembly's General Affairs

Committee came to a different conclusion. Reporting back to the Assembly on Monday, September 15, 1952, after a detailed study, it recommended instead a much more limited system of contacts. In the subsequent Council of Europe debate, Paul-Henri Spaak, Paul Reynaud and the MRP Resistance veteran Pierre-Henri Teitgen all sharply attacked the original project; and within a few months it was quietly buried. "Tragically," Nutting commented, "our initiative had only aroused suspicion that we were really trying to sabotage the unity of Europe." To some Europeans it certainly seemed so. But Monnet, whatever his private doubts, still went on looking for ways to bring Britain closer to the Community of the Six.[37]

He was already sixty-three when he took up his duties in Luxembourg as President of the ECSC High Authority; but from the first he set an exhausting pace. Lights burned until all hours in the headquarters' offices, soon established in an elderly brownstone building that had belonged to the Grand Duchy's railways. Officials' weekends were interrupted by urgent meetings: at least once, Monnet summoned an assistant from the woods, where he was enjoying a Sunday picnic with his family. Some newcomers complained that Luxembourg, despite its five night-clubs and seven cinemas, was hardly the gayest of capital cities: "Europe won't get built in night-clubs" was Monnet's reply. One evening he himself was due to leave on holiday: hotel rooms had been booked, seats reserved and baggage packed; but the High Authority was meeting, and Monnet insisted on staying to the end. One by one, urgent messages were passed to him: the train was leaving soon—it had gone—so had the next one; but every time he brushed them aside. It was exasperating, but exhilarating; and it helped to weld together a loyal international team.[38]

The High Authority's two Vice-Presidents were Franz Etzel, a tall, cool, gray-eyed lawyer who later became German Finance Minister, and the solid but energetic Albert Coppé, a Fleming who had been Belgian Minister of Economic Affairs. The other members were Léon Daum, a small, crisp, dapper French businessman and steel expert; the bony, white-haired Paul Finet, a former Belgian foundry worker who had been first President of the International Confederation of Free Trade Unions; Enzo Giacchero, an Italian Christian-Democrat and active federalist, who walked with a limp owing to a wartime wound; Heinz Potthoff, a serious-minded ex-steelworker from Germany who had served on the International Ruhr Authority; the taut, well-groomed Dirk Spierenburg, formerly head of the Dutch delegation to the OEEC and to the Schuman Plan Conference; and the stout, fatherly Albert Wehrer from Luxembourg. All were very different, by temperament as much as by political conviction; but under Monnet's chairmanship and in the relative isolation of the Grand Duchy, they quickly acquired the habit of seeing the Community's problems as common problems, transcending any purely national point of view.[39]

They held their first, ceremonial meeting on August 10, 1952—a Sunday, and ten days after the majority of Frenchmen and others would normally have left for their month-long holidays in the sun. The British Ambassador to Luxembourg was present at the ceremony, and Monnet declared: "We are determined to seek without delay, in direct talks, the means of fulfilling the British Government's stated intention to establish the closest association with the Community."[40]

The British Government responded on the very next day by announcing that it was ready for talks on the subject; and ten days later, on Thursday, August 21, 1952, Monnet was in London seeing the Minister of State at the Foreign Office, Selwyn Lloyd. The result was that on Monday, September 1, Britain accredited to the High Authority a delegation headed by Sir Cecil Weir, a Scottish businessman and civil servant whose most recent official post had been as Chairman of the Dollar Exports Board. One of his tasks was "to lay the foundations of an intimate and enduring association between the Community and the United Kingdom." As a first step, he helped to establish a joint Committee between the High Authority and the British Government; and at the Committee's first meeting, on Monday, November 17, 1952, Monnet explained the form of "association" that he had in mind. It was not, he said, a trade agreement or a cartel to share out overseas markets, but a system of joint action involving rights, responsibilities and obligations undertaken in common. As well as consultation and the exchange of information, this meant joint institutions and rules to be worked out and applied together. He suggested that the British Government and the High Authority begin by taking an over-all view of their future prospects—"just as if you were members of our Community."[41]

On Tuesday, February 10, 1953, the ECSC opened its "common market" in coal, followed on Friday, May 1, 1953, by the common market in steel. The way was now open, as Monnet saw it, for the drafting of a formal Treaty of Association with Great Britain; and the early versions of it prepared by the High Authority's staff showed how far-reaching Monnet's ambitions were. What he envisaged was the gradual establishment of a coal-steel common market between the Community and the United Kingdom. The question of institutions was left open; but Monnet clearly hoped that practical necessity would lead the British toward virtual or even actual membership of the ECSC—and thence, perhaps, to full membership of the political and defense Communities that were to be set up alongside it.[42]

It was important, however, not to alienate British opinion by too bold a proposal; and the project went through many drafts before Monnet and his colleagues were satisfied. Finally, on the morning of Christmas Eve, 1953, Monnet handed a formal Note to Sir Cecil Weir. In it, he no longer spoke explicitly of a "common market" with Britain, but he came as close to his original idea as he could without raising the specter of "supranationality." He proposed:

– an association between the markets, through the diminution and, if possible, the elimination of reciprocal protection and the institution of rules that each party pledges itself to respect;
– a procedure for joint action;
– joint institutions entrusted with the task of seeing that the system works, preparing joint action, and taking decisions arrived at by common accord.

The institutions, moreover, might include not only a Council of Association composed of members of the High Authority and the British Government, but also machinery for publicly discussing the Council's action and for interpreting the rules—in other words, a joint parliamentary Assembly and a Court.[43]

Monnet's letter requested a reply "as soon as possible"; but on Thursday, January 21, 1954, in answer to a parliamentary question, Anthony Eden explained that the proposal would require "careful study and consultation with the interests concerned." These, for contradictory reasons, were cool toward association. The British Iron and Steel Federation, representing industrialists, was suspicious of anything that might threaten further controls on private enterprise; the Government-run National Coal Board and Iron and Steel Board were reluctant to share—or diminish—their existing powers. It was hardly surprising that the British Government took four months to give a formal answer. Finally, on Thursday, April 29, 1954, Weir called on Monnet with a formal invitation to go to London to discuss the "precise form" of the future association. Within twenty-four hours, Monnet accepted, and a meeting was tentatively scheduled for early June. But then came an unforeseen obstacle, which in the end destroyed any hope that Britain's association with the Coal and Steel Community might bring her closer to—and thereby help to save EDC.[44]

For several years, Monnet had been under the strain of uninterrupted hard work and anxiety. Now, he fell seriously ill, and his doctors ordered a long rest. By the time he was better, July was almost over, and Europe was beginning its annual summer exodus. The London meeting was therefore postponed until September. When that month began, and newly bronzed officials came flocking back to Luxembourg, it was to a gloom that owed little to the Grand Duchy's climate. As an American observer put it, the Coal and Steel Community for which they worked was "no longer the advance guard of a strong movement toward integration: it was more like an isolated outpost." EDC was dead.[45]

The manner of its dying was undignified and dramatic; but its fate had long been foretold. Despite the encouraging example of the Coal and Steel Community, many Frenchmen were still afraid of facing Germany in EDC without Britain. In January 1953, when a further change of government brought in Georges Bidault to succeed Robert Schuman as Foreign Minister, France had demanded further concessions, including a European settlement for the Saar, still in dispute with Germany, and additional protocols to the EDC Treaty, to safeguard "the unity and integrity of the French Army and the French Union" and ensure, in particular, that France's voting power could never be outweighed by Germany's. What was more, Bidault asked for a firmer commitment by Britain. On Thursday, February 12, 1953, he and René Mayer, the new French Premier, visited London to request the British Government not only to maintain at least its existing strength on the Continent, but also to conclude a political association with the EDC Council and Assembly. Unfortunately, in the words of a British Minister, "their appeals fell upon deaf ears."[46]

By now, time was running out. Under the new administration of President Eisenhower and Secretary of State John Foster Dulles, the United States continued to press hard for EDC to be ratified: in December 1953 Dulles even threatened an "agonizing reappraisal" of American policy if it were to fail. But the death of Joseph Stalin and the subsequent softening of Soviet propaganda led many people—including Winston Churchill—to predict a "thaw" in East-West relations; and this impression was not effaced even after Soviet tanks had crushed an uprising in East Berlin on June 13, 1953. As the hope of *détente* grew, enthusiasm for EDC waned still further.[47]

In July 1953 René Mayer fell, to be replaced by Joseph Laniel at the head of a conservative cabinet including several Gaullists. He and his Ministers promised the National Assembly that they would not seek ratification of EDC until they were assured of British association with it. Eden, at this time, was recovering from a series of operations; and when on his return to the Foreign Office Anthony Nutting pressed him for a decision, he delayed it, partly because he was preoccupied with Churchill's eagerness for East-West

"summit" talks. At length, after the abortive four-power conference in Berlin in January 1954, Britain made her offer;
but it fell far short of French hopes. Instead of guaranteeing
to keep her present fighting strength on the Continent, she
agreed to consult with EDC before reducing it; instead of
British representation in the EDC Council and Assembly, she
proposed *ad hoc* discussion between Ministers; instead of
integrating all her forces on the Continent with those of
EDC, she promised to assign to the European army one
armored division. It was disappointing, but it was something.
On Tuesday, April 13, 1954, France and her partners signed
an agreement along these lines.[48]

Two months later, Laniel's Government fell, and was followed on Saturday, June 19, 1954 by a coalition of Radicals
and Gaullists under Pierre Mendès-France. He, whatever his
personal convictions, had never belonged to the compara-
tively small circle of the most active "Europeans"; and for
all his creative dynamism, he faced skeptical colleagues and
a Parliament deeply divided over EDC. He also had urgent
tasks outside Europe—to grant internal autonomy to Tunisia,
and above all to fulfill his promise that he would end the
war in Indochina within four weeks. Impressed but deeply
uneasy, his European partners determined to do their best to
keep EDC on Mendès-France's tight agenda. Their efforts
merely brought the latent crisis to a head.[49]

On Tuesday, June 22, three days after Mendès-France
had formed his government, Paul-Henri Spaak conferred with
his Benelux colleagues, and two days later they jointly proposed a meeting of the Six. The Germans and the Italians
accepted; but Mendès-France was overburdened by more
pressing anxieties, and Spaak therefore arranged to meet
him in Paris at 12:30 P.M. on Wednesday, June 30, 1954.
Their conversation, interrupted by a late lunch, lasted four
hours.[50]

Physically, there was little resemblance between the broad,
well-padded Spaak, with his air of Churchill's understudy,
and the slight, blue-chinned hooded-eyed Mendès-France.
Both in their different ways, however, were nervous, proud
and easily hurt; both, too, were compulsive doodlers, impa-

tient and rhetorical behind their respective masks of calm and irony. They were too alike to find it easy to agree.[51]

Mendès-France began by explaining his own awkward position. Until recently he had been against EDC, but had thought that the French Parliament would vote for it. Today, he still had objections: the existing project was too exclusively military and anti-Soviet; it contained too few safeguards, and was too dramatic a step toward supranationality; finally, Britain was not included, and there could be no progress in Europe without her presence and active support. On balance, however, a defense Community was desirable; but now that he had come around to supporting it, he was forced to realize that Parliament would not vote for it in its present form.[52]

Spaak raised skeptical eyebrows; but Mendès-France went on. What he proposed was to try to persuade French opponents and supporters of EDC to work out and agree on a compromise solution by July 20, when the Geneva conference on Indochina was due to conclude. If they failed, he himself would make new proposals by August 15, so that the National Assembly could cast its vote before the end of that month. What would this involve? There were three possibilities. Parliament might ratify EDC but postpone the application of some of its provisions; it might request changes; or it might approve parts of the Treaty while rejecting others.

Spaak pointed out that Germany, Belgium, the Netherlands, and Luxembourg had already ratified EDC as it stood. Were they now to have to wait for a *diktat* from the French Parliament, and start their own parliamentary procedure all over again? The Americans, he knew, were impatient for a decision: in April, Dulles had personally warned him that further delay might lead to cuts in U.S. military aid to Europe. As an alternative solution, there was now serious talk of simply admitting Germany to NATO. If France were to water down EDC into a mere military coalition, Spaak added, he would prefer the NATO solution himself. In that case, rather than force the other European countries to reject a diluted French version of the EDC Treaty, it might be better for France simply to say "No." But at the very least the Six should have a chance to discuss Mendès-France's counter-proposals before he put them to Parliament. Perhaps, after all, some compromise might be possible. Mendès-France promised to try this way out, and the two men parted amicably. But they both knew that the real difficulties remained.[53]

On Tuesday, July 20, 1954, only a few hours before his self-imposed time-limit, Mendès-France secured an armistice in Indochina. Some observers of the Geneva negotiations that led to it, including Raymond Aron, suspected that the Soviet Union had consented in the hope that the French Government might reciprocate by rejecting EDC. Twice—on Saturday, July 10 and Wednesday, July 21—Mendès-France was closeted alone with V. M. Molotov, the Soviet Foreign Minister; but to suspect that they had a tacit understanding would no doubt be an injustice. By his own account, Mendès-France refused to link the two questions; and when at their second meeting Molotov warned him that EDC would not "serve to bring together France and the Soviet Union," this was already twenty-four hours after the armistice agreement, and Mendès-France answered non-committally. His real difficulties were not with the Soviet Union, but with the National Assembly in France.[54]

There, supporters and opponents of EDC were as far as ever from being reconciled; and a fortnight after the Geneva Conference, Mendès-France held a series of secret cabinet meetings to expound new proposals of his own. These, he believed, could be embodied in protocols to the EDC Treaty which would only have to be signed by France's partners, whereas the French Parliament would have the chance to vote them. Briefly, they called for EDC to last as long as the Atlantic Alliance, ceasing to exist if that were denounced or if Germany were reunited; for military integration to be limited to units stationed in Germany; and for the "supranational" clauses of the Treaty to take effect only after eight years. "In other words," wrote Anthony Nutting, "Mendès-France was asking for a European army for the Germans and a French army for the French." Even so, he failed to satisfy three Gaullist members of his cabinet—General Pierre Koenig, Maurice Lemaire, and Jacques Chaban-Delmas. It was with their strictures still echoing that he left Paris for

Brussels on Wednesday, August 18, 1954, to present his proposals to his partners in the Six.[55]

From the start, the Brussels Conference was uneasy. The EDC Treaty had been signed two years earlier; since then, France had continually postponed ratification, and repeatedly asked for concessions; now, she was proposing changes yet again. Her new Premier, dynamic and unpredictable, was a newcomer to the circle of veterans round the table—Paul-Henri Spaak in the chair; Konrad Adenauer for Germany; Johan Willem Beyen for the Netherlands; Joseph Bech for Luxembourg; Attilio Piccioni for Italy. A few moments before the meeting opened, news came of the death of Alcide De Gasperi, Italy's greatest "European." To some, it seemed as if an epoch was ending.

Presenting his proposals, Mendès-France promised that the French Parliament would be able to vote them before the end of the year; but nothing else, he said, stood any chance of success. It was a story that had been heard too often to be believed: arguing the contrary, delegates pointed to articles in the French press by Robert Schuman and the Socialist leader André Philip in support of the original EDC Treaty. Spaak quoted a letter that he had received from Philip; Adenauer quoted optimistic forecasts by Maurice Faure. One after another, Beyen, Adenauer, and Bech repeated a further objection—Beyen with particular vehemence: the changes that Mendès-France demanded would mean going back to all the national parliaments, with no guarantee at all that the new draft would be accepted.[56]

In the hope of finding a way out, Spaak suggested that instead of protocols to be added to the Treaty, any changes take the form of a declaration of intent. He had done his best, he said, to draft one, which he now proposed to read. It began with a preamble summarizing EDC's long history, including previous hard-fought discussions with France. As soon as Mendès-France heard this, he interrupted. It was intolerable, he exclaimed, that his country should be accused in this fashion; and he insisted that the preamble be torn up then and there. Solemnly and a little sheepishly, the delegates destroyed their copies and promised never to reveal the contents. Then, with relative calm restored, the debate continued late into the night. Next day, officials of the Six labored to try to reconcile Mendès-France's and Spaak's proposals; and at 8:00 that evening the Ministers met again. At 11:00 P.M., Spaak proposed a brief adjournment, and retired to his office with Mendès-France. "We shan't agree," said Mendès-France, "I'm convinced of it"; and he drew from his pocket a paper that he had been preparing. "This is what I shall say when we realize we've failed," he explained. "I don't want to take the responsibility of breaking things off prematurely; but I can tell you that I've decided to say no."[57]

Nothing Spaak said could shake him. Despite the concessions already made, despite last-minute pleas when the Conference resumed, despite renewed American pressure in the form of a note from Dulles delivered to Spaak at 1:00 A.M. while the meeting was still in progress, Mendès-France insisted on making his declaration. What had been offered him, he said, was still not enough to satisfy the French Parliament: to all intents and purposes, he was going away empty-handed.[58]

That Sunday, August 22, 1954, he left Brussels for London. Winston Churchill met him at the airport, and they drove together to the Prime Minister's summer residence at Chartwell. There they were met by Anthony Eden, who had returned from holiday for the occasion. As Mendès-France argued afterward, he was unhappy that the price of Franco-German reconciliation in EDC should be a rift between France and Great Britain; but he was also anxious, no doubt, to forestall what Dulles had proposed in his note to Spaak: a conference of Benelux, Germany, Italy, the United States and Britain that would in fact have isolated France. Now, he made what one British Minister called "a final half-hearted attempt to bring Great Britain into the EDC." Churchill, although he had originally proposed the idea of a European army, would have none of it. "The best way out," he answered, would be if Mendès-France could persuade the French Parliament to ratify the existing Treaty with the declaration of intent proposed by Spaak and his partners. Its rejection, Churchill went on, would mean grave dangers to France and to the Western world. Mendès-France repeated that the French Parliament would certainly refuse to ratify it on any terms but those he was proposing. At this, Churchill and Eden together urged him to explain clearly in the debate that if EDC failed another solution would have to be found without delay. He agreed, and declared—characteristically setting a further time-limit—that this could be done within two months.[59]

Explicitly or not, what was now in prospect was a convergence of policy between the Governments of Britain and France. Both knew that the United States would insist on rearming the Germans; both were anxious to avoid too close or exclusive a link between Germany and America; both, however, were unwilling to accept—for themselves—a "supranational" European solution. Both bore some responsibility for EDC's difficulties, as did the overinsistence of John Foster Dulles.

On Saturday, August 28, 1954, despite a further last-minute compromise proposed by Spaak, Mendès-France submitted the original EDC Treaty to the French National Assembly. His speech was deliberately cool: he made it clear that he was neither endorsing EDC nor demanding a vote of confidence. Two days later, on Monday, August 30, the Assembly rejected the Treaty by 319 votes to 264 with 43 abstentions, on a merely procedural motion to postpone discussion indefinitely. Among the abstentions were Mendès-France and six of his Cabinet colleagues. Among the Noes were the Communist Party, the Gaullists, and more than half of both the Radicals and the Socialists. When the result was announced, the Opposition burst into the *Marseillaise*.[60]

God Save the Queen might have been almost as appropriate. Within two months, in fact, Britain had come to the rescue with a plan that Anthony Eden claimed later had come to him in his bath on the morning of Sunday, September 5—although it resembled the suggestion made to him two years earlier by Robert Schuman, that the Brussels Treaty should be extended to Germany and Italy. Was it also, perhaps, an echo of something that Mendès-France had said? At all events, on Wednesday, October 20, 1954, Spaak,

Mendès-France, Adenauer, Beyen, Bech, and Gaetano Martino met with Eden in Paris to sign on Saturday, October 23, an agreement enlarging the Brussels Treaty into Western European Union (WEU). It was a little more than a military alliance, and it had a consultative Assembly; but it bore no real resemblance to EDC. From Britain's point of view, its only provision that was even remotely "supranational" was the pledge that her four divisions and her tactical air force would not be withdrawn from the Continent—except in "an acute overseas emergency"—without the consent of a majority of WEU's member States. Germany, by contrast, faced notable constraints. The occupation régime was ended, and she was admitted to NATO; but her land contingent was limited to twelve divisions, and she was forbidden to manufacture atomic, biological or chemical weapons on her own soil.[61]

For many reasons, the establishment of WEU was a Pyrrhic victory. Those who had opposed a European army including Germans now faced the prospect of a German army within a looser, more or less traditional alliance. Those who had tried to achieve political unity in Europe by means of EDC and its attendant project for a Political Community now saw the ECSC as the sole survivor of their hopes. Those who had pressed for British participation now saw her a little more closely associated with her continental neighbors, but still not a member or even an associate of the only Community organization that remained.

At the Coal and Steel Community's headquarters in Luxembourg, some officials were frankly despondent: Europe, it seemed, had come to the end of the road. But Jean Monnet remained optimistic. Like Mendès-France, he recognized the importance of achieving economic unity as a basis for political and military integration. After a setback, the right course was to draw the lesson and continue building Europe by patient practical steps. Restored to health although no longer smoking his favorite cigars, he was now eager to press on with developing the ECSC and its association with Great Britain.

On Monday, September 6, 1954, just a week after the

defeat of EDC, Monnet had a preliminary talk with the head of the British Delegation, Sir Cecil Weir, and arranged to start unofficial discussions with Duncan Sandys, the Minister of Supply. Friendly as these were, they faced a number of difficulties. Already, the form of association now being worked out was far from Monnet's original idea of bringing Britain into the coal-steel common market; now, Monnet had a struggle to prevent its being weakened further still. In particular, although the British at length agreed to the High Authority's establishing a permanent delegation in London, they firmly rejected the notion of a joint Assembly and a Court. With WEU in the offing, they were anxious for quick results; but the High Authority, however "supranational," was handicapped as always by the need to secure agreement from all the Community's member States. The French Government was by far the most difficult: Mendès-France disliked the prospect of a bilateral link between the ECSC and Great Britain, and—perhaps on the WEU analogy—would have preferred to see her represented in the Community's Council of Ministers. At length, on Wednesday, December 8, 1954, after both private talks and a number of long six-nation discussions, Monnet and his colleagues were authorized to initial a draft agreement. It was formally signed in London on December 21, 1954. After ratification by all seven national Parliaments, it came into force on Friday, September 23, 1955.[62]

Britain's association with the ECSC undoubtedly proved useful. It led to a steady exchange of technical data; it installed in London a Community delegation with an influential information office; and in 1957 it produced an agreement to cut steel tariffs between Britain and the Community to a level on both sides around 10 per cent. For Monnet, these modest beginnings of consultation and joint action were a basis on which more ambitious projects might have been built. The British Government, however, clearly saw the Association Agreement not as a potential starting point for eventual membership, but rather—in the words of Alfred Robens, chief Opposition speaker in the debate on its ratification—as "the model of the association which we would be ready to accept in any organizations, any communities that may be set up in Europe to deal with things other than coal and steel."[63]

So the Echternach dance continued, five steps forward, three steps back. With only the Coal and Steel Community left, the first—"supranational"—stage in Europe's unification seemed to be over. Britain had embarked on a new relationship with the Continent, but she still retained her "special position." Having rejected EDC for its supranational features, she had made a practical pledge of British forces to the intergovernmental WEU. Having removed the supranational element from Monnet's original proposals of December 1953, she had taken the practical step toward tariff-cutting embodied in her Association Agreement with the ECSC. With that, for the time being, "Europeans" had to be satisfied. There was now a pause in the dance's rhythm before progress could begin again.

NEVER SO GOOD

What is Europe? Thought that is never contented.
                              Paul Hazard[1]

Greater virtues are needed to bear good fortune than
bad.   *François, duc de la Rochefoucauld*[2]

British foreign policy has usually been content to react
to the behaviour of others.   *A. J. P. Taylor*[3]

While Europe's statesmen and civil servants toiled and wran-
gled, others had not been idle—on farms and building sites,
in factories and offices, in schools and universities, in labora-
tories, hospitals, and homes. The same burst of creative energy
that had begun to transform international relations had also
been changing the face of the continent and the lives of its
inhabitants. Within ten years after World War II Western
Europe had not only recovered from most of war's effects;
it had entered a new phase of unprecedented peaceful
growth.

A bird's or airman's eye view of Europe now revealed a
more reassuring landscape. The scars and shadows of war
had largely—although not entirely—vanished. Along the temperate latitudes stretched familiar green miles of meadow,
field and woodland, smudged but made more prosperous by
the industrial towns and suburbs that thrust across them
from northwest to southeast, through Lancashire, London,
the Netherlands, Belgium, the Ruhr, and Munich, up the
Seine to Paris, through Lyon, spanning the Alps to Milan,
Turin, Genoa. Only the periphery, the bleak uplands and the
dry southern *maquis,* remained barren and poor.

Spreading like webs or wheelspokes from London, Paris,
Cologne, Milan, the railways were busy again, many of them
now electrified, and soon to rival the airlines with the smooth

speed and luxury of the Trans-Europ-Express. Motorways (*Autobahnen, autoroutes, autostrade* or express highways) were under construction, most notably in Germany, Italy, and France. The Rhine, the Weser, the Seine, and Europe's other great rivers and ship canals were once more crowded with barges; the rebuilt port of Rotterdam and its older competitors—London, Antwerp, Hamburg, Bremerhaven—were once more dealing with a prewar volume of traffic, as were Liverpool and Marseilles. The busiest airports—London, Paris, Frankfurt, Rome, Copenhagen, and Berlin—were each handling about a million passengers a year.[4]

People were traveling, and there were many more of them. Europeans spoke of a postwar "baby boom," a "population bulge," that was most marked in Finland, the Netherlands, France, and Portugal. Returning servicemen had been eager to be fathers, and the birth-rate in almost all European countries had risen sharply in 1946 and 1947. No less important, many more children were now surviving: Western Europe's infant death-rate for 1955 was little more than half that for 1939, and in some countries—Denmark, Finland, Spain, Switzerland, and the United Kingdom—it was rather less than half. The adult death-rate, too, was everywhere well below the 1939 level. Deaths from accidents, malignancies, and stress diseases were significantly increasing; but many of the illnesses that had once been killers—typhoid, smallpox, diphtheria and other epidemic diseases—had by now been largely tamed. Tuberculosis was being brought under control; bronchitis and pneumonia were being fought with new drugs. The combined result was that by mid-1955 Western Europe's population totaled nearly 300 million. They were most densely concentrated in Britain, the Netherlands, Belgium, the Ruhr, the Rhineland, the Paris region, Lombardy and the Campagna around Naples. More than half of them—161 million—lived in France, Germany, Italy, and the Benelux countries, forming the six-nation European Coal and Steel Community and, later, the Common Market. More than half of them, almost everywhere, were girls or women: only Iceland had an equal number of either sex, and only Luxembourg had fewer women than men.[5]

This increase in numbers was one reason for Western Europe's rapid economic expansion. By 1950, virtually all the member countries of OEEC had exceeded their prewar levels of production; by the beginning of 1955, all had done so. Now, Western Europe's total output was valued at more than 220 billion dollars. Her annual growth-rate had varied between 8.3 per cent in 1949–50 and 2.7 per cent in 1951–52; in 1954–55 it reached 6.7 per cent, well above the average for the whole decade. Since 1952, Western Europe had been enjoying a surplus in her over-all balance of payments; by 1955, her total reserves of gold and foreign currency, which in 1950 had been just below eleven billion dollars, stood at nearly sixteen billion. The only major exception was the United Kingdom, whose reserves had dropped, during the same five-year period, from 3.7 to 2.2 billion dollars.[6]

In world trade, Western Europe's relative position had been eroded since 1938; but in the general expansion her total imports from the rest of the world had now tripled, and her total exports quadrupled. The most notable single increase was in her imports of energy, which had risen from 7 per cent of her total consumption in 1937 to reach 25 per cent in 1955—four-fifths of it in the form of oil. Of her total imports, valued at eighteen billion dollars a year, nearly sixteen billion dollars' worth consisted of food, raw materials, fuel, ores, and base metals; of her total exports, valued at sixteen billion, eleven billion dollars' worth were capital and consumer goods and other manufactures. Western Europe, in other words, was still a workshop, in which many hands were gradually making lighter work.[7]

But her growing population was not the only reason for Europe's new prosperity. True, some countries with an ample labor force, like Germany, Italy, the Netherlands, and Switzerland, were enjoying spectacular growth-rates, while Belgium, Britain, and the Scandinavian countries, with limited labor supplies, grew more slowly. But France and Austria, equally hard-pressed for manpower, nevertheless expanded rapidly, the former at the cost of inflation, the latter with the aid of technical advance. This, reducing the so-called "backlog of unexploited technology," helped expansion everywhere. From 1950 to 1955, employment in Western Europe rose by only 7 per cent, and total man-hours by only 8.2 per cent.

Yet during the same period production increased by no less than 26.2 per cent, revealing a marked rise in productivity. This was made possible largely by new machinery, which in turn had required heavy capital investment. By 1955, Western Europe was investing forty-five billion dollars a year, or more than one-fifth of the value of its total production. Twenty per cent of these investments went to housing; but much of the rest was devoted to new industrial plant. Of the high-income countries, those with the lowest investment rates —Belgium and Great Britain—were among those with the slowest rate of growth.[8]

In all countries, investment was now partly supplied, enforced or encouraged by the State, which had come to play a far greater role in the economy. Of total government expenditure in 1955, five billion dollars—over 8 per cent—went to direct investment, making up more than 12 per cent of total capital supplies. Most railways, central banks and airlines were virtually or wholly government-owned, and in many countries the State had a sizable holding in heavy industry. Altogether, government revenue and expenditure amounted to some sixty billion dollars.[9]

Some of this greatly increased government outlay was earmarked for defense, on which Western Europe was now spending nearly 5 per cent of the value of her total production. This over-all figure was swollen, however, by the unusually high proportion—8 per cent—still being spent by Great Britain; for most countries, the figure was appreciably lower. A far more uniform element in government spending, and one that was more novel, was what was known in Britain as "the Welfare State." Primarily, this referred to the great expansion of social security: sickness and unemployment benefits, pensions and family allowances. In twenty years, the total spent on these had more than tripled: by the beginning of 1955 the average annual expenditure per head in Western Europe was 76 dollars, with the Saar the highest at 153 dollars, and Spain the lowest at 4.90 dollars. Except for Greece, Portugal, and Spain, where social security was rudimentary, and Austria, Finland, Ireland, and Italy, where it was still incomplete, most of Western Europe was now fully covered. Sweden and the United Kingdom had the most comprehensive systems, although in some cases Belgium, France, Germany, and Luxembourg gave higher benefits. Of the total of over twenty-two billion dollars—not all of which, by any means, came from the State—the highest single item of expenditure was on pensions (nearly eight billion dollars a year), followed by medical care and sickness benefits (six billion), with family allowances coming third.[10]

Government spending on education had also greatly increased by 1955, although it was still only half of that devoted to defense. The average annual expenditure was 2.4 per cent of total production, with peaks of 3.4 per cent in Finland, Iceland, and Sweden and troughs of 1.4 per cent in Greece and Spain and 1.2 per cent in Portugal. In absolute terms, education in Western Europe cost $5,312,000,000 in 1955, or 18 dollars per head of population. The highest national expenditure per head was in Sweden, with 41 dollars, followed by Iceland with 31.6 and Switzerland with 30.5; Britain came fourth, together with Belgium and Luxembourg, at 25.9 dollars per head. The lowest expenditure, again, was in Portugal—two dollars and fifty cents. In Western Europe as a whole, 81.8 per cent of all children between the ages of five and fourteen were at school, compared with nearly 100 per cent of American children, and only 15.9 per cent of those between fifteen and nineteen, compared with over 80 per cent in the United States. Higher education in Europe was open to only 4.5 per cent of the age-group between twenty and twenty-four. In primary schools, Britain had the highest percentage; but secondary education was relatively most widespread in Sweden, and higher education in Denmark. In all three categories, Portugal again came last, although even there the number of secondary-school enrollments had doubled since 1938.[11]

More numerous, more healthy, better cared for, and—in some degree—better educated, more Europeans were now beginning to enjoy material prosperity. By 1955, the annual value of total production per head of population in Western Europe had reached 747 dollars; but this average was brought down by Spain, Greece, and Portugal: in Belgium, Luxembourg, Sweden, Switzerland, and the United Kingdom, production per head was already more than a thousand dollars a year. For the whole of Western Europe, private consumption per head—at official exchange rates—now averaged 490 dollars a year. Switzerland was in the lead with 825 dollars, followed by Belgium with 765, Sweden with 745 and the United Kingdom with 700. To cope with this growing purchasing power, thirteen million people, 10.3 per cent of the total labor force, were now engaged in wholesale and retail trade, compared with ten million or 8.9 per cent, in the 1930s. Altogether, there were just over four million stores, market stalls and mobile shops, or one for every seventy-two inhabitants. Belgium with many family businesses—and a "Ministry of the Middle Classes" to protect them—had one for every thirty-four inhabitants; Iceland, at the other extreme, had one for every 158. Britain, once the nation of shopkeepers, had relatively fewer stores than most of her neighbors: soon, although less rapidly than Germany, she was to become a nation of supermarkets.[12]

More than half this army of retailers were sellers of food, on which Europeans were now spending an annual average of 177 dollars a head—rather more than one-third of the family budget. With the easing of supplies since the early postwar years, they had begun to eat less bread and fewer potatoes, and more fruit and meat. The annual consumption of cereals had fallen from 130 kilograms a head in 1948–49 to less than 120 in 1955; of potatoes, from over 120 kilograms to little more than 100. The consumption of fruit had risen from less than 40 kilograms to more than 60, and of meat from 30 to nearly 45. And if these had once been luxuries, Europeans could now afford others. They were now spending nearly 40 dollars a head each year on household equipment, furniture, and private cars—8 per cent of the family budget as against 6 per cent in 1949. One in five Europeans now had a radio set, as against one in ten before World War II; one in twelve had a telephone; one in twenty-five had a car. Some 16 per cent of families had television sets, 15 per cent had washing machines, and 10 per cent had refrigerators. All these numbers, moreover, were rapidly growing. In 1955 alone, two million new cars were driven on to European roads.[13]

It was two years later that Harold Macmillan told a British audience, "Most of our people have never had it so good"; but already the so-called "consumer society" had arrived. It contrasted sharply with the "austerity" of the recent past. Its uglier aspects included smog, traffic jams, property speculation, horror comics, and organized appeals to prurience, vanity, snobbery, and greed. To many, it seemed to be a world of advertising, public relations, and expense-account gluttony; of Edwardian suits and self-conscious connoisseurship; of espresso bars and vodka martinis; of "James Bond" fantasies and after-shave lotions; of soft-faced men who had done well out of the peace. Some, who had never been poor, derided the "materialism" of those who were eager for washing machines, refrigerators, and television sets; an older generation, remembering the '30s depression, deplored the "fecklessness" of families—eight out of every ten in Britain—who bought on hire purchase or deferred payment terms. What both types of critic found novel was the ability of "working-class" people, many of them young, to afford the products of their own labor. Privileges once reserved for the few could now be shared, at least, by the many. Unit trusts introduced them to the stock exchange on the same principle as the conducted tours that offered them foreign travel. However imperfectly, frozen foods, paperbacks, and do-it-yourself kits made widely available what had once been expensive or rare. It was not quite the world of equality and freedom so often imagined in wartime; but if gross inequality remained, both within European nations and between them, many more people had been freed—and freed by "the system"—from fear and want.[14]

With a new material environment came a new mood, curiously blending "realism" and fancy. In the various arts, the two were in counterpoint at different times. In painting, despite the isolated solidity of Renato Guttuso, "social" or representational art was now either rare or weak. Paris was giving place to New York as the center of finance and inspiration; and the chief thrust seemed to be inward, toward the abstract, sensuous in the work of Nicolas de Staël or Jackson Pollock, more cerebral in the hard-edged, perhaps defensive products of the "pop" and "op" art that was to come. In serious music, the trend seemed to be in the same direction, influenced by the "aleatory" methods and electronic techniques associated with Karlheinz Stockhausen; *mutatis mutandis*, popular music followed a similar course, both in the harmonic experiments of "progressive" jazz and in the inchoate move away from traditional ballads and Dixieland imitations, toward the more insistent, repetitive and hypnotic rhythms of rock-and-roll and the later "pop."

European cinema was also growing moodier, more introspective. Immediately after World War II, its characteristic tone might have seemed to be the romantic pessimism of Marcel Carné and his scriptwriter Jacques Prévert, the resurrected surrealism of Jean Cocteau's *Orphée*, or even the whimsicality of Great Britain's "Ealing comedies." But the most creative talents at that time had been engaged in work that was socially concerned, often explicitly "neo-realist"—Vittorio de Sica's *Sciuscia*, *Ladri di Biciclette*, and *Umberto D;* René Clément's *La Bataille du Rail* and *Les Jeux Interdits;* Georges Franju's short *Sang des Bêtes;* Luchino Visconti's *La Terra Trema;* Roberto Rossellini's *Paisà*. Then, in the early '50s, came a change. De Sica made his disappointing, part-American *Stazione Termini;* Clément ventured into ironic comedy with *Monsieur Ripois;* Franju launched into feature films; Visconti into the historical equivocations of *Senso;* Rossellini into a series of run-of-the-mill productions. "Neo-realism" was to have further brief flashes; but by 1955, broadly speaking, the most interesting talents seemed to be those of the introverts: Michelangelo Antonioni, with *Le Amiche*, from a story by Cesare Pavese; Ingmar Bergman, with *Smiles of a Summer Night* and, soon, *The Seventh Seal;* Federico Fellini, with *La Strada*. The French "new wave" was yet to come: its future members were for the most part making short "documentaries" or writing film criticism; but in this interim period their elders were already enlarging the scope of cinema, often with mannered bravura, to admit strange dreams.

In literature and the theatre there was a similar interaction. In France, the characteristic postwar figures seemed to be Jean-Paul Sartre, Simone de Beauvoir, and Albert

Camus. All struggled to square technical philosophical concepts with the irrational brute facts of existence; but their tortured *littérature engagée* was soon to be challenged by other experiments, partly linguistic—Nathalie Sarraute's *Portrait d'un Inconnu*, Alain Robbe-Grillet's *Le Voyeur*, Michel Butor's *L'Emploi du Temps*. In Italy, the "neo-realist" work of Carlo Levi, Vasco Pratolini and even Elio Vittorini began to be overshadowed by the more fanciful complexity of Italo Calvino, while Pier Paolo Pasolini moved on from the immediacy of *Ragazzi di Vita* to more reflective ventures, recording popular speech with an exactitude that was almost academic. The move away from simple realism was most marked in Germany, where only nightmares seemed capable of explaining nightmare. Older writers like Hans Werner Richter or Gerd Gaiser having explored the limits of traditional narrative, it was left to such newcomers as Günter Grass or Uwe Johnson to open trapdoors into darker depths.

In Britain, meanwhile, the process was partially reversed. Here, one immediate sequel to World War II seemed to have been a taste for the Gothic, if not the fey. The grotesque novels of Mervyn Peake; the fantasies of William Sansom; the juicy extravaganzas of Dylan Thomas; the charades of Christopher Fry or Ronald Duncan; the brave preciosity of Denton Welch—perhaps in this liminal territory the imagination had already sought a peacetime stimulus comparable to the demands of war. There was more than a suspicion, however, of dilettantism, of reaction against wartime drabness rather than an attempt to assimilate and reinterpret what had been deeply felt. This was especially so in the theatre. Even John Whiting, gifted and highly serious, seemed unable to engage his themes full-bloodedly; and while *Salad Days* vied for popularity with plays by Terence Rattigan, critics overpraised translations from Ugo Betti, Marcel Aymé, and Jean Anouilh. Once more, the change came in the mid-'50s. In 1953, John Wain published a "picaresque" first novel, *Hurry On Down*, followed in 1954 by Kingsley Amis's *Lucky Jim*; in May 1956 John Osborne's *Look Back in Anger* was staged at the Royal Court Theatre. Publicists lumped these three very different writers together, to their annoyance, as "angry young men"—chiefly because all three were equally impatient with postwar neo-gentility, but also because their idiom was vigorous and blunt. Partly concerned with English class nuances, their work seemed insulated from some of their continental colleagues' obsessions; but its robust directness, which in Amis's case owed something to the experience in the services that his generation had shared, marked a more serious—if less solemn—mood in English writing. Other examples were Robert Conquest's verse anthology, *New Lines*, which launched a short-lived "Movement" for stricter form and greater clarity, and in particular the taut, muscular poems of Philip Larkin and Thom Gunn. At the same time, however, an equally English tradition of puckish intellectual fantasy lived on in some of the novels of Iris Murdoch and Muriel Spark.

It was in architecture, finally, that fancy and "realism" were now most effectively blended. Much of Western Europe's postwar building, certainly, was uninspired. Identical cheap apartments or large commercial offices—both badly needed—were not promising subjects: too often, they seemed to treat human individuals as interchangeable units, belittled by sheer numbers, to be stacked like convicts in pale-gray blocks of more or less comfortable cells. But other assignments had already by 1955 produced undoubted masterpieces. Some were relatively orthodox, like the busy boxes of the Royal Festival Hall in London, Alison and Peter Smithson's stark, flatland Secondary School at Hunstanton, Norfolk, or Arne Jacobsen's icily austere Town Hall in Rødovre, Copenhagen. Others were comfortingly human, like the welcoming Lijnbaan shopping center in Rotterdam, Michael Scott's gay and efficient bus terminal at Beresford Place in Dublin, or the colorful honeycomb of the Gröndal apartment complex in Stockholm. But the most exciting were fantastic useful monuments—Le Corbusier's horned barbaric Church of Notre-Dame du Haut at Ronchamp in the Vosges; Stazione Termini in Rome, with its roof leaping from the ruins of the pre-Christian Servian Wall; the dazzling sunflower ceiling of Pier Luigi Nervi's Casino at Chianciano Terme near Lake Trasimeno; Danzeisen and Voser's astonishing Goldzack works at Gossau in Switzerland, with its stepped and corrugated roof like a row of gigantic transparent cable drums tipped slightly sideways. Together, such buildings as these spoke of hope and vision after the desolation of war. No: Europeans were far from finished. Indeed, they had barely begun.

Those who were working to unite Europe at this time badly needed such encouragement. By the beginning of 1955, most of their hopes had been disappointed. The OEEC, which some had once believed might be the basis of a European customs union, had become a useful but traditional body for co-operation between sovereign governments. The Council of Europe was virtually powerless. The European Coal and Steel Community, once thought of as the spearhead of unity, was now a blade without a shaft: the further projects for a European Defense Community and a European Political Community had finally been broken. Britain, it was true, had helped to form Western European Union, and had concluded an Agreement of Association with the surviving Coal and Steel Community; but Western European Union was just one more intergovernmental body, and the coal-steel Association Agreement was a means for consultation and little more. Joseph Stalin's death had reduced the incentive of fear that had once helped spur Europeans toward unity; the death of Alcide De Gasperi had removed one of Europe's foremost friends. Richer now, fat with peace, and no longer so frightened, had Europeans forgotten the hard lessons that war and poverty had taught them? Did they once more believe that their nation-states could solve their problems separately? Had they lost faith in the future they had sought to build together? It seemed so. On Thursday, November 11, 1954, when Jean Monnet announced in Luxembourg that he would not seek re-election as President of the coal-steel High Authority when his mandate expired in the following February, it seemed as if a generation were passing, as if an epoch of bright, misguided hopes were coming to an end.

And yet, within less than a year, this dismal climate had been totally transformed. Fears that the Coal and Steel Community, now isolated, might fail, had proved groundless. Monnet had been replaced at the High Authority, not by some obscure technocrat, but by a political figure who was also a convinced "European." Above all, Europe—as the phrase went—had been "relaunched"; and Britain too had begun to reconsider, if not yet radically to change, her policy toward it.

Monnet proposed to leave the High Authority, as he told his colleagues and the press, "in order to be able to take part with complete freedom of action and speech in the construction of European unity." Already, however, two days after the fatal Monday, August 30, 1954, on which the French Parliament had failed to ratify the Defense Community Treaty, he had begun to discuss the prospects for reviving the European idea. On Wednesday, September 1, 1954, he was in Paris consulting his friends among the "Europeans": it was the first of a whole series of such meetings throughout that autumn and the following spring. The list of those whom he saw made an impressive roll-call: Antoine Pinay, René Pleven, Robert Schuman, Guy Mollet, Paul Ramadier, Pierre Mendès-France, Pierre-Henri Teitgen; Paul-Henri Spaak, Jean Rey, Pierre Wigny; Joseph Bech; Giuseppe Pella, Emilio Battista; Ludwig Erhard, Eugen Gerstenmaier, Walter Hallstein, Konrad Adenauer, Walter Freitag, Heinrich Imig. The two last, German trade-unionists who had come to know and trust Monnet through their work with the Coal and Steel Community, were for the time being his line of communication with the German Socialist Party, still suspicious of the moves afoot to unite Western Europe. As time went on, however, contact and understanding grew here too. Patiently, Monnet pursued his consultations, traveling repeatedly to Paris, Bonn, Brussels and Strasbourg; when he was not deep in conversation with his visitors in Luxembourg, he seemed always to be on the telephone or on the train. As the weeks went by, plans for the relaunching of Europe gradually crystallized into action.[15]

Monnet's mandate as President of the High Authority was due to expire on Thursday, February 10, 1955, two years after the formal opening of the "common market" in coal, iron ore, and scrap. The anniversary date, it seemed, might be the moment for him to make a resounding political statement, a rallying-cry and a call for further action. What should that action be? One of Monnet's closest young associates, the

Englishman François Duchêne, suggested at one point that Monnet should stand for the French Parliament, in order to form an explicitly "European" party in France. If the idea ever tempted Monnet, he quickly thought better of it. What seemed far more appropriate was to form a "European" party on a European, not a national, basis. It might be a "European Front" or action group, composed not of individuals but of political parties and trade unions themselves.[16]

By January 1955, the idea of an action group had taken firm shape, and its proposed program was beginning to be sketched out. At first, this included plans for further integration in the fields of energy and transport, to be achieved by extending the powers of the Coal and Steel Community; for the establishment of new Community institutions to deal with armaments and the peaceful uses of atomic energy; for direct elections to the existing Common Assembly; and for the convening of a new "Ad hoc Assembly" to study and promote new steps toward unity. After further discussion, however, Monnet dropped the plan for an armaments pool, which was all too likely to arouse the same motley opposition as the Defense Community project. He also rebaptized his proposed action group, this time as a "Front for the United States of Europe." Then, in the last week of February, came a new idea—that all six Community member governments might issue a joint communiqué. What had begun as the notion of a resignation speech had turned into the plan for an action group. That in turn had led to a program for further unification. Now it was turning into proposals for action by governments.[17]

What had made this seem feasible was a change of Government in France. Over the weekend of February 5–6, 1955, Pierre Mendès-France's cabinet, already four times reshuffled, had finally fallen; and after Antoine Pinay, Pierre Pflimlin, and Christian Pineau had each in turn failed to form a Government, a cabinet headed by Edgar Faure had won a vote of confidence on Wednesday, February 23. It included several of those whom Monnet had been consulting: Pinay was Foreign Minister, Schuman Minister of Justice, and Teitgen Minister for France Overseas. With their support, it might now be possible to persuade the Six to take action;

and with this in mind, Monnet once more revised and sim-
plified his proposals. Now, they included the extension of
the Coal and Steel Community to cover energy and transport;
the establishment of a new Community for the peaceful uses
of atomic energy; and the formation of a European Full
Employment Insurance Fund.[18]

To achieve these aims, he envisaged a meeting of Foreign
Ministers; and at the beginning of April, after the French
Conseil de la République had approved the WEU agreements, Paul-Henri Spaak formally proposed that such a meeting be held in three weeks' time. Its aim, he wrote, would
be:

> . . . to relaunch the European idea by extending the attributions
> of the Coal and Steel Community. This extension of the Community
> could apply to all existing forms of energy (electricity, gas and fuel)
> and to means of transport (railways, river traffic, roads and airlines).
> The pooling of efforts for the peaceful development of atomic energy
> could also be entrusted to an organization dependent on the E.C.S.C.
> In order to achieve this extension, it would be urgently necessary
> to organize an international conference at which the idea would be
> examined practically, and whose aim would also be the drafting of
> a treaty. The chairman of this conference could be M. Monnet.[19]

All seemed well on the way to being settled, when Monnet
heard two pieces of bad news.

The first came on Tuesday, April 5, 1955, in a telephone
call from Hallstein in Bonn. Adenauer, who was due to receive Pinay at the end of April to discuss the Saar dispute
and the canalization of the Moselle, was anxious to avoid
complicating these delicate matters with a six-nation Foreign
Ministers' meeting, which also threatened to clash with some
speaking engagements of his own. He therefore proposed
that it be delayed until the end of May, after the next session of the coal-steel Common Assembly. What was more, he
felt that the question of further integration required more
detailed study. The reason underlying this was that pooling
atomic energy, which Monnet saw as the kernel of his project, was less popular in Germany than the prospect of freer
trade, perhaps within a general common market.[20]

The second piece of bad news came a week later, from
Paris. Here, the order of priorities was exactly the reverse:

except with the national atomic authorities, the idea of a nuclear pool was popular, while the lowering of tariffs was not. Edgar Faure, moreover, depended on the support of the Social Republicans, who were hostile to "supranationality" and wary of Monnet and the High Authority; as a result, his statements on Europe were understandably cautious. At a press conference on Wednesday, April 13, 1955, he spoke only of "certain formulae of European co-operation [*sic*] for atomic energy," and declared that the European organization of energy and transport would not necessarily be achieved within the framework of the ECSC.[21]

The next few days were anxious and uncertain. On Friday, April 15, it was provisionally agreed that the Foreign Ministers' meeting would be held on May 30; but so clouded were its prospects that Monnet was briefly tempted to seek a further postponement. Before he could do so, however, the train of events that he had helped to set in motion gave a farther lurch forward. This time, the impulse came from The Hague.[22]

Johan Willem Beyen, the Netherlands' joint Foreign Minister, had long been anxious to broaden the scope of European economic integration, which had hitherto been practiced and envisaged sector by sector. On April 4, 1955, he had sent to Spaak a memorandum in which he explained his reasons:

All partial integration tends to solve the difficulties in one sector by measures which harm other sectors or the consumers' interests, and it tends to exclude foreign competition. That is not the way to increase European productivity. Furthermore, sector integration does not help to strengthen the feeling of Europe's solidarity and unity in the same degree as general economic integration. To strengthen this feeling, it is essential that the notion of the European States' joint responsibility for the common good be incorporated in an organization adapted to the pursuit of the general interest, and whose executive body is responsible not to Governments but to a supranational Parliament. . . .

That is why it seems opportune for the three [Benelux] Governments to take a well-prepared initiative which might usefully be announced at the E.C.S.C. Foreign Ministers' meeting. Such an initiative would aim at establishing a supranational Community whose task it would be to achieve the economic integration of

Europe in the general sense, proceeding by means of a customs union to the establishment of an economic union. By clearly defining our point of view, we shall be able to put an end to the confusion and discouragement of those who support integration; and this seems to me to be of very particular interest for the future integration of Europe.

On Thursday, April 21, 1955, in a speech to the Netherlands Council of the European Movement, Beyen made these views public, and called for a study to be made of general economic integration, on supranational lines.[23]

Within twenty-four hours, Monnet had paid a lightning visit to Paul-Henri Spaak in Brussels; and on the following day, Saturday, April 23, Spaak himself was in The Hague. Together, he and Beyen agreed to ask Joseph Bech of Luxembourg to join them in submitting to the Foreign Ministers' meeting a joint Benelux Memorandum based partly on Beyen's and partly on Monnet's texts.[24]

When Pinay and Adenauer held their long-scheduled meeting on the following Friday and Saturday, April 29 and 30, they announced their agreement that the time had come "to give a new impulse to European co-operation," especially in the fields of transport, air navigation, aircraft-building, and research on atomic energy and its peaceful uses. Beyen's speech, perhaps, had forced the pace; but the reference to "European co-operation" was not reassuring; and it was clearly essential that the Benelux Memorandum form the agenda of the Foreign Ministers' meeting. For this, it had to be well drafted, and it had to be presented soon. From now on, Monnet kept in close touch with Spaak. At length, on Friday, May 6, Spaak announced that the reworked draft was ready. It came with a covering note: "Herewith your child."[25]

On Monday, May 9, 1955, the fifth anniversary of the Schuman Declaration, Monnet—still "caretaker" President of the High Authority—presented its annual Report to the Common Assembly. He said little of his projects for the future: but he took care to point out that there was no essential contradiction between extending unification to new sectors and pursuing general economic integration. In response, on the following Saturday, May 14, the Assembly unanimously voted a Resolution calling on the six Foreign Ministers, whose meeting was now fixed for June 1, to "charge an intergovernmental conference or conferences to work out, with the appropriate aid of the Community's institutions, the necessary draft treaties for the achievement of the next steps in European integration, of which the establishment of the European Coal and Steel Community was the beginning." On the previous day, moreover, the Assembly had asked Monnet to "intervene" with the six Governments to ensure that its views on social policy were heard. The "relaunching of Europe" was thus doubly linked, so far as the Assembly could ensure it, with the existing "supranational" institutions. For the time being, there was little more to do except wait.[26]

Eventually, on Friday, May 20, Monnet received two crucial telephone calls. The first was from Paul-Henri Spaak: the Benelux Memorandum was being officially submitted to the Foreign Ministers' Conference. The second call was from René Mayer in Paris: Edgar Faure and Antoine Pinay had just asked the French Cabinet to propose him as Monnet's successor on the High Authority. The first was a victory. The second was an irony.[27]

What was ironic was that just at this moment Monnet himself was preparing to withdraw his resignation. When he had originally announced it, in November 1954, the situation in Europe had looked bleak. Now, it was hopeful again—partly because of the influence that Monnet's position in Luxembourg had helped him to exert. There, he had material resources—offices, advisers, secretaries, drivers, telephones and telex machines, as well as an official platform: the material problems involved in all political work were easily solved. As long ago as December 1954, the ECSC's embryonic Parliament, the Common Assembly, had urged him to reconsider the decision to step down; and now it had voted two resolutions calling for the ECSC and Monnet himself to be given an active role in the "relaunching of Europe." Already, at the Assembly's Strasbourg session, Monnet had begun to think about staying on; and by the time he received Mayer's news on Friday, May 20, 1955, he had already written the first draft of a letter on the subject to the governments of the Six.[28]

He hesitated, but not for long. The French Cabinet was due to meet on the following Wednesday, May 25. On Saturday, May 21, Monnet sent off his letter; and three days later on Tuesday, May 24, he gave it to the press. In it he explained his reason: "In the face of the relaunching of policy undertaken by Governments, it would not be understood if I were not to declare myself ready once again to participate directly in the development of the task undertaken, should Governments wish to confirm the desire that several of them have insistently expressed to me."[29]

If this was a bid for reappointment to the presidency of the High Authority, there were arguments in its favor. René Mayer, a large, bass-voiced, Mr. Punch-like figure who had been a Radical Premier of France before retiring to private business, was a "European" and had had some hand in the original Schuman Declaration; but the "anti-Europeans" in Edgar Faure's Cabinet—particularly the Social Republicans Gaston Palewski, General Pierre Koenig, and General Edouard Corniglion-Molinier—were not without weight, and there was no guarantee that they would support him. It might prove harder to oppose Monnet, the present incumbent; and even if he were rejected, the fact that he too was in the running might make it easier for Mayer to be accepted as a compromise. Such a concession by the "Europeans" might then win them greater freedom on matters of substance when the Foreign Ministers met. The unaccustomed ambiguity of Monnet's letter, moreover, left it unclear whether he was in fact offering his services as President of the High Authority or for some other role in the "relaunching of Europe." At this stage, it was still uncertain whether the two would be separate or not.[30]

In the event, his offer was refused: when the French Cabinet met, on Wednesday, May 25, it chose René Mayer as France's official candidate. But on the question of substance, Monnet's action may have had some effect. At the same meeting, the Government gave a fairly broad mandate to Antoine Pinay, its delegate to the Foreign Ministers' Conference; as one of Pinay's assistants put it, France could not say "no" to everything. Next day, Edgar Faure addressed a news conference in unusually "European" terms. "A true organization," he said, "cannot be given too loose a formula, cannot become a mere club or a conference of ambassadors. If the term 'supranationality' is alarming, let us say that nevertheless it must be given powers of decision."[31]

So far, so good. With the French Government once more co-operative, the way seemed clear for the "relaunching of Europe." The Foreign Ministers were due to meet in Messina on the following Wednesday and Thursday, June 1 and 2. But now, at the last moment, came news of a further obstacle. In addition to the Memorandum from Benelux, the German Government too had submitted a draft paper which threatened to compromise the Community principle just when the French Government had at last endorsed it.

The Benelux Memorandum proposed further integration in a number of specific sectors—transport, energy, and atomic energy; it also proposed "the establishment of a European economic community," to integrate the economy as a whole. This, like the sectors to be integrated, required "the establishment of a common authority endowed with the necessary powers." The German paper, on the other hand, was far more loosely worded. "An attempt," it declared, "must be made to achieve European economic unity," and "close economic cooperation [*sic*] must be established between the States"; but this could be achieved by "constituting under the responsibility of the ECSC Council of Ministers a permanent consultative organ" with limited tasks. These views were those of Ludwig Erhard, Adenauer's stout, cigar-smoking and ultra-"liberal" Minister of Economic Affairs, who deeply distrusted both *dirigisme* and "supranationality"; but to have accepted them would have been a departure from past practice and a betrayal of existing hopes. "Co-operation" was no substitute for integration. A "consultative organ" responsible to the Council of Ministers, who represented the individual member States, would have been very different from the ECSC's independent High Authority, to say nothing of its Court and Assembly. Instead of continuing and developing the new method of pooling national sovereignty under common rules and common democratic institutions, begun by the Coal and Steel Community, the German Memorandum seemed to propose returning to the traditional method of

intergovernmental bargaining that experience had condemned.[32]

Yet, nevertheless, the German arguments had some point.
The Benelux Memorandum had called for "a common authority"; but how, asked one of Monnet's German colleagues,
could this work in the broader field of global economic integration? A body like the High Authority of the ECSC might
be suitable for dealing with specific sectors, where governments could agree on fairly detailed rules in advance; but
it could hardly tackle the whole range of the economy, even
supposing that governments were willing to give it such
broad and sweeping powers.[33]

With the benefit of hindsight, the way out of the dilemma
now seems clear. In practice, the ECSC High Authority, despite its name, seldom behaved like a "supranational" Government, ruling by *diktat*. Its essential quality was its
independence, not its direct power. As an impartial body responsible to the Common Assembly for the affairs of the Community as a whole, it worked in harness—in "dialogue," as
Community jargon put it—with the Council of Ministers,
whose opinion it sought more often than was legally required. A similar model, based on the High Authority's practice rather than its paper prerogatives, was at length to be
adopted for the future Common Market. Here, the independent body was to be the Commission, whose most
important role was to propose solutions for the problems that
it alone could see from an over-all Community viewpoint;
the main decisions were to be taken by the Council of Ministers, with the Commission sitting in. Gradually, the Common Market was to agree on what was virtually a series of
further Treaties, each prepared by the Commission with the
aid of the Assembly, and voted by the Council of Ministers
representing the member States. The difficulty of delegating
so much authority, daunting as it seemed at the outset, was
resolved by doing so gradually as successive problems were
broached.

Little of this could be foreseen, however, when the Foreign
Ministers' Conference opened in Messina. In the Mediterranean sunshine, they were taking a step in the dark. The set-

ting—Sicily in spring—was magnificent; but like many historic occasions, the meeting was less impressive at the time than it came to seem in retrospect. The delegates stayed in a former monastery, the Hotel San Domenico at Taormina, some twenty-five miles down the coast; in the late afternoon of Wednesday, June 1, 1955, they drove to Messina. Their talks were to last until the early hours of Friday, June 3. Their host was the dapper Gaetano Martino, Italian Foreign Minister and Rector of Messina University. The chairman was Joseph Bech, from Luxembourg, avuncular but shrewd behind his Santa Claus mustaches. The other participants were Paul-Henri Spaak, from Belgium; Antoine Pinay, from France, brisk and punctilious; Walter Hallstein, from Germany, in a slightly crumpled lightweight suit; and Johan Willem Beyen, from the Netherlands. Each had his own preoccupations. The Benelux Ministers took turns at explaining their Memorandum. Pinay approved it in principle, but pointed out that economic integration would raise many problems, among them the height of the future Common Market's outer tariff and the leveling up of wage rates as between the member countries. Martino, submitting a Memorandum on behalf of Italy, stressed the need to harmonize taxes and social security contributions; he also called for a European fund to retrain and resettle workpeople who had to change their jobs. Hallstein, a convinced "European" who had helped negotiate the ECSC Treaty but who as German Secretary of State was the only non-Minister heading a delegation, had the invidious task of presenting the patchy German Memorandum; but he made the most of its positive features—its call for a European atomic energy pool, and its sound analysis of what a general Common Market would involve. It was Hallstein, indeed, who toward the end of the day put the crucial question: "Are we agreed to do something on the basis of the Six?"[34]

They were; but at first sight it looked unspectacular. When the delegates finally parted, after a candle-lit dinner in their monastery, they had voted a Resolution several pages long. It took account of all three preparatory papers, and especially of the Benelux Memorandum, much of whose wording it adopted. "The Governments," it declared:

. . . believe that the time has come to make a fresh advance towards the building of Europe. [The Benelux Memorandum had refered to its 'integration'.] They are of the opinion that this must be achieved, first of all, in the economic field.

They consider that it is necessary to work for the establishment of a united Europe by the development of common institutions, the progressive fusion of national economies, the creation of a common market and the progressive harmonisation of their social policies.

Such a policy seems to them indispensable if Europe is to maintain her position in the world, regain her influence and prestige and achieve a continuing increase in the standard of living of her population.

But by way of practical decisions, the Messina Resolution seemed mainly to advocate a series of studies—of transport, energy, and atomic power, and of the gradual establishment of "a European market, free from all customs duties and all quantitative restrictions." "Conferences" were to be held "to work out treaties or other arrangements concerning the questions under consideration"; "the preparatory work" was to be done by "a Committee of Governmental representatives, assisted by experts, under the chairmanship of a political personality responsible for co-ordinating the work in the various fields."[35]

To many this seemed unduly cautious. "The Governments," wrote *Le Monde*, "have implicitly abandoned the idea of 'supranationality'." "Isn't all that very vague?" asked a journalist at Messina. "No," said the Ministers' patient Luxembourg Secretary-General, Christian Calmès; "proposing a statesman to run it is a guarantee that it will work, since he'll make it a point of honor to succeed."[36]

Calmès was to be proved right. Shortly afterward, Paul-Henri Spaak was chosen to head the new Committee. On Saturday, July 9, 1955, it held its first meeting, at the Belgian Ministry of Foreign Affairs; after that, it met in the Château de Val Duchesse, a modest mansion standing in its own grounds on the southeast outskirts of Brussels. Its mandate, although general, was fairly clear. Despite the national contrasts concealed in the Messina Resolution, the Governments had agreed on their broad objectives: the Committee's task was to discuss means, not ends. Spaak, admittedly, was no expert; but his parliamentary experience, his emotional power and oratorical skill, and above all his imposing physical presence, were invaluable as a goad. Pounding the table, imposing deadlines, threatening and cajoling, he forced the technicians to stick to the point. He was aided, moreover, by Jean Monnet and his associates. Although the Committee was composed of national delegates, it also included representatives from the High Authority—officially Dirk Spierenburg, semi-officially the ubiquitous Pierre Uri. Uri—"prodigiously brilliant, ditto vain, ditto kindly" was a colleague's private description—was still prominent in the so-called "Monnet grape-vine" that for some years had helped to disseminate "European" ideas, information and influence. Through him and others, as well as directly, Monnet kept in close touch with the Spaak Committee's work. For Monnet himself, however, one chapter was now closing. The Messina Conference, before discussing its Resolution, had quickly dispatched the main item on its original agenda: it had appointed René Mayer to succeed Monnet as President of the High Authority.[37]

So, on Thursday, June 9, 1955, Monnet had said his fare-wells to the staff in Luxembourg. On Friday, June 10 he had officially handed over to Mayer. On Saturday evening, June 11, his friend and assistant Max Kohnstamm had given a fork dinner for him; they had stayed up talking until 2:00 A.M. Then, on Monday, June 13, Monnet had tidied up his last official papers. He was sixty-six. He had "launched Europe," and now had helped to "relaunch" it. At this point, quite honorably, many men might have retired. Instead, Monnet went on his travels again, to bring together the "Front" or "Committee" for the United States of Europe that he had planned before the Messina meeting.[38]

His first stop was Paris. Here he saw Etienne Hirsch, Robert Marjolin, Hubert Beuve-Méry of *Le Monde*, Robert Schuman, Guy Mollet and Robert Bothereau of *Force-Ouvrière*. In London, he had talks with Campbell Secord, a Canadian engineer whose advice he sought on the proposed European atomic organization. In Bonn, he saw his trade-union friends Walter Freitag and Heinrich Imig, then Hall-

stein and Adenauer, then the Socialist leaders Erich Ollenhauer and Herbert Wehner. In Belgium, he called on the
Socialist Max Buset and a number of labor leaders, including
André Renard. In the Netherlands, he saw Sicco Mansholt,
Jelle Zijlstra and the president of the Dutch trade union federation. In Paris again after a brief August holiday, he had
further talks with Hirsch, Marjolin, Pierre Mendès-France,
and Louis Armand, the *polytechnicien* who had revolution-
ized French state railways and who now suggested the name
"Euratom" for the proposed atomic energy pool. All this time,
acceptances had been trickling in; and on Thursday, October
13, 1955, after six more weeks of travel, meetings, correspondence, and telephone calls, Monnet was at last able to announce
the formation of his "Action Committee for the United
States of Europe." It comprised, as corporate members, the
Socialist, Christian Democrat, and Liberal Parties, as well
as the non-Communist trade unions, of all six member countries of the ECSC. As one anonymous commentator later
said, it was "something like the collective democratic conscience of the European Community." Its thirty-three
founder delegates included such well-known names as Guy
Mollet, Erich Ollenhauer, Amintore Fanfani, Kurt Kiesinger,
Théo Lefèvre, Maurice Faure, Ugo La Malfa, René Pleven,
Auguste Cool, and Giulio Pastore. Their first aim, they declared, would be to demonstrate "to Governments, Parliaments, and public opinion their determination to see that the
Messina Resolution of June 2 becomes a veritable step towards the United States of Europe."[39]

Backed—and sometimes prodded—by Monnet's distinguished action group, the Spaak Committee toiled on in Val
Duchesse. At length, Spaak sent Uri, the German delegate
Hans von der Groeben, and one of his own Belgian assistants,
to a quiet retreat in the south of France—the Grand Hôtel
at St.-Jean-Cap-Ferrat—with instructions to draft a final report. When it was ready and broadly approved by the Committee, Spaak presented its findings to a special session of
the ECSC Assembly held in the Belgian Senate Chamber
on Tuesday, March 13, 1956. Just over five weeks later, on
Saturday, April 21, he submitted the printed Report to the
six Foreign Ministers. Meeting in Venice on Tuesday, May

29, they adopted it as a basis for formal negotiations, and the Spaak Committee turned into a Treaty-making conference, which began work in Val Duchesse on Tuesday, June 26. Here, once again, Spaak deployed all his boisterous talents to force the pace. On one typical occasion, when experts had haggled interminably about the tariff to be applied to banana imports, he deliberately lost his temper. "I give you two hours," he told them; "if it's not settled by then, I shall call the press in and announce that Europe won't be built after all, because we can't agree about bananas." Then he walked out. When he came back two hours later, the problem had been solved.[40]

Spaak's blend of chairmanship and gamesmanship was highly effective. It was helped, moreover, by two very serious crises in the summer and autumn of 1956. The first was over Suez, the second in Hungary. Both gave new impetus to the unification of Western Europe.

The origins of the Suez crisis can be traced back to the nineteenth century; but its immediate causes emerged only after World War II. Middle-Eastern politics were now polarized, both by the establishment of Israel in the midst of resentful Arab countries and by the revolution in Egypt that replaced puppet kings and pashas, first by General Mohammed Neguib, then by Colonel Gamal Abdel Nasser. Four external powers had interests in the area. For the Soviet Union and the United States, it was one focus of their global rivalry; for France and Britain, history gave the Suez Canal emotional as well as strategic and economic importance; the Suez Canal Company, moreover, was largely a French concern. All four had slightly ambiguous relationships with both Israel and Egypt. Broadly speaking, the Soviet Union backed Egypt and the United States backed Israel; but Nasser was reluctant to take sides in the "cold war," and Russian technicians made no secret of their impatience with Arab pupils; while the United States was anxious to set up a Middle East defensive system in which Egypt would be included. France, in the throes of the Algerian War, was grimly hostile to Nasser's pan-Arab aspirations, although she retained friends and influence in Lebanon; and Britain, although on bad terms with Israel, was growing increasingly uneasy at Nasser's attempts to play off the Soviet Union against the West. The scene was set for a convergence of Israeli, French, and British interests: it remained to be seen which way the United States would feel it safe to move. Tension, already latent, became acute when John Foster Dulles, the U. S. Secretary of State, refused finance for the building of the Aswan High Dam in Upper Egypt. Britain followed suit; and on Friday, July 20, 1956, Nasser retaliated by nationalizing the Suez Canal.[41]

There followed some weeks of anxious diplomacy, none of it very effective. This in itself helped dramatize the need to build Europe. Meeting in Paris on Wednesday and Thursday, September 19 and 20, 1956, Monnet's new Action Committee declared: "The events of the summer have revealed that only a United Europe can make its voice heard, and be respected, in the world of today." Western Europe, the Committee pointed out, was "the only great industrial region of the world that does not produce the power necessary to its development. Its life, in the near future, might be paralyzed by the cutting-off of its oil imports from the Middle East . . . In this respect, the Suez crisis is a grave warning. Even if, as we hope, it is solved by peaceful means, this fundamental lack of balance, with its threat to peace, will remain: namely, the weakness and growing dependence of Western Europe as regards its supplies of power." It was a fresh argument for hastening the Val Duchesse negotiations, and especially for establishing Euratom, which Monnet at that time regarded as the key feature of further integration, partly because it alone could persuade the French Government and Parliament to accept the general Common Market. The Committee therefore proposed that governments appoint "Three Wise Men" to report on Europe's atomic energy needs and possibilities; and on Tuesday, November 13, 1956, the governments did so, naming Louis Armand, Franz Etzel from the High Authority, and the bearded Italian physicist Francesco Giordani. The Report that they eventually submitted on Saturday, May 4, 1957, although initially overoptimistic, certainly helped to speed the Euratom and Common Market Treaties through the national parliaments, and to that extent left its mark.[42]

But the Suez crisis gave a further and sharper thrust to

events in Western Europe. When Guy Mollet had become French Prime Minister on Thursday, February 2, 1956, he had been expected as a Socialist to come to terms with the Algerian rebels; yet only four days later, howled down by a crowd of Algiers settlers and bombarded with stones and rotten tomatoes, he seemed to change his mind. His attitude to the Arabs now became abruptly hostile. Before the year was out, he acquiesced in—if he did not connive at—the kidnapping of the rebel leader Mohammed Ben Bella while flying over international waters on the night of Sunday, October 21. Next day, on Monday, October 22, at a secret meeting in Sèvres, he conspired with David Ben-Gurion, the Israeli Prime Minister, to make what amounted to a combined attack on Egypt. Also present were Christian Pineau, the French Foreign Minister; Maurice Bourgès-Maunoury, the Defense Minister; General Moshe Dayan, the Israeli Chief of Staff; and Shimon Peres, Secretary-General to the Israeli Ministry of Defense. Later they were joined by Mr. Selwyn Lloyd, Anthony Eden's Foreign Secretary, and Mr. (later Sir) Patrick Dean, then Deputy Under-Secretary at the British Foreign Office. All the principals were sworn to lifelong secrecy. It was not surprising, for they were putting the final touches to a plot that the French had suggested to Eden in an equally secret meeting at Chequers on the Sunday of the previous week. Crudely, what they planned was that Israel should invade Egypt across the Sinai Desert, and that Britain and France should intervene—supposedly to "separate the combatants," but in fact to seize the Canal and bring Nasser to his knees.[43]

The Israelis crossed the border on Monday, October 29, and advanced across the desert with great prowess and dash. But the rest of this dubious scheme was slower to move into action, and it quickly came to grief. Condemned by the United Nations and by many of the British people, threatened by the Soviet Union, and disavowed by the United States, which made no move to support sterling until £ 100 million had fled abroad, first Britain and then France had to call a halt and hand over to a United Nations peacekeeping force—but not before Nasser had seized a number of their assets and blocked the Suez Canal.[44]

The Suez adventure cost about 3,000 lives, many of them Egyptian. Britain lost twenty-two servicemen—and one badly shaken Prime Minister: Eden, already ill when the plot was hatched, had to step down in favor of one of its early supporters, Harold Macmillan. This, which helped make possible Macmillan's later bid for Britain to join the Common Market, was not the least of the consequences; but just as important was the effect on public opinion in Europe. For Britain, in particular, the Suez affair had shown that the United States —especially before an election—would refuse to be dragged into policies that it disapproved of. So long as Britain needed American support for the pound, her "special relationship" with Washington was bound to be one-sided. In the long run, fears for Europe's oil supplies were to prove excessive, since the Arab States had to sell in order to live. But the relative impotence of individual European countries had been shown unmistakably—all the more so since the Suez affair coincided with that year's other serious crisis, the Soviet invasion of Hungary.[45]

Signs of unrest in the eastern half of Europe had been growing ever since the death of Joseph Stalin; but it was in 1956 that they threatened to turn into revolt. It began in Poland, where "destalinization" in April and May brought the release of some 30,000 political prisoners, and a reduction of the sentences on 40,000 more. Then, in June and July, came a number of strikes and riots, notably in Poznan. Wladyslaw Gomulka, who had been victimized under Stalin, was now readmitted to the Communist Party, and soon became First Secretary. In this position, and confident of popular support, he was able to stand up moderately to the Soviet Union and dissuade it from using force to crush the new regime.

Hungary was less fortunate. Here, after Stalin's death, the once disgraced Imre Nagy had become Premier; but in 1955 he had again been ousted by the Stalinist Mátyás Rákosi. At this, the Hungarian Writers' Association, which had hitherto supported Rákosi, turned against him; and the Petöffi Circle of Hungarian intellectuals organized a series of mass public debates, calling for his resignation and demanding,

among other things, freedom of the press. In July 1956 the
Soviet Union dismissed him, partly for permitting these disorders, and replaced him by Ernö Gerö, another hard-line
Party man. Against Gerö, public feeling soon grew violent;
and on Tuesday, October 23, after a broadcast in which
he had attacked the "revolution," angry crowds swarmed
through Budapest shouting for Imre Nagy. Outside the radio
building, one group was fired on by the AVO security police:
but it fought back and manhandled them when they tried
to make arrests. In the City Park, another crowd pulled down
and smashed the giant metal statue of Stalin: it was like a
famous scene from Eisenstein's film *October*, but attacking a
Communist tyrant rather than a Czar. Gerö then called in
Soviet troops—but they were not enough to crush the rebellion, and three days later, on Friday, October 26, he was
replaced by Nagy. For a week there was heady excitement.
The one-party system was abolished; Cardinal Mindszenty
was released from his long imprisonment; freedom of teaching
was promised; and on Saturday, November 3, a new government was formed, including two non-Communists—the former
President Zoltán Tildy, and Béla Kovács, former Secretary-
General of the Smallholders' Party, to which Tildy also had
belonged. On the very next day, however, 6,000 Soviet
tanks converged on the capital. At 5:20 P.M. that same
Sunday, Nagy came to the radio to announce, "Our troops
are fighting"; but by then the situation was desperate. For
nearly three hours, Budapest went on broadcasting messages
and appeals for help. Then, at 8:07 P.M., the radio went
silent. That was that.[46]

At the time, it was tempting to believe that if the West
had not been occupied with Suez, the Soviet Union might
have held back; but what evidence there is suggests the
contrary. The very speed of the final invasion revealed its
careful planning, and the first fighting in Budapest actually
preceded the attack on Suez. Hungary, like Czechoslovakia
twelve years later, had overstepped the margin allowed by
Moscow: Suez provided good cover, but no pretext was
needed for the Soviet Union to act. On the other hand, this
sudden hardening of the "cold war" gave Western Europeans

a powerful, if crude, incentive for seeking unity. A more united Western Europe would certainly be stronger, and might well discourage aggression; and even if, in this instance, it could have done little to save Hungary, it was clear that a divided Western Europe could do even less.

Working against the clock and under these multiple pressures, the Val Duchesse negotiators completed the Euratom and Common Market Treaties in record time. From start to finish, it took them less than ten months. At length, on Monday, March 25, 1957, in the huge, ornate and crowded Sala degli Orazi e Curiazi of the Capitol in Rome, the Treaties were formally signed by the representatives of the Six—Spaak and Baron Snoy, for Belgium; Adenauer and Hallstein, for Germany; Christian Pineau and Maurice Faure, for France; Antonio Segni and Gaetano Martino, for Italy; Joseph Bech and Lambert Schaus, for Luxembourg; Joseph Luns and Johannes Linthorst Homan, for the Netherlands. The obstacle race was almost over. One by one, the national parliaments ratified the Treaties; and this process too was unwittingly assisted by the Soviet Union. On Friday, October 4, 1957, Soviet technicians put into orbit the world's first artificial satellite, Sputnik I, a 183-lb sphere nearly two feet across. It was a startling illustration of how far the countries of Western Europe lagged behind the giants; and Monnet and his friends were quick to use it as an argument for unity. Finally, in December 1957, the Rome Treaties cleared their last parliamentary hurdle; and on Wednesday, January 1, 1958, they came into force.

On Monday and Tuesday of the following week, January 6 and 7, the Foreign Ministers of the Six met in Paris to decide where Euratom and the Common Market should have their headquarters, and to appoint the Presidents and members of their respective Commissions. The latter task proved easier than the former. In 1952, the ECSC had settled in Luxembourg in default of a ministerial decision; now, it might have seemed logical for the new institutions to be set up alongside it, perhaps in a "European District" on the model of Washington, D.C. For a time, Monnet in particular canvassed this solution; but Luxembourg opinion—backed, it was said, by the Grand Duchess Charlotte and the Church

—was already very conscious of the High Authority's busy presence, and it feared a fresh influx of impatient foreigners. When the Government finally changed its mind, the chance had passed. Brussels, a larger and more lively capital with better communications, was now firmly in the running: not for nothing had the negotiations been conducted at Val Duchesse. Eventually, after long discussion, the Ministers decided that the new Community authorities should meet in Brussels and Luxembourg alternately. For a few weeks, this was attempted: the High Authority vacated some of its offices, and welcomed its new colleagues with a nervously eager embrace. But so much traveling quickly proved impracticable, and Brussels soon became the Commissions' de facto new home. At first, both Euratom and the Common Market were lodged in the same narrow, white-stone-faced building in rue Belliard. When they moved in, the lower floors were still not completed, and strangers wandered in and out of half-furnished offices to the tap of workmen's hammers and the buzz of drills. Within a few months, however, the Common Market Commission moved into roomier quarters in a similar new white building, appropriately located in the Avenue de la Joyeuse Entrée.[47]

As President of the Euratom Commission, the Ministers appointed Louis Armand. Its Vice-President was Enrico Medi, a highly volatile Italian physicist; the other three members were Paul Hubert De Groote, a lean, laconic former minister and Rector of Brussels Free University; Heinz Krekeler, who had been German Ambassador in Washington; and Emanuel Sassen, a former minister from the Netherlands who looked a little like Robert Boothby, and whose bulk and vocal power had been well known in the ECSC's Common Assembly.

The Common Market Commission had nine members to Euratom's five. Walter Hallstein became its President—a fifty-six-year-old bachelor who had been Rector of Frankfurt University before his appointment by Adenauer to the head of the German Foreign Office. Shy, rather solitary, sober-suited and bespectacled, with thinning hair above a C. P. Snow-like brow, he seemed very much the law professor, author of works like *Die Berichtigung des Gesellschaftskapitals* and *Wiederherstellung des Privatrechts*. But like most of his generation, he had lived through much more than the academic world could teach. As a boy growing up in the Rhineland, he had been told by one schoolmaster that the French across the frontier were his hereditary enemies. In 1944, conscripted into the German army, he had found himself fighting them. He was captured in Normandy by the Americans, and spent the rest of the war in Louisiana, where he organized a prison-camp "university," and was nearly murdered for his pains by Nazi fellow-captives. Since World War II he had been an active "European," and had represented Germany both at the Schuman Plan negotiations that had set up the ECSC, and at the recent Messina Conference. At times, his respect for law and protocol seemed rigid; but it sprang from a deep revulsion against anarchy and tyranny. Later, he was to sacri-fice his own post to his concern for principle. Meanwhile, he set to work with immense dedication. A serious, introspective man who saw few of even his senior staff regularly, he never-theless made it a point to accept speaking engagements. He was anxious to put the Commission on the map, in public view; perhaps, also, on the platform he felt both shielded and released. There was certainly a duality within him. Desk-bound, he looked back nostalgically to early skiing holidays. His official car was a gray Mercedes, but a convertible with red leather upholstery. And although work seemed to be his only hobby, he delighted in the theatre and in Berlin cabaret: at one official fancy-dress party, he astonished his fellow-guests by coming disguised as a tramp.[48]

His colleagues made a piquant contrast. There were three Vice-Presidents—Sicco Mansholt, a tall, weather-beaten Dutch Socialist, with a brown bald head who had won fame as a Resistance leader and as a postwar Minister of Agriculture, although his hobby was sailing, not farming; Piero Malvestiti, a stocky, plump Italian Christian Democrat who later be-came President of the ECSC High Authority, and who as a staunch Catholic favored what he called "a Guelph party in Europe"; and Jean Monnet's ex-colleague Robert Marjolin, formerly of OEEC, still at forty-six looking like a youthful college lecturer with his bright eyes behind dark-framed glasses, his springy step and his quick, wincing smile. The other members of the Commission were Hans von der Groeben, co-author of the Spaak Report, slightly resembling a younger, less Asiatic Adenauer; Robert Lemaignen, a gnarled, middle-aged French industrialist; the solid and dapper Giuseppe Petrilli, later to be head of IRI, the Italian state holding company; Michel Rasquin, a gaunt Socialist militant and former minister from Luxembourg; and Jean Rey, a friendly, lively, optimistic Belgian with heavy spectacles and a rapid, pouncing voice that made many of his remarks sound like successful tongue-twisters. A lawyer by profession and a Liberal in politics, Rey had been a prisoner-of-war in Germany and had later become Minister of Economic Affairs. In a country split by the language dispute between Walloons and Flemings, and repeatedly the victim of its bigger neighbors' quarrels, it was natural for him to be a federalist. Eventually he was to succeed Hallstein as President of the European Commission.[49]

Among the nine Common Market Commissioners, there were Catholics and Protestants, Socialists, Christian Democrats and Liberals. Several had served in the Resistance; several had been in prison-camps. Nearly all spoke French, and at least four spoke fluent English. At first they hardly knew each other. Lemaignen wrote eloquently later of the novelty and bewilderment of working in so mixed a group; and Malvestiti went so far as to have duplicated the speech that he planned to make at one of its early meetings, as if at some formal conference. But before long, in the small, deliberately cramped room near Hallstein's office on the top floor where the Commission met every Wednesday like a national cabinet, the atmosphere grew more relaxed and intimate. It was just as well. Looking out across the wintry roofs of Brussels, all nine felt the weight of what lay ahead. Backed by the Court of Justice and the 142-man European "Parliament," working in harness with the Council of Ministers that represented the national governments, their task was nothing less than to fuse six economies into one. They had just over a decade in which to do it.[50]

It was eight years since Jean Monnet had launched what became the Schuman Plan. It was six years since the Coal and Steel Community had been set up in Luxembourg. It was four years since EDC had been defeated. Now, Europe was on the move again, but in a different world. In the age of anxiety of the early 1950s, defense had seemed the key to Western Europe's unity: but with peace taken more and more for granted, and new prosperity beckoning, the hope of an American-sized Common Market was doubly attractive—as a means to greater wealth and a basis for political union. After the wild oats of EDC, it was a return to the more modest principles of the Schuman Declaration. "Thus will be realized . . . the fusion of interests which is indispensable to the establishment of an economic community; thus will be introduced the germ of a broader and deeper community between countries long opposed to one another by bloody conflicts." In those early months of 1958, Monnet's and Schuman's vision seemed to be coming true.[51]

For the moment, only one thing marred it: Great Britain still stood apart. This was one of Monnet's failures. Shortly after the Messina Conference, he had had another. Staying in Scotland with Sir Cecil Weir, his friend from the British Delegation in Luxembourg, he had tried his hand at an unaccustomed pastime. That night, he had noted in his diary: "I try to catch salmon in stream, without success." For salmon, the close-time came soon afterward; but there was no close season for Britain. Monnet had always believed that facts, not ideas, would eventually draw her into uniting Europe; and now, as the Common Market took shape in Brussels, at Val Duchesse and then in the Avenue de la Joyeuse Entrée, there came from across the Channel the first, hesitant signs that he was right.

THE LION AND THE UNICORN

> The lion and the unicorn
> Were fighting for the crown.
> *Nursery Rhyme*[1]

> I don't care to belong to any club that will have me
> as a member. *Groucho Marx*[2]

> We are no longer strong enough to stand alone, and if
> we fail to bring a Western European Union into being,
> we shall be obliged, in the long run, to subordinate our
> policy to that of one Great Power or the other.
> *George Orwell*[3]

Britain was not always an island. In the Tertiary geological
era, an isthmus blocked the Straits of Dover; even today,
over part of the Colbart, the ridge in mid-Channel between
Dungeness and Ambleteuse, there are only six feet of water
at low tide. Ever since the 1800s, attempts have been
made to bridge the Channel or to tunnel under it. Militarily, modern landing vessels, aircraft and missiles have
reduced it to little more than a ditch. But in the late 1950s,
the eighteen miles of choppy sea between Dover and Cap
Gris Nez still formed a psychological barrier—despite the
five million people who were crossing it every year. Then,
Britain was still tempted to think of Continental Europe, as
in the London *Times* of the period, under the general heading of "Overseas." To many British people, other European
countries seemed no less alien than other continents, and in
some respects more distant than English-speaking members
of the Commonwealth on the opposite side of the planet.[4]

In the Messina Resolution of June 1955, the Foreign Ministers of the Six promised to invite Britain, as a member of

WEU and an associate of the ECSC, to join the Spaak Committee set up to prepare the Common Market and Euratom. When Harold Macmillan, as British Foreign Secretary, accepted the invitation, he was careful to reserve his government's position. "There are, as you are no doubt aware," he wrote, "special difficulties for this country in any proposal for 'a European common market.' They [the British Government] will be happy to examine, without prior commitment and on their merits, the many problems which are likely to emerge from the studies and in doing so will be guided by the hope of reaching solutions which are in the interests of all parties concerned." The Government accordingly sent to the Spaak Committee the forty-nine-year-old R. F. Bretherton, a professional economist and amateur entomologist who was now Under-Secretary at the Board of Trade.[5]

At the Committee's first meeting, he pointed out that he was neither a delegate nor an observer, but a "representative" —presumably to stress Britain's midway position of being neither "in" nor "out." From the start, as Spaak put it, he was "discreet and sceptical": "While other countries' representatives took up their task with enthusiasm, he remained silent most of the time. When he intervened in the discussions, it was to express doubt whether his country could accept the ideas on which agreement seemed to be emerging."[6]

This was already discouraging, and worse was to come. On Tuesday, September 6, 1955, the Foreign Ministers met at Noordwijk on the Dutch coast to discuss the Committee's progress; but although the British Foreign Secretary was invited, he failed to appear. Then, in the second half of October, when the experts at Val Duchesse produced their first report, it revealed two basic clashes between the British and their colleagues. First, Britain opposed the idea of a common market based on a customs union: she preferred a free trade area, whose member States would retain their own existing tariffs on imports from non-members. Secondly, Britain wanted no new European institutions: she relied on the methods and machinery of the existing OEEC. "Existing" was in both cases the key word: above all, she wished to avoid change.[7]

On Monday, November 7, 1955, Spaak held a meeting of the heads of delegations to review the work of the experts. When Bretherton was called upon to comment, he again reserved the British position until further details were clarified; but he argued that it would be difficult for Britain, as a member of the Commonwealth, to join a European common market. On Euratom he was a little less chilling; but he still could make no formal promises. In reply, Spaak voiced the general disappointment that Britain was unwilling to go beyond intergovernmental co-operation as practiced in OEEC. He added that the experts' work was now completed, and that the next step was for the delegations to prepare a report for the Foreign Ministers. This, he made clear, would involve a political decision to proceed on the basis of the Messina Resolution. For Britain, it was the moment of choice. As it turned out, her choice was fateful. Bretherton returned to London, and the Spaak Committee continued on the basis of the Six.[8]

Once again, Britain had missed an opportunity. Both she and the future Common Market were to pay for the mistake. But at the time it seemed natural. The Six had plagued Britain to join EDC, and at the very least to form some link with it; yet when she had done so, EDC had failed. The new venture looked no closer to succeeding; unlike EDC, moreover, it seemed to be a matter of economics and trade, hardly enough to call for "supranational" institutions distinct from those of OEEC.

Mixed with British skepticism, there was also a measure of hostility, less to Euratom than to the Common Market. On Thursday, November 17, 1955, the British Government announced that it was unable to join the proposed atomic organization, partly because of its supranational institutions, partly because Britain's civil nuclear program was closely linked with defense, and partly because of existing bilateral links with Australia, Canada, and the United States. It added, however, that it had no desire to hinder the creation of Euratom if the Messina countries wished to proceed.[9]

The Common Market was another matter. Here, too, Britain repeatedly stressed that she was not opposed to the project; but to Continental Europeans, some of her actions seemed to belie her words. Anthony Eden, then British Prime Minister, made no secret of his fear that "these associations could lead to a high tariff group in Europe," and spoke of American "enthusiasm" for them in terms that showed how little he shared it. And a very clear demonstration of British policy was given on Tuesday, December 6, 1955, not in the Spaak Committee, but at a special unofficial meeting of the Heads of Delegation of OEEC, convened by the President in office, Sir Hugh Ellis-Rees.[10]

There was uncertainty and disquiet, said Ellis-Rees, about the future of OEEC. It was clear from the Messina Resolution, as from the later work of the Spaak Committee, that the Six's objectives were mainly political. It was also clear that they could lead to a reduplication of the work of OEEC and other bodies—something that the United Kingdom had repeatedly and officially opposed. Britain was not opposed to a greater political unity among the Six; but if they used economic means to achieve this end, it raised a problem for the other members of OEEC, none of whom had had the slightest hand in drawing up the Spaak Committee's reports. Given the difficulties that the Six must face, were they likely to achieve their economic aims more rapidly than OEEC could do by other means? As at present envisaged, the European Common Market would be an exclusive group, and could lead to the formation of a discriminatory block, nullifying part of OEEC's multilateral work. There was a danger that Western Europe might find itself divided into two camps. There was no question of proposing that the Six should cease their discussions, or hold them within the OEEC framework; but the relations between the Messina enterprise and the other member countries should be discussed by all the interested parties, with a view to general agreements to be worked out gradually through OEEC. The British Chancellor of the Exchequer, Mr. R. A. Butler, would make some proposals on these lines for discussion by the OEEC Ministers at their meeting in February 1956.[11]

Mr. Butler was renowned for his skillful use of ambiguity; and something of it seemed to pervade this statement by the Treasury's former Under-Secretary. In many respects, it was thoroughly reasonable. Was Britain opposed to a European Common Market? No: but she drew attention to its dangers. Did she believe that OEEC should take over the Six's project? No: but something might be worked out.

The type of arrangement that might be proposed was beginning to be clear in the case of Euratom. On Friday, June 10, 1955, just a week after the Messina Conference, OEEC had set up a working party on atomic energy. It reported back in January 1956; but Ellis-Rees, at the December meeting, was able to refer already to a plan whereby OEEC member States might collaborate or not, according to their needs and resources, in achieving well-defined aims. This was a fair description of what was to become OEEC's European Nuclear Energy Agency (ENEA). With far smaller resources than Euratom, it was to do well. But in the case of the Common Market, something far more elaborate was in prospect; and again it was highly ambiguous.[12]

In public, Britain repeated that while she could not join a European common market because of her Commonwealth commitments, she had no wish to thwart it. In private, in a Memorandum to the German Government on Monday, December 19, 1955, she appeared to suggest that Germany should break off the Spaak Committee negotiations and instead hold talks within OEEC.[13]

Spaak, informed of what seemed to him like an attempt to sabotage his efforts, was predictably incensed. In a calmer mood, he composed a long letter to Anthony Eden, which he finally sent on Tuesday, February 7, 1956. After recalling the unhappy history of EDC and the hopes aroused by Britain's association agreement with the European Coal and Steel Community, he described the progress made since Messina. "But now," he added:

. . . some weeks ago, a new and important event occurred, which may have very grave consequences for the future. Great Britain has not only declared that she will not associate herself with what may come into existence, but has added that she is against it. This is no longer benevolent and slightly sceptical neutrality, but hostility clearly expressed.

From the sides I hear the echoes of this opposition. I regret it and I should like to speak about it very frankly.

Let me summarize once again the many reasons that lead me to seek the integration of Europe.

First of all, this I believe is the real way to solve the German problem . . . A Germany which is integrated in European entities, and, through them, in the Atlantic Pact, will have defended herself against an individualism that too rapidly takes the form of nationalism, whose effects we know, and at the same time against the temptation to approach the Russians by herself in an attempt to solve with them, directly, the problems in dispute, without taking account of the general interests of the West. . . .

To this political conception are added some economic considerations. . . .

It seems clear to me that in this field the future belongs to the large communities of mankind. Automation, the progress of technology, the increase of production and productivity—all, to give their best results, require large markets. The Americans have achieved a material standard of living very much higher than that of European countries. Russia has announced a new Five-Year Plan. Even if we discount some of it as bluff, the size of its objectives is disquieting. What have we got to set alongside it? Not much, I am afraid. . . .

I recognize very willingly that if a European economic union is set up, with six countries and more than 150 million inhabitants, this raises serious problems for its neighbours—even if, as is the case, the union in question rejects all idea of self-sufficiency or excessive protectionism. To that, I might answer that our union is not exclusive, that on the contrary it is open to those who wish to join it, and that this applies above all to Great Britain. But I know that this reply is inappropriate, because Great Britain does not intend to join.

There remains, therefore, the subsidiary solution of an agreement between the new union and Great Britain. Is such an agreement possible? Quite clearly, the question must be thoroughly explored. What I dread is that Great Britain, by throwing her considerable weight into the balance of the talks, may succeed in wrecking our great projects and obliging us to accept the *fait accompli* of a negative policy, whose consequences for the future would I think be disastrous from all points of view.

If Great Britain is really afraid of our European ventures, would it not be better to discuss the subject frankly between ourselves? And is W.E.U. not the place where such discussions might be held?[14]

A few days later, on Monday, February 13, 1956, Spaak received an answer which he later described as "cordial but vague." Shortly afterward, Eden suggested that he talk with Harold Macmillan, who had now succeeded Butler at the

Treasury. For Whitehall, clearly, the "re-launching of Europe," although recognized as political, was still at this stage to be treated as economic, and referred to the Board of Trade and the Treasury rather than to the Foreign Office—still less to the Ministry of Defense. Nothing was made of Spaak's suggestion that talks be held in WEU, where Britain and the Six were closeted together. Instead, Britain continued to prefer the heterogeneous OEEC, whose eighteen member States ranged from members of NATO to neutrals, and from highly industrialized democracies to countries that both economically and politically were far less favored. As one of Spaak's former assistants remarked, if Britain feared that the Six were "dividing Europe," it was hard to claim that OEEC had united it.[15]

Ironies apart, however, the British response to the Six's plans was not completely negative. During the early meetings of the Spaak Committee, Britain had mooted the possibility of establishing a Free Trade Area in Europe; and on Wednesday and Thursday, March 14 and 15, 1956, the British economist James Meade published two articles on the subject in the *Manchester Guardian* that some believed to have been officially inspired. Finally, on Thursday, July 5, 1956, less than six weeks after the Spaak Report had been accepted by the six Foreign Ministers as a basis for negotiating Euratom and the Common Market, Sir Edward Boyle, then Economic Secretary to the Treasury, announced to the House of Commons that the Government was re-appraising the whole of its European policy. What this meant became clear some days later, at the July meeting of the OEEC Council of Ministers. There, with strong British backing, the Secretary-General René Sergent proposed a working party to study the possibility of setting up a Free Trade Area embracing all the OEEC countries, and including as one of its constitutents the Common Market of the Six.[16]

In retrospect, many people—including Spaak himself—came to believe that the proposed Free Trade Area would have dissolved the Common Market, as some of them put it, "like a lump of sugar in a British cup of tea." But the belief was slow in growing. When James Meade's articles were published, they were hailed by several of Monnet's associates, including one or two who were later very critical of the plan. Monnet himself favored it: on Thursday, September 20, 1956, the Action Committee called on Governments to "do all that lies in their power to hasten the conclusion of the Treaty for the European Common Market, and the completion of the studies undertaken in OEEC for the inclusion of this Common Market in a free trade area comprising the United Kingdom and the other members of OEEC." Even Walter Hallstein, as late as January 1958, when he had just been appointed President of the Common Market Commission, was to describe the Free Trade Area as its "necessary supplement."[17]

The OEEC working party duly reported back in January 1957; and on the 15th of that month Paul-Henri Spaak paid a visit to London to see the new Chancellor of the Exchequer, Peter Thorneycroft. The negotiations for Euratom and the Common Market were by this time far advanced; but Britain was anxious to ensure that the Common Market should not be set up before the Free Trade Area. Spaak pointed out that it would be impossible to hold up the negotiations, which the British conceded: he therefore suggested that if by the end of them Britain or other countries detected anything in the draft Treaty that seemed incompatible with a Free Trade Area, they should inform the Six. He further proposed that the Treaty contain a revision clause to cover the possibility of change if other countries were associated—although it would require unanimous agreement and parliamentary ratification. He then turned to the content of the proposed Free Trade Area. Fresh from his experiences in Brussels, he pointed out that to be effective it would have to deal with other barriers besides customs tariffs. The British seemed largely to agree. They refused, however, to include agriculture in the free trade system; as a compensation, they offered to maintain benevolent neutrality if the Common Market's own agricultural policy came under fire from other exporting countries in such international bodies as the General Agreement on Tariffs and Trade (GATT).[18]

The impression that Spaak brought back from his London talks was discouraging. The technical difficulty of establishing a Free Trade Area, already considerable, now looked even greater than before. Agriculture was to be excluded: this would deny outlets, in particular, to France and Italy, which as high-tariff countries would be making large concessions in the industrial field. Britain was worried at the prospect that the Six's colonies and ex-colonies might be linked with the Common Market; yet she herself proposed to stand at the crossroads of the Free Trade Area and the Commonwealth preference system, enjoying commercial privileges that her partners were denied. There was vagueness about the innumerable non-tariff problems with which the Brussels negotiators had grown familiar—revenue duties, subsidies to home industries, export rebates, tax discrimination, health and safety requirements, differential freight rates, cartels, monopolies, and price rings. There was hesitancy about institutions. There was doubt about the possible diversion of trade: how could imports through the low-tariff countries be prevented from slipping across the frontier into neighboring higher-tariff markets—unless there were a system of certificates of origin, which itself might be open to fraud? There was anxiety about the cohesion of the Common Market: if free trade—the most obvious of its benefits—were to be offered without the discipline of a common tariff, common rules and common institutions, might not its member States slide gradually into this convenient commercial arrangement, without ever approaching the economic union that was their formal goal? Finally, there was doubt about America. Was it reasonable for the OEEC countries—who were not embarking on economic or political union—to grant each other special privileges and establish tariff discrimination against the dollar area, just at the time when their newly favorable balance of payments position required them to remove the quota discrimination that the United States had accepted while they were poor? Washington welcomed the Common Market as a step toward European unity; but although it maintained a diplomatic silence, it was obviously embarrassed by the Free Trade Area proposal.

These difficulties were real. With many other technical problems, they occupied the negotiators for eighteen months, from the spring of 1957 until November 1958—first in expert committees of OEEC, then in a full-scale conference under the buoyant chairmanship of Reginald Maudling, who was also head of the British negotiating team. Conceivably, the problems might have been solved, and the Free Trade Area might have come into being—but for the dramatic events that now shook France and were soon to shake Europe itself.

At 3:00 P.M. on Tuesday, May 13, 1958, the sturdy, silver-haired Pierre Pflimlin, Catholic Mayor of Strasbourg, rose in the National Assembly to make his investiture speech as Prime Minister of France. Appointed by President René Coty to end a further month-long Government crisis, he faced a country torn apart by the three-and-a-half years of the Algerian War, an army on the brink of mutiny, and an unnerving multiplicity of threats, rumors, and genuine plots. Rightly or wrongly, both the settlers and the soldiers in Algeria suspected Pflimlin of being about to make terms with the Algerian rebels.[19]

Just two hours later, in Algiers, open riot broke out. A general strike was in progress, and the hot afternoon streets were crowded with young men. Unexpectedly, a mob of students and schoolboys attacked the Government Building, and invaded it with the help of paratroops supposedly called in to disperse them. When General Raoul Salan, the Army Commander-in-Chief, tried to restore order he was howled down. Thereupon, the paratroop general Jacques Massu announced the formation of a Committee of Public Safety; he also telegraphed Paris, demanding a government that would keep Algeria French. On the following day, Massu issued an appeal to the sixty-seven-year-old General de Gaulle to return to power; and Salan, prompted by a Gaullist plotter, half-inadvertently echoed this appeal next morning by ending a speech with the cry of *"Vive de Gaulle!"* De Gaulle had already heard from the conspirators, and with this he felt free to act. From his country retreat at Colombey-les-Deux-Eglises, he put himself forward as "ready to assume the powers of the Republic." After four more days of uproar in Algiers and suspense in Paris, he gave a resounding press conference, stating his views on Algeria in terms designed to appeal to both sides. Then, once more, he waited. On Sunday,

May 25, the blow fell: the Right-wing rebels seized the island of Corsica. The Government ordered the French navy to recapture it—but next day, in the face of a virtual refusal, it had to rescind the order. On Tuesday, May 27, after secret contacts with Pflimlin and with Guy Mollet, the Socialist leader, de Gaulle announced that he had begun "the regular process necessary to establish a republican Government capable of restoring the unity and independence of the country." In fact, to be on the safe side, he was also still in touch with the army insurrectionists. Next day, President Coty told the party leaders that they must choose between de Gaulle and a Popular Front Government that would surely spark off a revolt by the army. His own choice was now clear. On Thursday, May 29, he announced that he was asking de Gaulle to form a Government of National Safety; and on the evening of Sunday, June 1, 1958, with the necessary support of Guy Mollet's Socialists, de Gaulle was voted into office after an absence of over twelve years.[20]

At sixty-seven, de Gaulle described himself as an "old man, worn by suffering, detached from human concerns, feeling the approach of eternal cold, but never weary of watching in the shadows for the gleam of hope." It was the peroration of his war memoirs, following similar evocations of France and the whole earth; perhaps he added it after his return to power. As a literary artist whom critics compared to Bossuet and Pascal, he expressed very nobly the bleakness of his vision; but his rhetoric left a sense of strain and artifice. At worst, the grandeur of the style obscured the poverty of the content: too often, he was writing beyond his means.[21]

The same applied to many of de Gaulle's actions. His greatest skill was to use the grand manner to conceal his lack of resources. It was an art that he had learned in wartime London. Then, as now, his triumphs were essentially literary and histrionic—his broadcast appeal in June 1940; his masterly playing of the 1958 crisis; his later handling of the "barricades" rebellion, crushed largely by a single broadcast; finally, the four-minute speech with which he ended the disorders of May 1968. He was never quite without weapons: but to deploy them he used the power of words. Each time he had the courage, when lesser men were faltering, to stand up straight and say "No."

So astonished were some of his contemporaries that they looked for hidden subtleties in de Gaulle's political philosophy. They found them in his tactics—the shrewd, patient timing, the weighing of odds, the manipulation of rivalries, the feel for French public opinion, the sense of others' weaknesses, the use of hints, vague promises, ambiguous threats. But those who sought to construct a complicated system out of de Gaulle's twistings and turnings—his nods and winks to first one potential partner, then another—were fundamentally mistaken. In domestic as in foreign policy, de Gaulle's ideas were few and simple. Like his very great virtues, they were those of a soldier. He believed in efficiency, and he believed in France. To be efficient, it was essential to use the latest material techniques; it was also essential to practice the military art of "man management," partly by television, partly by profit-sharing, partly by the traditional wiles of leadership. Democracy was another matter. France had suffered from its excesses; and France must be restored. In the world of modern technology, this meant international co-operation. But no alliances could be eternally binding; no interests could be superior to the national interest; no pretended "merger of sovereignty" must tie the hands of France. And now, once again, "France" meant General Charles de Gaulle.

His return to power cast a cold shadow in the spring sunshine of Brussels. His views were well known. He and his party had opposed the Schuman Plan, the Common Market and Euratom; his new Prime Minister, Michel Debré, had passionately attacked the Spaak Report, and had been as fiercely attacked in his turn by Paul-Henri Spaak. At the same time, however, "Europeans" had read de Gaulle's memoirs, and had noted that at one point during World War II he had spoken of "a strategic and economic federation" in Western Europe, "to which Great Britain might be attached." The options, it seemed, were open. De Gaulle might well be persuaded to continue French support for the Common Market—provided that it showed clear advantages to France.[22]

The proposed Free Trade Area fulfilled no such condition. Lacking a single outer tariff, it would impose no collective discipline on its members; lacking an agreement on agriculture, it would provide no extra market for French farm produce; including Great Britain—and in a privileged position —it would challenge the tacit leadership that in the Common Market seemed to belong to France. For all these reasons, and not solely for fear of rivalry, de Gaulle decided to halt the negotiations. On the evening of Friday, November 14, 1958, the French Minister of Information, Jacques Soustelle, announced to the press that "it has become clear to France that it is not possible to set up the Free Trade Area as wished by the British." France's partners protested; but her opinion was shared by many of the Brussels Commission, although for different reasons. After much argument, two special reports by the Commission, and an American-sponsored re-organization of OEEC which turned it into an "Atlantic" body (OECD, the Organization for Economic Co-operation and Development) with the U.S. and Canada as full members, the hope of a Europe-wide Free Trade Area was finally buried. The lion and the unicorn had fought their first battle. Helped by some "Europeans," who feared the dissolvent effects of the Free Trade Area no less than the disruptive potential of General de Gaulle, the unicorn—for the time being —had won.

The second battle began three years later. In the meantime, the situation had changed. Britain, her hopes of a large Free Trade Area vanishing, had begun to form a small one: in Stockholm, on Friday, November 20, 1959, she signed the Convention establishing the EFTA, or European Free Trade Association, comprising Austria, Denmark, Norway, Portugal, Sweden, and Switzerland, in addition to Britain herself. This was partly a salvage operation, to secure whatever benefits were possible on a smaller and more scattered basis. In this respect it succeeded: eventually, it was to remove its internal tariff barriers more quickly than the Common Market, although many non-tariff obstacles remained. But in so far as EFTA was intended to bring pressure on the Common Market for a revival of the old Free Trade Area, in its early years it had very little success. It certainly dramatized the so-called "division of Europe," and news of its formation played some part in proposals for world-wide tariff-cutting made by the U. S. Under-Secretary of State, C. Douglas Dillon, shortly before the EFTA Convention was formally signed. But America continued to treat EFTA with extravagant coolness; and in the longer term its chief significance may have been as a stage in Britain's gradually greater involvement with the European continent.[23]

The Common Market, meanwhile, had survived the fears aroused by de Gaulle's return to office. By pushing through a 17.5 per cent devaluation of the franc on December 27, 1958, de Gaulle had actually made it possible for France to join in the first Common Market tariff reductions, due on January 1, 1959, without requesting a waiver. On May 12, 1960, the six member States agreed to the Commission's proposal to speed up the tariff-cutting process; and by mid-1961 the tariff barriers between them had been almost halved, while quota restrictions on industrial products were on their way to disappearing. Over-all production had increased by 20 per cent, and trade within the Common Market by 70 per cent. There was no watertight proof that this was due to the cutting of tariffs; but it seemed significant that trade with non-member countries had grown only half as fast. Already, in June and July 1959, two members of OEEC had drawn their own conclusions: Greece and Turkey had both applied for association with the Six.[24]

A similar process of rethinking had been going on in London. In October 1959, Harold Macmillan's government had been returned with an increased majority. Cartoonists were fond of portraying Macmillan as a slightly seedy Edwardian with almost heraldic mustaches; but under the archaic camouflage he was alert and sensitive, as much aware in Europe as in Africa of what he called "the wind of change." His manner was in part at least a sop to human conservatism, as misleading as de Gaulle's reassurance that he had "understood" the Algiers settlers. There was no real paradox, therefore, in Macmillan's being responsible for Britain's first decisive step toward uniting Europe. It was only unfortunate in being too cautious and too well disguised.

The first sign of change came on Thursday, January 21, 1960, at a meeting of the Consultative Assembly of the Council of Europe, when Selwyn Lloyd, the British Foreign Secretary, went so far as to admit: "I believe we made a mistake in not taking part in the negotiations which led to the formation of the Coal and Steel Community." In March, Macmillan went to Washington, and was startled to find how strongly the U. S. Administration backed the Common Market, if necessary to detriment of any "special relationship" with Britain: when, referring presumably to EFTA, he tactlessly recalled the "peripheral coalition" against Napoleon, his remarks were promptly leaked to the Washington *Post*. In April, the British Government announced that it could no longer afford to build the "Blue Streak" military rocket; in May, Nikita Khrushchev broke up the long-heralded "summit" meeting in Paris after President Eisenhower had admitted, with undiplomatic candor, his responsibility for the high-level "U-2" photographic reconnaissance aircraft, one of which had just been shot down near Sverdlovsk in the Urals. Both incidents set off a train of newspaper comment about Britain's relative impotence in world affairs and her inability by herself to match American technology. As a remedy, both *The Economist* and *The Observer* now began to advocate joining the Common Market. A similar conclusion was beginning to emerge from the Economic Steering Committee which the Government had set up under Sir Frank Lee, Permanent Secretary at the Treasury, to make a confidential study of the whole subject.[25]

In June 1960 the Cabinet itself edged a little further in this direction. Speaking in Paris at the Assembly of Western European Union, John Profumo, then Minister of State at the Foreign Office, affirmed that "the British Government, without regard to all that has happened in the last few years, will certainly be ready to consider anew the proposal that Britain should join Euratom, and indeed, the European Coal and Steel Community as well."[26]

Jean Monnet had been watching these developments with a mixture of anxiety and hope. Long after de Gaulle had rejected the old Free Trade Area, Monnet and the Action

Committee had continued to press for multilateral links between Britain and the Common Market, first in a European
framework, then in a broader context that would not exclude
the United States. Now, on Monday, July 11, 1960, the Committee made an unequivocal response to Profumo's statement.
"The acceleration of the Common Market," it declared:

. . . has shown the United Kingdom and the other European
countries that there is now no going back on European integration,
that it is beneficial, and also open to all.

Today it is possible to envisage the participation of all in the
common task of uniting Europe.

Accordingly the Action Committee, echoing the wishes of the vast
majority of citizens in our countries, earnestly hopes that the United
Kingdom and the other European countries will simultaneously become members of the Coal and Steel Community, Euratom, and the
Common Market, which are three facets of a single reality. This reality is the emerging European economic union that is paving the way
for a political unity, the exact nature of which cannot now be
foreseen.[27]

The British Government was not slow to take the point:
it realized the difficulty of joining two of the Community
organizations without joining the third. On Monday, July 25,
1960, when the House of Commons debated the question,
Selwyn Lloyd reviewed the three main groups of problems
that seemed to be raised by Common Market membership
—the Commonwealth, agriculture and EFTA—in terms that
revealed how far the discussion in Cabinet had gone. "I have
not pronounced against us going into some form of European
institution," he added, "but we have to be careful what
these institutions are, what they are to do, and what would
be our responsibilities in the matter." In fact, the Cabinet was
still divided.[28]

Conversations at that time in Whitehall and Westminster
revealed several reasons for Britain's hesitation. Some Ministers and officials still questioned whether a united Western
Europe was desirable or possible. Others, while accepting it
as an objective, doubted whether Britain could actually join
the Common Market without deserting and offending her
partners in the Commonwealth and EFTA. A third group,
finally, now urged British entry, but feared a possible rebuff.

There seemed no likelihood of a quick decision—until two events in the second half of 1960 combined to tip the scales. First, the Common Market Six began discussing political union. Secondly, John Fitzgerald Kennedy was elected President of the United States.

The impetus for political talks in Europe came from General de Gaulle. In a radio broadcast on Tuesday, May 31, 1960, he had said:

> To help to build Western Europe into a political, economic, cultural, and human group, organized for action, progress, and defence is the aim of the French Government. Already West Germany, Italy, the Netherlands, Belgium, and Luxembourg are co-operating directly with her in several fields. In particular the Common Market of the Six will on 31 December become a practical reality [when it was planned to make an extra internal tariff cut and begin establishing the common tariff on imports from outside]. Of course, the participants do not want this organization to injure the other countries of Europe, and we must expect a way to be found of accommodating their interests. Also, of course, the nations which are becoming associated must not cease to be themselves, and the path to be followed must be that of organized co-operation between states, while waiting to achieve, perhaps, an imposing confederation.

Listening in Brussels to this speech, some "Europeans" were suspicious. It was not so long since the General and his followers had denounced the "relaunching of Europe"; and as recently as September 17, 1958, he had formerly proposed to Eisenhower and Macmillan a Franco-British-American directorate of NATO that would have made impossible any equitable European Defense Community. The "organized co-operation between states" might mean little more than a traditional alliance, no doubt to be led by France; and although the term "confederation" was indeed imposing, it might well be a means of short-circuiting the Common Market's more truly federal institutions.[29]

Not everyone was so pessimistic. The only difference between a federation and a confederation, said some, was a French three-letter word. Others pointed out that even in a United States of Europe nations would never "cease to be themselves." If de Gaulle was seriously proposing co-operation among the Six on foreign policy, "culture," and defense, his partners should seize the opportunity; it might not be "political union," but it could be a step toward it. All that was essential was to ensure that the new moves strengthened rather than weakened the Common Market's structure, and that they took place within the Atlantic Alliance rather than seeking to establish an autonomous "third force."

On Friday, July 29, 1960, de Gaulle expounded his ideas to Dr. Adenauer at Rambouillet, the magnificent fifteenth-century château thirty miles southwest of Paris where Francis I had died. At the end of August, he saw J. E. De Quay and Joseph Luns, respectively Dutch Prime Minister and Foreign Minister; in early September he saw Amintore Fanfani and Antonio Segni, their Italian counterparts; later in the month he talked with Gaston Eyskens and Pierre Wigny from Belgium, and with Pierre Werner and Eugène Schaus from Luxembourg. After further diplomatic contacts, de Gaulle and Adenauer met again on Thursday, February 9, 1961; and on the Friday and Saturday the "Heads of State or Government"—President de Gaulle and the Prime Ministers—and the Foreign Ministers of the Six held a so-called "little summit" meeting to study, as they put it, "suitable means of organizing closer political co-operation. The establishment of links in other spheres will provide future bases for a progressively developing union. This union, for the moment confined to the Member States of the European Economic Community, could subsequently extend its boundaries." To make more concrete proposals, they set up an intergovernmental committee; and although the Dutch delegation there feared "that the system of European institutions might be compromised by the creation of a political superstructure of an intergovernmental character," when the Six held their next summit meeting, in Bonn on Tuesday, July 18, 1961, they had smoothed over the cracks. They decided, in the words of their final communiqué, "to give shape to the will for political union already implicit in the Treaties establishing the European Communities," and they set up a new committee to draft a political treaty.[30]

This committee—usually known as the "Fouchet Committee" after its first chairman, the French representative Christian Fouchet, although it was later chaired by Attilio Cattani from Italy—at length disbanded without reaching agreement. It was divided, in particular, about Europe's place in the Atlantic Alliance, about British membership of the proposed "political union," and about the need for a revision clause whereby the new institutions might be strengthened. If the Fouchet Committee had succeeded in its task, it might conceivably have helped avoid some of the later friction between the French Government and its partners. But it might equally have weakened the Common Market; and the institutions that it proposed to establish were themselves so feeble that they seemed unlikely to promote unity on subjects so intractable as foreign policy and defense. The first draft treaty put forward by France, her partners' counterproposal, a second French draft, and a compromise text canvassed just before the talks ended, all spoke of a "European Political Commission"; yet this would have consisted, not of independent persons like the members of the Common Market Commission, but simply of national representatives. All four drafts, not unnaturally, proposed a traditional Council of Ministers; but only that prepared by France's partners envisaged majority voting, and then only if all members of the Council unanimously agreed to it. All four mentioned the European Parliament; but none explicitly proposed that it be directly elected or have any specific powers. Neither French draft, finally, mentioned a Court of Justice; and although this was proposed by France's partners, it was virtually dropped from the final text. Broadly speaking, the Fouchet Committee retained Community terminology, but only to disguise its desertion of Community principles.[31]

At the time, this in no way discomfited the British Government; but far more disquieting was Britain's exclusion from the Six's plans. Only by joining the Common Market, it seemed, could she be sure of taking part in any collective political venture, and recovering as a member of the future union a share in the world influence she could no longer command alone.

Britain's relative loss of power was becoming very evident in her relations with Washington, where the "special relationship" was obviously less prized than in London. The

U. S. Presidential election of November 1960, which brought Kennedy to the White House in place of Eisenhower, accentuated this fact. Far from weakening America's support for the Common Market and her hope that Britain would join it, Kennedy and his team made them more articulate and active. The Francophile Douglas Dillon, rather to Eisenhower's annoyance, stayed on with the new Administration; and other convinced "Europeans" came in. Robert Bowie became a consultant to the new Secretary of State, Dean Rusk; McGeorge Bundy, the editor of Dean Acheson's speeches, became the President's special adviser on National Security Affairs; Paul Nitze became Assistant Secretary for International Security Affairs in the Pentagon; and the tough, genial George Ball, a close friend and associate of Jean Monnet's, became Under-Secretary of State for Economic Affairs, later succeeding Chester Bowles as Under-Secretary. He brought into his office three youngish State Department officials who were all energetic, gifted, and equally "European" —Robert Schaetzel, Stanley Cleveland, and Arthur Hartman.[32]

From this array of talent on "Fluff Row"—the State Department's top-level carpeted corridors—came a strong new impetus in America's relationship with Europe. Journalists later called it "the Grand Design," although it was no more than a reinvigorated version of what had been United States policy since World War II. It sought essentially what Kennedy called "an open partnership" between the United States and uniting Europe—"a relationship," as Jean Monnet's Action Committee said later, "of two separate but equally powerful entities, each bearing its share of common responsibilities in the world." Kennedy, again, was to echo these words just one week afterward; the "dialogue of continents" seemed to have begun. Its most concrete expression was the U. S. Trade Expansion Act, leading at long last to the "Kennedy Round" of tariff negotiations, whereby the United States, the Common Market and other countries eventually made tariff cuts of more than 30 per cent—and in some cases, of 50 per cent—on 40 billion dollars' worth of annual trade.[33]

Under a technicality in the Trade Expansion Act, the U. S. President's tariff-cutting powers would have been even greater had Britain joined the Common Market. It was drafted, in fact, with this in mind. Although Kennedy and his advisers stopped short of actual pressure, their eagerness for Britain to join the Common Market was very obvious. In London on Thursday, March 30, 1961, Edward Heath, the Lord Privy Seal, asked George Ball what America's attitude would be if she did. Ball answered that he had not discussed the question with the President. Nevertheless, he said:

. . . if Britain is now prepared to recognize that the Rome Treaty is not a static document but a process that could eventually lead to an evolving European community—something in the nature of a European federation—and if Britain can make the great national decision to join Europe on those terms, I am confident that my Government will regard this as a major contribution to Western solidarity and the stability of the free world. So long as Britain remains outside the European Community, she is a force for division rather than cohesion, since she is like a giant lodestone drawing with unequal degrees of force on each member State. But if Great Britain now decides to participate in the formidable efforts to unite Europe, she can, and I am sure will, apply her unique political genius—in which we have great confidence—toward the creation of a unity that can transform the Western world.

Harold Macmillan received a similar answer early in April when he put the same question to President Kennedy. So—somewhat to his surprise—did Walter Hallstein, President of the Common Market Commission, when he was in Washington in mid-May, 1961.[34]

By this time the British Government was approaching a decision. In the last week of June, 1961, the Ministerial Council of EFTA met in London and resolved that, if negotiations with the Common Market took place:

. . . the European Free Trade Association, the obligations created by the Convention between the Members, and the momentum towards integration within the Association, would be maintained at least until satisfactory arrangements have been worked out in negotiations to meet the various legitimate interests of all Members of EFTA, and thus enable them all to participate from the same date in an integrated European Market.

Britain pledged herself, in other words, not to make use of the denunciation clause allowing any member State to leave EFTA after twelve months' notice, and not to join the Common Market until all her EFTA partners were either about to join or about to make free-trade arrangements with it. At the time, it seemed a far-reaching commitment. No such promises were made, however, to the Commonwealth countries. In the hope of forestalling criticism, five British ministers visited their capitals, mostly during the first half of July; but the ensuing communiqués were inexplicit and brief.[35]

At last, on Monday, July 31, 1961, Harold Macmillan made his announcement to the House of Commons. One observer noted that it was delivered "in a surprisingly uninspired way"; but more important than Macmillan's fatigued manner was the substance of what he said. Britain was to ask for negotiations with the European Economic Community to see if mutually acceptable conditions could be worked out for British membership. "No British Government," he explained:

. . . could join the European Economic Community without prior negotiation with a view to meeting the needs of the Commonwealth countries, of our European Free Trade Association partners, and of British agriculture consistently with the broad principles and purposes which have inspired the concept of European unity and which are embodied in the Rome Treaty.

"The ultimate decision whether to join or not," he added:

must depend on the result of the negotiations. . . . No agreement will be entered into until it has been approved by the House after full consultation with other Commonwealth countries by whatever procedure they may generally agree.[36]

To Jean Monnet and his associates, Macmillan's announcement seemed curiously bitter-sweet. On the one hand, it was the culmination of their hopes and efforts; yet on the other it confirmed some lingering fears. Monnet knew very well the material problems involved in British entry; but to solve them he had for some time been urging a different procedural approach. His advice on the subject has been summarized as "sign now, negotiate later." This does it some injustice. More properly, what he was proposing may be described as "decide now, negotiate on essentials, sign, then solve the other problems from within the Common Market."[37]

His argument was roughly as follows. Speed, as in many important matters, was essential. An opportunity once lost might not recur for a long time; and when it recurred it might not be recognized. There was no certainty that General de Gaulle would welcome or even grudgingly accept British entry into the Common Market; and a long negotiation would make it easier for him to refuse. Delay, moreover, would only increase the number of new agreements within the Common Market that Britain would face when she finally entered: the sooner she joined, the more say she would have in the shape the Common Market took. Finally, the institutions themselves—the Commission, the Council of Ministers, the Court and the European Parliament—had been devised for the specific purpose of solving the member States' problems. To try to solve them from outside, without the help of the institutions, would be to start off on the wrong foot. Once Britain was in, however, her national concerns would be part of the Common Market's problems, which all its members had an interest in solving.

Monnet recognized, however, that some problems would brook no delay. British agriculture, he thought, had little to fear from competition with that of the Six; and if Britain joined the Community quickly enough, she could help shape its farm policy. Food imports from the former Dominions were more difficult, although here again early entry would enable Britain to influence policy. For New Zealand, and particularly for its butter, some standstill arrangement would have to be worked out, pending a permanent solution to be negotiated by the enlarged Common Market. For tropical primary products, the principle should be that Commonwealth producers in Africa deserved the same right of association with the Common Market as was offered to its founder-members' ex-colonies. For raw materials and manufactures, Britain would have to adopt the common outer tariff of the Six; but the duty on some products might be left to be settled by the institutions of the Common Market once Britain had joined. Finally, if some EFTA countries failed to join or associate with the Common Market, any trade problems that might arise for them would have to be discussed within OECD. What was above all essential, however, was that the number of questions to be settled before Britain's entry be reduced to a minimum, and that a firm decision be taken to join.[38]

Seen from London, there were several objections to such a course. First, it could be claimed that the provisions of the Rome Treaty, although mainly institutional and procedural, were also partly substantive: they included some precise agreements on material problems raised by one or other of the founder-members. The most obvious instance was the association with the Common Market of France's former colonies. Could Britain not claim something analogous for India, Ceylon, and Pakistan? Her responsibilities to the Commonwealth covered a far broader area than the overseas commitments of any of the Six; and although it might be argued that this made the problem far more difficult, the ethical principle was surely the same. By a similar token, the change involved for Britain in joining the Common Market could be considered more drastic than that undergone by any of the Six. Leaving aside the fact that she had not been defeated in war or invaded for the past nine centuries, leaving aside her Commonwealth ties and responsibilities, there were many technical differences between her legislative, judicial, and economic situation and those of the Six. In British law, for instance, no Parliament could bind its successors: some constitutional contortion would therefore be necessary for the House of Commons to ratify the Common Market Treaty, with no expiry date and no denunciation clause. British law was in many respects different from that of continental countries: this too would take time to adjust. Britain's national currency, unlike those of the Six, was still—however falteringly—a world reserve currency; her system of farm support, with low food prices and high subsidies to producers, was diametrically opposite to that of most of the Six; and while all the latter had been touched however unwillingly, by the Napoleonic Code and the metric system,

Britain had resisted Napoleon and missed his equivocal legacy.

Some of these objections had force, and in a perfect world they might have been sustained. But the world was far from perfect, and Britain had to make a choice. If she was not a founder-member of the Common Market, this was no fault of the Six: she must do her best to fit into the club as they had made it—although once inside she would find its rules more flexible than they looked. If she retained responsibilities as a leading member of the Commonwealth, the Common Market itself had comparable responsibilities as a leading industrial power. The Commonwealth preference system, together with the sterling area, could in this context be regarded as partial and imperfect attempts to solve world problems which the Common Market also faced. Britain's entry would merely restate them in more pressing terms; and their ultimate solution could only be sought by the enlarged Common Market with the aid of the United States. Finally, if Britain's changeover to Common Market membership caused her considerable upheaval, there was no question of her entering without a transition period in which to adapt herself. On the specific question of agriculture, where the adjustment problem seemed most acute, even the addition of Britain to the Common Market would not radically change the balance of supply and demand or the ratio of agriculture to industry. It would be understandable, therefore, if the Six asked Britain to accept the broad principles of what they themselves proposed as an agricultural policy—although the sooner she entered the greater say she would have.

Warnings and suggestions of this sort continued to reach London from a variety of quarters; but it was not easy for the British Government to respond. On Tuesday, August 1, 1961, Edward Heath told the WEU Council: "We shall be seeking the support of public opinion not just for British application for negotiations to join the European Economic Community but for the whole great enterprise which from now on we are, I trust, going to pursue together." But if this suggested that in Heath's mind at least the decision of principle was already taken, it remained formally necessary to keep up the "exploratory" stance. Characteristically, Macmillan's policy seemed to be to back into Europe. This was one reason that it failed.[39]

On Thursday, August 10, 1961, Great Britain formally requested the opening of negotiations. She was accompanied by Denmark, but overtaken by Ireland, which had applied to negotiate on August 1. On Tuesday, October 10, after further discussion among the Six, their Ministers met with Heath in Paris to hear a preliminary statement of Britain's case. It was in the same Salon de l'Horloge at the Quai d'Orsay that had seen so many European gatherings since the afternoon a decade ago when Robert Schuman had made his Declaration of May 9, 1950.

In many respects, Heath's speech was heartening:

> In saying that we wish to join the E.E.C., we mean that we desire to become full, whole-hearted and active members of the European Community in its widest sense and to go forward with you in the building of a new Europe. . . . In particular, we accept without qualification the objectives laid down in Articles 2 and 3 of the Treaty of Rome, including the elimination of internal tariffs, a common customs tariff, a common commercial policy, and a common agricultural policy.
>
> We are ready to accept, and to play our full part in, the institutions established under Article 4 and other Articles of the Treaty. . . .
>
> We are anxious that our accession to the Treaty should not tend to slow up the progress towards harmonization. . . .
>
> We are also ready, once we enter the Community, to make, in a single operation, the same cuts in tariffs on trade between Member States as you will have yourselves made by that date. In addition, we are prepared to move our M.F.N. [non-Commonwealth] tariff towards the new common tariff by a step equivalent to that which you have already taken. . . .
>
> We fully share the aims and objectives, political and otherwise, of those who drew up this Declaration [the Bonn Declaration on 'political union' of 18 July 1961], and we shall be anxious, once we are members of the Community, to work with you in a positive spirit to reinforce the unity which you have already achieved. . . .
>
> We in the United Kingdom will regard the successful conclusion of these negotiations as a point of departure, not as the end of the road. . . .[40]

This sounded far from "exploratory"; but the substance of Heath's speech was more disappointing. It would not be quite true to say that he gave away nothing in Paris that had not been announced in London: he did, after all, agree to make the tariff changes already gradually applied by the Six. The rest of his statement, however, gave the impression of trying to perpetuate in another form the economic and trading patterns that were crystallized in the Commonwealth and EFTA. By ingeniously adapting various provisions of the Rome Treaty, the speech implied, it would be possible for Britain to avoid—as the Six had avoided—imposing a tariff on trade where none had been in force before. The EFTA countries would join the Common Market or become associated with it in a free trade area; the African, Asian, and other "developing countries" of the Commonwealth would work out free access arrangements; "comparable outlets" would be found in the enlarged Common Market for foodstuffs from the former dominions, so that they could continue their exports as before. Only on one point did Heath's statement seem to allow for movement from this position of principle, hinting that it was a negotiating posture and not an inflexible stance. On manufactures from the Commonwealth, apart from those for which Britain proposed nil duties in the common outer tariff, he admitted that "we recognize that indefinite and unlimited continuation of free entry over the whole of this field may not be regarded as compatible with the development of the Common Market, and we are willing to discuss ways of reconciling these two conflicting considerations." In other respects, the system he initially proposed, if accepted by the Six, would have amounted not so much to Britain's joining the Common Market as to her embracing it and perhaps dissolving it in a quasi-worldwide system of free trade that would have included the whole of Western Europe, most of Africa, and all the rest of the British Commonwealth—discriminating, in other words, against the United States, Japan, Latin America and non-Commonwealth "developing countries." Clearly, this was impossible; and the main task of the negotiations was to force a slow retreat from this initial bargaining position toward a series of agreements much more like those that Monnet and his associates had already suggested.[41]

The negotiations formally began in Brussels on Wednesday, November 8, 1961, in a long narrow room at the top of Belgium's brand-new Foreign Ministry building in the rue des Quatre Bras. The British delegation sat at one end, in front of the interpreters' cabins; the President and Secretariat sat far away at the other, with the member States' and the Commission's delegations spread out along the sides. This led to problems. It was winter; the building was new, and was being dried out. The windows were therefore tight shut, and the central heating was oppressively efficient. Not only this, but several of the British had brought their pipes. It was not surprising that they pleaded for fresh air. At their request, windows were briskly opened, but then stealthily shut by those unlucky enough to be sitting in front of them. After several weeks of this running battle, the Belgians found a solution: directly above the British delegation they installed a ventilator pipe big enough to contain several spies or journalists. The tobacco-smoke vanished, the windows stayed shut, and the British delegation had its fresh air. In the euphoria of those early days, the incident seemed to symbolize all that the negotiators hoped.[42]

As the weeks went on, however, euphoria diminished. The British team was impressive: at ministerial level it was led by the bulky, shrewd and popular Edward Heath, a master of his dossiers; at official level, by the scholarly Sir Pierson Dixon, British Ambassador in Paris. It included Sir Eric Roll, Sir Roderick Barclay, Sir Henry Lintott, and Sir William Gorell Barnes—known collectively, because of their air trips to London, as "the flying knights." But despite this deployment of very able officials, the talks were extremely slow. Later, it was tempting to blame this on delaying tactics by the French delegation, whose leader at ministerial level was Maurice Couve de Murville, de Gaulle's icy Foreign Minister. But Couve de Murville's deputy was Bernard Clappier, who had been Robert Schuman's *Directeur de cabinet;* and although he was in a highly delicate position, he in fact played scrupulously fair. Nor, finally, could the Common

Market Commission be accused of obstruction. Headed at official level by an outstandingly able young Frenchman, Jean-François Deniau, who was later to be a Commission Member, it in fact produced all but one of the technical solutions that were found for Britain's problems before the end.[43]

It was April 1962, in fact, before the negotiators did more than elaborate fact-finding. By then, the Common Market had made further strides. At 5:32 A.M. on the morning of Sunday, January 14, 1962, after several all-night sessions and at least one ministerial heart attack, it had settled the broad lines of its farm support system, and had moved into the second four-year stage of its transition period—having "stopped the clock" at midnight on December 31 to maintain the legal fiction that it was on time. The agricultural agreement, strongly pressed by France, put paid to British and "European" hopes that Britain would be able to help shape the Common Market's farm arrangements. As Heath complained, it was like negotiating on a moving staircase.[44]

However, from April 1962 onward, the beginnings of solutions could be seen to emerge. The breakthrough came over manufactured goods imported from Canada, Australia, and New Zealand. On these, Britain agreed to phase out Commonwealth Preference and gradually apply the common outer tariff; the Common Market, meanwhile, agreed to consult on trade matters with the countries concerned. The process of transition was to be completed by 1970, but the steps involved were to be less steep than those prescribed by the Treaty of Rome.

A similar solution was found for imports from India, Pakistan, and Ceylon. Here too Commonwealth Preference was to be tapered off, but even more gradually. The enlarged Common Market was to give guarantees for Indian and Pakistani exports of textiles, and was to remove the tariff on tea: it was also to negotiate comprehensive trade agreements with all three countries to help promote their economic development.

To Commonwealth countries in Africa and the Caribbean, the enlarged Common Market offered association on the lines of that enjoyed by the ex-colonies of the Six. For those that might refuse association, comprehensive trade agreements were on offer, similar but not identical to those proposed to India, Pakistan, and Ceylon.

On agricultural imports from the temperate zones of the Commonwealth, full agreement was never reached; but what was envisaged was a tapering-off of Commonwealth Preference, accompanied by world-wide support agreements among the major supplying and importing countries—or, if they proved unco-operative, with Commonwealth countries alone.[45]

When the negotiating conference broke up for the summer recess in the early hours of Sunday, August 5, 1962, some crucial aspects of these and other Commonwealth problems—as well as those of EFTA—still remained to be settled. From September to the end of the year, however, the negotiators concentrated chiefly on the subject of home agriculture. Of all the main issues that the conference confronted, this seemed the least intractable technically. British farmers were efficient; the Common Market had not yet fixed the majority of its common price levels; complication rather than difficulty seemed to be the snag. But all parties, including the British, were inclined to be intransigent: on one occasion, delegates wasted a whole afternoon scoring debating points at each other's—and their own—expense. In principle, Britain accepted the Common Market's farm support system; one major point at issue, however, was whether she should adopt the transitional measures it included, or have a special transitional regime of her own. Several of the Six, and France in particular, feared that this might give her a privileged position, from which she would be hard to dislodge. These questions were stubbornly debated for several weeks. Finally, in December 1962, in the hope of breaking the apparent deadlock, the conference agreed to do what it might usefully have done from the beginning: it gave the Common Market Commission the task of finding common solutions instead of simply advising the Six on how they should negotiate with Britain. Under Sicco Mansholt, the Commission Vice-President chiefly responsible for agriculture, a special Ministerial Committee of Investigation sped through a sea of statistics and technical expertise, emerging in the early hours of Tuesday, January 15,

1963, with a voluminous but at last unanimous report. With this as a basis and the new working method as a model, it almost looked as if the Brussels negotiations might soon be completed. But by that time most people knew that they were dead.[46]

They had lasted nearly fourteen months. This was hardly the rapid progress that Monnet and his friends had urged. Instead of settling only a few questions before entering the Common Market, Britain had tried to solve the bulk of them. Instead of proposing solutions like those suggested by the "Europeans," the British delegation had been obliged, for domestic political reasons, to let itself be forced toward them, step by step. When the solutions emerged, they all had a similar pattern: in each case, Britain was given time to adapt to the Common Market's framework, while the Common Market accepted joint responsibility with Britain for what had once been mainly British concerns. In other words, the negotiation had simply provided transitional solutions—the steps whereby Britain would move from the Commonwealth Preference system into the Common Market. All the long-term solutions—trade agreements, and so on—were left to be dealt with by the enlarged Common Market. This looked very like what Monnet had suggested at the outset: but to get there had taken fourteen precious months.

It was not time alone, however, but General de Gaulle that killed the Brussels negotiations. Their length and detail no doubt gave him his opportunity; but the responsibility was his. On Monday, January 14, 1963, he told a press conference in Paris:

England in fact is insular, maritime, bound by her trade, her markets, her supplies, to countries that are very diverse and often very far away . . . The nature, the structure, the situation that are peculiar to England are very different from those of the continental countries. How can England, as she lives, as she produces, as she trades, be incorporated into the Common Market as it was conceived and as it works?

The question was rhetorical; but if de Gaulle had expected the Brussels talks to cease forthwith, he was disappointed.

In the rue des Quatre Bras, while officials in the corridors were listening to the General's words on pocket transistor radios, their colleagues in the conference-room worked on, that day and the next. Then, on the evening of Wednesday, January 16, 1963, Maurice Couve de Murville proposed to his colleagues of the Six that they discuss whether and how the negotiations should continue; and next day he formally requested their adjournment. For hours of tense argument, the other five and the Commission fought to keep the talks open; but all that they could secure was a postponement of the final blow. At last, on Tuesday, January 29, after further sharp exchanges, the seven delegations and the Commission met once again in the long familiar conference room that had heard so many speeches, so many arguments about canned salmon and East India kips, so many weak jokes and flowery compliments. Now, euphoria had given place to bitterness. One by one, the ministers made their farewell speeches: one German delegate sat weeping; Couve de Murville looked hunted and old.[47]

On one reckoning, this was the second battle between the lion and the unicorn; and again the unicorn had won. As Walter Hallstein commented afterward, "When the negotiations were suspended . . . it could not fairly be said that they had already failed on technical grounds, or that they were already on the verge of success. There is no need to conclude from the negotiations themselves, therefore, that future British membership has been proved to be unworkable: far from it." Britain had been denied a hearing, and condemned for the existence of those very problems that she was negotiating to solve. It was true that de Gaulle had suggested an interim "association" between her and the Common Market; but this disdainful consolation-prize amounted to little more than non-voting second-class citizenship, if that.

No less important than the fact of de Gaulle's veto was its motivation, real or supposed. In part, this may well have been fear of British rivalry in an enterprise that even before de Gaulle's return to office had been greatly influenced by France. Over the weekend of December 15 and 16, 1962, de Gaulle and Macmillan had already had a chilly meeting at Rambouillet, which now lived up to Marie Antoinette's description of it as a *"crapaudière,"* or toad-hole. Here, de Gaulle had virtually warned Macmillan that he planned to halt the negotiations; he also dropped a delicate hint about Anglo-French collaboration on missiles, to which Macmillan made no response. But it seems likely that de Gaulle's growing impatience was increased by suspicion of America, and by the feeling that Britain, as Gaullists frequently put it, was "an American Trojan Horse."[48]

The pretext for this reproach was the Nassau meeting between Macmillan and Kennedy on December 18–21, 1962. Ever since the Cuba missile crisis of October, de Gaulle had been even more painfully aware of America's nuclear supremacy, and ever more concerned to even the balance between the United States and Europe. France was struggling to build a nuclear arsenal; Britain was clinging to the remnants of her own: logically, there might have been a case for co-operation. But Britain was also relying on America, which had promised her the Skybolt air-ground missile—until Friday, November 9, 1962, when the U. S. Defense Secretary Robert S. McNamara telephoned his British counterpart Peter Thorneycroft to announce that he was thinking of abandoning it. With Britain's "independent deterrent" thus threatened, Macmillan flew to the Bahamas to try to reverse the American decision—having told de Gaulle that weekend what he hoped to do. He came back, not with a British Skybolt, but with a NATO Polaris missile, available to Britain under special circumstances, and offered also to France. De Gaulle, scenting American "hegemony," indignantly refused the offer; and it no doubt confirmed him in his suspicion of Britain.[49]

This additional encouragement to de Gaulle to halt the Brussels negotiations might have been avoided if they had not been so slow. It might also have been prevented. To have taken up de Gaulle's hint of bilateral Anglo-French co-operation on military matters might well have been unwise: it would certainly have troubled the Germans, and possibly the United States. But with the benefit of hindsight it certainly seems to have been inappropriate to talk so fulsomely about sharing the aims of the Bonn Declaration, while acting as if the bid to join the Common Market and to help unite

Europe were quite distinct from matters of defense. If, as some suggested directly after the veto, the British Government had announced that it would make over its nuclear missile forces to any future combined European component in NATO, it might have saved its own hopes of joining the Common Market, helped Europe toward unity, and tied her more closely to the United States. But as things were, it merely retired to lick its wounds. There were more to come.[50]

The year 1963 had begun in hope; it ended as a year of disaster. Britain was excluded from the Common Market; Kennedy had been killed, and the Grand Design seemed to have died with him; Adenauer had at last stepped down in Germany; in Britain, Harold Macmillan had retired in the wake of the Profumo scandal. No less dismaying was the state of the Common Market. General de Gaulle's veto had plunged it into a crisis from which it was not to recover for several years.

There was nothing technically illegal, of course, in General de Gaulle's having blackballed a would-be new member: everyone had the same right. But the manner of the veto—unannounced, undiscussed, unjustified—made it almost unconstitutional, a breach of unwritten law. The result was a crisis of confidence; and it was heightened by the almost simultaneous conclusion of the Franco-German Treaty of Friendship, signed in Paris on Tuesday, January 22, 1963, by Adenauer and General de Gaulle. This closely resembled an earlier French draft of a treaty for "political union" that had come before the Fouchet Committee. In reality, it merely sealed—and claimed the credit for—the reconciliation of the two countries that had already been achieved within the European Community: it also pleased its two elderly signatories, no doubt for subtly different reasons. But in the eyes of the smaller Community countries in particular, it threatened to pervert the Common Market's fair workings by establishing prior Franco-German consultation even on subjects due to be discussed later in the Council of the Six. As it was, the Bundestag, encouraged by some official "Europeans," insisted on voting in a Preamble to the Treaty which drew most of its sting. But within the Community, resentment against de Gaulle was now very powerful, and the Common Market ground almost to a halt. At length, in the spring of 1963, reprisals gave way to a method of work that Gerhard Schroeder, then German Foreign Minister, described as "synchronization." Essentially, this meant horse-trading. Its most obvious instance was the tacit agreement to synchronize progress on the Kennedy Round of tariff negotiations—of special interest to Germany, Belgium, and Holland—with work on the farm support system, of special interest to France.

"Synchronization" had been practiced before in the Common Market: there had always been some degree of package deals. But whereas in the past a country making a concession had sometimes been prepared to wait for "compensation" in the future, the watchword now was "payment on the nail." In practice, this was not always workable: the bulk of the Common Market's farm policy was in fact agreed on long before the end of the Kennedy Round. But the principle was now half-respectable; and the contagion spread.

It can, in fact, be blamed for the next serious crisis—or the next installment of the same crisis—which occurred in 1965. Then, the Commission itself attempted to promote a package deal compounded of three connected elements: the completion of the farm finance regulations, sought in particular by France; the independent financing of the Common Market out of its own resources, most desired by the Commission; and the granting of greater power to the European Parliament, demanded by the Parliament itself and by the Netherlands. Crudely, the Commission tried to make General de Gaulle pay a "supranational" price for his agricultural settlement.[51]

As might have been expected, the trick failed to work. At midnight on Wednesday, June 30, 1965, Maurice Couve de Murville, who was then chairman of the Council of Ministers, broke up the meeting—refusing to "stop the clock"— because it had not settled the farm finance question on time. Thereupon, the French Government virtually boycotted the Common Market for seven months. At length, after de Gaulle had been forced into a run-off in the Presidential elections of December 1965, partly owing to the efforts of the "European" candidate Jean Lecanuet, a so-called "Gentlemen's

Disagreement" was patched up. By this, de Gaulle did his best to cripple the Commission and eliminate majority voting from the Common Market, while the other five member States, showing unexpected cohesion partly under German leadership, did their best to resist. France reserved her "right" to the veto, despite the text of the Treaty; the "Five" reserved their right to overrule her. The most unfortunate victim of the whole affair was Walter Hallstein. The French Government's resentment led it to object to a further renewal of his mandate as President of the Common Market Commission; the German Government persuaded France to agree to appoint him for a shorter time than the statutory two years. Since this would have contravened the Treaty, Hallstein refused to accept it. His legalism had courage.

Hallstein's successor was Jean Rey, fresh from his success in negotiating for the Common Market in the Kennedy Round. He took his place on July 1, 1967 at the head of a Commission larger than Hallstein's, for by now the three Community organizations—the ECSC, Euratom, and the Common Market—had been merged under the terms of a Treaty signed in Brussels on April 8, 1965. Its ratification had been held up by the crisis; but now the way ahead once more seemed clear. The time had come, moreover, for a third brief round in the battle of the lion and the unicorn. On Wednesday, May 10, 1967, Harold Wilson, Britain's Labour Prime Minister, lodged her formal application to become a member of the Common Market.[52]

The process that had led the Labour Party to this decision was similar to that which had moved the Conservatives before them. Elected in October 1964, the Labour Government had been expected to canvass "Commonwealth," "EFTA," and even "neutralist" solutions to Britain's twin problems of slow economic growth and waning political influence. As early as February 1965, however, Harold Wilson had declared that if favorable conditions arose, Britain would be prepared to negotiate for membership of the Common Market, provided that essential British and Commonwealth interests could be assured. This was an echo of the "five conditions" put forward by the late Hugh Gaitskell during the first Common Market negotiations: safeguards for the Commonwealth, adequate arrangements for the other EFTA countries, suitable arrangements for British agriculture, freedom to pursue an independent foreign policy, and freedom to carry out national economic planning. At one time, these had seemed incompatible with Common Market membership; but times had changed. The 1961–63 negotiations had suggested how the Commonwealth and EFTA might be safeguarded. British agriculture, as such, had little to fear; and de Gaulle had demonstrated how easily national planning and a national foreign policy could be conducted by a full member of the Common Market. What was more, experience had changed the perspective. The Commonwealth remained a vital British interest; but trouble in Rhodesia and Nigeria, if nowhere else, had shown the limits of its cohesive force. Britain remained bound to EFTA; but her partners there had understandably reacted when she had felt herself obliged by the sterling crisis in October 1964 to slap a 15 per cent surcharge on all British imports. The United States, meanwhile, had contributed to the rethinking process. Lyndon Johnson, Kennedy's very different successor, had for some months pressed very hard the proposal for a mixed-manned multilateral NATO force of surface ships carrying Polaris missiles—the MLF—a project that had originated under Eisenhower and been developed by Kennedy, but never so much. Wellmeaning as this was, it underlined Britain's reduced status; and when Johnson abruptly dropped the MLF project in 1965, this caused some relief in Britain. But America was not the only source of not always welcome pressure. Equally powerful were the international bankers—the so-called "gnomes of Zurich"—whose influence on British national planning was at least as strong as the Common Market's would have been on Britain as a member. Finally, although Wilson was cautious in referring to European defense problems, the cutdown of British forces "East of Suez," imposed by economic necessity, was a further factor pointing toward Europe, as was the unpopularity, among many Labour Party members, of American military policy in southeast Asia.[53]

There was, moreover, one new element in the European equation that had not been so prominent in the past. This was technology. In essence, it had lain at the root of the Spaak Report: aircraft and atomic power, Spaak had said, required technical resources on a European scale. But more recent years had seen a growing realization that rapid economic growth now depended on high-technology industries; and these in turn depended not only on large markets, but also on large-scale government expenditure. Space and computers were the most obvious example where the United States had leaped ahead for this reason. Could Europe do the same? If she failed to, America would surely dominate her industries. One French author nicknamed the problem "the American challenge": the slogan, and the book of that title, had immense success.[54]

Others looked at the problem rather differently. Technology, in their eyes, was not an end in itself. What was important was to master it. Unless Europe did so, she would risk something worse than comparative backwardness: blind market forces would ensure that technology reached her, probably from America, but certainly out of her control. Individual European firms would be too small to withstand American takeovers; individual European countries might be no match for American corporations. To ensure that the quality of life should not suffer in a secondhand technological revolution, it was essential for Europeans to be rich, strong and united enough to make their new society civilized, and get their human priorities right.

Such was some of the thinking that lay behind Britain's second application to join the Common Market. Like the first, but more quickly, it was rebuffed. On Tuesday, October 3, 1967, the European Commission, at the request of the Council of Ministers, gave its Preliminary Opinion on Britain's application for membership. It concluded:

. . . in order to dispel the uncertainty which still attaches in particular to certain fundamental points, negotiations should be opened in the most appropriate forms with the States which have applied for membership, in order to examine in more detail, as is indeed necessary, the problems brought out in this document and to see whether arrangements can be made under which the indispensable cohesion and dynamism will be maintained in an enlarged Community.

Eight weeks later, on Monday, November 27, 1967, General de Gaulle gave another of his press conferences. This time, he stressed "the impossibility of bringing the Great Britain of today into the Common Market as it stands." Finally, on December 19, 1967, the Council Ministers issued a sadly revealing communiqué. "Five member States," it declared, "subscribed to the point of view of the Commission." France did not.

> One member State . . . expressed the opinion that this enlargement [of the Community] would modify profoundly the nature and the ways of administering the communities. . . .
> One member State considered that the process of restoring the British economy must be completed for Britain's application to be considered.

The unicorn had won a third round.[55]

But triumphs, like sorrows, are not always lasting. Before long, General de Gaulle himself was in difficulties. His personal magic had first seemed tarnished when he faced the run-off in the December 1965 election. In January 1966, he had ousted Valery Giscard d'Estaing from the French Finance Ministry, and started a running battle between the Gaullists and their "Independent Republican" allies. In March 1966, he had further alienated sections of French opinion by withdrawing France from NATO; in June he had paid an inconclusive visit to the Soviet Union; in August, in Djibouti, riots had forced him to cancel a speech. In the legislative elections of March 1967, the Gaullists had lost forty seats; in June, despite the General's admonitions, Israel had launched the six-day war. In July, the General had visited Quebec, cried *"Vive le Québec libre!"* and found himself *persona non grata* in Ottawa. In November he had alienated many Frenchmen—including civil servants and army officers— by making a verbal attack on Jewry. Then, in May 1968, France was rocked by student disorders and strikes. For a while, the General faltered. When he recovered, with the assurance of army backing, he made a brilliant four-minute broadcast which helped set off a carefully orchestrated movement of support. Now, for nearly twelve months, French political life remained calm. But the May disorders had shaken confidence; the closing months of 1968 saw France's reserves falling and a serious currency crisis. Then, in April 1969, the General staked his career on a referendum; and he lost. Promptly, without fuss, he retired; and Georges Pompidou was voted into his place.

Almost simultaneously, Jean Monnet's Action Committee held a further meeting, this time in Brussels. Now, it included the British Labour, Conservative, and Liberal Parties, all of them formally committed to "European" cause. It had before it reports on the main problems of British entry into the Common Market—agriculture, monetary policy, technology, and institutions. Without exception, the conclusion of their authors was that these problems could be solved.[56]

After the slow stagnation of the late 1960s, then, the unification of Western Europe began to make fresh and visible progress. The archaic battle between the lion and the unicorn could be forgotten—or at least transformed; and General de Gaulle's departure was only one of the reasons. Another was a quickening sense that the world was once more insecure. In the Middle East, in Asia, in Africa, in Latin America, violence had exploded; even in Europe, as was shown by Northern Ireland, it was still very close to the surface. Two past giants —Japan and China—were re-emerging in a new guise, the former as a commercial rival, the latter as an unknown factor in the global balance of power. Under President Nixon, the United States, so long Western Europe's protector, seemed to have concluded from the Vietnam tragedy that it was dangerous to give open-ended security guarantees to other countries: there was now increasing pressure to reduce American troop levels in Europe. Relations with Eastern Europe, which had thawed under Khrushchev, were uncertain under Brezhnev and Kosygin. The Soviet invasion of Prague in August 1968 was a grim commemoration of Czechoslovakia's fate twenty years earlier, and a repetition of Hungary's in 1956. Yet economic and commercial contacts between East and West continued to increase: there was even some fear in Western Europe that America might be tempted into deals with the Soviet Union at Europe's expense. With the world scene growing more complex, and the simplicities of the Kennedy era looking inadequate, unity in the Western half of the continent seemed more than ever essential both to Atlantic relations and to a true *détente*. This was made very clear when Willy Brandt's Social Democrats came to power in Germany after the elections of September 28, 1969. Although renowned—and in some quarters vilified—for his Ostpolitik of cautious contacts with Eastern Europe, Brandt repeatedly stressed that this was only possible within a European Community in the West. On this point, if on no other, Konrad Adenauer would have agreed with him.[57]

Although the Ostpolitik quite quickly led to a recognition of East Germany and therefore, in the eyes of West Germany's Right-wing Opposition, to a diplomatic surrender, the European response to all these various incentives to unity was at first less rapid than might have been hoped. The Common Market's morale had been sapped by years of crisis; the farm prices imposed by the professional lobbies had caused surpluses of wheat and butter but shortages of beef; and the absence of a common monetary policy—itself due to very deep divergences in economic policy—had led to increasing European disarray. At the "summit" meeting of the Six's Heads of State or Government, together with their Foreign Ministers, on December 1 and 2, 1969, in The Hague, it was agreed that economic and monetary union must be pursued, and political union studied; but practical progress was slow. Early in 1970, the Community settled its financial arrangements for the common farm policy, promising marginal budgetary powers to the European Parliament; in the summer, talks began with a view to British membership. At last, the Community was being enlarged: the French veto was in the process of being lifted.

The reasons for this change in official French policy appeared to be twofold. General de Gaulle's successor, President Georges Pompidou, seemed very much more a traditional politician, without de Gaulle's extraordinary charisma, but also without his recklessness: henceforth, decisions would be made on grounds of comparative advantage rather than doctrines of *grandeur*. And in this new context, it may have looked as if France's interests would be served by enlarging the Community to include Britain and other countries—not only to increase Europe's weight in a more uncertain world, but also to counterbalance the growing power of Germany within the Community itself. In the long run, and in strictly "European" terms, such counterbalancing was no doubt superfluous; but in the imperfect state of the Community's progress, and in the eyes of traditional politicians, balances of power were still important ingredients in policy. The only remaining uncertainty was Britain herself.

What obstacles stood between her and a uniting Europe? Lingering doubts in Britain were understandable. After so many rebuffs, it was natural to fear another; after living so long on food bought at dumping prices in the world market, it was painful to face the prospect of paying continental farmers' excessive costs. Lingering doubts were natural also in the Community of Six: Britain, after all, was a late convert to the cause. When negotiations for British membership at last began, however, under the leadership of Geoffrey Rippon, Chancellor of the Duchy of Lancaster, it soon became clear that the Conservative Government, now led by Edward Heath, was determined to meet whatever conditions were reasonable in order to join the Community. The last political doubts were removed by a "little summit" meeting of two—Heath and Pompidou—in June 1971, carefully prepared by Christopher Soames, Britain's burly Ambassador in Paris; the last technical obstacles were pared away in countless negotiating sessions by the experts in Brussels and Luxembourg. Finally, agreement was reached; and, on October 28, 1971, the House of Commons gave overwhelming approval to British entry by a majority of 112.

There were still hurdles ahead. It was another twelve-month and more before all the enabling legislation was passed by the British Parliament, often with narrower majorities: for the British Labour Party, under strong pressure from its extreme-Left supporters and trade unions, had by this time denounced the "Tory terms" secured by Edward Heath—although prominent "Europeans" in the Labour Shadow Cabinet doubted whether their own leader, Harold Wilson, could have secured entry on any other terms. As Britain finally entered the Community on January 1, 1973, therefore, the official Opposition remained divided on the subject, and for the time being was unwilling to play its part in the Community institutions.

A further absentee was Norway. Although the Government had successfully negotiated entry, it had unwisely pledged itself to submit the results to a popular referendum; and a *cartel des Non* compounded of the radical young, the poor, the old, and the farmers voted against the European Community. A few weeks later, when Britain, Ireland, and Denmark were seen to be joining the Community, Norwegian opinion polls once more swung in favor of following suit; but for the time being the enlarged Community was to be a Community of Nine, not Ten.

In longer perspective, however, the very real difficulties of this transitional phase, with the enlarged Community finding its feet, helping excluded neighbors, and beginning to negotiate with both the United States and the Soviet Union, remained unimportant compared with the opportunities that were now at hand. Even the fact that European unity remained half-finished was in some respects encouraging: with economic union only beginning, and common defense and foreign policies still unformed, new recruits to the task of unifying Europe had a real chance to share in the shaping of their common future. The present problems might seem daunting; but the possibilities were immense.

Europe, after all, was putting an end to centuries of armed conflict. It was getting rid of antiquated frontier controls, prejudice, narrow-mindedness, and cherished national stereotypes. It was harnessing the energies, now, of more than 250 million people for greater welfare and social justice. Together, they were seeking to recover the world influence that their separate nations had long since lost—to be a stronger force for peace and a better source of aid for the world's poor. Together with their allies across the Atlantic, they were trying to introduce into international affairs more stability and the beginnings of law and order—partly by their exertions, and partly by their example. Europe, in this sense, might be a small, imperfect, but nonetheless significant pointer to a better, more peaceful, and less anarchic future.

REMEMBERING THE FUTURE

The best Qualification of a Prophet is to have a good
Memory.   *George Savile, first Marquess of Halifax*[1]

To-morrow is an old deceiver, and his cheat never grows
stale.   *Dr. Samuel Johnson*[2]

If you have built castles in the air, your work need not
be lost; that is where they should be. Now put the foundations under them.   *Henry David Thoreau*[3]

This book began with a retrospect; it ends with a reminder.
The past thirty years have brought Europe and the world
an immense distance. A further generation will bring them
into the twenty-first century. The talismanic year 2000 is surprisingly near. Numerology apart, moreover, the future is already bearing down upon us far more rapidly than we often
realize. To secure its benefits and forestall some of its dangers,
we have no option but to look ahead.

Speculation about what may be in store for us has lately
become a growth industry; disused Utopias pile up yearly,
yet future-snobbery still abounds. It can hardly be surprising
that prophets are often at a loss when they are not at logger-
heads, since the extrapolation of current trends—one standard
procedure for forecasts—is more than usually misleading in
times of turmoil. Such is the pace of change at present that
many curves on the graph of "progress"—for the growth of
world steel production, of energy consumption, of accumu-
lated explosive power—are now almost vertical, apparently
heading for infinity within a few decades. This makes estimates rough-and-ready, and in many cases physically absurd.
They also ignore the inevitability of the unexpected and the
seemingly impossible. But if predictions, like compasses, are

almost always out of true, this is no reason for renouncing them. At least they tell us something about the present day.

Science and technology, in all likelihood, will continue to act as the ploughshare of future change. Increasingly, the distinction between them, as between their once separate disciplines, is becoming blurred. "Spin-off" is a characteristic feature of defense research, which has constant repercussions on civil technology; in this field, further spectacular results may be expected. But similar forces are at work among the "pure" sciences. Radio-astronomy provides one example; inter-disciplinary co-operation in the study and design of materials is another; and equally symptomatic are such terms as the familiar "biochemistry" and the less familiar "biometry" and "biophysics." The relatively recent exploration of the genetic code, indeed, is only one of the developments in biology that are likely to have profound and disturbing effects on human life.

Here, a number of tendencies may well converge. Man-machine symbiosis, already beginning with the improvement of artificial limbs and organs, may ultimately be completed by connecting miniaturized electronic units to the central nervous system; one day, for instance, there may be built-in radar for the blind. Some hereditary disabilities may be removed by "clonal" reproduction or by the chemical modification of the genes. Viral and bacterial diseases may increasingly be checked by immunization. A start may be made on creating a primitive form of artificial life, if only by the self-reproduction of molecules; tissue culture, meanwhile, may extend its success in facilitating further grafts of organs and the transfusion of cells. It may be that in this direction a cure will at length be found for cancer; and if, as may be hoped, arterial and degenerative diseases can be treated biochemically, some progress will have been made toward solving the problems of aging. Intelligence, likewise, may prove amenable to physical or chemical treatment. Non-narcotic drugs may be more widely used to reduce or eliminate some of the forms of mental illness or personality disorder at present treated—or left untreated—by other means; medicine may also find ways of raising the level of mental perception for specific tasks or of improving intelligence permanently.

Together with simpler contraception and more effective ways of increasing fertility, all these developments will give men and women—or those who can afford them—far greater control over processes once thought ineluctable: they will become forbiddingly responsible for their own bodies and minds. Misused, power of this order would have alarming possibilities. Even used with wisdom, it will present a very considerable challenge in philosophy, ethics, and politics. Who is to benefit first from the new discoveries—or to be their human guinea pigs? Whose authority should be required for operations on the genes, on the brain, on a fetus, on an ovum? If intelligence is a matter of medicine, what becomes of competitive examinations? If aging can be postponed indefinitely, what becomes of the world's population? Will individuals one day have to decide whether and when to die?

If biology may thus come to transform the framework of ordinary living, the progress of space research is doing so already. Seriously envisaged for the future are exploits even more striking than the first launchings of artificial satellites or the landings on the moon. Before long, systems will be devised for the regular rescue of cosmonauts. Not much later, a scientific research station may be established in orbit, followed by the development of rockets and orbital vehicles that can be serviced for reuse. Manned overflights of Mars and Venus might be possible in the 1970s, as is the establishment of a base on the moon. In the following decade, if not earlier, the first men could land on Mars. By the year 2000, rocket probes will probably have taken place outside the solar system, research stations may have been set up on some of the nearer planets, and the moon may well be the scene of mining operations. The early years of the twenty-first century could see a permanent base on Mars, a manned overflight of Pluto, and even perhaps some landings on the satellites of Jupiter. "Colonizing the planets" is a grandiose term for these sparse ventures into immensity; but the earliest European explorers of other continents, after all, were almost as few.

The exploration of space is affecting life on earth in at least two senses. Most immediately, its impact is practical. Artificial satellites will soon make possible truly world-wide television, as well as a marked improvement in weather forecasts. The actual control of weather will take much longer; but there seems every prospect of its being achieved—if only, at first, for military purposes—in the early '8os. By the turn of the century, high-altitude "space" gliders may well be in use for ballistic commercial transport.

No less real, however, are the psychological repercussions of space research. It already seems incongruous to see the moon as a "white goddess" now that machinery has been installed on it. Yet the function of myth is hardly to describe external reality, but rather to embody and respond to human fears and longings. Although known to be "untrue," it may come closer to everyday experience of the universe than a God's-eye view of the "objective" models of science; and whenever spectacular experiments or discoveries seem to break with such experience, the result is a psychological wrench. Similar dissociation or alienation was felt, more obviously, in the nineteenth century, when the findings of Darwin and Huxley appeared to clash with the revealed truth of the Bible. Abruptly, the normal tension between different "levels" of awareness becomes a strain. We find it harder than ever to see life as a whole, to keep simultaneously in focus the versions of reality perceived by the different components of our nature: the relatively inefficient two-legged machine, the intelligent animal that eats and defecates, the primitive human being afraid of the dark and of loneliness, the sensitive and quasi-autonomous but often unreliable computer, the reveller, the hero, the lover, the scientist, the citizen, the solitary dreamer. When these seeming contradictions become unbearable, we tend to deny or ignore one or other mode of perception. Some take refuge in a smug and simple scientism: they reduce once distant mysteries to prosaic terminal problems, coldly eying the conquered moon. In this way, the very magnitude of man's achievements in space may revive a geocentric self-importance that became anachronistic with Copernicus. Most scientists, however, are wary of complacency: they retain a sense of wonder, humility, and skepticism, knowing that they will never do more than laboriously nibble at the edges of the cosmos. Partly for this reason, and partly because research into outer space seems at once irrelevant and menacing, others again react to it with what one alert semi-layman described as "a certain sort of bored astonishment."[4] One further result of the space race, therefore, may be a slightly forced reassertion of private, personal values in a world where the individual feels increasingly lost.

Equally disturbing to habitual assumptions is the further growth of the computer. Here, the next generation will see a double development: far greater sophistication in computers themselves, and a vast extension of their use. These alone may prove quite as revolutionary as anything in computer development over the past twenty years.

One of the many nervous jokes made about computers in their early days was the stock description of them as "high-speed idiots." As far as speed is concerned, the immense acceleration of data processing that has taken place in the last generation is unlikely to be repeated in the future. Even so, computer speeds may yet increase more than a hundred-fold during the next few decades. What is almost certain, moreover, is that by the end of the century, and probably long before it, computers will in some respects have ceased to be idiots. If present progress continues, they will soon be far better able to learn from experience; and they may become capable of asking unexpected questions, sustaining a provocative dialogue, and taking the initiative. When this happens, a computer's "intelligence" may be less clearly limited by that of its programmer or its designer; and some will not need programming at all. They will still, of course, be essentially calculating machines of very great complexity; they may lack such human attributes as "intuition," moral sense, and persuasive power; nor is a "subconscious" likely to be built into them—unless, perhaps, their designers can work under hypnosis. But despite these ultimate limitations, the computers of the future will be very much more like so-called "thinking machines," and their speed will help to compensate, as now, for their residual naïveté. Perhaps it would be wise to avoid endowing such mechanical "brains" with efficient and powerful mechanical "bodies."

Even without such shadowy possibilities, the fairly primitive computers now in use have begun to have an immense influence on human affairs. This will grow very rapidly. Computers themselves are unlikely to become much larger, although their capacity will increase: on the contrary, their physical size is shrinking. Already, it is claimed, a six-foot cube could theoretically store the sum total of recorded knowledge; and for less ambitious purposes, microcircuitry may yet make possible computers little larger than transistor radio sets. Coupled with their mass production, expected by the '80s, this could open up some remarkable prospects. One is the development of a national, continental or global grid system of data storage, into which individual computers could be plugged to retrieve tailor-made information. This could have obvious applications for economic planning, for the stock exchange, for tax calculation, for legal advice, for marketing, and for scientific and other abstracts; it might also extend to automatic translation and interpretation, which in turn could be linked with an audio-visual telephone service, and with more responsive teaching machines. Nor need the flow of data be all one way. In some car factories, customers' individual orders have long been fed in at the start of the assembly line, on which all conceivable variants of each model travel nose to tail. With more sophisticated automation systems, custom-built mass production of this sort could be carried further, and into many other fields. Ultimately, its methods might be applied to politics, with automated polling at elections and quick referenda on specific issues, each elector dialing his vote from his own home.

Once again, however, there is no need to enter the realm of speculation to realize computers' potential impact. Transport, in particular, offers rapidly increasing scope. Ships have been built with computer-controlled engines; before long, they may have automated systems for collision warning, reckonings, and stability control. Airline bookings are already largely computerized; so is movement control at the major airports. The '70s may well see the surveillance of air traffic extended to cover all aircraft in flight over a broad area, and not merely within a short radius of the tower. On the railways, moreover, surveillance may be replaced by remote control.

Automated signaling and automatic coupling are already commonplace; within the next generation, the remote control of goods trains may begin with the processing of the original way-bill and only end with the transshipment of the containers for local delivery by road. The roads themselves, meanwhile, seem likely to change more slowly. Car design, it is true, may increasingly incorporate automatic features, and fully automatic underground parking lots are already being built. But human resistance to regimentation seems likely to delay the financing of automatic highways, where vehicles travel at fixed intervals under the control of a central computer system to which they can switch in at will. The social cost of road accidents will presumably have to rise even higher before such projects are seen to be economic.

Major innovations in transport will themselves involve both new materials and new forms of energy conversion or storage. High-speed express trains traveling in the region of 150 mph, require special steel rails with stronger embankments and sleepers. The electric car needs a cheap, light, and compact accumulator or fuel cell system; and submarine freight transport, which promises high efficiency, will almost certainly rely on nuclear power. Controlled thermonuclear fusion, as distinct from fission, may be achieved experimentally within the next two decades; and the end of the century should see its first adoption on an industrial scale. By that time, the world's energy consumption may have increased tenfold,[5] and a growing proportion of men's needs will have to be met by nuclear power, perhaps marginally supplemented by the conversion of solar heat into electricity. Of the fossil fuels, coal and oil may by then increasingly be used as chemical raw materials, since these, like energy, will be in very great demand. Many of the mineral resources that can be tapped by present methods may be in danger of exhaustion early in the twenty-first century.[6] The threat, if genuine, is less alarming than it sounds. Necessity is the mother of invention, and has often proved the mother of prospecting. Over the coming decades, materials science will undoubtedly develop new synthetic substances, many of them stronger, lighter and more flexible than those already in use; while some raw material and chemical needs may be met by deep drilling for molten magma, by mining the ocean bed, and by extracting metals from seawater—this last, perhaps, as one of the by-products of desalination research.

With such technological change in prospect, "scientific" Utopias and anti-Utopias have become an all too familiar literary form.

Switching on the domestic robot before leaving his plastic, tenant-owned apartment block, the man of the year 2000— let us call him 'John Future'—entrains on the high-speed monorail for the downtown section of his vast linear city. On the journey he buys some groceries; the store in the club car automatically debits his bank. This morning he has no need of the train's office facilities, for he delta-winged in last night from a five-hour conference in the antipodes, and got his overnight work done in the supersonic V.T.O.L. rocket. Through the panoramic window he can see that the city council has programmed a fine crisp day as usual, although weather control seems anachronistic now that industry is moving to the tropics to leave the temperate zones free for the automated ploughlands and prairies that the Farmer Giles of the twenty-first century runs from the console of his 'Sunnybrook-X' computer. Arriving at the office, John Future dials for the business page of his favourite newspaper, plays back the taped cassettes of the morning's mail, then settles down with the colour-TV phone for a planning discussion with his colleagues in Greater Paris, Novosibirsk, and the Osaka-Kyoto-Kobe urban complex. A friendly argument soon develops between them and their computer, which has meanwhile been analysing forward market trends. As usual, the computer—they fondly call it 'Old Know-all'—has the last word. The conference over, John Future spends a half-hour study period with his teaching machine switched into the Further Education (Western Hemisphere) Network, then his day's chores are done. Ready for relaxation, he hops the continuous conveyor belt out to the company's riding stables. His wife has arranged for a deputy to pilot her hovercar ambulance on the noon shift so that they can lunch together at an exclusive old-world cafeteria in one of the rural reservations. After the quiet clean air of the city, the din and dirt of the countryside are refreshing, although John's great-grandfather told him when they last played squash together that there was once more wildlife around. Over lunch—a luxury meal of fresh fish and newly fried potatoes—the Futures discuss their coming vacation. John is keen to try one of the new low-budget Adventure Weekends with the Club

Lunaire, leaving the children to play 'Independent Nations' at a Living History Camp. His wife, something of a stay-at-home, wants to split the time between Acapulco and Isfahan. 'But we do that *every* month,' objects John. Before a row can blow up, they both reach in their handbags and take their Darby and Joan pills. By coffee time, all's well once more.[7]

Most of these things are possible, and some of them are very likely. But what makes such vignettes so unconvincing —apart from their prose and characterization—is their reluctance to admit that the imagined society of the future will be only slowly, painfully and patchily achieved. All ages are "ages of transition," and the future is no exception. Even within the industrialized nations, many of the possibilities theoretically open to "twenty-first century man" will in fact be available only to a minority. Few cities will be built from nothing: most of them, as in the past, will grow up piecemeal around surviving buildings on existing sites. New forms of transport will co-exist with the old. Forecasting by computers may make possible faster economic growth, but lack of capital will continue to delay many public investment projects. New machines will be resisted for fear of unemployment; new jobs and retraining will have to be provided for those displaced. Apprenticeship courses, like education in general, will have to turn out growing numbers of electronics and other engineers to service ever more complex apparatus—until it can either service itself unaided or be replaced so cheaply as to become expendable. A few manual jobs that could be mechanized may continue for a time to be done by human beings: in one of the world's most modern automatic rolling mills, I myself have seen a solitary workman rubber-stamping the finished steel by hand. Some such tasks—many of them in the open air or the country—may be highly prized by those unwilling or unable to undertake others. In the factories, it may well be possible to adopt a thirty-hour week, forty weeks a year, and thirty-five years in a lifetime;[8] but this reduction of working hours, however modest, may not be universal. The organization of an increasingly prosperous mass-consumption society will demand a great deal of bureaucracy; and contrary to some predictions, not all of it seems likely to be automated. Even in the twenty-first century, offices will still probably employ enough people to keep them comfortably untidy: paperwork will still create paperwork, even if it takes the form of punched cards. Many of the staff, moreover, relieved of routine drudgery by the help of business machines, will act as intermediaries with the public, explaining procedures, meeting requests and complaints, settling priorities, and solving human problems within the growing complexities of large-scale administration. Such responsibilities will require not only high intelligence, technical knowledge, and judgment, but above all integrity, self-confidence, and the power of initiative in emergencies. This will be all the more necessary since power failures and electrical faults, despite all fail-safe systems and replacement circuits, will now and then produce unprecedented chaos.

Even without such technical imperfections, society will face some inevitable snags. The "problem of leisure," which greatly agitates those restless enough to fret about the distant future, may well turn out to be exaggerated. If the devil finds work for idle hands, man runs him a close second. Many people spend all their existing spare time in physical activity for which they would claim high wages if it were labeled "work"—using antiquated forms of transport (sailing or riding), propelling various projectiles (golf, tennis, cricket, football, motoring), or manufacturing items of furniture on an uneconomic scale. There seems no reason to believe that the appetite for these pursuits is easily surfeited. For the majority, the problem is not one of too much leisure, but of too much work; and more time for recreation will mean more work for those in the industries that service it. Increasingly, too, as human knowledge accumulates and becomes more readily available, self-education and refresher courses will compete for men's hours of freedom.

What is far more serious is the problem of numbers. In the field of leisure, this means clogged roads, spoiled countrysides, teeming holiday-resorts, crowded moorings, and meat-soup swimming pools. For a time, at least, the congestion could be relieved by staggering vacation times throughout the year and by exploiting still more distant regions; but life at home, for many people, will also become less private as numbers grow. More crowded cities will offer less separate living space, and will need more elaborate social engineering; this will require more comprehensive statistics, which better communications will help to assemble, digging deeper into individual lives. Whatever the political complexion of future governments, technology will inevitably emphasize the collective aspects of existence: a big corporation, just because it deals mechanically with very large numbers, is bound to seem in many ways as impersonal as the state.

This need not imply excessive standardization. Only in the primitive stages of a successful mass society may the individual have to put up with unimaginative minor officials, identical speculative houses and apartments, and the ubiquitous tastelessness of pre-cooked, pre-sliced, pre-wrapped, pre-masticated supermarket food. The better the machine, whether social or industrial, the better its products can be adapted to individual and even eccentric preferences. But total eccentricity, like the illusion of total privacy, will certainly become increasingly expensive. Personal service, custom-made tailoring, an isolated country cottage, and home-grown fruit and vegetables may more and more be regarded as luxury items, for special occasions only. Their day-to-day substitutes may be of even higher quality, as the products of today's best chain stores sometimes show; but the knowledge that their variety has limits may be frustrating in itself.

Comfortable, close-knit, and of necessity well-ordered, the society of the future may well have to guard against its appearing too tame. More and more, it will be vital to find outlets for men's natural anti-social impulses. Authorized rebellion, clearly, is a contradiction in terms. "Adventure playgrounds," despite their uses, will hardly satisfy the truly adventurous; and there are limits to the effective outlets that society itself can provide. Space travel, sometimes mooted as a safety-valve, is a highly organized and disciplined collective venture, sharing many drawbacks with the environment it purports to escape. Private flying, polar exploration, and solitary ocean cruising may recruit some stalwarts; big-game hunting or mercenary soldiering may attract others. But the real difficulty lies with those whose energies fall short of such endeavors, while yet overflowing the limits of an ever more tutelary state. Fifty years ago, William James foresaw the problem and proposed "instead of military conscription, a conscription of the whole youthful population to form for a certain number of years a part of the army enlisted against *Nature*"— a kind of compulsory Peace Corps. Whatever the solution, a continuing task for the industrialized nations will certainly be to treat their social and psychological casualties, to cope with crime and violence, and to find what James described as "the moral equivalent of war."[9]

In all these ways "the society of the year 2000" seems likely to confound its simpler prophets. Even more fundamentally, it will still be limited to a minority of mankind. In default of really drastic action, and perhaps in spite of it, twenty-first century prosperity and dark-age poverty will continue to co-exist on a shrinking planet; and the numbers of the poor and hungry will almost certainly grow.

Recent estimates of the world's population in the year 2000 have varied very widely. In 1945, one expert arrived at the figure of 3.3 billion; two others, in 1953, suggested 3.2 billion. Today, thirty years ahead of schedule, these numbers have already been attained. The next forecast was 6.3 billion, made by the United Nations in 1958: on that reckoning, the year 2000 would see as many people in non-Soviet Asia as now inhabit the entire globe. More recently, Rand Corporation experts have scaled down this estimate to 5.1 billion. But the reason that some of them gave was disquieting: they grimly predicted, for the less developed countries, a greater number of deaths from lack of food.[10]

Birth control may help to avert this catastrophe; but if it should prove impracticable or unacceptable, ways could still be found of producing food for six billion people. Insecticides, pesticides, fungicides, growth promotion agents and retardants, antibiotics and artificial fertilizers can greatly improve crop yields, especially in the less developed countries. Irrigation can help convert into foodstuffs some of the solar energy now wasted in the deserts, while reafforestation can curb their spread. Reclamation of the jungle could bring new areas under cultivation; water conservancy could more effectively harness the monsoons. Such measures as these might produce enough basic calories to ward off widespread famine; but because of the slowness of traditional livestock-breeding and the competition for fodder, the shortage of protein may have to be met by other means. These might include "sea farms" for large-scale fish rearing, by analogy with oysterbeds; collecting and possibly cultivating certain forms of plankton, including the tiny shrimp-like krill; and even, perhaps, manufacturing foodstuffs chemically by the synthesis of proteins in cell-free systems.

Despite the cost and difficulty of many of these projects, the biggest obstacles may not be technological, but human. By the end of the century, some of today's less developed countries may have profited from others' experience and by-passed the first industrial revolution. With the aid of nuclear power and computers, they may have taken a short-cut into advanced technology, and some of their manufactured output may well be highly competitive. But their economies are almost certain to have developed lopsidedly, with all the familiar contrasts that traditionally astonish the visitor, like the sight of barefoot women working as building laborers at India's Trombay center for nuclear research. Having joined the technology race at a stage when industry employs more machines and fewer workmen, such countries may find themselves saddled with a rural rather than an urban proletariat, impoverished peasants increasingly unable to produce enough food. Even in the richer nations, agriculture has until recently been a poor relation, only slowly mechanized, and never able to match the productive growth of industry. Short of intensive, laborious and electorally unrewarding efforts, it may lag even further behind in the developing countries; and their raw material producers, at the same time, will face even sharper competition from synthetics. If the gap between rich and poor nations is not to grow wider, therefore, it may prove necessary to reverse some of the accepted patterns of world trade. Instead of acting as quarries and home farms for the older industrialized nations, the less developed countries will have to import more food from them, meeting part of the bill by selling them more sophisticated manufactures.

The change, if it occurs, will not be rapid. For a long time to come, the richer countries may still have unsalable agriculture surpluses. As the world's population grows, however, they may well have to increase their production of certain foodstuffs, gearing it more closely to the less developed countries' needs rather than to their present-day purchasing power. If the recipient countries are to pay for their food imports—as ultimately they must—their manufactures will have to be given easier access to the markets of the richer countries. In some this will mean social and even political upheaval unless expansion continues fast enough to absorb the shock. Meanwhile, the less developed countries will have to develop livelier market research and salesmanship, and ensure that the food they receive in fact reaches the needy members of their own population. The latter in turn may have to be persuaded to accept an at first unfamiliar diet: wheat and beans instead of rice, for example, or fishmeal, krill, and even synthetic proteins. Finally, a vast campaign of education, land reform and investment will be needed to bring agriculture in these countries more nearly abreast of the industrial development and population growth to be expected in the decades to come.

To achieve this, habits and conventions in rich and poor countries alike will have to change. Piecemeal, perhaps, the change may be said to be beginning: more positive stockage policy, food aid, and the gradual disappearance of tariffs among the industrialized countries may already be signs of the times. But time presses; and unless more systematic and resolute efforts are made to meet a future that is already foreseeable, the results could be disastrous. In many places, famine is nearer than we think. At present, *vis-à-vis* the less developed countries, we are all in some degree practitioners of apartheid. Is our condemnation of it in others an oblique and cathartic criticism of ourselves?

Such are some of the shadows that mar the prospect of the future; but the darkest of all is the shadow of possible war. It would be naïve to imagine that in the midst of other technical progress, military technology will stand still. Some of its products, admittedly, may be welcomed: "non-mortal" means of persuasion and riot control, such as water guns and tear gases; effective nuclear bomb shelters; and anti-submarine defense. But less innocuous are some of the other developments already conceivable: an anti-ballistic missile race, kiloton "tactical" nuclear weapons, hydrogen bombs in orbit, and biological agents for killing and incapacitating, affecting men's sanity or sapping the will to resist. War, never clean, will grow dirtier. Even now it could destroy civilization.

General and controlled disarmament might seem the obvious safeguard; yet for at least twenty years it has proved impossible to achieve. Unilateral national disarmament has a few advocates: their opponents usually reply with variations on the couplet

> Pale Ebenezer thought it wrong to fight,
> But Roaring Bill, who killed him, thought it right.

Equally fruitless, so far, have been attempts to secure general disarmament in the nuclear field alone. One effective move in this broad direction was the 1968 treaty on non-proliferation, whose "nuclear" signatories have promised not to pass on atomic weapons to others, while the "non-nuclear" powers agreed not to acquire them. Despite the very real dangers that the treaty was intended to parry, it too ran into snags. Some non-nuclear powers have proved reluctant to accept it, fearing that their existing inferiority of status might become permanent, that inspection of their peaceful atomic plant might reveal industrial secrets, or that their dangerous neighbors might sign and then break their word. Others disliked on principle the whole notion of discrimination that underlay the treaty, and feared that it might kill the hope of a united Europe's one day equaling the United States. Finally, none of the three nuclear powers backing the treaty, seems remotely likely to pass on nuclear weapons, while the other two powers that possess them—France and Communist China—both refused to sign. However, like the Strategic Arms Limitation Talks (SALT) that began in 1969, the non-proliferation treaty at least had the great advantage of keeping the United States and the Soviet Union talking peaceably together—so long as they refrain from settling the fate of other countries over their heads.[11]

Will any of these efforts come to effective fruition in the near future? Past experience suggests that they may not, or that, if they do, their success will be only partial. There seems little hope of eliminating the instruments of war without tackling its basic causes, since these are precisely what makes agreement so difficult. If complete disarmament were possible, it would no longer be necessary. For the present, the most that seems likely is a series of conventions, probably tacit, to restrict new armaments, to maintain existing de facto spheres of influence, to limit anti-ballistic missiles and to demilitarize space. These, if achieved, would be very far from negligible; and they might bring world peace. At the very least, they would further acknowledge the common interest in avoiding a large-scale conflict, and they might succeed in staving it off. But smaller conflicts seem all too likely. In Latin America, economic progress is strengthening the demand for social changes that are long overdue; the inevitable upshot is political unrest. In the southern areas of Africa, continued white rule may lead to future explosions; to the north, new states are settling in with difficulty, often at odds with their neighbors, and sometimes a prey to civil war. The Middle East remains a potential battleground. Parts of southeast Asia have not known peace for over twenty years. The rise of Communist China, meanwhile, has added a third term to the East-West power equation. None of the giants may intentionally join battle; but they might be involved in war by their respective allies. Continuing insecurity, therefore, appears to be inescapable in the decades ahead.

Headlong, overcrowded, disunited, and dangerous, the world of the future may look forbidding; but for those with the zest and energy to face it, the prospect is surely a challenge. Now, as never before, men hold their destiny in their own hands. Will they succumb to *hubris,* or to squabbling over their new-found and future riches? Or will they have the wisdom, skill, and patience to devise a less unjust and uneasy form of international society, and a better way of settling disputes than by going to war? To these questions, Europe may furnish the modest beginnings of an answer.

Most of the world's present evils are familiar from Europe's history—disease and famine; the contrast of poverty and riches; tyranny and anarchy; commercial rivalry and pitiless war. Very gradually, Europeans have begun to overcome them. Since World War II, in particular, they have deliberately fostered a community of material interests between formerly implacable enemies. First in the European Coal and Steel Community, then in Euratom and the Common Market, six European countries have accepted the discipline of common rules and institutions, tempering the sovereignty of the nation-state. Often reluctantly, they have begun to apply to their dealings with each other those principles of law and order that in civilized communities keep the peace and settle disputes between private citizens. Haltingly, imperfectly, and in a limited field, they have begun to establish a new form of international society.

Already, this has had broader repercussions. Increasingly united by the institutions of the European Community, its members are beginning to act as one in their economic dealings with the rest of the world. In tariff negotiations, in international monetary discussions, their collective action has succeeded where individual efforts would have failed; and with British membership, this new European entity will be more effective still. The United States, although it also fears the rivalry of a prosperous united Europe, has welcomed its beginnings and sought to establish with it a new relationship of equals, healthier, closer, and more enduring than the present traditional alliance of many smaller countries with one giant. Progress toward this goal has been slow and not without friction; but the momentum of economic interest and political necessity remains powerful: Europe and America have far more in common than their obvious differences suggest. Gradually, as Europe gropes its way toward political unity, its "equal partnership" with America could develop in a similar direction. As equals, the United States and Europe could exert a moderating influence on each others' foreign policies. As partners, they could be more self-confident in their dealings with the Soviet Union and Communist China, without the suspicion and uneasiness prompted by either trying to act alone. Less tempted, because less able, to pursue its old policy of dividing the West, the East might be more prepared to come to terms with it. Unity in Europe, partnership across the Atlantic, and genuine peaceful coexistence between East and West would bind the world together in a network of institutions and agreements; national disruptive action would be more difficult, and less of a danger to peace. Within Europe, the barriers created by the "cold war" could be diminished: allowed once more to travel freely across the frontier, the German people could be in practice reunited without reviving a German Reich. In the wider world, the new international climate could put fresh life into the United Nations, and at last make it possible for East and West to co-operate on tasks that neither, however powerful, can successfully tackle without the other. Foremost among them would be a concerted effort to prevent famine, to eliminate disease and poverty, and to keep the peace.

Could the unification of Europe really begin such a process? Is the thought not simply a pipe dream, a typically European form of optimistic pride? With unity still incomplete in Western Europe, is there any real hope of reconciling East and West?

A generation ago, this question could have been asked of France and Germany. A true forecast, then, of present-day Western Europe would have seemed absurdly visionary. Yet visions of the future are what move men to act. And there is surely something noble about the vision of Europe, for so long a source of civilization and of conflict, so worn and weathered by history, so strong in spirit, so measured and so free, recovering its self-respect after so much shame and agony, achieving unity and assurance without losing its diversity, standing up once more for the old virtues—courage, wisdom, generosity, tolerance—in a world that so badly needs them, as Europe needed them in 1945.

Guilt is a paralyzing legacy, and it was harder than ever for Europeans to build the future when burdened by their recent past. Quite quickly, they cleared away the ruins; eagerly, and in some ways blindly, they grasped at a prosperity greater than they had ever known. Above all, patiently and doggedly, they began to civilize the relations between states by means of laws and institutions similar to those that keep the peace between fellow-citizens. Their task is far from ended. Performed in committees and councils instead of on the battlefield, disputing percentages and protocols instead of human lives, it seems undramatic and slow. But if there is one respect in which Europe today differs from the Europe of the past, this is its willingness, however fitful, to limit the self-righteousness of nations—its sense that a common interest binds even those who passionately disagree. World War II has often been called the last European civil war. That this can be said without irony is due to the efforts of those who set out to realize their vision of Europe; who failed; and who yet succeeded, because their aim was so high. The struggle continues. Its most appropriate epigraph was written in the year that Jean Monnet was born:

Men fight and lose the battle, and the thing they fought for comes about in spite of their defeat, and when it comes turns out to be not what they meant, and other men have to fight for what they meant under another name.[12]

Today, the name is Europe. Tomorrow, it could be the world.

REFERENCES

Chapter 1. A GENERATION OF CHANGE

1. *Averroës et l'Averroisme* (Paris, 1861), p. v (transl. R.M.)
2. *La Civilisation de 1975* (Paris, 1964), p. 7 (transl. R.M.)
3. *Table Talk and Omniana* (London, 1917), p. 434
4. Cf. Dwight D. Eisenhower, *Mandate for Change 1953–1956* (Signet edition, New York, 1965), p. 548
5. Christopher Isherwood, *Prater Violet* (London, 1946), p. 5
6. J. & F. Fourastié, *Les arts ménagers* (Paris, 1950), p. 73; estimate based on Reader's Digest European Surveys, *Products and People* (London, 1963), tables 5 and 55
7. Office Statistique des Communautés Européennes, *Statistiques de base de la Communauté: Comparaison avec certains pays européens, le Canada, les Etats-Unis d'Amérique et l'Union des Républiques Socialistes Soviétiques* (Brussels/Luxembourg, 1967), p. 152
8. E. G. Couzens & V. E. Yarsley, *Plastics in the Service of Man* (London, 1965), pp. 289–90; cf. the same authors' *Plastics* (London, 1941), pp. 154–8
9. Norman Lansdell, *The Atom and the Energy Revolution* (London, 1958), 60; Bertrand Goldschmidt, *L'Aventure atomique* (Paris, 1962), p. 94; Office Statistique des Communautés Européennes, *op. cit.* (n. 7, *supra*), p. 70
10. Sir George Thomson, *The Foreseeable Future* (Cambridge, 1955), p. 88. Léo Moulin, *La Société de demain dans l'Europe d'aujourd'hui* (Paris, 1966), pp. 29–30, appraises Thomson's predictions and those of W. Ley. For a convenient summary of space chronology and statistics, cf. D. & M. Frémy, *Quid?* (Paris, 1968), pp. 263–9. Further statistics from the U. S. National Aeronautics and Space Administration (NASA) and the Space Department of the Royal Aircraft Establishment, Farnborough, England
11. Jean Fourastié, *Les 40.000 heures* (Paris, 1965), p. 18
12. T. S. Ashton, *The Industrial Revolution 1760–1830* (Oxford, 1948), p. 99
13. A. J. P. Taylor, *English History 1914–1945* (Oxford, 1965), p. 132 n. 2
14. Lord Strang, *Home and Abroad* (London, 1956), p. 137; Taylor, *op. cit.*, p. 426 n. 2
15. Robert Murphy, *Diplomat Among Warriors* (London, 1964), pp. 258–9
16. Harry S. Truman, *Memoirs*, Vol. I, *1945: Year of Decisions* (Signet edition. New York, 1965), p. 444

17. Eisenhower, *op. cit.* (n. 4, *supra*), p. 586; *Waging Peace 1956–1961* (London, 1966), p. 415

18. Frémy, *op. cit.* (n. 10, *supra*), p. 959; Organisation for Economic Co-operation and Development (O.E.C.D.), *Tourism in O.E.C.D. Member Countries 1966* (Paris, 1966), p. 28; Wilfred Owen, "The Transport Revolution," in J. Frederic Dewhurst and others, *Europe's Needs and Resources* (New York, 1961), pp. 279–311 (p. 293); cf. also Bernard Dutoit, *L'Aviation et l'Europe* (Lausanne, 1959), *passim*

19. Fourastié, *op. cit.* (n. 11, *supra*), p. 17; Frémy, *op. cit.* (n. 10, *supra*), pp. 957–8, 988–9; *The Times* (London), January 5, 1967, p. 1; John Montgomery, *The Fifties* (London, 1965), p. 233

20. Dewhurst, *op. cit.* (n. 18, *supra*), appendices, pp. 913, 919

21. Cf. Peter Townsend, *The Family Life of Old People* (London, 1957), *passim*

22. Andrew Shonfield, *The Attack on World Poverty* (London, 1960), p. 83, J. Fourastié & C. Vimont, *Histoire de demain* (3rd ed., Paris 1964), pp. 15, 122–3; Hubert d'Hérouville, *L'économie mondiale* (4th ed., Paris, 1960), p. 12; Fritz Baade, *The Race of the Year 2000* (London, 1963), pp. 6–7, quoting L. Dudley Stamp, *Our Underdeveloped World* (London, 1952), p. 24; United Nations, *The Future Growth of World Population* (New York, 1958), *passim;* Carlo M. Cipolla, *The Economic History of World Population* (revised ed., London, 1964), pp. 91–106. The Italian edition of this last, *Uomini, tecniche, economie* (Milan, 1966), pp. 96–113, contains more recent figures

23. P. Lamartine Yates, *Food, Land and Manpower in Western Europe* (London, 1960), pp. 198–9; J. Fourastié, *La Civilisation de 1975* (Paris, 1964), p. 96; d'Hérouville, *op. cit.,* p. 51; John O. Coppock, "Land and Agricultural Resources" in Dewhurst, *op. cit.* (n. 18, *supra*), pp. 479–519 (pp. 494–5); d'Hérouville, *op. cit.,* p. 70; Dennis Gabor, *Inventing the Future* (London, 1963), pp. 75–85; Fourastié & Vimont, *op. cit.,* pp. 43–58

24. Cipolla, *Uomini, tecniche, economie* (Milan, 1966), pp. 50, 69; Office Statistique des Communautés Européennes, *op. cit.* (n. 7, *supra*), p. 78; J. Fourastié, *La Civilisation de 1975* (Paris, 1964), p. 83; d'Hérouville, *op. cit.* (n. 22, *supra*), pp. 64, 82; Office Statistique des Communautés Européennes, *Commerce extérieur: Statistique mensuelle* (Brussels/Luxembourg, monthly), *passim;* d'Hérouville, *op. cit.,* p. 90; Fourastié, *op. cit.,* p. 59; Fourastié, *Idées Majeures* (Paris, 1966), p. 99; Massimo Salvadori, "Capitalism in Postwar Europe," in Dewhurst, *op. cit.* (n. 18, *supra*), pp. 734–58 (p. 734); Angus Maddison, *Economic Growth in the West* (London, 1964), p. 220; P. Lamartine Yates, "Social Security," in Dewhurst, *op. cit.,* pp. 375–403 (p. 400); Yates, "Education," in Dewhurst, *op. cit.,* pp. 312–43 (p. 333); Maddison, *op. cit.,* p. 228; Dewhurst, "Needs and Re-

sources: Summary," in *op. cit.*, pp. 862–88 (p. 868); Dewhurst, "Manpower," in *op. cit.*, pp. 61–106 (p. 76); Maddison, *op. cit.*, p. 240; John O. Coppock, "Government Expenditure and Operations," in Dewhurst, *op. cit.*, pp. 404–42; Fourastié, *Le grand espoir du XXe siècle* (Edition définitive, Paris, 1963), p. 160; Dewhurst, "Consumption Levels and Patterns," in *op. cit.*, pp. 143–78 (p. 171); Yates, *Food, Land and Manpower in Western Europe* (London, 1960), pp. 32–4; Yates, "Household Operations," in Dewhurst, *op. cit.*, pp. 246–78 (p. 265); Dewhurst, *op. cit.*, appendices, pp. 1012–13; extrapolation from Office Statistique des Communautés Européennes, *Statistiques de base* (cf. n. 7, *supra*), p. 151

25. Cf. Gabor, *op. cit.* (n. 23, *supra*), pp. 23–4; C. Northcote Parkinson, *Parkinson's Law or the Pursuit of Progress* (London, 1958), chapter 1

26. Cf. Andrew Shonfield, *Modern Capitalism* (London, 1965), pp. 376–7, 385, 421–7

27. Robert Triffin, *The World Money Maze* (New Haven, Connecticut, and London, 1966), p. 349

28. Alexis de Tocqueville, *Democracy in America*, transl. Henry Reeve (Oxford, 1946), pp. 286–7

29. Pierre George, *Géographie industrielle du monde* (Paris, 1957), pp. 67–9

30. Office Statistique des Communautés Européennes, *Statistiques de base* (cf. n. 7, *supra*), pp. 43, 64, 80, 82, 90, 143–53

31. André Gide, *Retour de l'U.R.S.S.* (Paris, 1936), p. 14

32. League of Nations, *Industrialization and Free Trade* (Geneva, 1945), II, A. 10, p. 13; Norman S. Buchanan & Friedrich A. Lutz, *Rebuilding the World Economy* (New York, 1947), p. 185; Richard Mayne, *The Community of Europe* (London, 1962; New York, 1963), pp. 61–2

33. Leonard Beaton, *Must the Bomb Spread?* (London, 1966), pp. 42, 47, 141

34. Buchanan & Lutz, *loc. cit.* (cf. n. 32, *supra*)

35. Organisation for Economic Co-operation and Development (O.E.C.D.), Economic Surveys, *Japan* (Paris, December 1965), pp. 6, 7; Office Statistique des Communautés Européennes, *Statistiques de base* (7e. édition, Brussels/Luxembourg, 1967), pp. 15, 64, 80, 90, 91; Norman Macrae, "The Risen Sun," in *The Economist*, vol. CCXXIII, Nos. 6457 & 6458 (London, May 27–June 2 & June 3–9, 1967); cf. *International Management*, December 1967, pp. 41–3

36. J. Fourastié, *Les 40.000 heures* (Paris, 1965), pp. 17–18; Institute of Strategic Studies, *The Military Balance 1968–69* (London, 1969); Jean Cocteau, *Portrait d'un inconnu* (Paris, 1953), p. 31

37. Cf. Evan Luard (ed.), *The Cold War: A Reappraisal* (London, 1964) and André Fontaine, *Histoire de la guerre froide* (2 vols., Paris, 1965 and 1967). For the traditional "Western" view, cf.

David Rees, *The Age of Containment* (London, 1967); for the opposite, D. F. Fleming, *The Cold War and its Origins 1917–1960* (2 vols., London, 1961) and David Horowitz, *From Yalta to Vietnam* (revised edition, London, 1967). Louis J. Halle, *The Cold War as History* (London, 1967) is a scrupulous attempt to see the issue from both sides. On later changes, cf. especially Ghita Ionescu, *The Break-up of the Soviet Empire in Eastern Europe* (London, 1965), Edward Crankshaw, *The New Cold War: Moscow v. Pekin* (revised edition, London, 1965) and Peter Bender, *Offensive Entspannung* (Cologne/Berlin, 1964)

38. M. M. Postan, *An Economic History of Western Europe 1945–1964* (London, 1967), pp. 12, 16; Alfred Nydegger, "Foreign Trade and Capital Movements," in Dewhurst, *op. cit.* (n. 18, supra), pp. 635–73 (p. 655); Dewhurst, *op. cit.*, appendices, pp. 1097–8; 1103–4

39. Cipolla, *op. cit.* (n. 24, supra), p. 60; d'Hérouville, *op. cit.* (n. 22, supra), p. 87; Albert Kervyn, "Exchange and Currency Problems," in Dewhurst, *op. cit.*, pp. 674–707 (p. 707); Dewhurst, *op. cit.*, appendices, pp. 1106–7

40. D. Swann & D. L. McLachlan, *Concentration or Competition: A European Dilemma* (London, 1967), p. 19; Frémy, *op. cit.* (n. 10, supra), pp. 397–9

Chapter 2.   THE WASTE LAND

1. *Table Talk*, ed. S. W. Swinger (3rd ed., London, 1860), p. 210
2. "Alle Tage," from *Die gestundete Zeit* (1953), reprinted in Horst Bingel (ed.), *Deutsche Lyrik: Gedichte seit 1945* (DTV edition, Munich, 1963), p. 9 (transl. R.M.)
3. *La Pelle* (Economica Vallecchi edition, Florence, 1965), p. 36 (transl. R.M.)
4. Lionel Trilling, *The Middle of the Journey* (Penguin edition, London, 1963), p. 313
5. Harry C. Butcher, *My Three Years with Eisenhower* (New York, 1946), p. 836
6. P. E. Schramm (ed.), *Die Niederlage 1945* (DTV edition, Munich, 1962), pp. 433 & 451n.; William D. Leahy, *I Was There* (New York, 1950), pp. 357–8; Dwight D. Eisenhower, *Crusade in Europe* (Dolphin edition, New York, 1961), p. 453; Harry S. Truman, *Memoirs*, Vol. I, *1945: Year of Decisions* (Signet edition, New York, 1965), p. 230; John Toland, *The Last Hundred Days* (Bantam edition, New York, 1967), p. 644; Butcher, *op. cit.* (n. 5, supra), p. 834
7. Field-Marshal the Viscount Montgomery of Alamein, K.G., *Memoirs* (Fontana edition, London, 1960), pp. 345–50; Dönitz Diary, May 7, 1945, in Schramm, *op. cit.*, p. 433; Leahy, *loc. cit.* and Eisenhower, *op. cit.*, p. 455, both corrected and greatly amplified by Toland, *op. cit.*, pp. 644–7 (n. 5, supra). On the

Caserta surrender, cf. Allen Dulles, *The Secret Surrender* (London, 1967)

8. Leahy, *op. cit.*, p. 361; Toland, *op. cit.*, p. 647; Truman, *op. cit.*, p. 232; Leahy, *op. cit.*, p. 359 (n. 6, *supra*)

9. Truman, *op. cit.*, p. 231; Leahy, *op. cit.*, pp. 362–3; Arthur Bryant, *Triumph in the West 1943–1946* (Alanbrooke War Diaries, vol. II), (Fontana edition, London, 1965), p. 357; Toland, *op. cit.*, pp. 647, 654n. (n. 6, *supra*); cf. *The Papers of Dwight David Eisenhower: The War Years* (5 Vols. Baltimore, 1970), *passim*

10. Private information; Robert Murphy, *Diplomat Among Warriors* (London, 1964), pp. 296–7; Bryant, *loc. cit.*; Toland, *op. cit.*, p. 645; Philip E. Mosely, "Dismemberment of Germany," in *Foreign Affairs*, vol. XXVIII, No. 3 (April, 1950), pp. 487–98, reprinted in *Ibid.*, *The Kremlin in World Politics* (Vintage books edition, New York, 1960), pp. 131–54 (pp. 148–52)

11. Toland, *op. cit.*, pp. 657–60 and Schramm, *op. cit.*, pp. 454–5 (n. 6, *supra*); Cornelius Ryan, *The Last Battle* (London, 1966), photograph in plates between pp. 320 and 321; Butcher, *op. cit.* (n. 5, *supra*), p. 844

12. Murphy, *op. cit.* (n. 10, *supra*), p. 298; H. R. Trevor-Roper, *The Last Days of Hitler* (revised Pan edition, London, 1962), p. 240; Schramm, *op. cit.* (n. 6, *supra*), pp. 413–17, 420, 429, 434

13. Schramm, *op. cit.*, pp. 419, 431–2, 433, 441–2; Trevor-Roper, *op. cit.*, pp. 236, 237, 255; Lionel Kochan, *The Struggle for Germany 1914–1945* (Edinburgh, 1963), pp. 94–6, 127; Rebecca West, *The Meaning of Treason* (revised Penguin edition, London, 1965), p. 127; Murphy, *op. cit.*, pp. 297–300. Cf. also Walter Lüdde-Neurath, *Die Regierung Dönitz* (Göttingen, 1950) & Karl Dönitz, *Zehn Jahre und zwanzig Tage* (Bonne, 1958), *passim*

14. On the Eastern campaign, cf. Alan Clark, *Barbarossa* (Penguin revised edition, London, 1966); on Russian behavior in Germany, Ryan, *op. cit.* (n. 11, *supra*), and Anon., *A Woman in Berlin,* transl. James Stern (London, 1965); on Russia's "defensive expansion," Louis J. Halle, *The Cold War as History* (London, 1967), esp. pp. 11–19; on the effects of "unconditional surrender," Jean Laloy, *Entre guerres et paix 1945–1965* (Paris, 1966), esp. pp. 32–3, 67

15. Jacques Dumaine, *Quai d'Orsay 1945–1951,* transl. Alan Davidson (London, 1958), p. 226

16. U.N. Economic Commission for Europe, *The European Housing Problem: a Preliminary Review* (E/ECE/110, Geneva, 1949); R. G. Hawtrey, "The Economic Consequences of the War," in A. & V. M. Toynbee (ed.), *The Realignment of Europe* (London, 1955), pp. 36–51 (p. 39); Michael Balfour, "Germany," in A. Toynbee (ed.), *Four-Power Control in Germany and Austria 1945–1946* (London, 1956), pp. 1–265 (p. 7); John Gunther,

Inside Russia Today (London, 1958), p. 65; Paul Alpert, *Twentieth-Century Economic History of Europe* (New York, 1951), pp. 253–4; Bruno Foa, *Monetary Reconstruction in Italy* (New York, 1949), p. 23; Katharine Duff, "Liberated Italy: from September 1943 to February 1947," in A. & V. M. Toynbee, *op. cit.*, pp. 409–53 (p. 441)

17. John Lukacs, *Decline and Rise of Europe* (New York, 1965), p. 15; R. C. Mowat, *Ruin and Resurgence 1939–1965* (London, 1966), pp. 85–94; Balfour, *op. cit.* (n. 16, *supra*), pp. 7–8; Truman, *op. cit.* (n. 6, *supra*), p. 378; Lucius D. Clay, *Decision in Germany* (London, 1950), pp. 21, 32; Eugene Davidson, *The Death and Life of Germany* (London, 1959), p. 66; J.-F. Angelloz, "En Allemagne: Berlin–Hambourg," in *Mercure de France*, No. 1007 (Paris, July 1, 1947), pp. 456–66 (p. 457)

18. Balfour, *op. cit.*, p. 9, & Alpert, *op. cit.*, p. 251 (n. 16, *supra*), G. R. Gayre, *Italy in Transition* (London, 1946), pp. 26–7; Robert Aron, *Histoire de la libération de la France* (*Livre de poche* edition, Paris, 1967), vol. 1, p. 466; David Thomson, *Europe Since Napoleon* (2nd ed. revised, London, 1962), p. 775

19. Hawtrey, *op. cit.*, p. 39, Balfour, *op. cit.*, p. 9, Alpert, *op. cit.*, p. 252 (n. 16, *supra*); Clay, *op. cit.*, p. 188, Davidson, *op. cit.*, p. 70 (n. 17, *supra*)

20. Marcel Jouanique & Lucien Morice, *La Navigation intérieure en France* (Paris, 1951), p. 16; Hawtrey, *op. cit.*, pp. 40, 42, Balfour, *op. cit.*, p. 9, Alpert, *op. cit.*, p. 252 (n. 16, *supra*); Theodore H. White, *Fire in the Ashes: Europe in Mid-Century* (New York, 1953), p. 140; Muriel Grindrod, *The Rebuilding of Italy* (London, 1955), p. 38

21. Hawtrey, *op. cit.*, p. 40, Balfour, *op. cit.*, p. 11, Alpert, *op. cit.*, pp. 252–3 (n. 16, *supra*); Grindrod, *op. cit.*, pp. 39, 155; White, *loc. cit.* (n. 20, *supra*); Norman Kogan, *A Political History of Postwar Italy* (London, 1966), p. 43

22. Howard K. Smith, *The State of Europe* (London, 1950), p. 10; Alpert, *op. cit.* (n. 16, *supra*), p. 254; Italy, Instituto Poligrafico dello Stato, *Lo Sviluppo dell'Economia Italiana* (Rome, 1952), p. 3; Grindrod, *op. cit.* (n. 20, *supra*), pp. 38–9; Libero Lenti, *Inventario dell'economia italiana* (Milan, 1966), pp. 20–4; A. J. P. Taylor, *English History 1914–1945* (Oxford, 1965), p. 599; Hawtrey, *op. cit.* (n. 16, *supra*), pp. 41–2, 47–8; T. Balogh, "The International Aspect," in G. D. N. Worswick & P. H. Ady, *The British Economy 1945–1950* (Oxford, 1952), pp. 476–510; Anthony Harrison, *The Framework of Economic Activity* (London, 1967), p. 83; Norman S. Buchanan & Friedrich A. Lutz, *Rebuilding the World Economy* (New York, 1947), p. 78; Balfour, *op. cit.* (n. 15, *supra*), p. 9; J.F., "De l'économie de guerre à l'économie de paix," in *Mercure de France* No. 1010 (Paris, October 1, 1947), pp. 198–205; "Christopher Felix," *The Spy and his Masters* (London, 1963), p. 173

23. Cf. Michel van der Plas, *Mooie Vrede: een documentaire over Nederland in de jaren 1945–1950* (Utrecht, 1966), p. 15
24. Hawtrey, *op. cit.*, p. 38, Alpert, *op. cit.*, p. 253, Duff, *loc. cit.* (n. 16, *supra*), Truman, *op. cit.*, (n. 6, *supra*), p. 252
25. Hawtrey, *loc. cit.*, Alpert, *op. cit.*, p. 255 (n. 16, *supra*); J.F. *op. cit.*, (n. 22, *supra*), p. 203; H. Riemans, *Perspectief voor Nederland* (Amsterdam, 1957), p. 63
26. Janet Flanner, *Paris Journal 1944–1965* (London, 1966), p. 5; Aron, *op. cit.* (n. 18, *supra*), pp. 464–5; Edmund Wilson, *Europe Without Baedeker* (London, 1948), p. 146; Smith, *op. cit.* (n. 22, *supra*), p. 215
27. United Nations, Economic and Social Council, *Preliminary Report of the Temporary Sub-Commission on Economic Reconstruction of Devastated Areas* (September 18, 1946), 26–7; Hawtrey, *op. cit.* (n. 16, *supra*), pp. 38–9; René Masseyeff, *La Faim* (Paris, 1956), p. 92; Smith, *op. cit.* (n. 22, *supra*), p. 170
28. Smith, *op. cit.* (n. 22, *supra*), p. 10; D. & M. Frémy, *Quid?* (Paris, 1968), pp. 493–5, J. Frederic Dewhurst, "Population," in J. Frederic Dewhurst & associates, *Europe's Needs and Resources* (New York, 1961), 32–60 (p. 32, n. 1); Balfour, *op. cit.* (n. 16, *supra*), p. 10; United Nations, Economic Commission for Europe, *Growth and Stagnation in the European Economy* (Geneva, 1954), p. 236; D. V. Glass & E. Grebenik. "World Population, 1800–1950," in H. J. Habakkuk & M. Postan (ed.), *The Cambridge Economic History of Europe*, vol. II, *The Industrial Revolutions and After: Incomes, Population and Technological Change* (Cambridge, 1965), pp. 56–138 (p. 61)
29. Malcolm J. Proudfoot, *European Refugees: 1939–52* (London, 1957), pp. 303–17; Eugen Kogón, *Der SS-Staat und das System der deutschen Konzentrationslager* (Munich, 1946), transl. as *The Theory and Practice of Hell* (New York, 1951); Gerald Reitlinger, *The Final Solution: the Attempt to Exterminate the Jews of Europe, 1939–1945* (London, 1953); *ibid.*, The SS: *Alibi of a Nation* (London, 1956); *Trial of the Major War Criminals before the International Military Tribunal*, 42 vols. (Nuremberg, 1947–49); *Trials of War Criminals before the Nuremberg Military Tribunals*, 15 vols. (Washington, 1951–52); Alan Moorehead, "Glimpses of Germany: II–Belsen," in *Horizon*, vol. XII, No. 67 (London, July 1945), pp. 26–35; William L. Shirer, *The Rise and Fall of the Third Reich* (Crest edition, New York, 1962), pp. 1234–88; Rudolf Hoess, *Commandant of Auschwitz*, transl. Constantine FitzGibbon (London, 1959); Constantine FitzGibbon, "Auschwitz," in *Random Thoughts of a Fascist Hyena* (London, 1963), pp. 33–57; Robert Merle, *La Mort est mon métier* (Paris, 1953); Jean-François Steiner, *Treblinka* (Paris, 1966)
30. Proudfoot, *op. cit.* (n. 29, *supra*), pp. 32, 34; Davidson, *op. cit.* (n. 17, *supra*), p. 53; Joseph B. Schechtman, *European Population Transfers, 1939–1945* (New York, 1946), pp. vii, viii; *ibid.*,

The Refugee in the World: Displacement and Integration (New York/London, 1963), pp. 3, 13, 47; Montgomery, *op. cit.* (n. 7, *supra*), p. 407; Clay, *op. cit.* (n. 17, *supra*), p. 15; Balfour, *op. cit.* (n. 16, *supra*), p. 13

31. Schechtman, *The Refugee in the World* (n. 30, *supra*), p. 14; Elizabeth Wiskemann, *Germany's Eastern Neighbours* (London, 1957), pp. 121–2; Robert Kee, *Refugee World* (London, 1961), p. 21; Inez Holden, "U.N.R.R.A. in Germany," in Reginald Moore & Edward Lane (ed.), *The Windmill* (London, 1946), pp. 13–32 (pp. 15–16); Proudfoot, *op. cit.* (n. 29, *supra*), pp. 170–5; Peter Rodd, "The Psychology of Refugees," in *Horizon*, vol. x, No. 59 (London, November 1944), pp. 312–19

32. Malaparte, *op. cit.* (n. 3, *supra*), p. 68; René Fallet, *Banlieue Sud-Est* (*Livre de poche* edition, Paris, 1967), pp. 109–11 (transl. R.M.)

33. Wyndham Lewis, *The Writer and the Absolute* (London, 1952), p. 68; Proudfoot, *op. cit.* (n. 29, *supra*), pp. 128–9, 175–8, 313; Ryan, *op. cit.* (n. 11, *supra*), pp. 361–3, 366–7, 382–9; van der Plas, *op. cit.* (n. 23, *supra*), pp. 77–135; Aron, *op. cit.* (n. 18, *supra*), p. 455; *ibid.*, *Histoire de l'épuration*, vol. I (Paris, 1967), p. 433; M. R. D. Foot, *SOE in France* (London, 1966), pp. 418–23; Anon., *op. cit.* (n. 14, *supra*), *passim;* Peter Novick, *The Resistance versus Vichy* (London, 1968), pp. 71, 202–8

34. Shirer, *op. cit.* (n. 29, *supra*), p. 1482

35. Thomson, *op. cit.* (n. 18, *supra*), p. 877

36. G. M. Gilbert, *Nuremberg Diary* (New York, 1947), p. 31; Davidson, *op. cit.* (n. 17, *supra*), p. 108, n. 1

37. Whitney R. Harris, *Tyranny on Trial: the Evidence at Nuremberg* (Dallas, 1954), p. 16, Robert H. Jackson, *Report* (Department of State Publication 3080, Washington, 1949), pp. 340–4; Davidson, *op. cit.* (n. 17, *supra*), pp. 105, n. 107, 122, n. 3; Gordon Young, *The Fall and Rise of Alfred Krupp* (London, 1960), p. 81

38. Young, *op. cit.* (n. 37, *supra*), p. 88

39. For an example perhaps deliberately paradoxical, cf. A. J. P. Taylor, *The Origins of the Second World War* (Penguin edition with Foreword. London, 1964), pp. 96ff

40. *The New York Times*, August 9, 1932; *Trial of Major War Criminals* (n. 29, *supra*), vols. II, p. 154, XIX, pp. 399, 448; Jackson, *op. cit.* (n. 37, *supra*), p. 295; Davidson, *op. cit.* (n. 17, *supra*), pp. 102, nn. 7, 8, 9; 117, n. 1. On the Nuremberg trial in general, and particularly its atmosphere, cf. also R. W. Cooper, *The Nuremberg Trials* (London, 1946)

41. Wilson, *op. cit.* (n. 26, *supra*), p. 24

Chapter 3. THE NEW FRONTIER

1. Milovan Djilas, *Conversations with Stalin*, transl. Michael B. Petrovich (Penguin edition, London, 1963), p. 90

2. *Memoirs*, vol. I, *1945: Year of Decisions* (Signet edition, New York, 1965), p. 354

3. *Through the Looking-Glass and what Alice Found There* (Miniature edition, London, 1908), p. 153

4. John Toland, *The Last Hundred Days* (Bantam edition, New York, 1967), pp. 500–9, which misprints the date as April 26 (p. 502); Cornelius Ryan, *The Last Battle* (London, 1966), pp. 371–2; Dwight D. Eisenhower, *Crusade in Europe* (Dolphin edition, New York, 1961), p. 434; Arthur Bryant, *Triumph in the West 1943–1946* (Alanbrooke War Diaries, vol. II (Fontana edition, London, 1965), p. 353; Chester Wilmot, *The Struggle for Europe* (Fontana edition, London, 1959), p. 802

5. John Colville, Churchill's assistant private secretary, quoted by Lord Moran, *Churchill: The Struggle for Survival* (Boston, 1966), p. 194

6. Cf. Ludwig Dehio, *The Precarious Balance*, transl. Charles Fullman (New York, 1962), esp. pp. 247–88; Wilfrid Knapp, "The Partition of Europe" in Evan Luard (ed.), *The Cold War: A Reappraisal* (London, 1964), pp. 45–61; John Lukacs, *Decline and Rise of Europe* (New York, 1965), pp. 25–56

7. D. F. Fleming, *The Cold War and its Origins 1917–1960* (London, 1961), vol. I, pp. 145–8

8. Sidney Lowery, "Poland," in A. & V. M. Toynbee (ed.), *The Realignment of Europe* (London, 1955), pp. 126–245 (pp. 164–82); Hugh Seton-Watson, *The East European Revolution* (London, 1950), pp. 83–98, 104–5; Fitzroy Maclean, *Disputed Barricade* (London, 1957), p. 291; W. H. McNeill, "Greece, 1944–1946," in Toynbee, *op. cit.*, pp. 389–408 (p. 392); Winston Churchill, *The Second World War* (Cassell paperback edition, vol. XI, *The Tide of Victory*, London, 1964), pp. 187, 188, 203

9. Churchill, *op. cit.* (n. 8, *supra*), p. 200; Moran, *op. cit.* (n. 5, *supra*), p. 207

10. Churchill, *op. cit.* (n. 8, *supra*), pp. 200–1; André Fontaine, *Histoire de la guerre froide*, vol. I (Paris, 1965), p. 246

11. Polish Government in Exile, *Facts and Documents Concerning Polish Prisoners of War, Captured by the U.S.S.R. during the 1939 Campaign* (London, 1944); Joseph Mackiewicz, *The Katyn Wood Murders* (London, 1951); Lowery, *op. cit.* (n. 8, *supra*), pp. 138–47; Jean Laloy, *Entre guerres et paix 1945–1965* (Paris, 1966), pp. 68–9

12. Stanislaw Mikolajczyk, *The Pattern of Soviet Domination* (London, 1948), pp. 78–87, 102, 328; Churchill, *op. cit.* (n. 8, *supra*), p. 208; Laloy, *op. cit.* (n. 11, *supra*), pp. 70–2; Lowery, *op. cit.* (n. 8, *supra*), pp. 171–3, 177–8

13. Mikolajczyk, *op. cit.* (n. 12, *supra*), pp. 103–8; Churchill, *op. cit.* (n. 8, *supra*), p. 200; Jan Ciechanowski, *Defeat in Victory* (New York, 1947), pp. 328–9, 338; Wladyslaw Anders, *An Army in Exile* (London, 1949), pp. 237–9, 243; James F. Byrnes,

Speaking Frankly (New York, 1947), p. 29; William D. Leahy, *I Was There* (New York, 1950), p. 249; Robert E. Sherwood, *Roosevelt and Hopkins: An Intimate History* (New York, 1948), pp. 833–4; Lowery, *op. cit.* (n. 8, *supra*), pp. 182–4

14. Ciechanowski, *op. cit.* (n. 13, *supra*), pp. 333–4, 342–3, 345; Mikolajczyk, *op. cit.* (n. 12, *supra*), pp. 109–11, 114; Anders, *op. cit.* (n. 13, *supra*), pp. 240–2; Churchill, *op. cit.* (n. 8, *supra*), pp. 208, 210, 212–13; Hansard, *House of Commons debates*, 5th series, vol. 404, cols. 493–5 & vol. 406, cols. 1478–578; Lowery, *op. cit.* (n. 8, *supra*), pp. 184–9

15. Lowery, *op. cit.* (n. 8, *supra*), pp. 191–4, 202 n. 1, 206 n. 5; U.K. Foreign Office, *Report of the Crimea Conference* (Cmd. 6598, London, 1945); Leahy, *op. cit.* (n. 13, *supra*), p. 370

16. Laloy, *op. cit.* (n. 11, *supra*), p. 95

17. McNeill, *op. cit.* (n. 8, *supra*), pp. 393–8; Hugh Seton-Watson, "Yugoslavia," in Toynbee, *op. cit.* (n. 8, *supra*), pp. 352–71 (p. 359); Byrnes, *op. cit.* (n. 13, *supra*), p. 31

18. Cf. Knapp, *op. cit.* (n. 6, *supra*), p. 46

19. *Foreign Relations of the United States, 1943*, vol. I, pp. 708–10, 762–3; *Correspondence between the Chairman of the Council of Ministers of the U.S.S.R. and the Presidents of the U.S.A. and the Prime Ministers of Great Britain during the Great Patriotic War of 1941–45* (Moscow, 1957), vol. I, No. 186, p. 154; Laloy, *op. cit.* (n. 11, *supra*), pp. 43, 52–3

20. Laloy, *op. cit.* (n. 11, *supra*), pp. 42–5; Norman Kogan, *A Political History of Postwar Italy* (London, 1966), pp. 4–5; L. M. Goodrich & M. J. Carroll (ed.), *Documents on American Foreign Relations, 1943–1944* (Boston, 1945), p. 228; Hansard, *House of Commons debates*, 5th series, vol. 392, col. 99; Katharine Duff, "Liberated Italy: from September 1943 to February 1947," in Toynbee, *op. cit.* (n. 8, *supra*), pp. 409–53 (pp. 418–20); Peirgiovanni Permoli, *La Costituente e i Partiti Politici Italiani* (Rocca San Casciano, 1966), pp. 70–6

21. Lionel Kochan, *The Struggle for Germany 1914–1945* (Edinburgh, 1963), pp. 79–80, 84, 89–90; *Foreign Relations of the United States, Diplomatic Papers: The Conferences at Cairo and Teheran, 1943* (Washington, 1961), pp. 600–1; Laloy, *op. cit.* (n. 11, *supra*), pp. 103–4; Arthur Conte, *Yalta ou le partage du monde* ("J'ai lu" edition, Paris, 1965), p. 332; *Pravda*, May 10, 1945; *Foreign Relations of the United States, Diplomatic Papers: The Conference of Berlin, 1945* (Washington, 1960), vol. II, p. 61

22. *Foreign Relations of the United States, 1942: Europe, Vol. III*, pp. 517–18; Kochan, *op. cit.* (n. 21, *supra*), pp. 80, 82, 84; *The Conferences at Cairo and Teheran, 1943* (n. 21, *supra*), *loc. cit.*; Lukacs, *op. cit.* (n. 6, *supra*), p. 36; Laloy, *op. cit.* (n. 11, *supra*), p. 62

23. Eugene Davidson, *The Death and Life of Germany* (London, 1959), pp. 6–10; Cordell Hull, *Memoirs* (New York, 1948), vol. II, pp. 1265–6; Sumner Welles, *The Time for Decision* (New York, 1944), pp. 336–61; *The Conferences at Cairo and Teheran, 1943* (n. 21, *supra*), *loc. cit.*; Leahy, *op. cit.* (n. 13, *supra*), p. 186; Lukacs, *op. cit.* (n. 6, *supra*), pp. 32–3; Robert Murphy, *Diplomat Among Warriors* (London, 1964), p. 281

24. Ray S. Cline, *Washington Command Post: The Operations Division* (Washington, 1951), p. 217; Herbert Feis, *Churchill, Roosevelt, Stalin: The War They Waged and the Peace They Sought* (Princeton, 1957), p. 360; Sir Llewellyn Woodward, *British Foreign Policy in the Second World War* (London, 1962), p. 438; Laloy, *op. cit.* (n. 11, *supra*), pp. 31, 55, 56 n. 1; Hull, *op. cit.* (n. 23, *supra*), pp. 1255–6, 1285; Kochan, *op. cit.* (n. 21, *supra*), p. 86; Edgar McInnis, Richard Hiscocks & Robert Spencer, *The Shaping of Postwar Germany* (Toronto/London, 1960), pp. 93–4

25. Philip Mosely, "The Occupation of Germany," in *Foreign Affairs,* vol. XXVIII, No. 4 (July, 1950), pp. 580–604, reprinted in *Ibid., The Kremlin in World Politics* (Vintage books edition, New York, 1960), pp. 155–88 (p. 157 n. 4); *The Conferences at Cairo and Teheran, 1943* (n. 21, *supra*), p. 183; *Foreign Relations of the United States, 1943,* vol. I (Washington, 1963), pp. 720–1; Laloy, *op. cit.* (n. 6, *supra*), pp. 55–6; Kochan, *op. cit.* (n. 21, *supra*), p. 86

26. Winston Churchill, *The Second World War* (Cassell paperback edition, vol. XII, *Triumph and Tragedy,* London, 1964), p. 159; Feis, *op. cit.* (n. 24, *supra*), p. 360; John L. Snell, *Wartime Origins of the East-West Dilemma over Germany* (New Orleans, 1959), p. 46

27. Lord Strang, *Home and Abroad* (London, 1956), pp. 203, 204, 207, 208, 212, 220; Nikolaus Pevsner, *The Buildings of England: London, Vol. I: The Cities of London and Westminster* (London, 1957), p. 447; Mosely, *op. cit.* (n. 25, *supra*), and "Dismemberment of Germany," in *Foreign Affairs,* vol. XXVIII, No. 3 (April, 1950), pp. 487–98, also reprinted in *Ibid., The Kremlin in World Politics* (n. 25, *supra*); *Foreign Relations of the United States, 1944,* vol. I, pp. 17ff; E. F. Penrose, *Economic Planning for Peace* (Princeton, 1953), *passim*

28. Woodward, *op. cit.* (n. 24, *supra*), p. 442; Mosely, *The Kremlin in World Politics* (n. 25, *supra*), p. 168; Sir Frederick Morgan, *Overture to Overlord* (London, 1950), p. 124; Strang, *op. cit.* (n. 27, *supra*), p. 218

29. Strang, *op. cit.* (n. 27, *supra*), pp. 213–14; Ryan, *op. cit.* (n. 4, *supra*), pp. 125–6; Mosely, *op. cit.* (n. 25, *supra*), pp. 169–71; Kochan, *op. cit.* (n. 21, *supra*), p. 87

30. Strang, *op. cit.* (n. 27, *supra*), pp. 213–15; Mosely, *op. cit.* (n. 25, *supra*), pp. 167, 171

31. Ryan, *op. cit.* (n. 4, *supra*), pp. 115–29, 134 (reproduction of *National Geographic* map); *Foreign Relations of the United States, Diplomatic Papers, 1944*, vol. 1: *General* (Washington, 1966), pp. 195–6 (with inset map); Murphy, *op. cit.* (n. 23, *supra*), pp. 284–7; Dwight D. Eisenhower, *Waging Peace 1956–1961* (London, 1966), p. 335, n. 5

32. Private information; Mosely, *The Kremlin in World Politics* (n. 25, *supra*), pp. 171–3; George Kennan, *Memoirs 1925–1950* (London, 1968), pp. 168–71

33. Mosely, *The Kremlin in World Politics* (n. 25, *supra*), pp. 166–7; Ryan, *op. cit.* (n. 4, *supra*), pp. 124–5; *Foreign Relations of the United States, Diplomatic Papers, 1944* (n. 31, *supra*), pp. 100–9

34. Strang, *op. cit.* (n. 27, *supra*), p. 215

35. *Foreign Relations of the United States, Diplomatic Papers: The Conference at Malta and Yalta, 1945* (Washington, 1955), pp. 612, 624; Kochan, *op. cit.* (n. 21, *supra*), p. 86

36. Private information; Murphy, *op. cit.* (n. 23, *supra*), p. 281; Churchill, *op. cit.* (n. 26, *supra*), p. 159

37. Byrnes, *op. cit.* (n. 13, *supra*), pp. 50–2, 54–5, 60; R. H. Markham, *Rumania under the Soviet Yoke* (Boston, 1949), pp. 207–12; Lowery, *op. cit.* (n. 8, *supra*), pp. 210–14; Churchill, *op. cit.* (n. 26, *supra*), p. 124

38. Ryan, *op. cit.* (n. 4, *supra*), pp. 133–5. On friction, cf. Churchill, *op. cit.* (n. 26, *supra*), pp. 114–25, 156–68, 200–2; Dwight D. Eisenhower, *Crusade in Europe* (Dolphin edition, New York, 1961), pp. 325–6, 419–27; Field-Marshal the Viscount Montgomery of Alamein, K.G., *Memoirs* (Fontana edition, London, 1960), pp. 281–3, 287–90, 341–2; Bryant, *op. cit.* (n. 4, *supra*), pp. 346–53; Omar Bradley, *A Soldier's Story* (London, 1952), p. 537; Wilmot, *op. cit.* (n. 4, *supra*), pp. 553–62, 606–9, 612–14, 782–3, 788–95, 815–16

39. Montgomery, *op. cit.* (n. 38, *supra*), pp. 281, 290, 294; Eisenhower, *op. cit.* (n. 38, *supra*), pp. 326–7

40. Bryant, *op. cit.* (n. 4, *supra*), pp. 347, 350; Montgomery, *op. cit.* (n. 38, *supra*), p. 341; Ryan, *op. cit.* (n. 4, *supra*), p. 185; Eisenhower, *op. cit.* (n. 38, *supra*), pp. 419–20

41. Churchill, *op. cit.* (n. 26, *supra*), pp. 117–25; Bryant, *op. cit.* (n. 4, *supra*), pp. 347–51; Eisenhower, *op. cit.* (n. 38, *supra*), p. 422; Ryan, *op. cit.* (n. 4, *supra*), pp. 178, 180

42. Churchill, *op. cit.* (n. 26, *supra*), p. 117; Ryan, *op. cit.* (n. 4, *supra*), pp. 186–95

43. Bryant, *op. cit.* (n. 4, *supra*), p. 353; Ryan, *op. cit.* (n. 4, *supra*), pp. 252–3, 259–60; Wilmot, *op. cit.* (n. 4, *supra*), pp. 791–4; Leahy, *op. cit.* (n. 13, *supra*), p. 351; F. C. Pogue, "The Decision to Halt on the Elbe, 1945," in Greenfield and Kent (ed.) *Command Decisions* (London, 1960)

44. Leahy, *op. cit.* (n. 13, *supra*), pp. 349–50; Churchill, *op. cit.* (n. 26, *supra*), p. 161; Truman, *op. cit.* (n. 2, *supra*), pp. 237–45

Chapter 4. SELF-HELP

1. *Terre des hommes* (*Livre de poche* edition, Paris, 1961), p. 59, quoting his fellow-pilot Guillaumet on his survival after a forced landing in the Andes (transl. R.M.)

2. *Maximen und Reflexionen,* ed. Paul Stöcklein (Munich, 1963), p. 111 (transl. R.M.)

3. *Self-Help: with Illustration of Conduct and Perseverance* (New edition, London, 1887), p. 1

4. Hansard, *House of Commons debates,* 5th series, vol. 364, cols. 1161–2; Arnold Toynbee, "Introductory Note" to F. Ashton-Gwatkin, "The United Nations Relief and Rehabilitation Administration," in A. & V. M. Toynbee, *The Realignment of Europe* (London, 1955), pp. 51–125 (p. 52)

5. Ashton-Gwatkin, *op. cit.* (n. 4, *supra*), pp. 72–4, 77, 83–4, 102–7, 110; George Woodbridge & others, *UNRRA: The History of the United Nations Relief and Rehabilitation Administration* (3 vols., New York, 1950), vol. II, pp. 320, 451–2; Inez Holden, "U.N.R.R.A. in Germany," in Reginald Moore & Edward Lane (ed.), *The Windmill* (London, 1946), pp. 14–32 (pp. 21, 31); Edmund Wilson, *Europe Without Baedeker* (London, 1948), pp. 205–6

6. Ashton-Gwatkin, *op. cit.* (n. 4, *supra*), pp. 53–4, 62, 68

7. Ashton-Gwatkin, *op. cit.* (n. 4, *supra*), pp. 68, 70, 77–8, 89, 111–17; *UNRRA* Council, 1st Session, Resolution 14, Section 16; Woodbridge, *op. cit.* (n. 5, *supra*), vol. I, pp. 81–3, vol. III, pp. 33ff; Richard Mayne, *The Community of Europe* (London, 1962; New York, 1963), pp. 59–60

8. Ashton-Gwatkin, *op. cit.* (n. 4, *supra*), p. 104; Woodbridge, *op. cit.* (n. 5, *supra*), vol. III, pp. 428–97

9. Ashton-Gwatkin, *op. cit.* (n. 4, *supra*), pp. 77, 78, 88

10. Cf. Saul Friedländer, *Hitler et les Etats-Unis, 1939–41* (Geneva, 1963), revised by the author and translated by Aline B. & Alexander Werth as *Prelude to Downfall: Hitler and the United States 1939–1941* (New York, 1967), pp. 165–75

11. Allan Nevins, *America in World Affairs* (Oxford, 1941), pp. 131–2; A. J. P. Taylor, *English History 1914–45* (Oxford, 1965), pp. 513, 533; R. G. Hawtrey, "The Economic Consequences of the War," in A. & V. M. Toynbee, *op. cit.* (n. 4, *supra*), pp. 36–51 (p. 45); Norman S. Buchanan & Friedrich A. Lutz, *Rebuilding the World Economy* (New York, 1947), pp. 78–9; J.-B. Duroselle, *De Wilson à Roosevelt: politique extérieure des Etats-Unis* (Paris, 1960), p. 310; Harry S. Truman, *Memoirs,* vol. I, *1945: Year of Decisions* (Signet edition, New York, 1965), p. 262

12. L. M. Goodrich & M. J. Carroll (ed.), *Documents on American Foreign Relations, July 1942–June 1943* (Boston, 1944), pp. 264–5; Ashton-Gwatkin, *op. cit.* (n. 4, *supra*), p. 66

13. William D. Leahy, *I Was There* (New York, 1950), pp. 272–3, 280

14. Nevins, *op. cit.* (n. 11, *supra*), p. 132; Harry Dexter White, Memorandum on meeting in Hull's office, September 20, 1944, in *Foreign Relations of the United States, Diplomatic Papers: The Conference at Malta and Yalta* (Washington, 1955), pp. 136–9

15. White, *loc. cit.* (n. 14, *supra*), Truman, *op. cit.* (n. 11, *supra*), pp. 257–8

16. Truman, *op. cit.* (n. 11, *supra*), pp. 254–5

17. Truman, *op. cit.* (n. 11, *supra*), pp. 255–8; James F. Byrnes, *Speaking Frankly* (New York, 1947), p. 62

18. Truman, *op. cit.* (n. 11, *supra*), pp. 255–6, 260, 524; Leahy, *op. cit.* (n. 13, *supra*), p. 414; Hawtrey, *op. cit.* (n. 11, *supra*), p. 42 n. 2

19. R. F. Harrod, *The Life of John Maynard Keynes* (London, 1951), p. 595

20. Harrod, *op. cit.* (n. 19, *supra*), p. 596; T. Balogh, "The International Aspect," in G.D.N. Worswick & P. H. Ady (ed.), *The British Economy 1945–50* (Oxford, 1952), pp. 476–510 (p. 490); Hugh Dalton, *High Tide and After: Memoirs 1945–1960* (London, 1962), p. 68

21. Dalton, *loc. cit.* (n. 20, *supra*), Harrod, *op. cit.* (n. 19, *supra*), p. 595

22. R. N. Gardner, *Sterling-Dollar Diplomacy* (Oxford, 1956), p. 186 & n.; Buchanan & Lutz, *op. cit.* (n. 11, *supra*), p. 78

23. Truman, *op. cit.* (n. 11, *supra*), p. 524; P. J. D. Wiles, "Prewar and Wartime Controls," in Worswick & Ady, *op. cit.* (n. 20, *supra*), pp. 125–58 (pp. 153–4); Dalton, *op. cit.* (n. 20, *supra*), pp. 71–2

24. Dalton, *op. cit.* (n. 20, *supra*), pp. 70, 73–4, 75 n. 1; Harrod, *op. cit.* (n. 19, *supra*), pp. 596–7

25. Hawtrey, *op. cit.* (n. 11, *supra*), pp. 47–8

26. Balogh, *loc. cit.* (n. 20, *supra*); Dalton, *op. cit.* (n. 20, *supra*), p. 81

27. Dalton, *op. cit.* (n. 20, *supra*), p. 73

28. Woodbridge, *op. cit.* (n. 5, *supra*), vol. I, pp. 327–31; Ashton-Gwatkin, *op. cit.* (n. 4, *supra*), pp. 92–3; Susan Cooper, "Snoek Piquante," in Michael Sissons and Philip French (ed.), *Age of Austerity 1945–51* (Penguin edition, London, 1964), pp. 35–57 (pp. 38–42)

29. Francis Williams, *A Prime Minister Remembers: The War and Post-war Memoirs of the Rt. Hon. Earl Attlee, K.G., P.C., O.M., C.H.* (London, 1961), pp. 135–48; Truman, *op. cit.* (n. 11, *supra*), p. 514

30. Truman, *op. cit.* (n. 11, *supra*), pp. 512, 513, 515–16, 519–22; *Ibid.*, vol. II, *1946–1952: Years of Trial and Hope* (Signet edition, New York, 1956), p. 389; Williams, *op. cit.* (n. 29, *supra*), p. 140

31. Williams, *op. cit.* (n. 29, *supra*), pp. 135, 138–9

32. Winston Churchill, *The Second World War* (Cassell paperback

edition, vol. XII, *Triumph and Tragedy*, London, 1964), p. 164; Lucius D. Clay, *Decision in Germany* (London, 1950), p. 265; Eugene Davidson, *The Death and Life of Germany* (London, 1959), p. 135; Williams, *op. cit.* (n. 29, *supra*), p. 148

33. Byrnes, *op. cit.* (n. 17, *supra*), p. 182; Cordell Hull, *Memoirs* (New York, 1948), vol. II, p. 1603; Henry L. Stimson & McGeorge Bundy, *On Active Service in Peace and War* (New York, 1947), p. 573

34. Byrnes, *op. cit.* (n. 17, *supra*), p. 181; Henry Morgenthau, *Germany is our Problem* (New York, 1945), pp. 12–15; Ernest F. Penrose, *Economic Planning for the Peace* (Princeton, 1953), pp. 244–50; Michael Balfour, "Germany," in A. Toynbee (ed.), *Four-Power Control in Germany and Austria 1945–1946* (London, 1956), pp. 1–255 (p. 19); *Le Monde* (Paris, February 8, 1967), p. 19

35. Stimson & Bundy, *op. cit.* (n. 33, *supra*), p. 578; Morgenthau, letter to Edward R. Stettinius, September 20, 1944, quoted by H. Freeman Matthews, Deputy Director of Office of European Affairs, U. S. State Department, in Memorandum of September 20, 1944, reprinted in *The Conferences at Malta and Yalta* (n. 14, *supra*), p. 134; Lord Moran, *Churchill: The Struggle for Survival* (Boston, 1966), p. 190; Edmund Burke, *Speech moving his Resolutions for Conciliation with the Colonies, 22 March, 1775*, in *Select Works* (ed. E. J. Payne, Oxford, 1874), vol. I, p. 192: "I do not know the method of drawing up an indictment against a whole people."

36. Cf. C. P. Snow, *Science and Government* (Four Square edition, London, 1963), p. 26; R. F. Harrod, *The Prof* (London, 1959), *passim;* The Earl of Birkenhead, *The Professor and the Prime Minister* (Boston, 1962), *passim;* Davidson, *op. cit.* (n. 32, *supra*), p. 37; Moran, *op. cit.* (n. 35, *supra*), pp. 191–2; Byrnes, *op. cit.* (n. 17, *supra*), p. 184

37. Churchill, *op. cit.* (n. 32, *supra*), pp. 19–20; *Ibid.*, vol. XI, *The Tide of Victory*, p. 138

38. Davidson, *op. cit.* (n. 32, *supra*), pp. 6–14; Department of State *Bulletin*, vol. XIII, (Washington, 1945), pp. 596–607; Stimson & Bundy, *op. cit.* (n. 33, *supra*), p. 570; Clay, *op. cit.* (n. 32, *supra*), pp. 6, 11, 17–18; Theodore H. White, *Fire in the Ashes* (New York, 1953), pp. 138–40

39. Byrnes, *op. cit.* (n. 17, *supra*), pp. 28–9; U.K. Foreign Office, *Protocol of the Proceedings of the Berlin Conference, 2 August, 1945* (H.M.S.O., Cmd. 7087, London, 1947), pp. 7–8; Balfour, *op. cit.* (n. 34, *supra*), pp. 77–8, 87; Clay, *op. cit.* (n. 32, *supra*), pp. 120–1; William Henry Chamberlin, *The German Phoenix* (London, 1964), p. 35; Howard K. Smith, *The State of Europe* (London, 1950), pp. 104, 107; Nicolas Nabokov, *Old Friends and New Music* (London, 1951), p. 211; John P. Nettl, *The Eastern Zone and Soviet Policy in Germany* (London, 1951), p. 204; Mayne, *op. cit.* (n. 7, *supra*), p. 59

40. Henry C. Wallich, *Mainsprings of the German Revival* (New Haven, 1955), p. 370; Chamberlin, *op. cit.* (n. 39, *supra*), p. 71; Clay, *op. cit.* (n. 32, *supra*), p. 124

41. Karl W. Roskamp, *Capital Formation in West Germany* (Detroit, 1965), p. 39; personal knowledge

42. Konrad Adenauer, *Erinnerungen 1945–1953* (Stuttgart, 1965), pp. 36–7; Robert F. Kennedy, *Just Friends and Brave Enemies* (Popular Library edition, New York, 1963), pp. 139–40; Harold Zink, *The United States in Germany, 1944–1955* (New York, 1957), p. 136; Chamberlin, *op. cit.* (n. 39, *supra*), pp. 40–2; Davidson, *op. cit.* (n. 32, *supra*), pp. 84–5; Field-Marshal the Viscount Montgomery of Alamein, K.G., *Memoirs* (Fontana edition, London, 1960), p. 380

43. Balfour, *op. cit.* (n. 34, *supra*), pp. 169–265; Raymond Ebsworth, *Restoring Democracy in Germany: The British Contribution* (London, 1960), *passim;* Clay, *op. cit.* (n. 32, *supra*), pp. 67–70, 98–9, 258–62, 287–8, 298–302

44. Balfour, *op. cit.* (n. 34, *supra*), pp. 203–4, 212–15, 219–26, 231; H. H. Wollenberg, *Fifty Years of German Film* (transl. Ernst Sigler, London, 1948), p. 47; William L. Shirer, *The Rise and Fall of the Third Reich* (Crest Books edition, New York, 1962), p. 333; Ebsworth, *op. cit.* (n. 43, *supra*), p. 22

45. Simone de Beauvoir, *La Force des Choses* (Paris, 1963), p. 14 (transl. R.M.)

46. Federico Chabod, *L'Italia Contemporanea 1918–1948* (Piccola biblioteca Einaudi edition, Turin, 1965), p. 133 (transl. R.M.); Michel van der Plas, *Moie Vrede: een documentaire over Nederland in de jaren 1945–1950* (Utrecht, 1966), p. 142 (transl. R.M.); Margot Lyon, "The Christian Democratic Parties and Politics," in *Journal of Contemporary History*, vol. II, No. 4 (London, October 1967), pp. 69–87; Peter H. Merkl, *Germany Yesterday and Tomorrow* (New York, 1965), p. 204; Dalton, *op. cit.* (n. 20, *supra*), p. 3

47. M. M. Postan, *An Economic History of Western Europe 1945–1964* (London, 1967), pp. 217–29; Vera Lutz, "The French 'Miracle'," in Jossleyn Hennessy, Vera Lutz & Giuseppe Scimone, *Economic "Miracles"* (London, 1964), pp. 75–167 (pp. 79–80)

48. Paul Alpert, *Twentieth-Century Economic History of Europe* (New York, 1951), pp. 289–90; David Thomson, *Europe Since Napoleon* (London, revised ed., 1963), pp. 775–6

Chapter 5. THE RELUCTANT ST. GEORGE

1. *High Tide and After: Memoirs 1945–1960* (London, 1962), p. 187

2. *Autobiography* (Everyman edition, London, 1948), p. 118

3. *1066 and All That* (26th edition, London, 1938), p. 115

4. Harry S. Truman, *Memoirs*, vol. II, *1946–1952: Years of Trial and Hope* (Signet edition, New York, 1965), p. 122; Joseph

Marion Jones, *The Fifteen Weeks* (Harbinger edition, New York, 1964), pp. 3–4; David Watt, "Withdrawal from Greece," in Michael Sissons & Philip French (ed.), *Age of Austerity 1945–1951* (Penguin edition, London, 1964), pp. 106–31 (p. 107); Dalton, *op. cit.* (n. 1, *supra*), p. 208; Dean Acheson, *Present at the Creation* (London, 1970), p. 217

5. Jones, *op. cit.* (n. 4, *supra*), pp. 5, 59–77; Dalton, *op. cit.* (n. 1, *supra*), p. 206; personal knowledge; George F. Kennan, *Memoirs 1925–1950* (London, 1968), pp. 316–17

6. Truman, *op. cit.* (n. 4, *supra*), pp. 221–2

7. Dalton, *op. cit.* pp. 187–8, 193, 199, 201–3, 210; Watt, *op. cit.* p. 106; Howard K. Smith, *The State of Europe* (London, 1950), pp. 20–1

8. Dalton, *op. cit.* (n. 1, *supra*), pp. 206–7

9. Dalton, *op. cit.* (n. 1, *supra*), pp. 220–1, 257, 259–60, 262 & n. 2

10. *Ibid.*, pp. 193, 197, 221

11. Maulana Abul Kalam Azad, *India Wins Freedom* (Bombay, 1959), pp. 57ff; Taya Zinkin, *India* (London, 1965), pp. 73ff; Ronald Segal, *The Crisis of India* (London, 1965), pp. 115ff. Cf. also Michael Brecher, *Nehru: A Political Biography* (Oxford, 1953); V. P. Menon, *The Transfer of Power in India* (Bombay, 1961); Penderal Moon, *Divide and Quit* (London, 1962)

12. Personal knowledge

13. Jones, *op. cit.* (n. 4, *supra*), p. 44

14. Harry S. Truman, *Memoirs*, vol. I, *1945: Year of Decisions* (Signet edition, New York, 1965), pp. 464–5; William D. Leahy, *I Was There* (New York, 1950), p. 430; Barbara Ward, *The West at Bay* (New York, 1948), p. 14

15. David J. Dallin, *The Big Three: United States, Britain, Russia* (New Haven, 1945); Cf. also John Mander, *Great Britain or Little England?* (London, 1963), pp. 26–30

16. James F. Byrnes, *All In One Lifetime* (London, 1960), pp. 368–9, 400–2; Jones, *op. cit.* (n. 4, *supra*), p. 54; Truman, *Memoirs*, vol. II (n. 4, *supra*), p. 125; *Ibid.*, vol. I (n. 14, *supra*), pp. 86–7, 98–9, 606; Watt, *op. cit.* (n. 4, *supra*), p. 121; D. F. Fleming, *The Cold War and its Origins 1917–1960* (London, 1961), vol. I, pp. 441–2

17. Private information

18. Jones, *op. cit.* (n. 4, *supra*), p. 3

19. *Ibid.*, pp. 129, 132, 136–8, 144–7; Kennan, *op. cit.* (n. 5, *supra*), p. 314; Truman, *Memoirs*, vol. II (n. 4, *supra*), pp. 122–3, 126–7; Acheson, *op. cit.* (n. 4, *supra*), pp. 217–19

20. Truman, *Memoirs*, vol. II (n. 4, *supra*), pp. 127–8; Jones, *op. cit.* (n. 4, *supra*), pp. 76–7, 269–74; Acheson, *op. cit.* (n. 4, *supra*), pp. 220–3

21. Jones, *op. cit.* (n. 4, *supra*), pp. 160–1; U.N. General Assembly, *Resolution of 13 December, 1946*

22. Jones, *op. cit.* (n. 4, *supra*), pp. 154–5, 163; Kennan, *op. cit.* (n. 5, *supra*), pp. 314–15, 317

23. *Ibid.*, pp. 320–2
24. Jones, *op. cit.* (n. 4, *supra*), p. 190; Kennan, *op. cit.* (n. 5, *supra*), p. 321
25. Ward, *op. cit.* (n. 14, *supra*), pp. 10–14; Harry Bayard Price, *The Marshall Plan and Its Meaning* (Ithaca, New York, 1955), pp. 29–32; Howard S. Ellis, *The Economics of Freedom* (New York, 1950), p. 62; Organisation for European Economic Co-operation, *Second Report* (Paris, 1950), p. 21; R. Mayne, *The Community of Europe* (London, 1962 & New York, 1963), pp. 74–5
26. Theodore H. White, *Fire in the Ashes* (New York, 1953), pp. 45, 135; Ward, *op. cit.* (n. 14, *supra*), pp. 17, 160–1; United Nations, Economic Commission for Europe, *Growth and Stagnation in the European Economy* (Geneva, 1954), p. 255; Norman J. G. Pounds & William N. Parker, *Coal and Steel in Western Europe* (Bloomington, Indiana, 1957), p. 296
27. Personal knowledge; Ward, *op. cit.* (n. 14, *supra*), p. 12; Price, *op. cit.*, Eugene Davidson, *The Death and Life of Germany* (London, 1959), p. 172
28. Price, *op. cit.* (n. 25, *supra*), p. 9; E. F. Penrose, *Economic Planning for Peace* (Princeton, 1953), *passim*
29. Asher Isaacs, *International Trade: Tariff and Commercial Policies* (Chicago, 1948), pp. 790–7, 816–17; Mayne, *op. cit.* (n. 25, *supra*), pp. 73–4; Jones, *op. cit.* (n. 4, *supra*), pp. 207, 233
30. Personal knowledge; Jones, *op. cit.* (n. 4, *supra*), pp. 199–201, 242–4; Max Beloff, *The United States and the Unity of Europe* (London, 1963), pp. 15–18; Ernst H. van der Beugel, *From Marshall Aid to Atlantic Partnership* (Amsterdam/London/New York, 1966), pp. 44–6
31. Jones, *op. cit.* (n. 4, *supra*), pp. 199–201, 228; Lippmann in New York *Herald Tribune*, March 20, 1947; van der Beugel, *op. cit.* (n. 30, *supra*), p. 39; Truman, *Memoirs*, vol. 1, *1945: Year of Decisions* (Signet edition, New York, 1965), pp. 519–22
32. Donald Watt, "Germany," in Evan Luard (ed.), *The Cold War: A Reappraisal* (London, 1964), pp. 84–119 (pp. 99)
33. Watt, *op. cit.* (n. 32, *supra*), pp. 100–103; Philip E. Mosely, "Some Soviet Techniques of Negotiation," in Raymond Dennett & Joseph E. Johnson (ed.), *Negotiating with the Russians* (Boston, Mass., 1951), pp. 271–303; *L'Année Politique 1946* (Paris, 1947), pp. 399–401; *L'Année Politique 1947* (Paris, 1948), pp. 49–58, 79–88; Lucius D. Clay, *Decision in Germany* (London, 1950), p. 151; van der Beugel, *op. cit.* (n. 30, *supra*), p. 34; Jones, *op. cit.* (n. 4, *supra*), pp. 221–3
34. Kennan, *op. cit.* (n. 5, *supra*), pp. 325–6
35. Kennan, *op. cit.* (n. 5, *supra*), pp. 330, 332–3
36. Jones, *op. cit.* (n. 4, *supra*), pp. 206–7; text of speech, *Ibid.*, pp. 274–81; Acheson, *op. cit.* (n. 4, *supra*), pp. 227–30
37. Jones, *op. cit.* (n. 4, *supra*), pp. 249–52; Kennan, *op. cit.* (n. 5,

supra), pp. 335–8, 341; Price, *op. cit.* pp. 22–3 ("Western" omitted on p. 22)

38. Jones, *op. cit.* (n. 4, *supra*), pp. 246–8; Beloff, *op. cit.* (n. 30, *supra*), p. 19
39. Kennan, *op. cit.* (n. 5, *supra*), p. 342; Price, *op. cit.* (n. 25, *supra*), pp. 23–4; Jones, *op. cit.* (n. 4, *supra*), pp. 31–3, 249, 252–5
40. Full text in Jones, *op. cit.* (n. 4, *supra*), pp. 281–4; cf. Policy Planning Staff memorandum quoted on p. 101, *supra*
41. Price, *op. cit.* (n. 25, *supra*), pp. 24–7
42. Jones, *op. cit.* (n. 4, *supra*), pp. 212, 255–6; Leonard Miall, "How the Marshall Plan Started," in *The Listener* (London, May 4, 1961), pp. 779–80
43. Jones, *op. cit.* (n. 4, *supra*), p. 256; Price, *op. cit.* (n. 25, *supra*), p. 27; Hansard, House of Commons, vol. 438 (June 19, 1947), cols. 2353–4; Dean Acheson, *Sketches from Life* (New York, 1961), p. 2
44. *L'Année Politique 1947* (Paris, 1948), pp. 134–5, 352

Chapter 6. EUROPE OF THE STATES

1. *A Midsummer-Night's Dream*, Act III, Scene 2, lines 208–10
2. *Introductio ad Prudentiam* (2nd edition, London, 1740), vol. II, p. 131
3. *L'Ancien régime et la révolution*, Book I, Chap. i, last sentence (transl. R.M.)
4. *L'Année politique 1947* (Paris, 1948), pp. 134–5, 353; *The Times* (London), June 14 and 20, 1947; Ministère des Affaires Etrangères, *Documents de la Conférence des Ministres des Affaires Etrangères de la France, du Royaume Uni et de l'URSS tenue à Paris du 27 juin au 3 juillet 1947* (Paris, 1947), pp. 15–16
5. *L'Année politique 1947* (Paris, 1948), pp. 135, 353–4 (Bidault, transl. R.M.); *The Times* (London), June 24, 1947; D. F. Fleming, *The Cold War and its Origins 1917–1960* (London, 1961), vol. I, p. 479
6. *Pravda* (Moscow), June 16 and 25, 1947; Fleming, *loc. cit.* (n. 5, *supra*); Harry Bayard Price, *The Marshall Plan and its Meaning* (Ithaca, New York, 1955), p. 28; *L'Année politique 1947* (Paris, 1948), p. 136; Ministère des Affaires Etrangères, *op. cit.* (n. 4, *supra*), pp. 38–42
7. Price, *op. cit.* (n. 6, *supra*), p. 27; Fleming, *loc. cit.* (n. 5, *supra*)
8. Ministère des Affaires Etrangères, *op. cit.* (n. 4, *supra*), pp. 44–6
9. *Ibid.*, p. 49
10. Ministère des Affaires Etrangères, *op. cit.* (n. 4, *supra*), pp. 52–3; official translation except for "voluntarily" (replacing official "willingly") in second sentence
11. *Ibid.*, pp. 58–61; Fleming, *op. cit.* (n. 5, *supra*), pp. 479–80
12. Ministère des Affaires Etrangères, *op. cit.*, pp. 62–5; *L'Année politique 1947* (Paris, 1948), p. 137 (transl. R.M.)

13. *Ibid.*, p. 354 (transl. R.M.)
14. Price, *op. cit.* (n. 6, *supra*), p. 28; Ernst H. van der Beugel, *From Marshall Aid to Atlantic Partnership* (Amsterdam/London/New York, 1966), p. 62; William C. Mallalieu, "The Origins of the Marshall Plan," in *Political Science Quarterly*, vol. LXIII (1958), pp. 483–91; Hubert Ripka, *Czechoslovakia Enslaved* (London, 1950), pp. 52–3
15. W. W. Rostow, *The United States in the World Arena* (New York, 1960), p. 211, quoted by David Horowitz, *From Yalta to Vietnam* (Penguin edition, 1967, of *The Free World Colossus*, London, 1965), p. 72; cf. also Fleming, *loc. cit.* (n. 11, *supra*)
16. Theodore H. White, *Fire in the Ashes* (New York, 1953), pp. 39–40; Price, *op. cit.* (n. 6, *supra*), pp. 27–8 (interview with Dean Acheson); Fleming, *loc. cit.* (n. 11, *supra*)
17. Private information
18. Price, *op. cit.* (n. 6, *supra*), pp. 26, 36–7, 39–48, 50–5, 61; Committee of European Economic Co-operation, vol. I, *General Report* (Paris/London, 1947); William Diebold, Jr., *Trade and Payments in Western Europe* (New York, 1952), p. 25; van der Beugel, *op. cit.* (n. 14, *supra*), pp. 86–9, 97–8, 174; Robert A. Dahl, *Congress and Foreign Policy* (New York, 1950), pp. 128–30
19. Price, *op. cit.* (n. 6, *supra*), pp. 63–5; Arthur H. Vandenberg, Jr. (ed.), *The Private Papers of Senator Vandenberg* (Boston, 1952), p. 389
20. Price, *op. cit.* (n. 6, *supra*), p. 70; David M. Crawford, "United States Foreign Assistance Legislation, 1947–1948," in *Yale Law Journal*, May 1949, pp. 877–921
21. Price, *op. cit.* (n. 6, *supra*), pp. 71–3; Paul G. Hoffman, *Peace Can Be Won* (New York, 1951), p. 87
22. Price, *op. cit.* (n. 6, *supra*), pp. 76–7; White, *op. cit.* (n. 16, *supra*), p. 60
23. U. S. Department of Commerce, *Foreign Aid by the United States Government 1940–1951*, Supplement to the *Survey of Current Business* (Washington, 1952), pp. 7, 12, 57, 60–1; Price, *op. cit.* (n. 6, *supra*), pp. 88–90
24. New York *Times*, July 13, 1947; Committee of European Economic Co-operation, *op. cit.* (n. 18, *supra*), p. 22; van der Beugel, *op. cit.* (n. 14, *supra*), pp. 80, 127–8; Price, *op. cit.* (n. 6, *supra*), p. 285; personal knowledge
25. van der Beugel, *op. cit.* (n. 14, *supra*), pp. 147, 149–65
26. Organisation for European Economic Co-operation, 9th Report, *A Decade of Co-operation: Achievements and Perspectives* (Paris, 1958), pp. 55, 60, 61; Diebold, *op. cit.* (n. 18, *supra*), pp. 164–6; Michael Palmer & others, *European Unity: A Survey of the European Organisations* (London, 1968), pp. 101–2; R. Mayne, *The Community of Europe* (London, 1962; New York, 1963), p. 76
27. Organisation for European Economic Co-operation, *op. cit.*

(n. 26, *supra*), pp. 76–8; Robert Triffin, *Europe and the Money Muddle* (New Haven, Conn., 1957), p. 153; Diebold, *op. cit.* (n. 18, *supra*), p. 64; O.E.E.C. Information Department, Mimeographed document Press D (50) 14, July 7, 1950; private information; M. J. Colebrook, *Dialogue of the Deaf: Franco–British Relations and European Integration 1945–1950* (unpublished thesis, Geneva, 1968), Chapter II B, "The Payments Issue"

28. G. D. N. Worswick, "The British Economy 1945–50," in G. D. N. Worswick and P. H. Ady (ed.), *The British Economy 1945–1950* (Oxford, 1952), pp. 1–34 (pp. 32–4); William Adams Brown, Jr. and Redvers Opie, *American Foreign Assistance* (Washington, 1953), p. 201; van der Beugel, *op. cit.* (n. 14, *supra*), pp. 152–6, 169

29. Personal knowledge; Georgette Elgey, *Histoire de la IVe République*, vol. II, *La République des Contradictions 1951–1954* (Paris, 1968), pp. 207–8. Cf. also Marcus Cunliffe, "Europe and America," in *Encounter*, vol. XVII, No. 6 (London, December 1961), pp. 19–29, and Melvin J. Lasky, "America and Europe," in *Encounter*, vol. XVIII, No. 1 (London, January 1961), pp. 66–82

30. George F. Kennan, *Memoirs 1925–1950* (London, 1967), p. 417; Max Beloff, *The United States and the Unity of Europe* (London, 1963), pp. 2–3

31. Beloff, *op. cit.* (n. 30, *supra*), pp. 7, 11, 14; Count Coudenhove-Kalergi, *An Idea Conquers the World* (London, 1953), p. 260; private information; U. S. Senate, 2nd Session, Part II, p. 54; John C. Campbell, *The United States in World Affairs 1945–1947* (New York, 1947), p. 471; Joseph Marion Jones, *The Fifteen Weeks* (Harbinger edition, New York, 1964), p. 220; van der Beugel, *op. cit.* (n. 14, *supra*), p. 39

32. Cf. pp. 97–8, *supra;* Beloff, *op. cit.* (n. 30, *supra*), pp. 15–18; van der Beugel, *op. cit.* (n. 14, *supra*), pp. 44–6

33. Cf. p. 102, *supra;* Jones, *op. cit.* (n. 31, *supra*), pp. 246–8; Beloff, *op. cit.* (n. 30, *supra*), pp. 19–20

34. Cf. Chapter V, p. 101, *supra;* Beloff, *op. cit.* (n. 30, *supra*), p. 23; Kennan, *op. cit.* (n. 30, *supra*), p. 337; private information; Price, *op. cit.* (n. 6, *supra*), p. 44; van der Beugel, *op. cit.* (n. 14, *supra*), pp. 86, 88, 90–1, 182–3; *European Recovery and American Aid*, Report by the President's Committee on Foreign Aid (Washington, D.C., 1947); U. S. Select Committee on Foreign Aid, *Final Report on Foreign Aid*, House of Representatives, 80th Congress, 2nd Session, 1948; Paul Hoffman, speech to the O.E.E.C. Ministerial Council, October 31, 1949, O.E.E.C. Document C (49) 176

35. Sforza in *Relazioni Internazionali*, January 24, 1948, p. 57 (transl. R.M.); Diebold, *op. cit.* (n. 18, *supra*), p. 354

36. Private information; van der Beugel, *op. cit.* (n. 14, *supra*), pp. 74, 78–80

37. Committee of European Economic Co-operation, vol. I, *General Report* (Paris/London, 1947), pp. 19–20; Diebold, *op. cit.* (n. 18, *supra*), pp. 305–11; European Customs Union Study Group (E.C.U.S.G.), *General Report of the Economic Committee* (mimeographed, Brussels, October 1948), vol. I, p. 11; E.C.U.S.G., *First Report* (mimeographed, Brussels, March 1948), p. 91

38. Diebold, *op. cit.* (n. 18, *supra*), pp. 377–83

39. *Customs Unions: A League of Nations Contribution to the Study of Customs Union Problems* (New York, 1947), pp. 47, 75; J. E. Meade, *Problems of Economic Union* (London, 1953), pp. 9ff, 82; Jacob Viner, *The Customs Union Issue* (New York/London, 1950), p. 41; Pierre Uri, "The meaning of economic integration," in *Aspects of European Integration* (London/Paris, 1962), pp. 1–2; Walter Hallstein, *United Europe: Challenge and Opportunity* (Cambridge, Mass./Oxford, England, 1962), pp. 30–57; Mayne, *op. cit.* (n. 26, *supra*), pp. 119–28; *Ibid.*, "Economic Integration in the New Europe," in Stephen Graubard (ed.), *A New Europe?* (Boston, Mass., 1964), pp. 174–99 (pp. 175–9)

40. Cf. van der Beugel, *op. cit.* (n. 14, *supra*), pp. 68–9

41. Ministère des Affaires Etrangères, *op. cit.* (n. 4, *supra*), pp. 44–6, 52–3; New York *Times*, July 13, 1947

42. van der Beugel, *op. cit.* (n. 14, *supra*), pp. 92, 132; *The Times* (London), August 16, 1947; private information; Beloff, *op. cit.* (n. 30, *supra*), p. 45

43. *Foreign Relations of the United States, Diplomatic Papers: The Conference of Berlin, 1945* (Washington, 1960), vol. I, pp. 253, 256–7 (Documents 223 & 224, Briefing Book papers of July 4, 1945, Summaries and Recommendations); Jan Christian Smuts, *Thoughts on a New World* (Empire Parliamentary Association, London, 1943); Hansard, House of Commons, 5th Series, vol. 403, vols. 704–6

44. Alan Bullock, *The Life and Times of Ernest Bevin*, vol. I (London, 1960), pp. 360–1, 371, 387–8, 633; *Milwaukee Leader*, November 6, 1926. In the first quotation above "an ability" is interpolated: Bullock, *op. cit.*, p. 387, quoting the T.U.C. *Report*, reads "a mobility," which seems likely to have been a mishearing or an error of transcription by the T.U.C. secretariat

45. Bullock, *op. cit.* (n. 44, *supra*), pp. 440–2; F. S. Northedge, *British Foreign Policy: The Process of Readjustment 1945–1961* (London, 1962), pp. 13–32; *Foreign Relations of the United States, Diplomatic Papers: The Conference of Berlin, 1945* (Washington, 1960), vol. I, p. 258 (Memorandum of June 28, 1945); Hansard, House of Commons, 5th Series, vol. 416, cols. 759–846; vol. 427, cols. 1487–1623; vol. 446, cols. 383–622; vol. 450, cols. 1105–1222; vol. 456, cols. 89–107; Mayne, *op. cit.* (n. 26, *supra*), pp. 132–7; private information

46. Diebold, *op. cit.* (n. 18, *supra*), pp. 40–1, 64–70; Colebrook, *loc. cit.* (n. 27, *supra*), O.E.E.C., *Memorandum by the Chancellor of the Exchequer*, Consultative Group of Ministers, CGM(49)16 Annexe I, Paris, June 1, 1949; O.E.E.C., *Memorandum by the French Minister of Finance and Economic Affairs*, Consultative Group of Ministers, CGM(49)16, Annexe II, Paris, June 2, 1949; O.E.E.C., *Present Positions on the Principles of the Payments Scheme for the 1949–50 Financial Year*, CGM(49)16, June 27, 1949; O.E.E.C., *54th Council Meeting* (Ministerial Level), C/M(49)11, June 29 to July 1, 1949

Chapter 7. THE AGE OF ANXIETY

1. *The French Revolution* (London, 1837), vol. III, p. 112
2. *Under Western Eyes* (9th Edition, London, 1924), p. 8
3. *Diplomacy* (2nd edition, Oxford, 1950), p. 140
4. Kenneth Ingram, *History of the Cold War* (London, 1955), pp. 20–1; David Horowitz, *From Yalta to Vietnam* (Penguin edition, 1967, of *The Free World Colossus*, London, 1965), p. 74; Anton Zischka, *The Other Europeans* (English translation by Brian Battershaw, London, 1962, of *Auch Das ist Europa*, Gütersloh, 1960), p. 243
5. Louis J. Halle, *The Cold War as History* (London, 1967), p. 151; Frederick L. Schuman, *Russia Since 1917* (New York, 1957), pp. 362–3
6. Sidney Lowery, "Poland" in A. & V. M. Toynbee (ed.), *The Realignment of Europe* (London, 1955), pp. 126–245 (pp. 216–17); *Ibid.*, "Hungary," in A. & V. M. Toynbee, *op. cit.*, pp. 317–32 (p. 324); Hugh Seton-Watson, "Yugoslavia," in A. & V. M. Toynbee, *op. cit.*, pp. 352–71 (pp. 363–4, 369); *Ibid.*, "Albania," in A. & V. M. Toynbee, *op. cit.*, pp. 371–6 (pp. 374–5); Elizabeth Wiskemann, "Czechoslovakia: Spring 1945 to the Signing of the Peace Treaties, February 1947," in A. & V. M. Toynbee, *op. cit.*, pp. 376–88 (p. 387); Milovan Djilas, *Conversations with Stalin* (transl. from the Serbo-Croat by Michael B. Petrovich, Penguin edition, London, 1963), p. 100
7. Ghita Ionescu, *The Break-up of the Soviet Empire in Eastern Europe* (London, 1965), pp. 29–31; Hugh Seton-Watson, *The East European Revolution* (London, 1950), p. 314; *Ibid.*, "Yugoslavia," in A. & V. M. Toynbee, *op. cit.* (n. 6, *supra*), pp. 352–71 (pp. 365–7); Djilas, *op. cit.* (n. 6, *supra*), pp. 136–7 (February 10, 1948)
8. Cf. Chapter III, pp. 47–9, *supra*; Sidney Lowery, "Poland," in A. & V. M. Toynbee, *op. cit.* (n. 6, *supra*), pp. 126–245 (pp. 194–242); R. E. Sherwood, *Roosevelt and Hopkins: An Intimate History* (New York, 1948), pp. 887–912; Stanislaw Mikolajczyk, *The Pattern of Soviet Domination* (London, 1948), pp. 147–9, 180–212; Seton-Watson, *op. cit.* (n. 7, *supra*), pp. 171–9; R. C. Mowat, *Ruin and Resurgence, 1939–1965* (London, 1966), pp. 162–4

9. Sidney Lowery, "Bulgaria," in A. & V. M. Toynbee, *op. cit.*
    (n. 6, *supra*), pp. 301–17; Zischka, *op. cit.* (n. 4, *supra*), p. 120;
    Mowat, *op. cit.* (n. 8, *supra*), pp. 164–5; Seton-Watson, *op. cit.*
    (n. 7, *supra*), pp. 211–19; *Ibid., Nationalism and Communism*
    (London, 1964), pp. 93–7; U. S. Military Intelligence, *The Com-
    munist Bloc in Europe* (H.Q., U. S. Army Europe, March 10,
    1959), pp. 292–3

10. Sidney Lowery, "Rumania," in A. & V. M. Toynbee, *op. cit.*
    (n. 6, *supra*), pp. 285–301; D. F. Fleming, *The Cold War and
    its Origins 1917–1960* (London, 1961), vol. I, p. 208; A. Cretz-
    ianu (ed.), *Captive Rumania* (New York, 1956), pp. 51, 56;
    Mowat, *op. cit.* (n. 8, *supra*), pp. 168–71; James F. Byrnes,
    Speaking Frankly (London, 1947), pp. 50–2; Zischka, *op. cit.*
    (n. 4, *supra*), p. 142; Seton-Watson, *Nationalism and Commu-
    nism* (n. 9, *supra*), p. 98

11. Sidney Lowery, "Hungary," in A. & V. M. Toynbee, *op. cit.*
    (n. 6, *supra*), pp. 317–32; Ferenc Nagy, *The Struggle Behind
    the Iron Curtain* (London, 1948), pp. 52, 101, 112, 145–51, 159–
    64, 311–70; P. E. Zinner, *Revolution in Hungary* (New York,
    1962), pp. 33, 37; Zischka, *op. cit.* (n. 4, *supra*), p. 186; U. S.
    Military Intelligence, *op. cit.* (n. 9, *supra*), pp. 261–3; Mowat,
    op. cit. (n. 8, *supra*), pp. 165–8; Seton-Watson, *op. cit.* (n. 10,
    supra), pp. 146–53

12. Sidney Lowery, "Finland," in A. & V. M. Toynbee, *op. cit.* (n. 6,
    supra), pp. 261–85 (pp. 277–84); Isaac Deutscher, *Stalin: A
    Political Biography* (revised Pelican edition, London, 1966),
    pp. 187, 435; Howard K. Smith, *The State of Europe* (London,
    1950), pp. 363–7

13. Hugh Seton-Watson, "Albania," in A. & V. M. Toynbee, *op. cit.*
    (n. 6, *supra*), pp. 371–6; Zischka, *op. cit.* (n. 4, *supra*), p. 89

14. Hugh Seton-Watson, "Yugoslavia," in A. & V. M. Toynbee, *op.
    cit.* (n. 6, *supra*), pp. 352–71; Mowat, *op. cit.* (n. 8, *supra*),
    pp. 275–8; Djilas, *op. cit.* (n. 6, *supra*), p. 90

15. Wiskemann, *op. cit.* (n. 6, *supra*), pp. 376–7; Mowat, *op. cit.*
    (n. 8, *supra*), p. 178; Hubert Ripka, *Czechoslovakia Enslaved*
    (London, 1950), p. 38; Dwight D. Eisenhower, *Crusade in
    Europe* (Dolphin edition, New York, 1961), p. 442

16. Wiskemann, *op. cit.* (n. 6, *supra*), pp. 377–8; P. E. Zinner,
    Communist Strategy and Tactics in Czechoslovakia 1914–48
    (London, 1963), pp. 118–19, 174; W. Jaksch, *Europe's Road to
    Potsdam* (London, 1963), pp. 429ff; Mowat, *op. cit.* (n. 8,
    supra), p. 179

17. Wiskemann, *op. cit.* (n. 6, *supra*), pp. 380–7; Hubert Ripka,
    Eastern Europe in the Post-War World (London, 1961), p. 73;
    Jaksch, *op. cit.* (n. 16, *supra*), p. 434; Mowat, *op. cit.* (n. 8,
    supra), pp. 180–1; Zinner, *op. cit.* (n. 16, *supra*), pp. 124, 156

18. Mowat, *op. cit.* (n. 8, *supra*), pp. 182–3; Celia Phelps, "The
    Death of Jan Masaryk: An Interview with his Private Secretary,"
    in R. Macdonald & M. West (ed.), *Eurovista '69* (St. Andrews,

1969), pp. 11–12; Howard K. Smith, *The State of Europe* (London, 1950), pp. 334–47; André Fontaine, *Histoire de la guerre froide,* vol. I (Paris, 1965), pp. 399–403

19. Peter Novick, *The Resistance Versus Vichy* (London, 1968), pp. 72–6; John Steward Ambler, *The French Army in Politics 1945–1962* (Columbus, Ohio, 1966), pp. 79–81; M. R. D. Foot, *SOE in France* (London, 1966), pp. 444–5; Crane Brinton, *The Americans and the French* (Cambridge, Mass., 1968), p. 91; Viscount Chilston, "Western Europe," in A. & V. M. Toynbee, *op. cit.* (n. 6, *supra*), pp. 523–53 (pp. 540, 542); Katharine Duff, "Italy," in A. & V. M. Toynbee, *op. cit.* (n. 6, *supra*), pp. 409–53 (pp. 427, 432); Norman Kogan, *A Political History of Postwar Italy* (London, 1966), p. 10; Royal Institute of International Affairs, *The Soviet–Yugoslav Dispute* (London, 1948), p. 51; Ripka, *op. cit.* (n. 17, *supra*), p. 68 (Soviet letter of May 4, 1948 to Central Committee of Yugoslav Communist Party)

20. Chilston, *op. cit.* (n. 19, *supra*), pp. 513 n. 1, 520, 539, 545, 548 & n. 1; *L'Année politique 1946* (Paris, 1947), pp. 11–12, 145, 158, 285; Duff, *op. cit.* (n. 19, *supra*), pp. 426, 429; W. Hilton-Young, *The Italian Left* (London, 1949), pp. 184–5, 187, 189; Maxime Mourin, *Histoire des Nations Européennes,* vol. III (Paris, 1963), pp. 115–17; *L'Année politique 1944–1945* (Paris, 1946), pp. 5, 352; *L'Année politique 1947* (Paris, 1948), pp. 7–8; Piergiovanni Permoli, *La Costituente e i Partiti Politici Italiani* (Rocca San Casciano, 1966), pp. 85–91, 114–23; Federico Chabod, *L'Italia Contemporanea (1918–1948)* (9th edition, Turin, 1965), pp. 143, 161–2

21. Sergio Bologna et al. (ed.), *Fascismo e antifascismo: Lezioni e testimonianze* (Milan, 1962), vol. II, *1936–1948,* p. 645 (transl. R.M.)

22. Mourin, *op. cit.* (n. 20, *supra*), pp. 116–17; Chilston, *op. cit.* (n. 19, *supra*), p. 551; *L'Année politique 1947* (Paris, 1948), pp. 39–43, 65–6, 91–3; Hilton-Young, *op. cit.* (n. 20, *supra*), pp. 191–4; Kogan, *op. cit.* (n. 19, *supra*), 47–53; H. Stuart Hughes, *The United States and Italy* (Cambridge, Mass., 1953), pp. 155–9; Chabod, *op. cit.* (n. 20, *supra*), pp. 161–9; personal knowledge

23. J. V. Stalin, *Problems of Leninism* (11th edition, Moscow, 1940), pp. 3, 52, 79, 156–7, 657

24. John Foster Dulles, *War or Peace* (New York, 1950), pp. 12–13

25. *Ibid.,* p. 175; F. W. Mulley, *The Politics of Western Defence* (London, 1962), pp. 32–46

26. Harry S. Truman, *Memoirs,* vol. II, *1946–1952: Years of Trial and Hope* (Signet edition, New York, 1965), p. 280; Ernst H. van der Beugel, *From Marshall Aid to Atlantic Partnership* (Amsterdam/London/New York, 1966), pp. 121–2; Paul Stehlin, *Retour à Zéro* (Paris, 1968), pp. 47–9; *L'Année politique 1948* (Paris, 1949), pp. 14–15, 33–4, 44–6, 381–2 (Text of Brussels Treaty); personal knowledge

27. Cf. Heinrich von Brentano, *Speech on denazification, July 4, 1947*, reprinted in *Ibid., Deutschland, Europa und die Welt*, transl. by Edward Fitzgerald as *Germany and Europe: Reflections on German Foreign Policy* (London, 1964), pp. 19–29 (p. 22); Hermann Eich, *The Unloved Germans*, transl. by Michael Glenny (London, 1965); Gudrun Tempel, *Deutschland? Aber Wo Liegt Es?*, transl. by Sophie Wilkins as *Speaking Frankly About the Germans* (London, 1963); Hans Herzfeld, "The Splitting of Berlin in 1948," in Charles B. Robson (transl. & ed.), *Berlin—Pivot of German Destiny* (Chapel Hill, North Carolina, 1960), pp. 47–66 (p. 52); personal knowledge

28. Siegfried Kracauer, *From Caligari to Hitler: a Psychological History of the German Film* (Princeton, 1947), pp. v, 11

29. Cf. Ralf Dahrendorf, *Gesellschaft und Demokratie in Deutschland* (Munich, 1965), *passim;* Enzo Bettiza, *L'Altra Germania* (Milan, 1968), pp. 20–1

30. Potsdam final communiqué, paras. III A 1, III B 14; Ernst Deuerlein (ed.), *Potsdam 1945* (Munich, 1963), pp. 350, 357

31. Eugene Davidson, *The Death and Life of Germany* (London, 1959), pp. 70–1, 74, 76, 132–3, 140, 179; German Federal Government, *Germany Reports* (Wiesbaden, 1953), p. 70; Thilo Vogelsang, *Das geteilte Deutschland* (Munich, 1966), pp. 53–6; Wolfgang Leonhard, *Die Revolution entlässt ihre Kinder* (Cologne/Berlin, 1955), p. 448; Michael Balfour, "Germany," in A. Toynbee (ed.), *Four-Power Control in Germany and Austria 1945–1946* (London, 1956), pp. 3–265 (pp. 205–7, 239–40); Gordon Schaffer, *Russian Zone,* (London, 1947), p. 72

32. Davidson, *op. cit.* (n. 31, *supra*), p. 141 and n. 2; Lucius D. Clay, *Decision in Germany* (London, 1950), pp. 88–91; Richard Lukas, *Zehn Jahre Sowjetische Besatzungszone Deutschlands* (Mainz/Wiesbaden/Düsseldorf, 1955), p. 17; William Henry Chamberlin, *The German Phoenix* (London, 1964), p. 126; German Federal Government, *op. cit.* (n. 31, *supra*), p. 71; Richard Hiscocks, "Divided Germany," in Edgar McInnis (ed.), *The Shaping of Postwar Germany* (London/Toronto, 1960), pp. 57–89 (p. 69); Balfour, *op. cit.* (n. 30, *supra*), pp. 208–9

33. Cf. pp. 78–9, *supra;* Clay, *op. cit.* (n. 32, *supra*), pp. 78, 121; Byrnes, *op. cit.* (n. 10, *supra*), pp. 195–7; Elmer Plischke, *Contemporary Government of Germany* (London, 1964), p. 18

34. Clay, *op. cit.* (n. 32, *supra*), p. 174; Plischke, *op. cit.* (n. 33, *supra*), p. 183; German Federal Government, *op. cit.* (n. 31, *supra*), p. 71

35. *L'Année politique 1948* (Paris, 1949), pp. 31–2, 46–7; Clay, *op. cit.* (n. 32, *supra*), pp. 180–1

36. *L'Année politique 1948* (Paris, 1949), p. 47; Alfred Grosser, *La République Fédérale d'Allemagne* (Paris, 1963), p. 15; Plischke, *op. cit.* (n. 33, *supra*), p. 184; Clay, *op. cit.* (n. 32, *supra*), pp. 355–6; Wolfgang Heidelmeyer & Guenter Hindrichs

(ed.), *Documents on Berlin 1943–1963* (Second ed., revised, Munich, 1963), pp. 55–6

37. *L'Année politique 1948* (Paris, 1949), pp. 107–9, 400–3; Davidson, *op. cit.* (n. 31, *supra*), pp. 223–4; Ludwig Erhard, *Wohlstand für Alle*, transl. by E. T. Roberts & J. B. Wood as *Prosperity Through Competition* (London, 2nd ed., 1959), pp. 13–14; Grosser, *op. cit.* (n. 36, *supra*), p. 69; personal knowledge

38. Clay, *op. cit.* (n. 32, *supra*), pp. 63, 208–9

39. William H. Conland, *Berlin: Beset and Bedevilled* (New York, 1963), pp. 239–41; Clay, *op. cit.* (n. 32, *supra*), pp. 358–62

40. Clay, *op. cit.* (n. 32, *supra*), pp. 365–6, 376, 381–2, 386; Truman, *op. cit.* (n. 26, *supra*), pp. 149–53

41. Truman, *op. cit.* (n. 26, *supra*), pp. 278–9, 281–8; North Atlantic Treaty, Article 5; Paul-Henri Spaak, *Combats Inachevés*, vol. I (Paris, 1969), p. 263

42. Plischke, *op. cit.* (n. 33, *supra*), p. 23 & n. 7

43. German Federal Government, *op. cit.* (n. 31, *supra*), p. 72; Plischke, *op. cit.* (n. 33, *supra*), p. 185

44. Plischke, *op. cit.* (n. 33, *supra*), pp. 23–5

45. Plischke, *op. cit.* (n. 33, *supra*), pp. 185–6

46. German Federal Government, *op. cit.* (n. 31, *supra*), p. 112

Chapter 8. EUROPE AND THE ISLANDS

1. *The Dog Beneath the Skin* (with Christopher Isherwood, London, 1935), p. 11

2. *The Hot Gates* (Pocket Books edition, New York, 1967), p. 37

3. *The Texts*, Book XXVI

4. Verbatim note of a discussion at Chatham House, February 1939, quoted by Alan Bullock, *The Life and Times of Ernest Bevin*, vol. I (London, 1960), pp. 631–2

5. Fritz Nova, *Contemporary European Governments* (Baltimore/Dublin, 1963), p. 603

6. *Constitution of the Fourth Republic*, in Philip M. Williams, *Crisis and Compromise: Politics in the Fourth Republic* (London, 1964), pp. 478–92 (p. 479); *Costituzione della Repubblica Italiana*, in Senato della Repubblica/Camera dei Deputati, *Manuale Parlamentare, Legislatura IV* (Rome, 1964), pp. 13–54 (p. 16) (transl. R.M.)

7. R. Mayne, *The Community of Europe* (London, 1962; New York, 1963), pp. 29–52, 68–9, 78–80; Denys Hay, *Europe: the Emergence of an Idea* (Edinburgh, 1957); Federico Chabod, *Storia dell'idea dell'Europa* (Universale ed., Bari, 1967); Achille Albonetti, *Préhistoire des Etats-Unis d'Europe* (Paris, 1963); Bernard Voyenne, *Petite histoire de l'idée européenne* (Paris, 1965); J.-B. Duroselle, *L'Idée européenne dans l'Histoire* (Paris, 1965); Hendrik Brugmans, *L'Idée européenne 1918–1965* (Bruges, 1965); Lord Gladwyn, *The European Idea* (London, 1966); Altiero Spinelli, "European Union in the Resistance," in

Government & Opposition, vol. II, No. 3 (April-July, 1967), pp. 321–9; Denis de Rougemont, "The Campaign of the European Congresses," *Ibid.*, pp. 329–49

8. *L'Année politique 1948* (Paris, 1949), p. 126; *Le Monde*, July 22, 1948, p. 2; private information; Royal Institute of International Affairs, *Survey of International Affairs, 1947–1948*, pp. 143–4; European Movement, *The European Movement and the Council of Europe* (London, 1949), p. 52; private information

9. Private information

10. *L'Année politique 1948* (Paris, 1949), pp. 217, 236; Royal Institute of International Affairs, *op. cit.* (n. 8, *supra*), p. 145; *Ibid.*, *Survey of International Affairs 1949–1950*, p. 169; private information

11. Private information; Royal Institute of International Affairs, *op. cit.* (n. 10, *supra*), p. 170; European Movement, *op. cit.* (n. 8, *supra*), pp. 61–2

12. Mayne, *op. cit.* (n. 7, *supra*); personal knowledge; Paul-Henri Spaak, *Combats Inachevés*, vol. II, (Paris, 1969), pp. 28, 51

13. Mayne, *op. cit.* (n. 7, *supra*), pp. 81–4

14. Merry & Serge Bromberger, *Les Coulisses de l'Europe* (Paris, 1968), pp. 9–12; "Then Will It Live . . . ," *Time*, vol. LXXVIII, No. 14 (October 6, 1961), pp. 20–7 (p. 23); R. Mayne, "The Role of Jean Monnet," *Government and Opposition*, vol. II, No. 3 (April-July, 1967), pp. 349–71 (pp. 352–3); *Ibid.*, "Jean Monnet—Portrait of a European," *The Listener*, vol. LXXX, No. 2072 (December 12, 1968), pp. 787–9 (p. 787)

15. Bromberger, *op. cit.* (n. 14, *supra*), pp. 14–20; *Time*, *loc. cit.* (n. 14, *supra*), Mayne, *locc. citt.* (n. 14, *supra*)

16. Personal knowledge; Mayne, *locc. citt.* (n. 14, *supra*); John Davenport, "M Jean Monnet of Cognac," *Fortune*, vol. XXX, No. 2 (August, 1944), pp. 121–126; Bromberger, *op. cit.* (n. 14, *supra*), pp. 20–1; *Time*, *loc. cit.* (n. 14, *supra*)

17. Bromberger, *op. cit.* (n. 14, *supra*), pp. 21–6; *Time*, *loc. cit.*; Mayne, *locc. citt.*; private information; personal knowledge

18. Private information; John M. Haight, "France, the United States, and the Munich Crisis," *Journal of Modern History*, vol. XXXII, No. 1 (December 1960), pp. 340–58; *Ibid.*, "Roosevelt and the Aftermath of the Quarantine Speech," *Review of Politics*, vol. XXIV, No. 2 (April 1962), pp. 233–59; *Ibid.*, "Les Négociations françaises pour la fourniture d'avions américains (I), *Forces Aériennes Françaises*, No. 198 (December, 1963), pp. 807–39; *Ibid.*, "France's First War Mission to the United States," *The Airpower Historian*, vol. XI, No. 1 (January 1964), pp. 11–15; *Ibid.*, "Les Négociations relatives aux achats d'avions américains par la France pendant la période qui précéda immédiatement la guerre," *La Revue de l'Histoire de la 2e Guerre Mondiale*, No. 58 (April 1965), pp. 1–34; *Ibid.*, "Jean Monnet and the Opening of the American Arsenal," paper to the Franco-American Historical Colloquium, September 1964; *The Times*

(London), November 28, 1939; W. K. Hancock & M. M. Gowing, *British War Economy* (London, 1949), pp. 192 n. 1, 195

19. Private information; Max Beloff, "The Anglo-French Union Project of June 1940," *Mélanges Pierre Renouvin* (Paris, 1966), pp. 199–219; Winston Churchill, *The Second World War* (Cassell paperback edition, London, 1964), vol. III, pp. 183–7; Charles de Gaulle, *Mémoires de Guerre* (*Livre de poche* edition, Paris, 1959), vol. I, pp. 80–7; J.-R. Tournoux, *Secrets d'Etats*, vol. II: *Pétain et de Gaulle* (Paris, 1964), pp. 426–41; Davenport, *loc. cit.* (n. 16, *supra*)

20. *Time, loc. cit.* (n. 14, *supra*); Mayne, *locc. citt.* (n. 14, *supra*); Bromberger, *op. cit.* (n. 14, *supra*), pp. 37–66; Robert Murphy, *Diplomat Among Warriors* (London, 1964), pp. 223–8; Harold Macmillan, *The Blast of War 1939–1945* (London, 1967), pp. 297–8, 300, 312, 317–19, 321, 328–31; Georgette Elgey, *La République des Illusions* (Paris, 1965), pp. 413–34

21. Private information; personal knowledge; Elgey, *loc. cit.* (n. 20, *supra*); Bromberger, *op. cit.* (n. 14, *supra*), pp. 14, 26

22. Personal knowledge; Mayne, *op. cit.* (n. 7, *supra*), pp. 90–1

23. Davenport, *loc. cit.* (n. 16, *supra*)

24. Private information

25. *L'Année politique 1947* (Paris, 1948), pp. 31, 351; Agence France Presse dispatch April 30, 1947

26. *L'Année politique 1948* (Paris, 1949), pp. 12–14, 67, 87, 196–7, 236; *L'Année politique 1949* (Paris, 1950), pp. 456–7; Bromberger, *op. cit.* (n. 14, *supra*), pp. 96–7; Elgey, *op. cit.* (n. 20, *supra*), pp. 439–40; Etienne Hirsch, "L'Angleterre fera-t-elle antichambre?," Les Cahiers de la République, No. 51 (January, 1963), pp. 9–16

27. Private information; personal knowledge

28. Private information; Bromberger, *loc. cit.* (n. 14, *supra*), Elgey, *loc. cit.* (n. 20, *supra*), *L'Année politique 1949* (Paris, 1950), pp. 160–1; Hirsch, *loc. cit.* (n. 26, *supra*)

29. *L'Année politique 1949* (Paris, 1950), p. 167; Don Cook, *Floodtide in Europe* (New York, 1965), pp. 110–12; *L'Année politique 1950* (Paris, 1951), p. 93; Mayne, "The Role of Jean Monnet" (n. 14, *supra*), p. 356

30. Private information; Pierre Gerbet, "La Genèse du Plan Schuman," *Revue Française de Science Politique*, vol. VI, No. 3 (Paris, 1956), pp. 525–53 (p. 544); Elgey, *op. cit.* (n. 20, *supra*), p. 445; Bromberger, *op. cit.* (n. 14, *supra*), p. 119

31. Quotations from the Schuman Declaration of May 9, 1950, based on Monnet's drafts; text in *L'Année politique 1950* (Paris, 1951), pp. 306–7 (transl. R.M.)

32. Mayne, *op. cit.* (n. 7, *supra*), pp. 43, 90–1; Bromberger, *op. cit.* (n. 14, *supra*), pp. 116–19; Fritz Stern, "Adenauer and a Crisis in Weimar Democracy," *Political Science Quarterly* (March 1958), p. 22, n. 55; William Diebold, Jr., *The Schuman Plan*

(New York, 1959), pp. 25–6, 35–6; Konrad Adenauer, *Erinnerungen 1945–1953* (Stuttgart, 1965), pp. 41, 303, 311–16;
Regierung des Landes Nordrhein-Westfalen *et al.*, *Das Abkommen über die Errichtung einer Internazionalen Ruhrbehörde*
(Düsseldorf, 1949), p. 5; *L'Année politique 1950* (Paris, 1951),
pp. 63, 93–4

33. *Ibid.*, pp. 93–4; Bromberger, *op. cit.* (n. 14, *supra*), pp. 114–15
34. Personal knowledge; Bromberger, *op. cit.* (n. 14, *supra*), pp.
103–4, 121–2; Elgey, *op. cit.* (n. 20, *supra*), pp. 445–6
35. Jean Monnet, *Allocution à Scy-Chazelles le 3 octobre 1965*
(mimeographed, Paris, 1965); Robert Schuman, *Pour l'Europe*
(Paris, 1963), p. 207
36. Bromberger, *op. cit.* (n. 14, *supra*), pp. 121–3 (but with dates
confused); Elgey, *op. cit.* (n. 20, *supra*), pp. 445–7; Mayne, *op.
cit.* (n. 7, *supra*), pp. 85–91; private information
37. François Fontaine, *La Nation frein* (Paris, 1965), pp. 99–101;
Bromberger, *loc. cit.* (n. 36, *supra*); Elgey, *loc. cit.* (n. 36,
supra); Cook, *op. cit.* (n. 29, *supra*), pp. 124–5; private information
38. Dean Acheson, *Sketches from Life* (New York, 1961), pp. 35–9;
Ibid., *Present at the Creation* (London, 1970), pp. 382–6
39. Ulrich Sahm, "Grossbritanniens Haltung zum Schuman-Plan,"
in Walter Hallstein and Hans-Jürgen Schlochauer (ed.), *Zur
Integration Europas: Festschrift für Carl Friedrich Ophüls*
(Karlsruhe, 1965), pp. 153–65; transl. as "Britain and Europe,
1950," in *International Affairs*, vol. XLIII, No. 1 (London, January, 1967), pp. 12–24, with a comment by Kenneth Younger,
Ibid., pp. 24–8 (pp. 24, 26); *Keesing's Contemporary Archives*,
1950, p. 10705
40. Gilles Anouil, *La Grande-Bretagne et la Communauté Européenne du Charbon et de l'Acier* (Issoudun, 1960), pp. 45–7;
*Anglo-French Discussions regarding French proposals for the
Western European Coal, Iron and Steel Industries, May-June,
1950* (H.M.S.O. Cmd. 7970), p. 5; *The Times* (London), May
12, 1950
41. Cmd. 7970 (Cf. n. 40, *supra*), p. 6; private information
42. Cmd. 7970 (Cf. n. 40, *supra*), p. 6; *Hansard*, vol. 475, col. 587
(1950)
43. Raymond Racine, *Vers une Europe nouvelle par le Plan Schuman* (Neuchâtel, 1954), pp. 62ff; Hirsch, *op. cit.* (n. 26, *supra*),
p. 10; private information
44. Cmd. 7970 (Cf. n. 40, *supra*), p. 6; Jean Monnet, *Interview
with German television* (typescript, Paris, July 21, 1965), pp.
2–3; private information; Adenauer, *op. cit.* (n. 32, *supra*), pp.
336–7
45. Private information; Cmd. 7970 (Cf. n. 40, *supra*), pp. 7–9,
translation corrected from original version in *La Documentation
Française*, No. 1339 (June 13, 1950), pp. 4–5
46. Cmd. 7970 (Cf. n. 40, *supra*), pp. 6–7

47. Agence France Presse dispatch of May 25, 1950; Cmd. 7970, p. 8
48. Cmd. 7970 (Cf. n. 40, *supra*), p. 9; Younger in *International Affairs, loc. cit.* (n. 40, *supra*), p. 27
49. Private information; Cmd. 7970 (Cf. n. 40, *supra*), pp. 9–11, translation and punctuation corrected from original version in *La Documentation Française, loc. cit.* (n. 45, *supra*), pp. 5–6
50. *Note verbale de l'Ambassadeur des Pays-Bas,* May 31, 1950; cf. Mayne, *op. cit.* (n. 14, *supra*), pp. 359–60
51. Cmd. 7970 (Cf. n. 40, *supra*), pp. 11–12
52. Elgey, *op. cit.* (n. 20, *supra*), pp. 448–9 (transl. R.M.)
53. Cmd. 7970 (Cf. n. 40, *supra*), p. 12
54. Cmd. 7970 (Cf. n. 40, *supra*), pp. 13–14
55. *Ibid.,* pp. 14–15, translation corrected from *La Documentation Française, loc. cit.* (n. 45, *supra*), p. 8

Chapter 9.   THE ECHTERNACH DANCE

1. *Absalom and Achitophel* (London, 1681), lines 799–800
2. Motto to Ludwig Wittgenstein, *Philosophical Investigations* (Oxford, 1953) (transl. R.M.)
3. *The Making of the President 1960* (Cardinal edition, New York, 1961), p. 429
4. République Française, Ministère des Affaires Etrangères, *Rapport de la délégation française sur le Traité instituant la Communauté Européennes du Charbon et de l'Acier et la Convention relatives aux dispositions transitoires signés à Paris le 18 avril 1951* (Paris, October, 1951), pp. 11–12; Schuman, lecture at the College of Europe, Bruges, 1953
5. Max Kohnstamm, "The European Tide," in Stephen R. Graubard (ed.), *A New Europe?* (Boston, 1964), pp. 140–73 (pp. 151–2)
6. André Fontaine, *Histoire de la guerre froide,* vol. II (Paris, 1967), pp. 13–22; *L'Année politique 1950* (Paris, 1951), pp. 144–5, 364 (Security Council resolution of June 27, 1950)
7. *L'Année politique 1950* (Paris, 1951), p. 145; Fontaine, *op. cit.* (n. 6, *supra*), p. 14; Philip Mosely, *The Kremlin in World Politics* (Vintage Books edition, New York, 1960), p. 327; Barbara Ward, *Policy for the West* (New York, 1951), p. 101, n. 2; Georgette Elgey, *La République des Illusions* (Paris, 1965), p. 458; personal knowledge
8. *L'Année politique 1950* (Paris, 1951), p. 144; Fontaine, *op. cit.* (n. 6, *supra*), p. 19; Elgey, *op. cit.* (n. 7, *supra*), p. 460; Drew Middleton, *The Defense of Western Europe* (New York, 1952), pp. 76–7; Royal Institute of International Affairs, *Britain in Western Europe* (London, 1956), p. 25; Paul-Henri Spaak, *Combats Inachevés* (Paris, 1965), vol. I, p. 269
9. Ward, *op. cit.* (n. 7, *supra*), p. 101, n. 1; Fontaine, *op. cit.* (n. 6, *supra*), p. 47; Elgey, *op. cit.* (n. 7, *supra*), p. 461; Jacques Fauvet, *La IV ème République* (Paris, 1959), p. 168; Jules

Moch, *Histoire du réarmement allemand depuis 1950* (Paris, 1965), pp. 46–7; Royal Institute of International Affairs, *op. cit.* (n. 8, *supra*), p. 26; Konrad Adenauer, *Erinnerungen 1945–1953* (Stuttgart, 1965), pp. 350–62

10. Fontaine, *loc. cit.* (n. 9, *supra*); Elgey, *op. cit.* (n. 7, *supra*), p. 462; "Sirius" (Beuve-Méry) in *Le Monde* (Paris, April 6, 1948)

11. *The Plain Dealer* (Cleveland, Ohio, December 3, 1949); Adenauer, *op. cit.* (n. 9, *supra*), pp. 341–9; Pierre Billotte, *Le Temps du choix* (Paris, 1950), *passim;* Richard Mayne, *The Community of Europe* (London, 1962; New York, 1963), p. 101; Arthur Koestler, *The Trail of the Dinosaur* (London, 1955), pp. 204–14

12. Private information

13. Moch, *op. cit.* (n. 11, *supra*), pp. 60–139; Elgey, *op. cit.* (n. 7, *supra*), pp. 461–3

14. Private information; Elgey, *op. cit.* (n. 7, *supra*), p. 462; Merry and Serge Bromberger, *Les Coulisses de l'Europe* (Paris, 1968), pp. 132–8

15. Présidence du Conseil, Secrétariat-Général du Gouvernement, *L'Organisation de l'Europe Occidentale* (*1948–1955*), (Paris, July 19, 1955), p. 45

16. *Ibid.;* Paul Stehlin, *Retour à Zéro* (Paris, 1968), pp. 83–4

17. Présidence du Conseil, *op. cit.* (n. 15, *supra*), pp. 45–6, 48–56, 61–5; Mayne, *op. cit.* (n. 11, *supra*), pp. 102–3; *Ibid., The Institutions of the European Community* (London, 1968), p. 11

18. Mayne, *op. cit.* (n. 11, *supra*), p. 103; Présidence du Conseil, *op. cit.* (n. 15, *supra*), p. 63

19. *Ibid.*, p. 46

20. Personal knowledge; Mayne, *op. cit.* (n. 11, *supra*), p. 104; *Ibid.*, "Castellammare and E.D.C.," *New Statesman* (London, April 14, 1954); Daniel Lerner & Raymond Aron (ed.), *France Defeats EDC* (New York, 1957), *passim*

21. Cf. Chapter VIII, *supra;* Hansard, House of Commons, 1950, vol. 472, col. 320; Ulrich Sahm, "Grossbritanniens Haltung zum Schuman-Plan," in Walter Hallstein & Hans-Jürgen Schlochauer (ed.), *Zur Integration Europas: Festschrift für Carl Friedrich Ophüls* (Karlsruhe, 1965), pp. 153–65 (p. 158), transl. as "Britain and Europe, 1950," in *International Affairs*, vol. XLIII, No. 1 (London, January 1967), pp. 12–24 (p. 17); Churchill, speech in the House of Commons, June 27, 1950; *L'Année politique 1950* (Paris, 1951), p. 140; Hugh Dalton, *High Tide and After: Memoirs 1945–1960* (London, 1962), p. 334; National Executive Committee of the British Labour Party, *European Unity* (London, May 1950), p. 8

22. R. C. Mowat, *Ruin and Resurgence 1939–1965* (London, 1966), p. 227; *L'Année politique 1950* (Paris, 1951), pp. 140–1; official minutes of the Schuman Plan Conference, unpublished

23. Sahm, *op. cit.* (n. 21, *supra*), pp. 161–2 (original), 20–21

(translation); *Anglo-French Discussions regarding French pro-posals for the Western European Coal, Iron and Steel Industries, May-June, 1950* (H.M.S.O., Cmd. 7970), p. 15; *Europa-Archiv*, 1950, p. 3173; *Hansard*, House of Commons, 1950, vol. 476 (June 15, 1950), cols., 551, 554; Gilles Anouil, *La Grande-Bretagne et la Communauté Européenne du Charbon et de l'Acier* (Issoudun, 1960), pp. 91–2; Raymond Racine, *Vers une Europe Nouvelle par le Plan Schuman* (Neuchâtel, 1954), p. 66; A.F.P. dispatch of 4:00 P.M., June 5, 1950; *Le Monde* (Paris, June 7 & 20, 1950); private information

24. Cf. Chapter VI, *supra;* Anthony Sampson, *Macmillan: A Study in Ambiguity* (Pelican edition, London, 1968), pp. 90–92; Harold Macmillan, *Tides of Fortune 1945–1955* (London, 1969), pp. 193–5, 204; Council of Europe, *Documents de Séance*, 1950, pp. 719–24; Anouil, *op. cit.* (n. 8, *supra*), pp. 93–5; Nora Beloff, *The General Says No* (London, 1963), pp. 58–9

25. Sampson, *loc. cit.* (n. 24, *supra*); Beloff, *op. cit.* (n. 24, *supra*), pp. 59–60

26. Anouil, *loc. cit.* (n. 23, *supra*); Racine, *loc. cit.* (n. 23, *supra*); *Le Monde* (Paris, July 27, 1950)

27. Council of Europe, Consultative Assembly, 2nd Session, *Reports*, Part I, p. 136; *Hansard*, House of Commons, 1950, vol. 476 (November 7, 1950); A.F.P. dispatch, May 1, 1951; private information

28. H. J. Heiser, *British Policy with regard to the unification efforts on the European Continent* (Leyden, 1959), p. 41; the Rt. Hon. Sir Anthony Eden, K.G., P.C., M.C., *Memoirs: Full Circle* (London, 1960), pp. 31–2; *The Times* (London, July 14, 1950), editorial

29. Associated Press dispatch from London, November 23, 1951; R. S. Churchill (ed.), *The Sinews of Peace: Postwar Speeches by Winston S. Churchill* (London, 1948), p. 199; Eden, *op. cit.* (n. 28, *supra*), pp. 30, 32–3, 36; Council of Europe, Consultative Assembly, *Official Report*, 3rd Session, 1951, pp. 513–14; Mayne, *op. cit.* (n. 11, *supra*), pp. 79, 138

30. Eden, *op. cit.* (n. 28, *supra*), pp. 34–5, 37–8, 40–41

31. Eden, *op. cit.* (n. 28, *supra*), pp. 42–4

32. *Ibid.*

33. *Ibid.*, p. 44

34. Conseil de l'Europe, Assemblée Consultative, 4ème Session ordinaire, AS (4) 11: *Demande d'avis du Comité des Ministres sur les meilleurs moyens de mettre en application les proposi-tions du Royaume-Uni* (Strasbourg, May 24, 1952); Eden, *op. cit.* (n. 28, *supra*), pp. 47–8; Anthony Nutting, *Europe Will Not Wait* (London, 1960), p. 42

35. Nutting, *op. cit.* (n. 34, *supra*), p. 43

36. Nutting, *op. cit.* (n. 34, *supra*), pp. 42, 44

37. Council of Europe, *Documents*, 4th Session, Document 33, pp. 409–29; Anouil, *op. cit.* (n. 23, *supra*), pp. 115–17; Nutting, *op. cit.* (n. 34, *supra*), p. 46

38. Private information; personal knowledge

39. Personal knowledge

40. Anouil, *op. cit.* (n. 23, *supra*), p. 121; private information

41. *Le Monde* (Paris, August 13, 1952); Anouil, *op. cit.* (n. 23, *supra*), pp. 121–6; private information

42. Private information; High Authority Information Service, *Chronology of Association with the United Kingdom* (Luxembourg, October 16, 1954)

43. Private information; High Authority, *Correspondance concernant les relations entre la Communauté Européenne du Charbon et de l'Acier et le Royaume-Uni* (Luxembourg, May 3, 1954), pp. 1–5

44. *Hansard*, House of Commons, 1954, vol. 552, col. 190; British Iron and Steel Federation, *Monthly Statistical Bulletin* (London, March 1954); private information; High Authority, *loc. cit.* (n. 43, *supra*)

45. Private information; William Diebold, Jr., *The Schuman Plan* (New York, 1959), p. 641

46. Arnold J. Zurcher, *The Struggle to Unite Europe 1940–1958* (New York, 1958), pp. 114–18; New York *Times*, March 4, 1953; Nutting, *op. cit.* (n. 34, *supra*), pp. 47–8

47. New York *Times*, December 15, 1953; Nutting, *loc. cit.* (n. 46, *supra*)

48. Nutting, *op. cit.* (n. 34, *supra*), pp. 50, 55–6, 59–64

49. Mayne, *op. cit.* (n. 11, *supra*), pp. 104–5; *Ibid.*, "Le Rouge et le Noir," *New Statesman* (London, June 26, 1954)

50. Pierre Rouanet, *Mendès-France au Pouvoir 1954–1955* (Paris, 1965), pp. 220–2; Spaak, *op. cit.* (n. 8, *supra*), pp. 276–7

51. Personal knowledge; private information

52. Spaak, *op. cit.* (n. 8, *supra*), p. 278; Pierre Mendès-France in *Le Figaro* (Paris, February 17, 1969)

53. Rouanet, *op. cit.* (n. 50, *supra*), pp. 224–31; Spaak, *op. cit.* (n. 8, *supra*), pp. 277–80

54. Mayne, *op. cit.* (n. 11, *supra*), pp. 104–5; Daniel Lerner and Raymond Aron (ed.), *France Defeats E.D.C.* (New York, 1957), p. 17; Rouanet, *op. cit.* (n. 50, *supra*), pp. 122–3, 231–40

55. Rouanet, *op. cit.* (n. 50, *supra*), pp. 248–54; Nutting, *op. cit.* (n. 34, *supra*), p. 67

56. Spaak, *op. cit.* (n. 8, *supra*), pp. 286–7; Rouanet, *op. cit.* (n. 50, *supra*), pp. 255–63

57. Spaak, *op. cit.* (n. 8, *supra*), pp. 287–90; Rouanet, *op. cit.* (n. 50, *supra*), pp. 263–75; Mendès-France, *loc. cit.* (n. 52, *supra*)

58. Spaak, *op. cit.* (n. 8, *supra*), pp. 290–5; Rouanet, *op. cit.* (n. 50, *supra*), pp. 265–75

59. Spaak, *op. cit.* (n. 8, *supra*), pp. 295–7; Rouanet, *op. cit.* (n. 50, *supra*), pp. 276–81; Mendès-France, *loc. cit.* (n. 52, *supra*); Nutting, *op. cit.* (n. 34, *supra*), p. 67

60. Spaak, *op. cit.* (n. 8, *supra*), pp. 297–9; Mayne, *op. cit.* (n. 11, *supra*), p. 105; Zurcher, *op. cit.* (n. 46, *supra*), p. 124

61. Eden, *op. cit.* (n. 28, *supra*), p. 151; *Documents agreed on by the Conference of Ministers held in Paris, 20-23 October 1954* (London, H.M.S.O., Cmd. 9304, November 1950)

62. Private information; Anouil, *op. cit.* (n. 23, *supra*), pp. 174, 184

63. *Bulletin from the European Coal and Steel Community*, vol. IV, No. 5 (London, November 1957), p. 4; High Authority, *Sixth General Report*, vol. I (Luxembourg, 1958), pp. 83–5; *Hansard*, House of Commons, February 21, 1955, col. 897

Chapter 10. NEVER SO GOOD

1. *La Crise de la conscience européenne* (*Idées* edition, Paris, 1968), vol. II, p. 295 (transl. R.M.)

2. *Maximes*, ed. F. C. Green (Cambridge, 1945), p. 60, No. 25 (transl. R.M.)

3. *English History 1914–1945* (Oxford, 1965), p. 425

4. *Statistiques des aéroports de l'Europe de l'Ouest* (Paris, annual), *passim*

5. J. Frederic Dewhurst and others, *Europe's Needs and Resources* (New York, 1961), pp. 36, 40, 50, 347–53; European Economic Community, Commission, *Report on the Economic Situation in the Countries of the Community* (Brussels, September 1958), pp. 23, 30; European Community Information Service, *The Community in Maps* (Brussels/Luxembourg, 1967), map 2

6. Charles P. Kindleberger, *Europe's Postwar Growth: The Role of Labor Supply* (Cambridge, Massachusetts, 1967), *passim*; Dewhurst, *op. cit.* (n. 5, *supra*), pp. 17, 27, 120, 676, 706; O.E.E.C. *General Statistics* (Paris, July 1960); I.M.F. *International Financial Statistics* (Washington, June 1960)

7. Dewhurst, *op. cit.* (n. 5, *supra*), pp. 576, 651, 655, 1106–7, 1145–6

8. Kindleberger, *op. cit.* (n. 6, *supra*), pp. 24–86; Dewhurst, *op. cit.* (n. 5, *supra*), pp. 113, 444–5; Angus Maddison, *Economic Growth in the West* (New York/London, 1964), pp. 76–98; Jossleyn Hennessy and others, *Economic "Miracles"* (London, 1964), *passim*

9. Dewhurst, *op. cit.* (n. 5, *supra*), pp. 407, 431, 433, 437, 439

10. Dewhurst, *op. cit.* (n. 5, *supra*), pp. 138, 378–9, 398–9, 413

11. Dewhurst, *op. cit.* (n. 5, *supra*), pp. 138, 313, 315, 330; Raymond Poignant, *L'Enseignement dans les pays du Marché commun* (Paris, 1965), pp. 28, 76

12. Dewhurst, *op. cit.* (n. 5, *supra*), pp. 123, 146; James B. Jeffreys & Derek Knee, *Retailing in Europe* (London, 1962), pp. 8, 24–5, 106–7

13. Dewhurst, *op. cit.* (n. 5, *supra*), pp. 147, 185, 189, 258, 265–6, 306; O.E.E.C., *Agricultural and Food Statistics* (Paris, 1956 and 1959)

14. Harold Macmillan, speech to an open-air rally at Bedford, July 20, 1957; John Montgomery, *The Fifties* (London, 1965), p. 270; Clive Irving and others, *Scandal '63* (London, 1963), p. 3

15. Statement to the High Authority on November 9, 1954, the Council of Ministers and the press on November 11, and the Common Assembly on November 30; *Débats de l'Assemblée Commune*, No. 7 (Luxembourg, 1955), p. 21; private information

16. Private information

17. Private information

18. Private information

19. Private information; Paul-Henri Spaak, *Combats Inachevés*, vol. II (Paris, 1969), pp. 62–3 (transl. R.M.)

20. Private information

21. *L'Année politique 1955* (Paris, 1956), p. 381

22. Private information

23. Spaak, *op. cit.* (n. 19, *supra*), pp. 64–5 (transl. R.M.); *L'Année politique 1955* (Paris, 1956), p. 382

24. *L'Année politique 1955* (Paris, 1956), p. 382

25. *L'Année politique 1955* (Paris, 1956), pp. 375–6; private information

26. *L'Année politique 1955* (Paris, 1956), pp. 409–13

27. Private information

28. Private information

29. *L'Année politique 1955* (Paris, 1956), p. 415

30. Personal knowledge; R. Mayne, "The Role of Jean Monnet," in *Government and Opposition*, vol. II, No. 3 (April-July, 1967), pp. 349–71 (pp. 366–7)

31. *L'Année politique 1955* (Paris, 1956), p. 416; Miriam Camps, *Britain and the European Community 1955–1963* (London, 1964), p. 23; Merry & Serge Bromberger, *Les Coulisses de l'Europe* (Paris, 1968), p. 193

32. Benelux Memorandum in *L'Année politique 1955* (Paris, 1956), pp. 714–16; German Memorandum, *Ibid.*, pp. 716–17 (transl. R.M.)

33. Private information

34. Personal knowledge; private information; Bromberger, *loc. cit.* (n. 31, *supra*); Camps, *op. cit.* (n. 31, *supra*), pp. 24–9; Jean Lecerf, *Histoire de l'unité européenne* (Paris, 1965), pp. 56–9

35. Lecerf, *op. cit.* (n. 34, *supra*), p. 60; Messina Resolution in British White Paper (Cmd. 9525, H.M.S.O., London, July 1955), pp. 7–9, and Camps, *op. cit.* (n. 31, *supra*), pp. 520–2

36. *Le Monde* (Paris, June 5-6, 1955); Camps, *op. cit.* (n. 31, *supra*), pp. 28–9; Lecerf, *op. cit.* (n. 34, *supra*), pp. 60–1

37. Personal knowledge; private information; R. Mayne, *The Com-*

munity of Europe (London, 1962; New York, 1963), pp. 108–9
38. Private information
39. Private information; Action Committee for the United States of Europe, *Statements and Declarations 1955–67* (London, 1969), pp. 7–11; "Setting the Pace for Unity," in *Common Market*, vol. IV, No. 6 (The Hague, June 1964), pp. 104–6 (p. 106); Walter Yondorf, "Monnet and the Action Committee: the Formative Period of the European Communities," in *International Organization*, vol. XIX, No. 4 (1965), pp. 885–912; Mayne, "The Role of Jean Monnet," *op. cit.* (n. 30, *supra*), pp. 367–71; Mayne, *The Community of Europe, op. cit.* (n. 37, *supra*), pp. 109–10
40. Spaak, *op. cit.* (n. 19, *supra*), pp. 85, 89; Bromberger, *op. cit.* (n. 31, *supra*), p. 218; personal knowledge
41. On Suez, cf. Hugh Thomas, *The Suez Affair* (London, 1967); Anthony Nutting, *No end of a lesson* (London, 1967); Anthony Moncrieff (ed.), *Suez ten years after* (London, 1967); Henri Azeau, *Le piège de Suez* (Paris, 1964); Terence Robertson, *Crisis* (London, 1965); Merry and Serge Bromberger, *Les Secrets de l'expédition d'Egypte* (Paris, 1957); also private information
42. Action Committee, *op. cit.* (n. 39, *supra*), pp. 17–19; Mayne, *op. cit.* (n. 37, *supra*), pp. 112–13; *A Target for Euratom, Report submitted by Mr. Louis Armand, Mr. Franz Etzel and Mr. Francesco Giordani at the request of the governments of Belgium, France, German Federal Republic, Italy, Luxembourg and the Netherlands* ([Luxembourg], May 1957)
43. John Steward Ambler, *The French Army in Politics 1945–1962* (Columbus, Ohio, 1966), pp. 214, 228; Thomas, *op. cit.* (n. 41, *supra*), pp. 112–15; Nutting, *op. cit.* (n. 41, *supra*), pp. 90–9, 101; Moncrieff, *op. cit.* (n. 41, *supra*), pp. 93–4
44. Moncrieff, *op. cit.* (n. 41, *supra*), p. 25; Thomas, *op. cit.* (n. 41, *supra*), pp. 145–7
45. Thomas, *op. cit.* (n. 41, *supra*), p. 151
46. P. E. Zinner, *Revolution in Hungary* (New York, 1962), pp. 135, 182, 223, 226 & *passim;* Moncrieff, *op. cit.* (n. 41, *supra*), pp. 118–26; Anton Zischka, *The Other Europeans* (English translation by Brian Battershaw, London, 1962, of *Auch Das ist Europa,* Gütersloh, 1960), pp. 190–9; R. C. Mowat, *Ruin and Resurgence 1939–1965* (London, 1966), pp. 305–12; L. B. Bain, *The Reluctant Satellites* (New York, 1960), *passim;* Doris Scarlett, *Window onto Hungary* (Bradford, mimeographed, n.d.), *passim*
47. Personal knowledge; private information; Mayne, *op. cit.* (n. 37, *supra*), pp. 109, 113; *Ibid., The Institutions of the European Community* (London, 1968), pp. 60–1
48. Personal knowledge; private information
49. Personal knowledge; private information; Piero Malvestiti, *Parte guelfa in Europa* (Milan, 1945)

50. Personal knowledge; Robert Lemaignen, *L'Europe au berceau: souvenirs d'un technocrate* (Paris, 1964)
51. Schuman Declaration in *L'Année politique 1950* (Paris, 1951), pp. 306–7 (transl. R.M.)

Chapter 11. THE LION AND THE UNICORN

1. Iona & Peter Opie (ed.), *The Oxford Dictionary of Nursery Rhymes* (2nd edition, Oxford, 1952), p. 269
2. *Groucho and Me* (Dell Books edition, New York, 1960), p. 240
3. "In Defence of Comrade Zilliacus," in *Collected Essays, Journalism, and Letters* (ed. by Sonia Orwell & Ian Angus (London, 1968), vol. IV, pp. 395–400 (p. 398)
4. Deryck Abel, *Channel Underground* (London, 1961), pp. 7–8, 46, 68–9; O. M. Watts (ed.) *Stanford's General Chart of the English Channel, Eastern Section* (London, 1969)
5. *Correspondence arising out of the Meeting of the Foreign Ministers of the Governments of Belgium, France, the Federal Republic of Germany, Italy, Luxembourg and the Netherlands held at Messina on 1–2 June 1955* (H.M.S.O., Cmd. 9525, London, July 1955)
6. Miriam Camps, *Britain and the European Community 1955–1963* (London, 1964), p. 30; Paul-Henri Spaak, *Combats Inachevés*, vol. II (Paris, 1969), p. 73 (transl. R.M.)
7. Camps, *op. cit.* (n. 6, *supra*), pp. 33, 34
8. Camps, *op. cit.* (n. 6, *supra*), pp. 43–5
9. Private information
10. Private information; the Rt. Hon. Sir Anthony Eden, K.G., P.C., M.C., *Memoirs: Full Circle* (London, 1960), p. 337
11. Private information
12. Private information; Christopher Layton, *European Advanced Technology: A Programme for Integration* (London, 1969), p. 106
13. Spaak, *op. cit.* (n. 6, *supra*), pp. 74–5
14. Spaak, *op. cit.* (n. 6, *supra*), pp. 75–9 (transl. R.M.)
15. Personal knowledge; Spaak, *op. cit.* (n. 6, *supra*), pp. 80–1
16. *The Manchester Guardian* (Manchester, March 14 and 15, 1956); Camps, *op. cit.* (n. 6, *supra*), p. 95 and n. 6, pp. 96–9
17. Spaak, *op. cit.* (n. 6, *supra*), p. 82; personal knowledge; Action Committee for the United States of Europe, *Statements and Declarations 1955–67* (London, 1969), p. 17; R. Mayne, *The Community of Europe* (London, 1962 & New York, 1963), p. 141
18. Private information
19. *L'Année politique 1958* (Paris, 1959), p. 54; personal knowledge
20. Merry and Serge Bromberger, *Les 13 Complots du 13 Mai* (Paris, 1959), *passim*; *L'Année politique 1958* (Paris, 1959), pp. 57–71; Aidan Crawley, *De Gaulle* (London, 1969), pp. 332–53; Alexander Werth, *De Gaulle: a Political Biography*

(Third edition, London, 1969), pp. 11–52; Paul-Marie de la Gorce, *De Gaulle entre deux mondes* (Paris, 1964); pp. 535–6

21. Charles de Gaulle, *Mémoires de Guerre*, vol. III, *Le Salut* (Livre de poche edition, Paris, 1961), p. 337

22. Charles de Gaulle, *op. cit.* (n. 21, *supra*), vol. II, *L'Unité* (Livre de poche edition, Paris, 1960), p. 481

23. Mayne, *op. cit.* (n. 17, *supra*), pp. 144–6

24. Mayne, *op. cit.* (n. 17, *supra*), pp. 15–17, 143

25. Council of Europe, *Debates, Eleventh Ordinary Session* (Strasbourg, January 1960), pp. 760–4; The *Economist* (London, June 11, 1960); The *Observer* (London, July 3, 1960); Camps, *op. cit.* (n. 6, *supra*), pp. 278, 280–1, 283–4, 287

26. W.E.U., *Debates, Sixth Ordinary Session, First Part* (June, 1960), p. 137; Camps, *op. cit.* (n. 6, *supra*), p. 298

27. Action Committee, *op. cit.* (n. 17, *supra*), p. 50

28. *Hansard*, House of Commons (July 25, 1960), cols. 1099–1218; Camps, *op. cit.* (n. 6, *supra*), p. 298

29. *L'Année politique 1960* (Paris, 1961), pp. 647–9; on NATO, cf. esp. Spaak, *op. cit.* (n. 6, *supra*), pp. 180–7

30. European Parliament, Political Committee, *Towards Political Union: A Selection of Documents with a Foreword by Mr. Emilio Battista* (London, January 1964), pp. 6–11; Camps, *op. cit.* (n. 6, *supra*), pp. 302–12, 329; R. Mayne, *The Institutions of the European Community* (London, 1968), p. 74

31. Mayne, *op. cit.* (n. 30, *supra*), pp. 74–7; Miriam Camps, *What Kind of Europe?* (London, 1965), pp. 89–116; *Ibid., European Unification in the Sixties* (New York, 1966), pp. 27, 126, 223, 225

32. Dwight D. Eisenhower, *Waging Peace* (London, 1966), p. 603; Joseph Kraft, *The Grand Design: From Common Market to Atlantic Partnership* (New York, 1962), pp. 24–5; personal knowledge

33. Kraft, *op. cit.* (n. 32, *supra*), title; J. F. Kennedy, *Message to Congress*, January 25, 1962; *Ibid., Speech at Philadelphia*, July 4, 1962; Action Committee, *op. cit.* (n. 17, *supra*), pp. 64–5 (Joint Declaration of June 26, 1962)

34. George W. Ball, *The Discipline of Power* (Boston, 1968), pp. 78–9; Camps, *op. cit.* (n. 6, *supra*), pp. 336–7; personal knowledge

35. EFTA, *Bulletin* (Geneva, July 1961), p. 8; *Commonwealth Consultations on Britain's Relations with the European Economic Community* (H.M.S.O., Cmd. 1449, London, July 1961); Camps, *op. cit.* (n. 6, *supra*), pp. 338–56

36. *Hansard*, House of Commons, vol. 645, no. 159 (July 31, 1961), cols. 928–31

37. Camps, *op. cit.* (n. 6, *supra*), pp. 287, 357

38. Private information

39. Private information

40. *The United Kingdom and the European Economic Community* (H.M.S.O., Cmd. 1565, London, November 1961)

41. *Ibid.*

42. Personal knowledge. Cf. Camps, *op. cit.* (n. 6, *supra*), pp. 367–506; Nora Beloff, *The General Says No* (London, 1963), pp. 113–71

43. Personal knowledge. Cf. Piers Dixon, *Double Diplomat: The Life of Sir Pierson Dixon, Don and Diplomat* (London, 1968), pp. 279–314

44. Personal knowledge

45. E.E.C. Commission, *Report to the European Parliament on the State of the Negotiations with the United Kingdom* (Brussels, February 26, 1963)

46. Personal knowledge

47. Personal knowledge; *L'Année politique 1963* (Paris, 1964), p. 400 (transl. R.M.)

48. Robert Kleiman, *Atlantic Crisis* (New York, 1964), pp. 48–9

49. *Ibid.*, pp. 50–61

50. Private information

51. Mayne, *op. cit.* (n. 30, *supra*), pp. 42–50; John Newhouse, *Collision in Brussels* (London, 1968), *passim*

52. Uwe Kitzinger, *The Second Try: Labour and the EEC* (London, 1968), p. 177

53. Pierre Uri (ed.), *From Commonwealth to Common Market* (London, 1968), pp. 51–88

54. Jean-Jacques Servan-Schreiber, *Le défi américain* (Paris, 1967)

55. Texts in Kitzinger, *op. cit.* (n. 52, *supra*), pp. 299, 316, 317, 319

56. *Problems of British entry into the EEC: Reports to the Action Committee for the United States of Europe* (London, September 1969)

57. Cf. Z. E. B. Zeman, *Prague Springs: A Report on Czechoslovakia 1968* (London, 1969); Willy Brandt, *A Peace Policy for Europe* (London, 1969)

Chapter 12. REMEMBERING THE FUTURE

1. "Miscellaneous Thoughts and Reflections," in *Complete Works*, ed. by Walter Raleigh (Oxford, 1912), p. 249

2. *Letters*, ed. by G. B. Hill (London, 1897), vol. I, p. 221

3. *Walden* (Scott Library edition, London, n.d. [1905?]), p. 321

4. Dr. Jonathan Miller, in Henry Brandon, *Conversations With* (London, 1966), p. 253

5. Fritz Baade, *The Race to the Year 2000* (London, 1962), p. 122

6. Dennis Gabor, *Inventing the Future* (London, 1963), pp. 49–50; Penguin edition (London, 1964), p. 42

7. This example, perhaps needless to say, is imaginary

8. This thesis is developed in Jean Fourastié, *Les 40.000 heures* (Paris, 1965)

9. William James, "The Moral Equivalent of War," in *Memories and Studies* (London, 1911)

10. 1945 estimate by Frank W. Notestein; W. S. & E. S. Woytinsky, *World Population and Production: Trends and Outlook* (New York, 1953), pp. 257–62; United Nations, *The Future Growth of World Population* (New York, 1958); J. Fourastié & C. Vimont, *Histoire de demain* (3rd ed., Paris, 1964), pp. 14–17; "Les savants scrutent l'avenir," in *Réalités* (Paris, September and October, 1965); NATO Defense College, Course 30, Segment 3, *The Way Ahead* (Rome, 1967), pp. 33–50 (pp. 38, 47)

11. NATO Defense College, *op. cit.* (n. 10, *supra*), pp. 44–6

12. William Morris, *The Dream of John Ball*, chap. IV, in G. D. H. Cole (ed.) William Morris, *Stories in Prose, Stories in Verse, Shorter Poems, Lectures and Essays* (London, 1948), p. 214

BIBLIOGRAPHY

Abel, Deryck. *Channel Underground*. London, 1961.

Abendroth, Wolfgang. *Sozialgeschichte der Europäischer Arbeiter-bewegung*. Frankfurt-am-Main, 1965.

Abosch, Heinz. *The Menace of the Miracle*. London, 1962.

Acheson, Dean. *Sketches from Life*. New York, 1961.

    Present at the Creation. London, 1970.

Action Committee for the United States of Europe. *Statements and Declarations 1955–1957*. London, 1969.

Adenauer, Konrad. *Erinnerungen 1945–1953*. Stuttgart, 1965.

    Erinnerungen 1953–1955. Stuttgart, 1966.

    Erinnerungen 1955–1959. Stuttgart, 1967.

"Adstans." *Alcide De Gasperi nella Politica Estera Italiana*. Milan, 1953.

Agar, Herbert. *A Time for Greatness*. London, 1944.

Agence France Presse. *Dispatches*.

Agenor.

The Air-Power Historian.

Albenski, Henry S., and Pettit, Lawrence K. (eds.). *European Political Processes*. Boston, Mass., 1967.

Albonetti, Achille. *Préhistoire des Etats-Unis d'Europe*. Paris, 1963.

Albrecht-Carrié, René. *The Unity of Europe*. London, 1966.

Alexandre, Philippe. *Le Duel de Gaulle Pompidou*. Paris, 1970.

    L'Elysée en peril. Paris, 1969.

Allais, Maurice. *L'Europe unie, route de la prosperité*. Paris, 1960.

Allen, H. C. *The Anglo-American Predicament*. London, 1960.

Allen, James Jay. *The European Common Market and the G.A.T.T.* Washington, 1960.

Alperovitz, Gar. *Atomic Diplomacy: Hiroshima and Potsdam*. London, 1966.

Alpert, Paul. *Twentieth-Century Economic History of Europe*. New York, 1951.

Ambler, John Steward. *The French Army in Politics 1945–1962*. Columbus, Ohio, 1966.

Anders, Wladyslaw. *An Army in Exile*. London, 1949.

Andrews, William G. (ed.). *European Politics I: The Restless Search*. Princeton, N.J., 1966.

L'Année Politique. Paris, annual.

Anonymous (transl. James Stern). *A Woman in Berlin*. London, 1965.

Anouil, Gilles. *La Grande-Bretagne et la Communauté Européenne du Charbon et de l'Acier*. Issoudun, 1960.

Armand, Louis, and Drancourt, Michel. *Le Pari européen*. Paris, 1968.

Plaidoyer pour l'avenir. Paris, 1961.

and Etzel, Franz, and Giordani, Francesco. *A Target for Euratom*. Luxembourg, 1957.

Aron, Raymond. *Démocratie et totalitarisme*. Paris, 1965.

Dimensions de la conscience historique. Paris, 1960.

Dix-huit leçons sur la société industrielle. Paris, 1962.

La Lutte des classes. Paris, 1964.

L'Opium des intellectuels. Paris, 1955.

Trois essais sur l'âge industriel. Paris, 1966.

Aron, Robert. *Histoire de l'épuration*, Vol. 1. Paris, 1967.

Histoire de la libération de la France. Pocket edition, Paris, 1967.

Ashcroft, Edward. *De Gaulle*. London, 1952.

Ashton, T. S. *The Industrial Revolution 1760–1830*. Oxford, 1948.

Aubrey, Henry G. *Atlantic Economic Co-operation*. London/New York, 1967.

Behind the Veil of International Money. New York, 1969.

Azad, Maulana Abul Kalam. *India Wins Freedom*. Bombay, 1959.

Azeau, Henri. *Le piège de Suez*. Paris, 1964.

Baade, Fritz (transl. Ernest Pavel). *The Race to the Year 2000*. London, 1963.

Bagrit, Leon. *The Age of Automation*. Paperback edition, London, 1965.

Bain, L. B. *The Reluctant Satellites*. New York, 1960.

Bank for International Settlements. *Eight European Central Banks*. London, 1963.

Ball, George W. *The Discipline of Power*. Boston, Mass., 1968.

Ball, M. Margaret. *Nato and the European Unity Movement*. New York, 1959.

Barraclough, Geoffrey. *An Introduction to Contemporary History*. London, 1964.

The Origins of Modern Germany. Oxford, 1946.

Bartoli, Domenico. *La Fine della Monarchia*. Milan, 1947.

Barzanti, Sergio. *The Underdeveloped Areas within the Common Market*. Princeton, N.J., 1965.

Basile, Joseph. *Les Atoufs de L'Europe*. Paris, 1970.

Bayliss, Brian T. *European Transport*. London, 1965.

Beaton, Leonard. *Must the Bomb Spread?* London, 1966.

The Politics of Arms Control. New York, 1969.

and Maddox, John. *The Spread of Nuclear Weapons*. London, 1962.

Beaufre, André. *Introduction à la stratégie*. Paris, 1963.

Beaumont, P. de. *La IVe République: politique intérieure et européenne*. Brussels, 1960.

Beauvoir, Simone de. *La Force des choses*. Paris, 1963.

Beddington-Behrens, Edward. *Is There Any Choice? Britain Must Join Europe*. London, 1966.

Bedell Smith, W. *Moscow Mission 1946–1949*. London, 1950.

Beever, R. Colin. *European Unity and the Trade Union Movement.* Leyden, 1961.
 Trade Unions and Free Labour Movement in the EEC. London, 1969.
Bell, Coral. *Negotiation from Strength.* London, 1962.
Bellotto, Adriano. *La Televisione Inutile.* Milan, 1962.
Beloff, Max. *Europe and the Europeans.* London, 1957.
 The Future of British Foreign Policy. London, 1969.
 New Dimensions in Foreign Policy. London, 1961.
 The United States and the Unity of Europe. London, 1963.
Beloff, Nora. *The General Says No.* London, 1963.
Bender, Peter. *Offensive Entspannung.* Cologne/Berlin, 1964.
Benoit, Emile. *Europe at Sixes and Sevens.* New York, 1961.
 and Boulding, Kenneth E. (eds.). *Disarmament and the Economy.* New York, 1963.
Berliner, Joseph S. *Soviet Economic Aid.* New York, 1958.
Bettini, Emilio (ed.). *Il Trattato contro la Proliferazione Nucleare.* Bologna, 1968.
Bettiza, Enzo. *L'Altra Germania.* Milan, 1968.
Birkenhead, The Earl of. *The Professor and the Prime Minister.* Boston, Mass., 1962.
Birrenbach, Kurt. *Die Zukunft der Atlantischen Gemeinschaft.* Freiburg-im-Breisgau, 1962.
Black, C. E. *The Transformation of Russian Society.* Cambridge, Mass., 1960.
Blanc, André. *L'Economie des Balkans.* Paris, 1965.
 Géographie des Balkans. Paris, 1965.
Blijstra, R. *Nederlandse Bouwkunst na 1900.* Utrecht/Antwerp, 1962.
Boarman, Patrick. *Germany's Economic Dilemma: Inflation and the Balance of Payments.* New Haven, Conn./London, 1964.
Bocca, Giorgio. *I Giovani Leoni del Neocapitalismo.* Bari, 1963.
Bölling, K. (transl. Jean Steinberg). *Republic in Suspense: Politics, Parties, and Personalities in Post-War Germany.* London, 1964.
Bologna, Sergio, and others (eds.). *Fascismo e Antifascismo: Lezioni e Testimonianze.* 2 volumes, Milan, 1962.
Bonanni, Massimo (ed.). *La Politica Estera della Repubblica Italiana.* 3 volumes, Milan, 1967.
Bowie, Robert R., and Friedrich, Carl J. (eds.). *Studies in Federalism.* Boston, Mass., 1954.
 and Geiger, Theodore. *The European Economic Community and the United States.* Washington, 1961.
Bradley, Omar. *A Soldier's Story.* London, 1962.
Brandt, Willy. *A Peace Policy for Europe.* London, 1969.
Brecher, Michael. *Nehru: A Political Biography.* Oxford, 1953.
Brentano, Heinrich von. *Deutschland, Europa, und die Welt* (transl. Edward Fitzgerald as *Germany and Europe: Reflections on German Foreign Policy*). London, 1964.

Brinton, Crane. *The Americans and the French.* Cambridge, Mass., 1968.

British Iron and Steel Federation. *Monthly Statistical Bulletin.*

Broad, Roger, and Jarrett, Robert. *Community Europe.* London, 1967.

Bromberger, Merry and Serge. *Les Coulisses de l'Europe.* Paris, 1968.
  Les Secrets de l'expédition de Suez. Paris, 1957.
  Les 13 complots du 13 mai. Paris, 1959.

Brown, J. F. *The New Eastern Europe.* New York, 1966.

Brown, William Adams, Jr., and Opie, Redvers. *American Foreign Assistance.* Washington, 1953.

Brugmans, Henri. *L'Idée européenne 1918–1965.* Bruges, 1965.
  Les Origines de la civilisation européenne. Liège, 1958.

Bruhat, Jean. *Histoire de l'U.R.S.S.* 7th edition, Paris, 1964.

Bryant, Arthur. *Triumph in the West 1943–1946.* Paperback edition, London, 1965.

Brzezinski, Zbigniew. *Alternative to Partition.* New York, 1965.

Buchan, Alastair (ed.). *Europe's Future, Europe's Choices.* London, 1969.

Buchanan, Norman S., and Lutz, Friedrich A. *Rebuilding the World Economy.* New York, 1947.

Buckley, Christopher. *The Road to Rome.* London, 1945.

Bullock, Alan. *Hitler: A Study in Tyranny.* Paperback edition, London, 1962.
  The Life and Times of Ernest Bevin. London, 1960.

Butcher, Harry C. *My Three Years with Eisenhower.* New York, 1964.

Byrnes, James F. *All in One Lifetime.* London, 1960.
  Speaking Frankly. New York, 1947.

Les Cahiers de la République.

Calder, Nigel (ed.). *The World in 1984.* 2 volumes, London, 1965.

Callender, Harold. *A Preface to Peace.* New York, 1944.

Calleo, David. *Britain's Future.* London, 1968.
  Europe's Future. New York, 1965.

Calmann, John (ed.). *Western Europe: A Handbook.* London, 1967.

Calzini, Paolo (ed.). *Evoluzione delle Economie Orientali e Prospettive degli Scambi Est-ovest.* Rome, 1968.

Campbell, Alan, and Thompson, Dennis. *Common Market Law.* London, 1962.

Campbell, John C. *The United States in World Affairs 1945–1947.* New York, 1947.

Camps, Miriam. *Britain and the European Community 1955–1963.* London, 1963.
  European Unification in the Sixties. New York, 1966.
  What Kind of Europe? London, 1965.

Carlyle, Margaret. *The Awakening of Southern Italy.* London, 1962.
  Modern Italy. London, 1957.

Carr, E. H. *The Soviet Impact on the Western World*. London, 1946.

Carter, W. Horsfall. *Speaking European*. London, 1966.

Cartier, Raymond. *Les 19 Europes*. Paris, 1960.

Catlin, George E. G. *The Atlantic Commonwealth*. London, 1969.

Cattaneo, Carlo. *I Problemi dello Stato Italiano*. Verona, 1966.

Caute, David. *The Left in Europe Since 1789*. London, 1966.

Cavallari, Alberto. *L'Europa su Misura*. Florence, 1963.

Ceccarini, Ennio, and others. *La Nato nell'era della Distensione*. Bologna, 1966.

Céré, Roger. *Entre la guerre et la paix*. Paris, 1962.

Chabod, Federico. *L'Italia Contemporanea 1918–1948*. Paperback edition, Turin, 1965.

   Storia dell' Idea dell' Europa. Paperback edition, Bari, 1967.

Chamberlin, William Henry. *The German Phoenix*. London, 1964.

Charpentier, Maryse (ed.). *Dossier de l'Europe des Six*. Paris, 1969.

Churchill, R. S. (ed.). *The Sinews of Peace: Postwar Speeches by Winston S. Churchill*. London, 1948.

Churchill, Winston S. *The Second World War*. 12-volume paperback edition, London, 1964.

Ciechanowski, Jan. *Defeat in Victory*. New York, 1947.

Cipolla, Carlo M. *The Economic History of World Population*. Paperback edition, London, 1964.

Clark, Alan. *Barbarossa*. Paperback edition, London, 1966.

Clark, Douglas. *Three Days to Catastrophe*. London, 1966.

Clarke, Arthur C. *Profiles of the Future*. London, 1962.

Clay, Lucius D. *Decision in Germany*. London, 1950.

Cleveland, Harold Van B. *The Atlantic Idea and its European Rivals*. New York, 1966.

Cline, Ray S. *Washington Command Post: The Operations Division*. Washington, 1951.

Cole, J. P. *Geography of World Affairs*. London, 1959.

Colebrook, M. J. *Dialogue of the Deaf: Franco–British Relations and European Integration 1945–1950*. Unpublished thesis, Geneva, 1968.

Colombo, Arturo. *Rapporto sull Universita Italiana*. Milan, 1962.

Committee of Economic Co-operation. *General Report*. Paris/London, 1957.

Common Market.

Conland, William H. *Berlin: Beset and Bedevilled*. New York, 1963.

Conquest, Robert. *Common Sense About Russia*. London, 1961.

Conte, Arthur. *Yalta ou le partage du monde*. Pocket edition, Paris, 1965.

Cook, Don. *Floodtide in Europe*. New York, 1965.

Coombes, David. *Towards a European Civil Service*. London, 1968. *Politics and Bureaucracy in the European Community*. London, 1970.

Cooper, R. W. *The Nuremberg Trials*. London, 1946.

Corbett, J. P. *Europe and the Social Order*. Leyden, 1959.

Correspondence between the Chairman of the Council of Ministers of the U.S.S.R. and the Presidents of the U.S.A. and the Prime Minister of Great Britain during the Great Patriotic War of 1941–1945. Moscow, 1957.

Coston, Henry. *L'Europe des banquiers.* Paris, 1963.

Coudenhove-Kalergi, Richard. *An Idea Conquers the World.* London, 1953.

Council of Europe. *Debates.*

Dix Ans de Coopération Européenne. Strasbourg, 1958.

Couzens, E. G., and Yarsley, V. E. *Plastics.* London, 1941.

Plastics in the Service of Man. London, 1965.

Crankshaw, Edward. *Khrushchev's Russia.* London, 1959.

The New Cold War: Moscow v. Pekin. London, 1965.

Crawley, Aidan. *De Gaulle.* London, 1969.

Cretzianu, A. (ed.). *Captive Rumania.* New York, 1965.

Criddle, Brian. *Socialists and European Integration.* London, 1969.

Crozier, Michel. *Le monde des employés de bureau.* Paris, 1965.

Curzon, Gerald. *Multilateral Commercial Diplomacy.* London, 1965.

Dahl, Robert A. *Congress and Foreign Policy.* New York, 1950.

Dahrendorf, Ralf. *Gesellschaft und Demokratie in Deutschland.* Munich, 1865.

Dallin, David J. *The Big Three: The United States, Britain, Russia.* New Haven, Conn., 1945.

Dalton, Hugh. *High Tide and After: Memoirs 1945–1960.* London, 1962.

Davidson, Eugene. *The Death and Life of Germany.* London, 1959.

Davidson, Ian. *Britain and the Making of Europe.* London, 1971.

Davis, Melton S. *All Rome Trembled.* London, 1957.

Who Defends Rome? London, 1972.

Davison, W. Phillips. *The Berlin Blockade.* Princeton, N.J., 1958.

Deakin, F. W. *The Last Days of Mussolini.* Paperback edition, London, 1966.

De Gasperi, Maria. *De Gasperi, Uomo Solo.* Milan, 1965.

de Gaulle, Charles. *Mémoires de guerre.* 3 volumes, Paris, 1954–9. *Mémoires d'Espoir.* Paris, 1970.

Dehio, Ludwig (transl. Charles Fullman). *The Precarious Balance.* New York, 1962.

Del Bo, Dino. *Traguardo Europa.* Florence, 1966.

Dell, Sidney. *Trade Blocs and Common Markets.* London, 1963.

Deniau, J. F. *The Common Market.* Second edition, London, 1961.

Dennett, Raymond, and Johnson, Joseph E. (ed.). *Negotiating with the Russians.* Boston, 1951.

Denton, Geoffrey. *Planning in the E.E.C.* London, 1967.

(ed.). *Economic Integration in Europe.* London, 1969.

de Rougemont, Denis. *The Meaning of Europe.* London, 1965.

Despicht, Nigel. *The Transport Policy of the European Communities.* London, 1969.

Deuerlein, Ernst. (ed.). *Potsdam 1945.* Munich, 1963.

Deutsch, Karl W., and others. *Political Community and the North Atlantic Area*. Princeton, N.J., 1957.

Deutscher, Isaac. *Stalin: A Political Biography*. Revised paperback edition, London, 1966.

De Vree, J. K. *Political Integration*. The Hague/Paris, 1972.

Dewhurst, J. Frederick, and others. *Europe's Needs and Resources*. New York, 1961.

d'Hérouville, Hubert. *La Communauté économique atlantique*. Third edition, Paris, 1964.

L'Economie méditerranéenne. Paris, 1958.

L'Economie mondiale. Fourth edition, Paris, 1960.

Diebold, William, Jr. *The Schuman Plan*. New York, 1959.

Trade and Payments in Western Europe. New York, 1952.

Dill, M. *Germany: A Modern History*. Michigan, 1961.

Dixon, Piers. *Double Diplomat: The Life of Sir Pierson Dixon, Don and Diplomat*. London, 1968.

Djilas, Milovan (transl. Michael B. Petrovitch). *Conversations with Stalin*. Paperback edition, London, 1963.

La Documentation Française.

Dolci, Danilo. *Conversazioni Contadini*. Turin, 1962.

(transl. R. Munroe). *The Outlaws of Partinico*. London, 1960.

(transl. P. D. Cummins). *Poverty in Sicily*. London, 1959.

Dönitz, Karl. *Zehn Jahre und Zwanzig Tage*. Bonn, 1958.

Donnelly, Desmond. *Struggle for the World*. London, 1965.

Donnison, F. S. V. *Civil Affairs and Military Government: N.W. Europe 1944–1946*. New York, 1961.

Dosser, Douglas, and Han, S. S. *Taxes in the E.E.C. and Britain: The Problem of Harmonization*. London, 1968.

Drouin, Pierre. *L'Europe du marché commun*. Paris, 1963.

Ducci, Roberto, and Olivi, Bino (ed.). *L'Europa incompiuta*. Padua, 1970.

Dulles, Allen. *The Secret Surrender*. London, 1967.

Dulles, E. L. *The Bank for International Settlements at Work*. New York, 1932.

Dulles, John Foster. *War or Peace*. New York, 1950.

Dumaine, Jacques (transl. Alan Davidson). *Quai d'Orsay 1945–1951*. London, 1958.

Duroselle, J.-B. *De Wilson à Roosevelt: politique extérieure des Etats-Unis*. Paris, 1960.

L'Idée européenne dans l'histoire. Paris, 1965.

Dutoit, Bernard. *L'Aviation et l'Europe*. Lausanne, 1959.

Ebsworth, Raymond. *Restoring Democracy in Germany: The British Contribution*. London, 1960.

The Economist.

Eden, The Rt. Honourable Sir Anthony, K.G., P.C., M.C. *Memoirs: Full Circle*. London, 1960.

Eich, Hermann (transl. Michael Glenny). *The Unloved Germans*. London, 1965.

Einaudi, M., and Goguel, F. *Christian Democracy in Italy and France.* Notre Dame, Indiana, 1952.

Einzig, Paul. *The Euro-Dollar System.* London, 1964.

Foreign Dollar Loans in Europe. London, 1965.

Eisenhower, Dwight D. *Crusade in Europe.* Paperback edition, New York, 1961.

Mandate for Change. Paperback edition, New York, 1961.

The Papers of Dwight David Eisenhower: The War Years. 5 vols., Baltimore, 1970.

Waging Peace. London, 1966.

Elgey, Georgette. *Histoire de la IVe République, Volume I: La République des illusions.* Paris, 1965.

Volume II: La République des contradictions. Paris, 1968.

Ellis, Howard S. *The Economics of Freedom.* New York, 1950.

Encounter.

Erhard, Ludwig. *Deutschlands Rückkehr zum Weltmarkt.* Düsseldorf, 1953.

(transl. J. A. Arengo Jones and J. S. Thomson). *The Economics of Success.* London, 1963.

(transl. Edith Temple Roberts and J. B. Wood). *Prosperity Through Competition.* Second edition, London, 1959.

Etzioni, Amitai. *Political Unification: a comparative study of leaders and forces.* New York, 1965.

European Coal and Steel Community. *Bulletin.*

Common Assembly. *Debates.*

Correspondance concernant les relations entre la Communauté Européenne du Charbon et de l'Acier et le Royaume-Uni. Luxembourg, 1954.

General Reports.

European Community Information Service. *The Community in Maps.* Brussels/Luxembourg, 1967.

European Customs Union Study Group. *First Report.* Brussels, March 1948.

General Report of the Economic Committee. Brussels, October 1948.

European Economic Community, Commission. *Report on the Economic Situation in the Countries of the Community.* Brussels, 1958.

Report to the European Parliament on the State of the Negotiations with the United Kingdom. Brussels, 1963.

European Free Trade Association. *Bulletin.*

European Movement. *The Economic Future of Europe.* London, 1954.

The European Movement and the Council of Europe. London, 1949.

European Parliament. *Debates.*

Political Committee. *Towards Political Union: A Selection of Documents with a Foreword by Mr. Emilio Battista.* London, 1964.

Everts, P. P. (ed.). *The European Community in the World*. Rotterdam, 1972.

Fabra, Paul. *Y a-t-il un marché commun?* Paris, 1965.
Faculté des Lettres et Sciences Humaines de Paris. *Mélanges Pierre Renouvin*. Paris, 1966.
Fauvet, Jacques. *La IVième République*. Paris, 1959.
Feis, Herbert. *Between War and Peace: The Potsdam Conference*. London, 1960.
    Churchill, Roosevelt, Stalin: The War They Waged and the Peace They Sought. Princeton, N.J., 1957.
Fejtö, François. *Budapest '56*. Paris, 1966.
"Felix, Christopher." *The Spy and his Masters*. London, 1963.
Le Figaro.
Fitz Gibbon, Constantine. *Random Thoughts of a Fascist Hyena*. London, 1963.
Flanner, Janet. *Paris Journal 1944–1965*. London, 1966.
Fleming, D. F. *The Cold War and its Origins 1917–1960*. Two volumes, London, 1961.
Florinsky, Michael T. *Integrated Europe*. New York, 1955.
Foa, Bruno. *Monetary Reconstruction in Italy*. New York, 1949.
Fontaine, André. *Histoire de la guerre froide*. Two volumes, Paris, 1965–7.
Fontaine, François. *La Nation frein*. Paris, 1956.
Foot, M. R. D. *S.O.E. in France*. London, 1966.
Forces Aériennes Françaises.
Foreign Affairs.
Foreign Relations of the United States, 1942: Europe Vol. III.
    1943: Vol. I.
    1944: Vol. I.
    Diplomatic Papers: The Conference of Berlin, 1945. Washington, 1960.
    The Conferences at Cairo and Teheran, 1943. Washington, 1961.
    The Conferences at Malta and Yalta, 1945. Washington, 1955.
Fortune.
Fougeyrollas, Pierre. *Pour une France fédérale*. Paris, 1968.
Fourastié, J. *La Civilisation de 1975*. Paris, 1964.
    Le Grand espoir du XXe siècle. Paris, 1963.
    Idées majeures. Paris, 1966.
    Les 40.000 heures. Paris, 1965.
    and F. *Les arts ménagers*. Paris, 1950.
    and Vimont, C. *Histoire de demain*. Third edition, Paris, 1964.
Fraenkel, H. *Farewell to Germany*. London, 1959.
Frank, Isaiah. *The European Common Market*. New York, 1961.
Frankel, Joseph. *International Relations*. London, 1964.
Frankel, P. H. *Mattei: Oil and Power Politics*. London, 1966.
Frémy, D., and M. *Quid?* Paris, annual.
Freymond, Jacques. *The Saar Conflict 1945–1955*. London/New York, 1960.

Western Europe Since the War. London/New York, 1964.

Friedländer, Saul. *Hitler et les Etats-Unis 1939–1941*. Geneva, 1963. (Revised by the author and transl. Aline B. & Alexander Werth as *Prelude to Downfall: Hitler and the United States 1939–1941*. New York, 1967).

Friedmann, Georges. *Le Travail en miettes*. Paris, 1964.

Fulop, Christina. *Competition for Consumers*. London, 1964.

Gabor, Dennis. *Inventing the Future*. London, 1963.

Galante, Pierre and Miller, Jack. *The Berlin Wall*. London, 1965.

Galli, Giorgio. *Il Bipartismo Imperfetto*. Bologna, 1966.
  and Facchi, Paolo. *La Sinistra Democristiana*. Milan, 1962.

Gardini, T. L. *Towards the New Italy*. London, 1943.

Gardner, R. N. *Sterling-Dollar Diplomacy*. Oxford, 1956.

Gayre, G. R. *Italy in Transition*. London, 1946.

George, Pierre. *Géographie industrielle du monde*. Paris, 1957.
  Géographie de l'Italie. Paris, 1964.

German Federal Government. *Germany Reports*. Wiesbaden, 1953.

Giacchero, Enzo. *Il Mezzogiorno nel Mercato Italiano*. Luxembourg, 1957.

Gide, André. *Retour de l'U.R.S.S.* Paris, 1936.

Gilbert, G. M. *Nuremberg Diary*. New York, 1947.

Gilbert, Martin. *The European Powers 1900–45*. London, 1965.

Ginestet, Pierre. *L'Assemblée parlementaire européenne*. Paris, 1959.

Giordano, Renato. *Il Mercato Comune e i suoi Problemi*. Rome, 1958.

Gladwyn, Lord. *The European Idea*. London, 1966.
  De Gaulle's Europe. London, 1969.

Golay, J. F. *The Founding of the Federal Republic of Germany*. Chicago, 1958.

Goldschmidt, Bertrand. *L'Aventure atomique*. Paris, 1962.
  Les Rivalités atomiques. Paris, 1967.

Gollancz, Victor. *In Darkest Germany*. London, 1947.

Goodrich, L. M. and Carroll, M. J. (eds.). *Documents on American Foreign Relations July 1942–June 1943*. Boston, 1945.
  Documents on American Foreign Relations 1943–1944. Boston, 1945.

Gorce, Paul-Marie de la. *De Gaulle entre deux mondes*. Paris, 1964.

Gorell Barnes, Sir William. *Europe and the Developing World*. London, 1967.

Government and Opposition.

Graham, B. D. *The French Socialists and Tripartisme 1944–1947*. London, 1965.

Granick, David. *The European Executive*. New York, 1962.

Graubard, Stephen R. (ed.). *A New Europe?* Boston, Mass., 1964.

Grindrod, Muriel. *Italy*. London, 1964.
  The Rebuilding of Italy. London, 1955.

Grosser, Alfred. *La IVe République et sa politique extérieure*. Paris, 1961.
  La République Fédérale d'Allemagne. Paris, 1963.

The Guardian.

Gunther, John. *Inside Europe Today.* Revised edition, New York, 1962.

Inside Russia Today. London, 1958.

Guyard, Jacques. *Le Miracle français.* Paris, 1965.

Haas, Ernst B. *The Uniting of Europe.* Revised edition, Stanford, Calif., 1968.

Habakkuk, H. J., and Postan, M. M. (eds.). *The Cambridge Economic History of Europe, Vol. VI.* Cambridge, 1965.

Halecki, Oscar. *The Limits and Divisions of European History.* London, 1950.

Halle, Louis J. *The Cold War as History.* London, 1967.

Hallstein, Walter. *Europe in the Making.* London, 1972.

United Europe: Challenge and Opportunity. Cambridge, Mass./ Oxford, 1962.

and Schlochauer, Hans-Jürgen (eds.). *Zur Integration Europas: Festschrift für Carl-Friedrich Ophüls.* Karlsruhe, 1965.

Hambis, Louis. *La Sibérie.* Paris, 1957.

Hancock, W. K. and Gowing, M. M. *British War Economy.* London, 1949.

Hansard. *Parliamentary Debates.*

Harris, Whitney R. *Tyranny on Trial: the Evidence at Nuremberg.* Dallas, 1954.

Harrison, Anthony. *The Framework of Economic Activity.* London, 1967.

Harrod, R. F. *The Life of John Maynard Keynes.* London, 1951.

The Prof. London, 1959.

Hartmann, Frederick H. *Germany Between East and West: The Reunification Problem.* Englewood Cliffs, N.J., 1965.

Hartog, F. *European Trade Cycle Policy.* Leyden, 1959.

Haviland, H. Field, Jr. (ed.). *The United States and the Western Community.* Haverford, Pa., 1957.

Hay, Denys. *Europe: The Emergence of an Idea.* Edinburgh, 1957.

Heidelberg, Franz C. *Das Europäische Parlament.* Baden-Baden/ Bonn/Frankfurt-am-Main, 1959.

Die Berlin-Frage. Frankfurt/Strasbourg, 1965.

Heidelmeyer, Wolfgang and Hindrich, Günter (eds.). *Documents on Berlin 1943–1963.* Second edition, revised, Munich, 1963.

Heidenheimer, A. T. *Adenauer and the C.D.U.* The Hague, 1960.

Heinemann, Dannie N. *Esquisse d'une Europe nouvelle.* Brussels, 1931.

Heiser, H. J. *British Policy with regard to the Unification Efforts on the European Continent.* Leyden, 1959.

Henig, Stanley, and Pinder, John (ed.). *European Political Parties.* London, 1969.

Hennessy, Jossleyn; Lutz, Vera, and Scimone, Giuseppe. *Economic "Miracles."* London, 1964.

Héraud, Guy. *Peuples et langues d'Europe*. Paris, 1966.

Herz, Martin. *Beginnings of the Cold War*. Bloomington, Ind., 1966.

Hildebrand, George H. *Growth and Structure in the Economy of Modern Italy*. Cambridge, Mass., 1965.

Hinshaw, Randall. *The European Community and American Trade*. New York, 1964.

(ed.). *Monetary Reform and the Price of Gold*. Baltimore, 1967.

Hirsch, Fred. *Money International*. London, 1967.

Hodgkins, Jordan A. *Soviet Power: Energy Resources, Production, and Potentials*. Englewood Cliffs, N.J., 1961.

Hoehler, Fred K. *Europe's Homeless Millions*. New York, 1945.

Hoess, Rudolf (transl. Constantine Fitz Gibbon). *Commandant of Auschwitz*. London, 1959.

Hoffmann, Paul G. *Peace Can Be Won*. New York, 1951.

Hoffmann, Stanley and others. *France: Change and Tradition*. London, 1963.

Holt, Stephen. *The Common Market: the Conflict of Theory and Practice*. London, 1967.

Six European States. London, 1970.

Horizon.

Hornstein, Erika von (ed.). *Beyond the Berlin Wall*. London, 1962.

Horowitz, David. *From Yalta to Vietnam*. London, 1967.

Howard, Michael. *Disengagement in Europe*. London, 1958.

Hudson, G. F. *The Hard and Bitter Peace*. London, 1966.

Hughes, H. Stuart. *Contemporary Europe: A History*. Englewood Cliffs, N.J., 1961.

The United States and Italy. Cambridge, Mass., 1953.

Huizinga, J. H. *Confessions of a European in England*. London, 1958.

Mr Europe. London, 1961.

Hull, Cordell. *Memoirs*. Two volumes, New York/London, 1948.

Huntley, James R. *The Nato Story*. New York, 1965.

Ingram, Kenneth. *History of the Cold War*. London, 1955.

International Affairs.

International Institute for Strategic Studies. *Adelphi Papers*.

The Military Balance. London, annual.

International Monetary Fund. *International Financial Statistics*.

International Organization.

Ionescu, Ghita. *The Break-up of the Soviet Empire in Eastern Europe*. London, 1965.

(ed.). *The New Politics of European Integration*. London, 1972.

Irving, Clive and others. *Scandal '63*. London, 1963.

Irving, David. *The Destruction of Dresden*. Paperback edition, London, 1966.

Isaacs, Asher. *International Trade: Tariffs and Commercial Policies*. Chicago, 1948.

Isolera, Italo. *Roma Moderna*. Turin, 1962.
Istituto Poligrafico dello Stato. *Lo Sviluppo dell'economia Italiana*. Rome, 1952.

Jacobsen, Hans-Adolf and Stenzl, Otto (eds.). *Deutschland und die Welt*. Munich, 1964.
Jaksch, W. *Europe's Road to Potsdam*. London, 1963.
Jackson, Robert H. *Report*. Washington, 1949.
Jasny, N. *The Soviet Economy During the Plan Era*. Stanford, 1951.
Jay, Douglas. *After the Common Market*. London, 1968.
Jefferys, James B. and Knee, Derek. *Retailing in Europe*. London, 1962.
Jennings, W. Ivor. *A Federation for Western Europe*. Cambridge, 1940.
Jones, Joseph Marion. *The Fifteen Weeks*. Paperback edition, New York, 1964.
Jouanique, Marcel and Morice, Lucien. *La Navigation intérieure en France*. Paris, 1951.
Journal of Contemporary History.
Journal of Modern History.
Jouvenel, Bertrand de. *Quelle Europe?* Paris, 1947.
Junckerstorff, H. K. *International Manual on the European Economic Community*. St. Louis, Mo., 1963.

Kahn, Herman and Wiener, Anthony J. *The Year 2000*. New York, 1967.
Kee, Robert. *Rufugee World*. London, 1961.
Keesing's Contemporary Archives.
Kennan, George F. *American Diplomacy 1900–1950*. London, 1952.
    Memoirs 1925–1950. London, 1968.
    Russia and the West. New York, 1962.
Kennedy, John F. *Why England Slept*. Paperback edition, New York, 1962.
Kennedy, Robert F. *Just Friends and Brave Enemies*. Paperback edition, New York, 1963.
Kidder Smith, G. E. *The New Architecture of Europe*. London, 1962.
Kimball, Warren F. *The Most Unsordid Act: Lend-Lease 1939–1941*. Baltimore, 1969.
Kindleberger, Charles P. *Economic Growth in France and Britain 1851–1950*. Cambridge, Mass., 1964.
    Europe's Postwar Growth: The Role of Labor Supply. Cambridge, Mass., 1967.
Kissinger, Henry. *The Necessity for Choice*. Paperback edition, New York, 1962.
    The Troubled Partnership. Paperback edition, New York, 1965.
Kitzinger, U. W. *Britain, Europe, and Beyond*. Leyden, 1964.
    The Challenge of the Common Market. Oxford, 1961.
    Diplomacy and Persuasion. London, 1973.

German Electoral Politics. Oxford, 1960.

(ed.). *The Second Try: Labour and the E.E.C.* London, 1968.

Kleiman, Robert. *Atlantic Crisis*. New York, 1964.

Kochan, Lionel. *The Struggle for Germany 1914–1945*. Edinburgh, 1963.

Koestler, Arthur. *The Trail of the Dinosaur*. London, 1955.

Kogan, Norman. *A Political History of Postwar Italy*. London, 1966.

Kogon, Eugen. *Der SS-Staat und das System der deutschen Konzentrationslager*. Munich, 1946.

Kracauer, Siegfried. *From Caligari to Hitler*. Princeton, N.J., 1947.

Kraft, Joseph. *The Grand Design: from Common Market to Atlantic Partnership*. New York, 1962.

Kumar, Dharma. *India and the European Economic Community*. Bombay, 1966.

Laloy, Jean. *Entre guerres et paix 1945–1965*. Paris, 1966.

Lambert, John. *Britain in a Federal Europe*. London, 1968.

Lamfalussy, Alexander. *The United Kingdom and the Six*. London, 1963.

Lansdell, Norman. *The Atom and the Energy Revolution*. London, 1958.

La Palombara, Joseph. *Interest Groups in Italian Politics*. Princeton, N.J., 1964.

Lapie, Pierre-Olivier. *Les trois communautés*. Paris, 1960.

Laqueur, Walter. *Europe since Hitler*. London, 1970.

Russia and Germany: A Century of Conflict. London, 1965.

Laurat, Lucien. *Bilan de vingt-cinq ans de plans quinquennaux*. Paris, 1955.

Lavrillère, Jacques. *L'Industrie des banquiers*. Paris, 1966.

Layton, Christopher. *European Advanced Technology: A Programme for Integration*. London, 1969.

League of Nations. *Industrialization and Free Trade*. Geneva, 1945.

Leahy, William D. *I Was There*. New York, 1950.

Lecerf, Jean. *Histoire de l'unité européenne*. Paris, 1965.

Lechat, Paul. *Italie*. Paris, 1954.

Ledre, C. *Robert Schuman*. Paris, 1954.

Leith, C. K., and others. *World Minerals and World Peace*. Washington, 1943.

Lekachman, Robert. *The Age of Keynes*. London, 1967.

Lemaignen, Robert. *L'Europe au berceau*. Paris, 1964.

Lenti Libero. *Inventario dell'Economia Italiana*. Milan, 1966.

Leonhard, Wolfgang. *Die Revolution entlässt ihre Kinder*. Cologne/Berlin, 1955.

Leonhardt, Rudolf Walter. *This Germany*. Greenwich, Conn., 1964.

Lerner, Daniel, and Aron, Raymond. *France Defeats E.D.C.* New York, 1957.

and Gorden, Morton. *Euratlantica*. Cambridge, Mass., 1969.

Lewis, Norman. *The Honoured Society*. London, 1964.

Lichtheim, George. *Europe and America*. London, 1963.
Lindberg, Leon N. *The Political Dynamics of European Economic Integration*. Stanford, Cal., 1963.
    and Scheingold, Stuart A. *Europe's Would-Be Polity*. Englewood Cliffs, N.J., 1970.
    (ed.). *Regional Integration*. Cambridge, Mass., 1971.
Lindsay, Kenneth. *European Assemblies*. New York, 1960.
Lippmann, Walter. *The Communist World and Ours*. London, 1959.
    Western Unity and the Common Market. Boston, 1962.
The Listener.
Lister, Louis. *Europe's Coal and Steel Community*. New York, 1960.
Locatelli, Silvio. *Konrad Adenauer*. Milan, 1965.
Luard, Evan (ed.). *The Cold War: A Reappraisal*. London, 1964.
Lüdde-Neurath, Walter. *Die Regierung Dönitz*. Göttingen, 1950.
Lukacs, John. *Decline and Rise of Europe*. New York, 1965.
Lukas, Richard. *Zehn Jahre Sowjetische Besatzungszone Deutschlands*. Mainz/Wiesbaden/Düsseldorf, 1955.
Lyon, Margot. *Belgium*. London, 1970.

McCreary, Edward A. *The Americanization of Europe*. New York, 1964.
Macdonald, R. and West, M. *Eurovista '69*. St. Andrews, 1969.
McInnis, Edgar; Hiscocks, Richard and Spencer, Robert. *The Shaping of Postwar Germany*. Toronto/London, 1960.
Mackay, R. W. G. *Towards a United States of Europe*. London, 1961.
Mackiewicz, Joseph. *The Katyn Wood Murders*. London, 1951.
Maclean, Fitzroy. *Disputed Barricade*. London, 1957.
MacLennan, Malcolm. *French Planning: Some Lessons for Britain*. London, 1963.
Macmahon, Arthur W. (ed.). *Federalism: Mature and Emergent*. New York, 1955.
Macmillan, Harold. *Memoirs. Vol. II: The Blast of War 1939–1945*. London, 1967.
    III: Tides of Fortune 1945–1955. London, 1969.
McNeill, W. H. *The Rise of the West*. Chicago, 1963.
Madariaga, Salvador de. *Portrait of Europe*. New edition, London, 1967.
Maddison, Angus. *Economic Growth in the West*. New York/London, 1964.
Mahotière, Stuart de la. *Towards One Europe*. London, 1970.
Maillet, Pierre. *La Croissance économique*. Paris, 1966.
Malvestiti, Piero. *Parte Guelfa in Europa*. Milan, 1945.
Mander, John. *Berlin: Hostage for the West*. London, 1962.
    Great Britain or Little England? London, 1963.
Marc, Alexandre. *L'Europe, terre décisive*. Paris, 1959.
Markevitch, Igor (transl. Darina Silone). *Made in Italy*. London, 1949.

Markham, R. H. *Rumania under the Soviet Yoke*. Boston, Mass., 1949.

Martin, Laurence W. (ed.). *Diplomacy in Modern European History*. New York, 1966.

Mason, Henry L. *The European Coal and Steel Community*. The Hague, 1955.

Masseyeff, René. *La Faim*. Paris, 1956.

Massip, Roger. *Voici l'Europe*. Paris, 1958.

Mathijsen, Pierre. *Le Droit de la Communauté Européenne du Charbon et de l'Acier*. The Hague, 1958.

Maxwell, Gavin. *God Protect Me From My Friends*. London, 1956.

Mayne, Richard. *The Community of Europe*. London, 1962.
    The Europeans. London/New York, 1972.
    (ed.). *Europe Tomorrow*. London, 1972.
    The Institutions of the European Community. London, 1968.

Meade, J. E. *Negotiations for Benelux*. Princeton, N.J., 1957.
    Problems of Economic Union. London, 1953.

Meinecke, F. *The German Catastrophe*. Cambridge, Mass., 1950.

Meisel, J. H. *The Fall of the Republic*. Michigan, 1962.

Menon, V. P. *The Transfer of Power in India*. Bombay, 1961.

Mercure de France.

Merkl, Peter H. *Germany Yesterday and Tomorrow*. New York, 1965.

Meyer, F. V. *The Seven*. London, 1960.

Middleton, Drew. *Crisis in the West*. London, 1965.
    The Defense of Western Europe. New York, 1952.
    The Supreme Choice. London, 1963.

Midgley, John. *Germany*. London, 1968.

Mikolajczyk, Stanislaw. *The Pattern of Soviet Domination*. London, 1948.

Miles, W. (ed.). *The Forrestal Diaries*. London, 1952.

The Milwaukee Leader.

Ministère des Affaires Etrangères. *Documents de la conférence des Ministres des Affaires Etrangères de la France, du Royaume-Uni, et de l'U.R.S.S. tenue à Paris du 27 juin au 3 juillet 1947*. Paris, 1947.

Moch, Jules. *Histoire du réarmement allemand depuis 1950*. Paris, 1965.

Moncrieff, Anthony (ed.). *Britain and the Common Market 1967*. London, 1967.
    Suez Ten Years After. London, 1967.

Le Monde.

Monnet, Jean. *Les Etats-Unis d'Europe ont commencé*. Paris, 1955.

Montgomery of Alamein, Field-Marshal the Viscount, K.G. *Memoirs*. Paperback edition, London, 1960.

Montgomery, John. *The Fifties*. London, 1965.

Moon, Penderel. *Divide and Quit*. London, 1962.

Moonman, Eric (ed.). *Science and Technology in Europe*. London, 1968.

Moore, Ben T. *Nato and the Future of Europe*. New York, 1958.
Moore, Reginald, and Lane, Edward (eds.). *The Windmill*. London, 1946.
Moran, Lord. *Churchill: The Struggle for Survival*. London, 1966.
Morandi, Rudolfo. *Storia della Grande Industria in Italia*. Turin, 1966.
Morgan, Sir Frederick. *Overture to Overlord*. London, 1950.
Morgenthau, Henry. *Germany is our Problem*. New York, 1945.
Morris, James. *The World Bank: A Prospect*. London, 1958.
Mosely, Philip E. *The Kremlin in World Politics*. Paperback edition, New York, 1960.
    The Soviet Union Since Khrushchev. New York, 1966.
Moulin, Léo. *La Société de demain dans l'Europe d'aujourd'hui*. Paris, 1966.
Moulton, Harold G. and Pasvolsky, Leo. *War Debts and World Prosperity*. Washington, 1932.
Mourin, Maxime. *Histoire des nations européennes*, Vol. III. Paris, 1963.
Mowat, R. C. *Ruin and Resurgence 1939–1965*. London, 1966.
Muhlen, Norbert. *The Survivors: A Report on the Jews in Germany Today*. New York, 1962.
Mulley, F. W. *The Politics of Western Defence*. London, 1962.
Murphy, Robert. *Diplomat Among Warriors*. London, 1964.

Nabokov, Nicolas. *Old Friends and New Music*. London, 1951.
Nagy, Ferenc. *The Struggle Behind the Iron Curtain*. London, 1948.
Nettl, John P. *The Eastern Zone and Soviet Policy in Germany*. London, 1951.
Neuvecelle, Jean. *Eglise capitale Vatican*. Paris, 1954.
Nevins, Allan. *America in World Affairs*. Oxford, 1941.
Newhouse, John. *Collision in Brussels*. London, 1968.
The New Statesman.
The New York *Herald Tribune*.
The New York *Times*.
North Atlantic Treaty Organization, Defence College. *The Way Ahead*. Rome, 1967.
Northedge, F. S. *British Foreign Policy: The Process of Readjustment 1945–1961*. London, 1962.
Northrop, F. S. C. *European Union and United States Foreign Policy*. New York, 1954.
Nova, Fritz. *Contemporary European Governments*. Baltimore/ Dublin, 1963.
Novick, Peter. *The Resistance versus Vichy*. London, 1968.
Nutting, Anthony. *Europe Will Not Wait*. London, 1960.
    No End of a Lesson. London, 1967.

The Observer.
Office Statistique des Communautés Européennes. *Commerce Extérieur: Statistique Mensuelle*.

Statistiques de base de la Communauté Européenne: Comparaison avec certains pays européens, le Canada, les Etats-Unis d'Amérique, et l'U.R.S.S. Brussels/Luxembourg, annual.

Ogburn, W. F. (ed.). *Technology and International Relations.* Chicago, 1949.

Olivi, Bino. *L'Europa Difficile.* Milan, 1964.

Organisation for Economic Co-operation and Development. *Economic Surveys.*

Tourism in O.E.C.D. Member Countries 1966. Paris, 1966.

Organisation for European Economic Cooperation. *Council Meetings, Reports.*

Memorandum by the Chancellor of the Exchequer. Paris, June 1, 1949.

Memorandum by the French Minister of Finance and Economic Affairs. Paris, June 2, 1949.

Present Positions on the Principles of the Payments Scheme for the 1949–50 Financial Year. Paris, June 27, 1949.

Reports.

Orwell, George. *Collected Essays, Journalism, and Letters* (ed. Sonia Orwell and Ian Angus). Four volumes, London, 1968.

Palmer, Michael, and others. *European Unity: A Survey of the European Organizations.* London, 1968.

Pantaleone, Michele. *Mafia e Politica.* Turin, 1962.

Paranque, Régis. *La Semaine de trente heures.* Paris, 1964.

Parker, Geoffrey. *The Logic of Unity.* London, 1969.

Parkinson, C. Northcote. *Parkinson's Law.* London, 1958.

Payne, R. *General Marshall.* London, 1952.

Penrose, E. F. *Economic Planning for the Peace.* Princeton, N.J., 1953.

"Pentad." *The Remaking of Italy.* London, 1941.

Permoli, Piergiovanni. *La Costituente e i Partiti Politici Italiani.* Rocca San Casciano, 1966.

Pevsner, Nikolaus. *The Buildings of England: London, Vol. I: The Cities of London and Westminster.* London, 1957.

Peyret, Henry. *La Stratégie des trusts.* Paris, 1961.

Pflimlin, Pierre, and Legrand-Lane, Raymond. *L'Europe Communautaire.* Paris, 1966.

Phillips, Cabell. *The Truman Presidency.* New York, 1966.

Pickles, Dorothy. *The Fifth French Republic.* Third edition, London, 1965.

Pickles, William. *Not with Europe: The Political Case for Staying Out.* London, 1962.

Pinder, John. *Britain and the Common Market.* London, 1961.

Europe Against De Gaulle. London, 1963.

and Pryce, Roy. *Europe After De Gaulle.* London, 1969.

Pingaud, Bernard. *Hollande.* Paris, 1954.

Pisani, Edgard and others. *Problems of British Entry into the E.E.C.:*

Reports to the Action Committee for the United States of Europe. London, 1969.

Plischke, Elmer. *Contemporary Government of Germany.* London, 1964.

Summit Diplomacy. College Park, Md., 1958.

Poignant, Raymond. *L'Enseignement dans les pays du marché commun.* Paris, 1965.

Polish Government in Exile. *Facts and Documents concerning Polish Prisoners of War Captured by the U.S.S.R. During the 1939 Campaign,* London, 1944.

Political and Economic Planning (London). *Aspects of European Integration.* London/Paris, 1962.

European Organizations. London, 1959.

The Political Science Quarterly.

Poos, Jacques F. *Luxembourg et le marché commun.* Luxembourg/Lausanne, 1961.

Posner, M. V., and Woolf, S. J. *Italian Public Enterprise.* London, 1967.

Postan, M. M. *An Economic History of Western Europe 1945–1964.* London, 1967.

Pounds, Norman J. G. *The Economic Pattern of Modern Germany.* London, 1963.

and Kingsbury, Robert C. *An Atlas of European Affairs.* London, 1964.

and Parker, William N. *Coal and Steel in Western Europe.* Bloomington, Ind., 1957.

Pravda.

Présidence du Conseil, Secrétariat-General du Gouvernement. *L'Organisation de l'Europe occidentale* (*1948–1955*). Paris, 1955.

Price, Harry Bayard. *The Marshall Plan and Its Meaning.* Ithaca, N.Y., 1955.

Priouret, Roger. *Les Managers européens.* Paris, 1970.

Proudfoot, Malcolm J. *European Refugees 1939–52.* London, 1957.

Pryce, Roy. *The Political Future of the European Community.* London, 1962.

Quin, Claude; Boniface, Jean, and Gaussel, Alain. *Les Consommateurs.* Paris, 1965.

Racine, Raymond. *Vers une Europe nouvelle par le Plan Schuman.* Neuchâtel, 1954.

Reader's Digest European Surveys. *Products and People.* London, 1963.

Réalités.

Reed, Laurance. *Europe in a Shrinking World.* London, 1967.

Ocean-Space: Europe's New Frontier. London, 1969.

Rees, David. *The Age of Containment.* London, 1967.

Regierung des Landes Nordrhein-Westfalen and others. *Das Abkommen über die Errichtung einer Internazionalen Ruhrbehörde.* Düsseldorf, 1949.

Reitlinger, Gerald. *The Final Solution: The Attempt to Exterminate the Jews of Europe 1939–1945.* London, 1953.

  The SS: Alibi of a Nation. London, 1956.

Relazioni Internazionali.

Repubblica Italiana, Senato dell Repubblica/Camera dei Deputati. *Manuali Parlamentari.*

République Française, Ministère des Affaires Etrangères. *Rapport de la délégation française sur le Traité instituant la Communauté Européenne du Charbon et de l'Acier et la Convention relative au dispositions transitoires signés à Paris le 18 avril 1951.* Paris, 1951.

The Review of Politics.

La Revue Française de Science Politique.

La Revue de l'Histoire de la 2e Guerre Mondiale.

Reynaud, Paul. *La Politique étrangère du Gaullisme.* Paris, 1964.

Riemans, H. *Perspectief voor Nederland.* Amsterdam, 1957.

Ripka, Hubert. *Czechoslovakia Enslaved.* London, 1950.

  Eastern Europe in the Postwar World. London, 1961.

Robertson, A. H. *European Institutions.* New York, 1959.

Robertson, Terence. *Crisis.* London, 1965.

Robson, Charles B. (transl. and ed.). *Berlin—Pivot of German Destiny.* Chapel Hill, N.C., 1960.

Rodens, Franz. *Konrad Adenauer.* Munich/Zurich, 1965.

Rogow, Arnold. *Victim of Destiny.* London, 1966.

Romano, Salvatore F. *Storia della Mafia.* Paperback edition, Verona, 1966.

Roskamp, Karl W. *Capital Formation in West Germany.* Detroit, 1965.

Rostow, W. W. *The United States in the World Arena.* New York, 1960.

Rothstein, Andrew. *A History of the U.S.S.R.* London, 1950.

Rouanet, Pierre. *Mendès-France au pouvoir 1954–1955.* Paris, 1965.

Rovan, Joseph. *L'Europe.* Paris, 1966.

Royal Institute of International Affairs. *Britain in Western Europe.* London, 1956.

  The Soviet-Yugoslav Dispute. London, 1948.

  Surveys of International Affairs.

Rueff, Jacques, and others. *Le Marché commun et ses problèmes.* Paris, 1958.

Ryan, Cornelius. *The Last Battle.* London, 1966.

Sampson, Anthony. *Macmillan: A Study in Ambiguity.* Paperback edition, London, 1968.

  The New Europeans. London, 1968.

Sannwald, Rolf, and Stohler, Jacques. *Wirtschaftliche Integration.* Basel/Tübingen, 1958.

Sayers, R. S. (ed.). *Banking in Western Europe*. Oxford, 1962.

Scarlett, Doris. *Window onto Hungary*. Bradford, n.d.

Schaffer, Gordon. *Russian Zone*. London, 1947.

Scheingold, Stuart A. *The Rule of Law in European Integration*. New Haven, Conn./London, 1965.

Schlachter, Gustav. *The Italian South*. New York, 1965.

Schechtman, Joseph B. *European Population Transfers 1939–1945*. New York, 1946.

   The Refugee in the World: Displacement and Integration. New York/London, 1963.

Schoenbrun, David. *As France Goes*. London, 1957.

Schramm, P. E. (ed.). *Die Niederlage 1945*. Paperback edition, Munich, 1962.

Schuman, Robert. *Pour l'Europe*. Paris, 1963.

Schur, Val, and Curzon, Gerard (eds.). *East-West Trade*. London, 1965.

Schwab-Felisch, Hans (ed.). *Der Ruf*. Munich, 1962.

Scitovsky, Tibor. *Economic Theory and Western European Integration*. London, 1958.

Scott, John. *Democracy is Not Enough*. New York, 1960.

   The Soviet World. New York, 1966.

Seale, Patrick, and McConville, Maureen. *French Revolution 1968*. London, 1968.

Segal, Ronald. *The Crisis of India*. London, 1965.

Servan-Schreiber, Jean-Jacques. *Le Défi americain*. Paris, 1967.

Seton-Watson, Hugh. *The East European Revolution*. London, 1950.

   From Stalin to Malenkov. London, 1953.

   Nationalism and Communism. London, 1964.

   The New Imperialism. London, 1961.

   The Pattern of Communist Revolution. London, 1953.

Shanks, Michael, and Lambert, John. *Britain and the New Europe*. London, 1962.

Sherwood, Robert E. *Roosevelt and Hopkins: An Intimate History*. New York, 1948.

Shirer, William L. *The Rise and Fall of the Third Reich*. Paperback edition, Greenwich, Conn., 1962.

Shonfield, Andrew. *The Attack on World Poverty*. London, 1960.

   British Economic Policy Since the War. Revised edition, London, 1959.

   Modern Capitalism. London, 1965.

Siegfried, A. *De la IVe à la Ve République*. Paris, 1958.

Siegler, Heinrich von. *Dokumentation der Europäischen Integration 1946–1961 mit besonderer Berücksichtigung des Verhältnisses EWG-EFTA*. Bonn/Vienna/Zurich, 1961.

Silbermann, Alphons. *Vom Wohnen der Deutschen*. Frankfurt/Hamburg, 1966.

Silvestri, Stefano (ed.). *Il Mediterraneo: Economia, Politica, Strategia*. Rome/Bologna, 1968.

Simpson, E. S. *Coal and the Power Industries in Postwar Britain.* London, 1966.

Sissons, Michael, and French, Philip (eds.). *Age of Austerity 1945–51.* Paperback edition, London, 1964.

Smith, Howard K. *The State of Europe.* London, 1950.

Smuts, Jan Christian. *Thoughts on a New World.* London, 1943.

Snell, John L. *The Meaning of Yalta.* New York, 1956.
   Wartime Origins of the East-West Dilemma over Germany. New Orleans, 1959.

Snow, C. P. *Science and Government.* Paperback edition, London, 1963.

Snoy et d'Oppuers, Baron. *La Formation du Zollverein (1815–1867): une leçon pour l'Europe contemporaine.* Brussels, 1957.

Spaak, Paul-Henri. *Combats Inachevés.* Two volumes, Paris, 1969.
   Why Nato? London, 1959.

Spanier, David. *Europe, Our Europe.* London, 1972.

Spanier, J. W. *American Foreign Policy Since World War Two.* New York, 1960.

Speier, Hans. *Divided Berlin.* London, 1961.

Spinelli, Altiero. *The European Adventure.* London, 1972.
   Rapporto sull'Europa. Milan, 1965.

Stalin, Joseph V. *Correspondence with Churchill, Attlee, Roosevelt, and Truman.* London, 1952.
   Problems of Leninism. Eleventh edition, Moscow, 1940.

Stamp, L. Dudley. *Our Underdeveloped World.* London, 1952.

Steel, Ronald. *The End of Alliance.* London, 1964.

Stehlin, Paul. *Retour à Zéro.* Paris, 1968.

Steiner, Jean-François. *Treblinka.* Paris, 1966.

Sternberg, Fritz. *Wer beherrscht die zweite Hälfte des 20. Jahrhunderts?* Paperback edition, Munich, 1963.

Stettinius, E. R. *Roosevelt and the Russians.* London, 1950.

Stimson, Henry L., and Bundy, McGeorge. *On Active Service in Peace and War.* New York, 1947.

Stolper, Wolfgang. *Germany Between East and West.* Washington, 1960.

Strang, Lord. *Home and Abroad.* London, 1956.

Strange, Susan. *The Sterling Problem and the Six.* London, 1967.

Strauss, E. *Common Sense About the Common Market.* London, 1958.
   European Reckoning. London, 1962.

Strauss, Franz-Josef. *Challenge and Response.* London, 1969.
   The Grand Design. London, 1965.

Swann, D., and McLachlan, D. L. *Concentration or Competition: A European Dilemma.* London, 1967.

Szokoloczy-Syllaba, Janos. *Les Organisations professionnelles françaises et le marché commun.* Paris, 1965.

Taber, George M. *John F. Kennedy and a United Europe.* Bruges, 1969.

Taylor, A. J. P. *English History 1914–1945*. Oxford, 1965.
    Europe: Grandeur and Decline. London, 1967.
    The Origins of the Second World War. Paperback edition, London, 1964.

Tempel, Gudrun (transl. Sophie Wilkins). *Speaking Frankly About the Germans*. London, 1963.

Thomas, Hugh. *Europe: the Radical Challenge*. London, 1973.
    The Spanish Civil War. Paperback edition, London, 1965.
    The Suez Affair. London, 1967.

Thomson, David. *Democracy in France Since 1870*. Fifth edition, London, 1969.
    Europe Since Napoleon. Second edition, London, 1962.

Thomson, George. *The Foreseeable Future*. Cambridge, 1955.

Time.

The Times.

Tocqueville, Alexis de (transl. Henry Reeve). *Democracy in America*. Oxford, 1946.

Toland, John. *The Last Hundred Days*. Paperback edition, New York, 1967.

Tournoux, J.-R. *Secrets d'Etat, Vol. II: Pétain et de Gaulle*. Paris, 1964.
    La Tragédie du Général. Paris, 1967.

Townsend, Peter. *The Family Life of Old People*. London, 1957.

Toynbee, A. (ed.). *Four-Power Control in Germany and Austria 1945–1946*. London, 1956.
    and V. M. (eds.). *The Realignment of Europe*. London, 1955.

Trempont, Jacques. *L'Unification de l'Europe*. Amiens/Brussels, 1955.

Trevor-Roper, H. R. *The Last Days of Hitler*. Revised paperback edition, London, 1962.

Trial of the Major War Criminals before the International Military Tribunal. Forty-two volumes, Nuremberg, 1947–49.

Trials of War Criminals before the Nuremberg Military Tribunals. Fifteen volumes, Washington, 1951–52.

Triffin, Robert. *Europe and the Money Muddle*. New Haven, Conn., 1957.
    The World Money Maze. New Haven, Conn., 1966.

Truman, Harry S. *Memoirs*. Two volumes, paperback edition, New York, 1965.

United Kingdom Foreign Office. *Protocol of the Proceedings of the Berlin Conference, 2nd August 1945*. London, 1947.
    Report of the Crimea Conference. London, 1945.
    H.M.S.O. *Anglo-French Discussions regarding the French Proposals for the Western European Coal, Iron, and Steel Industries, May–June 1950*. London, 1950.
    Commonwealth Consultations on Britain's Relations with the European Economic Community. London, 1961.
    Correspondence arising out of the meeting of the Foreign Minis-

ters of the Governments of Belgium, France, the Federal Republic of Germany, Italy, Luxembourg, and the Netherlands, held at Messina on 1–2 June 1955. London, 1955.

Documents agreed on by the Conference of Ministers held in Paris, October 20–23, 1954. London, 1954.

The United Kingdom and the European Economic Community. London, 1961.

United Nations. *Customs Unions: A League of Nations Contribution to the Study of Customs Union Problems.* New York, 1947.

The Future Growth of World Population. New York, 1958.

Economic Commission for Europe. *The European Housing Problem: a Preliminary Review.* Geneva, 1949.

Growth and Stagnation in the European Economy. Geneva, 1954.

Economic and Social Council. *Preliminary Report of the Temporary Sub-Committee on Economic Reconstruction of Devastated Areas.* Geneva, 1946.

General Assembly. *Resolutions.*

United States, Department of Commerce. *Foreign Aid by the United States Government 1940–1951.* Washington, 1952.

Department of State. *Bulletin.*

Military Intelligence. *The Communist Bloc in Europe.* Headquarters, U. S. Army in Europe, 1959.

Presidential Committee on Foreign Aid. *European Recovery and American Aid.* Washington, 1947.

Select Committee on Foreign Aid. *Final Report on Foreign Aid.* Washington, 1948.

Uri, Pierre. *Partnership for Progress.* New York, 1963.

(ed.). *From Commonwealth to Common Market.* London, 1968.

Urwin, D. W. *Western Europe Since 1945.* London, 1968.

Valentine, D. G. *The Court of Justice of the European Coal and Steel Community.* The Hague, 1954.

Valentino, Nino. *L'Elezione di Segni.* Milan, 1963.

Vallette, Geneviève, and Bouillon, Jacques. *Munich 1938.* Paris, 1964.

Vandenberg, Arthur H., Jr. (ed.). *The Private Papers of Senator Vandenberg.* Boston, Mass.

van der Beugel, Ernst. *From Marshall Aid to Atlantic Partnership.* Amsterdam/London/New York, 1966.

Van der Molen, G. H. J., and others (eds.). *The United Nations: Ten Years' Legal Progress.* The Hague, 1956.

van der Plas, Michel. *Mooie Vrede: een documentaire over Nederland in de jaren 1945–1950.* Utrecht, 1966.

Vaussard, Maurice. *Histoire de l'Italie contemporaine 1870–1946.* Paris, 1950.

Verburg, M. C. *Nederland in de europese ruimte.* Amsterdam, 1966.

Vernay, Alain. *Les Paradis fiscaux.* Paris, 1968.

Viansson-Ponté, Pierre. *Les Politiques.* Paris, 1967.

Viner, Jacob. *The Customs Union Issue.* New York, 1950.

Vogelsang, Thilo. *Das geteilte Deutschland*. Munich, 1966.

Votaw, Dow. *The Six-Legged Dog: Mattei and E.N.I.—a Study in Power*. Berkeley/Los Angeles, 1964.

Voyenne, Bernard. *Histoire de l'idée européenne*. Paris, 1964.

Waites, Neville (ed.). *Troubled Neighbours*. London, 1971.

Wall, Edward. *Europe: Unification and Law*. London, 1969.

Wallich, Henry C. *Mainsprings of German Revival*. New Haven, Conn., 1955.

Walsh, W. B. *Russia and the Soviet Union*. Michigan, 1958.

Ward, Barbara. *Policy for the West*. New York, 1951.

The West at Bay. New York, 1948.

Warley, T. K. *Agriculture: The Cost of Joining the Common Market*. London, 1967.

Waterlow, Charlotte. *Tribe, State, and Community*. London, 1967.

Watt, D. C. *Britain Looks At Germany*. London, 1965.

Watts, O. M. *Stanford's General Chart of the English Channel*. London, 1969.

Weil, Gordon L. (ed.). *A Handbook on the European Economic Community*. Washington/New York/London, 1965.

Welles, Sumner. *The Time for Decision*. New York, 1944.

Where we are Heading. London, 1946.

Wellisz, Stanislaw. *The Economics of the Soviet Bloc*. New York, 1964.

Werth, Alexander. *De Gaulle: A Political Biography*. Third edition, London, 1969.

The Strange History of Pierre Mendès France. London, 1957.

West, Rebecca. *The Meaning of Treason*. Revised edition, London, 1965.

Western European Union, Assembly. *Debates*.

Reports.

White, Theodore H. *Fire in the Ashes: Europe in Mid-Century*. New York, 1953.

Williams, Francis. *A Prime Minister Remembers: The War and Postwar Memoirs of the Rt. Hon. Earl Attlee, K.G., P.C., O.M., C.H.* London, 1961.

Williams, Gertrude. *Apprenticeship in Europe*. London, 1963.

Williams, Philip M. *Crisis and Compromise: Politics in the Fourth Republic*. London, 1964.

and Harrison, M. *De Gaulle's Republic*. London, 1960.

Willis, F. Roy. *France, Germany, and the New Europe, 1945–1967*. London, 1969.

Wilmot, Chester. *The Struggle for Europe*. Paperback edition, London, 1959.

Wilson, Edmund. *Europe Without Baedeker*. London, 1948.

Wiskemann, Elizabeth. *Europe of the Dictators 1919–1945*. London, 1966.

Germany's Eastern Neighbours. London, 1957.

Italy. London, 1947.

Wollenberg, H. H. *Fifty Years of German Film*. London, 1948.

Woodbridge, George, and others. *U.N.R.R.A.: The History of the United Nations Relief and Rehabilitation Administration*. Three volumes, New York, 1950.

Woodward, Sir Llewellyn. *British Foreign Policy in the Second World War*. London, 1962.

Worswick, G. D. N., and Ady, P. H. (eds.). *The British Economy 1945–1950*. Oxford, 1952.

Woytinsky, W. S., and E. S. *World Population and Production: Trends and Outlook*. New York, 1953.

The Yale Law Journal.

Yates, P. Lamartine. *Food, Land, and Manpower in Western Europe*. London, 1960.

Young, Gordon. *The Fall and Rise of Alfried Krupp*. London, 1960.

Young, Wayland. *The Italian Left*. London, 1949.

   The Montesi Scandal. London, 1959.

Zaring, J. L. *Decision for Europe*, Baltimore, 1969.

Zebot, Cyril A. *The Economics of Competitive Coexistence: Convergence Through Growth*. New York, 1964.

Zeman, Z. E. B. *Prague Spring: A Report on Czechoslovakia 1968*. London, 1969.

Zink, Harold. *American Military Government in Germany*. New York, 1947.

   The United States in Germany 1944–1955. New York, 1957.

Zinkin, Taya. *India*. London, 1965.

Zinner, P. E. *Communist Strategy and Tactics in Czechoslovakia 1914–1948*. London, 1963.

   Revolution in Hungary. New York, 1962.

Zischka, Anton (transl. Brian Battershaw). *The Other Europeans*. London, 1962.

Zurcher, Arnold J. *The Struggle to Unite Europe 1940–1958*. New York, 1958.

INDEX

ANCHOR BOOKS

HISTORY

9Ab

ANCHOR BOOKS

POLITICAL SCIENCE AND GOVERNMENT

ANCHOR BOOKS

SOCIOLOGY (cont'd)

SOCIOLOGY *(cont'd)*

Volume II: How to Manage an Urbanized World—H. Wentworth Eldredge, ed., A593a, b

THE TOOLS OF SOCIAL SCIENCE—John Madge, A437

UNION DEMOCRACY—Seymour Martin Lipset, Martin A. Trow, and James S. Coleman, Foreword by Clark Kerr, A296

THE URBAN COMPLEX—Robert C. Weaver, A505

URBAN RENEWAL: People, Politics, and Planning—Jewel Bellush and Murray Hausknecht, eds., A569

VILLAGE OF VIRIATINO: An Ethnographic Study of a Russian Village from Before the Revolution to the Present—Sula Benet, trans. and ed., A758

WALK THE WHITE LINE: A Profile of Urban Education—Elizabeth M. Eddy, Ph.D., A570

WHITE MAN, LISTEN!—Richard Wright, A414

WHO DESIGNS AMERICA?—Laurence B. Holland, ed., A523

WHO NEEDS THE NEGRO?—Sidney Willhelm, A789

ANCHOR BOOKS

17Ab